60

FARRAR
STRAUS
GIROUX

CROSS-X

CROSS-X

JOE MILLER

FARRAR, STRAUS AND GIROUX | NEW YORK

FARRAR, STRAUS AND GIROUX
19 Union Square West, New York 10003

Copyright © 2006 by Joe Miller
All rights reserved
Distributed in Canada by Douglas & McIntyre Ltd.
Printed in the United States of America

ISBN-13: 978-0-7394-8257-5

Designed by Gretchen Achilles

TITLE-PAGE PHOTOGRAPH: (*back row, left to right*) Adrienne, unidentified student,
Brandon Dial, Jane Rinehart, Dionne, Day Brown, Rahman McGill; (*front row, left to right*)
DiAnna Saffold, Marcus Leach, Leo Muhammad, Kerra McCorkle.
(Photograph © Michael McClure)

FOR ALLIE JOHNSON AND KATHRYN MORGAN

Brick by brick, stone by stone, the prison of individual, institutional and cultural racism can be destroyed.

JOSEPH BARNDT

Rather than standing above or outside their society, "specific intellectuals" are immersed within it. They cite, analyze, and engage in struggles not in the name of the oppressed, but alongside them, in solidarity with them.

TODD MAY

Nigga, you white! You can't dictate the revolution!

MARCUS LEACH

CONTENTS

PART ONE: THE CONSTRUCTIVES

PART TWO: THE REBUTTALS

PART THREE: THE BALLOT

PART FOUR: THE POST-ROUND CRITIQUE

PART ONE

THE CONSTRUCTIVES

ONE

FIRST DAY

JANE RINEHART began the best and worst year of her teaching career in a familiar pose: hands on hips, lips pinched in a downward twist, one eyebrow cocked above the other. Seven kids slumped at their desks and scowled back at her. She only knew one of them—Ebony Rose, a gangly sixteen-year-old with a ghetto accent so thick people often had to ask him to repeat himself three or four times before they could understand what he'd said. The rest were strangers who wound up in her beginning debate class because the new hires in the school's counseling office were, like so many administrators in Kansas City, Missouri's notoriously dysfunctional school district, inept or lazy or both.

The previous spring she and her team of debaters canvassed Central High School in search of new recruits. They looked everywhere—in the cavernous lunchroom, the noisy study halls, the history classes full of bored teens scratching answers onto photocopied worksheets. They even checked the windowless room where cutups sit for hours on end to atone for their sins. ("In an inner-city school, in-school suspension is one of the best places to find good debaters," Rinehart often said.) They tracked down tips from fellow students and teachers who had learned years ago to steer smart kids to Rinehart's program, one of the few bright spots in a school where more than half the incoming freshmen drop out before their senior year. Within a few weeks, she hand-delivered a list of eighteen prospective debaters to the counseling office well before the cutoff date.

But they lost it. So she turned in another. She even offered to type the names into the school's computer system herself. "No, no," one of the counselors told her. "We can handle it."

They couldn't. When Rinehart opened up her schedule packet a few days before the start of school, she found that *not one* of her recruits had been enrolled in beginning debate. When she brought this to the attention of her assistant principal, the administrator shrugged. "They're new," her boss said of the school's counselors. "What do you expect?"

As Rinehart sized up her meager prospects, a girl with long, skinny braids threw open the door and marched two steps into the room. Rinehart turned and stared her down.

"This ain't no required class, is it?" the girl asked.

"This *isn't any*?" Rinehart replied without hesitation.

The girl's shoulders dropped. "Do we gotta take this class?!"

"You don't *gotta* take anything."

"I mean . . ." the girl sputtered.

"This isn't a mandated class, if that's what you want to know."

"That's what I wanted to know."

"But if you only go through life doing the minimum," Rinehart said as the girl plopped herself into one of the twenty empty desks, "the minimum is all you'll get out of life."

RINEHART CROSSED HER ARMS and glanced around her classroom, which, only two hours into the school year, looked as if a gale had blown through and tossed around all the desks and books and files. Room 109, the one-window headquarters for Central's debate program, contains too much bustle to be as orderly as a typical high school room. Even before the school year started, with summer's free days dwindling, kids flitted in and out of Rinehart's domain to seek advice on the cases they were building for the coming season or simply to escape the bleak streets of Kansas City's East Side.

Rinehart moved to the dry-erase board, uncapped a purple marker, and wrote, "Resolved: That the federal government should substantially increase public mental health services for mental health care in the United States." She turned to face the students, who were stretched so far back in their chairs they were nearly horizontal. Each kid grudgingly wore a baggy version of the school's mandatory uniforms: khaki or navy blue pants with navy blue or white shirts.

"I'm Mrs. Rinehart," she said cheerily, trying to shake off her bad mood. "This is the debate class. You are the beginners. You are the novices. You are the hope for the future. You are the ones who are going to win trophies like this." She gestured toward a handsome copper chalice rising from an old audiovisual cart stuffed with books and papers and plastic cups full of pencils and pens. "We run with the big dogs."

A few of the kids chuckled at this short white woman who stood before them in her prim silk blouse and matching marigold skirt, trying to talk trash.

"We *do*," she insisted, hands back on her hips.

She rattled off an abbreviated list of accomplishments: the trophy case near the principal's office stuffed with shiny metal; the victories at out-of-state tournaments; the scholarships. "Last year one of my top debaters, Donnell, got a full scholarship to the University of Northern Iowa because of his debate skills," she said. "All he has to do is argue in college and they pay for him to go."

"I want some of that," said a girl with bright red hair sprouting from the top of her crown.

"Yeah," Rinehart said. "All he has to do is argue with *attitude*."

She paused to let that sink in. Even for cocky kids, it was difficult to fathom such success at a school like Central. Over the past half century, the school had become a nationally recognized symbol for the despair of urban education. It was the flash point of Kansas City's riots in the late 1960s. In the early 1970s the school's security guards carried handguns as they roamed the halls. Through the 1980s and '90s, ABC, *60 Minutes*, scores of newspapers, and even Jesse Jackson paid visits to Central—all to tell virtually the same stories of failure or slim hope. And then, in 2001, as if for final emphasis, Missouri education officials put the school on alert, declaring it "academically deficient."

The students stared at Rinehart blankly. "At this point," she continued, "if you don't know anything about debate, don't worry about it. That's my problem. If you don't know anything about it in six months, then maybe it'll be your problem. But for now it's my problem."

She told the students to form a circle, and they sluggishly scooted their desks across the tile floor. "Debate is basically arguing," she said, sitting down, crossing her legs off to the side, and leaning forward on the desk. "And this is what we're going to be arguing this year." She cocked her head toward the board and again read aloud the resolution to improve mental health services in the United States, the topic selected by coaches from across the country for the year ahead.

"What does that mean?" she asked, facing the kids again. "What is mental health?"

The teens blinked back at her.

Finally one boy offered, "Health is healthy."

"Your brain," added another.

"People who have mental health problems, what do we call them?" Rinehart asked.

After another long pause, one student looked up and said, in a bored voice, "Mentally ill."

"Don't we have some not-so-nice words for them?" Rinehart asked.

Silence. Then a skinny boy with cornrows muttered, "Retarded."

"Okay," she said. "Retarded. What else?"

More silence.

"Come on!" Rinehart said, waving her hands in the air. "Crazy! Loony! Insane! Don't we have expressions? Off his rocker! Mad as a hatter!"

A few of the kids looked around at each other and raised their eyebrows.

"Statistics say 85 percent of the public is mentally ill," Rinehart continued, unfazed. "Don't you think we should help these people?"

Apparently, none did. Again, blank stares.

"Our job," she said, "if we're in a debate round, and we're on the affirmative team, we have to figure out how to help people who are mentally ill. How are we going to help them?"

She shifted in her chair. "Let's start with attention deficit disorder, because most of us know someone on Ritalin," she said. "Let's say we're the affirmative team and we've got lots of ADD kids we want to help. We decide we're gonna give them some Ritalin. But if you're on the negative, your job is to poke holes in that plan."

"What about the side effects?" one of the students, Phillip White, said suddenly, in a soft, high-pitched voice that betrayed the hard facade he was trying to maintain. All morning he'd leered at Rinehart from under the hood of his navy blue sweatshirt, the way his father might stare down fellow inmates at a penitentiary back in Phillip's home state of Ohio.

"*Ooooh!*" Rinehart said, her eyes widening. "You think there might be side effects?"

"There's always side effects," he said, sitting up a little straighter.

"What are some of them?" she asked.

"I dunno," he replied. "Paranoid. Tired."

"What happens in the long run if you keep taking the pills?" Ebony Rose blurted.

"Addiction," Phillip answered.

"Yeah," Ebony said, leaning back with his fingers laced behind his head.

Rinehart's eyes scanned her tiny class. "That's a debate, guys," she said quietly, as though she were spilling a well-guarded secret. "That's basically what you guys have just done. You've had a mini little debate. That's all it is. It's a game. Success in life is a game."

"It hard," Ebony said, shuffling in his seat. "The rules are hard. The game is hard." Unlike the other kids, Ebony had some experience with debate. For three weeks during the summer, he sat through hours and hours of lessons at beginning debate camp at the University of Missouri–Kansas City. He was the only one of Rinehart's recruits who made it to class, even though his schedule, put together by the bumbling counselors, said he should be in aerobics.

"Yes, it's hard." Rinehart nodded. "But it's worth it when you make the other team cry. You're gonna be so proud of yourself." She turned to one of her varsity debaters, who had sneaked in after the bell because, owing to an administrative mix-up in the district's central office, she had nowhere else to go. "How many teams did we make cry last year?"

"Three," the senior replied, glancing nonchalantly at her long bright red fingernails.

At this, Phillip leaned forward and removed his hood. A few other kids straightened up as well. "You will be amazed at how much you're going to learn in the next six months," Rinehart said.

She started breaking down the structure of a debate round, explaining each of its eight speeches, its cross-examination periods—the question-and-answer portions of debates commonly known as cross-x. But a few minutes into the lecture, the students slid back into their supine poses and glazed expressions.

"I can tell you guys are freaking out," she said.

She got up and rooted through a tall gray file cabinet until she found a thin stack of photocopied papers. She passed them out to the students. The kids looked at them. The sheets read "NEWSLETTER" in big bold letters along the left-hand side and contained two short articles about Humpty Dumpty falling off a wall, one titled "South Side Gangs Continue to Play Chicken," the other, "Dumpty Boy Found Dead by Wall."

Ebony cringed at his copy. "This is a joke, right?"

Standing between the encircled desks, Rinehart began reading aloud in a faux newscaster voice: "Cripts and Bloods led by Little Boy Blue and Little Red Riding Hood have been terrorizing citizens on the South Side." Then she switched into the role of Little Boy Blue, reading in what might be the worst imitation of a thug the kids had ever heard. "Yeah," she groused. "I've pushed a few eggs, but I was just playing. I would never really push an egg hard, or over the wall or anything. Man, it's just innocent fun."

The students looked back at her slack-jawed, not sure whether to be offended or to burst out in laughter. "Nobody's even laughing," she said. "I mean, come on!"

She continued through both stories. The first seemed to suggest that Humpty Dumpty had jumped off the wall in response to a dare. The second quoted a police officer, Lucky Ducky, as saying, "I suspect foul play."

Apparently, the residents of Mother Goose Village had been receiving pamphlets from a radical group known as the E.G.G.B.E.A.T.E.R.S., members of which had been convicted for the murders of Chicken Little, Half-Chick, and the Gingerbread Man.

"The only good egg is a boiled egg," Rinehart continued in the gruff voice of one of the E.G.G.B.E.A.T.E.R.S. "That Dumpty family has been uppity ever since they made friends with the king. Well, let's see what the king and his men can do now. I hate eggs."

She looked up at the class. "Okay," she said. "We have evidence that Humpty was pushed. And we have evidence that it was an accident."

She divided the class into two groups and passed out blank sheets of paper, which she instructed them to fold in half. On one side, she wanted them to list evidence suggesting an accident; on the other, facts indicating foul play.

Ebony volunteered to be secretary for his group. Phillip did the same for the opposing team. The kids huddled around Ebony, scanning the short columns of text. Finally a boy in cornrows offered, "There was a handprint."

"Handprint." Ebony nodded, writing it down. Minutes passed with no more evidence. Ebony tapped his pen against the page. Rinehart strode by and glanced over their shoulders. "You have a brain, too," she said. "Not every argument has to come from the articles."

"Little Boy Blue pushed him," someone finally suggested.

"And Little Red Riding Hood," another said. "She in it, too. They was cousins."

"Hood and Blue."

"They was a tag team."

"They was cousins."

Now both teams were chattering away, building their cases. Rinehart paced between them, smiling. "You guys are doing great," she said. "You're already doing advanced debate work. You're cutting cards. You're writing arguments. This is the name of the game."

When the teams had completed their lists, Rinehart lined them up standing opposite each other. She fished a quarter out of her pocket. "Call it in the air," she said, lobbing the coin and watching it clink across the floor.

"What part of 'call it in the air' didn't you understand?"

She tried again. Ebony called heads and lost. Phillip's team chose to argue that Humpty Dumpty had been killed. After Rinehart laid out the rules, the kids took turns arguing both sides, getting more and more excited as the game proceeded.

"In the article it says Little Boy Blue was pushing eggs," one girl said, shuffling her feet and chopping her hands in the air. "So maybe he pushed Humpty Dumpty a little too hard."

By the time it was Phillip's turn, he could barely contain himself. "It was Jack that did it," he said, stomping his foot and punching the air. "See, he was part of them E.G.G.B.E.A.T.E.R.S. And his mama said she didn't like no eggs. She say the only good egg is boiled egg. So it was murder. And Jack did it."

Ebony delivered the last speech for his team. "I ain't got nothing to say," he said, shrugging and glancing coolly to the side. "First of all, y'all didn't have proof. Second, eggs don't have hands. How you even know Humpty Dumpty was on the wall? I mean, he's an egg. Eggs don't even got arms."

"Nah, man," Phillip yelled, spinning around and jumping up and down. "Humpty Dumpty *do* have arms!"

"Where's the proof?!" Ebony demanded.

Phillip and his team huddled for the final argument. One of his partners pointed at a line in the fake newsletter and Phillip clenched his fist, grinning at the other team. He got up to close it out. "First of all, this is a fairy tale, right?" he said, smiling broadly. "So in a fairy tale, almost anything can happen. It says in the article that Humpty Dumpty was in a creative writing class. That he got teased in there. So that proves it. Eggs in creative writing class has to have hands."

Just then the principal's voice crackled across the PA system—morning announcements, the end of class.

"All right, guys," Rinehart said. "Wasn't that fun? Welcome to debate. You guys are now officially debaters."

TWO

ACADEMICALLY DEFICIENT

A YEAR AND A HALF EARLIER, in the spring of 2001, just as Ebony was nearing the end of his stint in middle school, I paid my first visit to Central High. I came as a reporter for *The Pitch*, a news and entertainment magazine published weekly in Kansas City, at the invitation of Bryan Dial, the school's student body president. I met him at a contentious school board meeting at the district's central offices, where he spoke out on behalf of his recently demoted principal. It was a time of political turmoil in the district, which had been operating for nearly two years without state accreditation. Less than a week before I met Bryan, a slim majority of school board members called an illegal secret meeting to fire the superintendent, the nineteenth in twenty years. The next day the federal judge who oversaw Kansas City's twenty-four-year-old desegregation case reinstated the superintendent. But the damage was done; the following day the superintendent very publicly declined the job, calling the school district's governance "fatally flawed." This drew headlines nationwide, further spreading the school district's reputation as one of the worst in the country. After the meeting, while my fellow reporters crowded around board members for quotations, I sidled up to Bryan. He was eager to talk to me. He felt personally insulted by the media's coverage of Kansas City's public school system, where he had spent most of his eighteen years. It was his world. And the constant flow of negative stories seemed to say that he and all the people he grew up with were inferior, almost worthless. He wanted a reporter to spend some time in his school and meet more kids like him: just as bright and capable as any other.

The next morning I got in my car and drove east across town, a trek I would make many, many times over the next several years. To bisect Kansas City this way is to fully experience its split personality. It's a journey many white Kansas Citians don't dare make. For me, it began two blocks in on the Missouri side of the border with Kansas, where my apartment was located, on Thirty-ninth Street, also known as Restaurant Row. With its funky used-book stores and coffee shops, and bistros offering everything from lamb curry and saffron rice to bubble teas and vegetarian spring rolls, it's one of those stylish nooks that make cities bearable for people like me. Three-story homes, flowering lawns, and lush, full-grown trees surround the hip commercial zone, spreading in all directions and broken up here and there by clean, quiet parks. As one heads east, the blocks of stately homes are interspersed more and more with tall, compact apartment buildings bearing the flourishes of early twentieth-century architecture, columned porches and balconies, and intricately carved cornices, some a bit run-down with age, but not so much as to destroy the homeyness of the neighborhoods.

Then, at Troost Avenue, a long commercial thoroughfare of mostly vacant storefronts, the landscape shifts abruptly. Suddenly the blocks resemble broken smiles with wide gaps between rotting teeth. Every other house, it seems, has been torn down, its lot left to grow weedy and litter-strewn. Many of those still standing appear to be close to falling down, with sagging porches and peeling paint, a few with boarded windows and NO TRESPASSING signs tacked on their front doors. Crossing the busy north-south streets, one sees ghosts of a long-dead economy, one- and two-story buildings that housed grocery and shoe stores and haberdasheries fifty years ago. Most have windows covered with opaque paint and braced with slabs of plywood. Unlike neighborhoods to the west of Troost, though, these streets are full of activity, with dozens of people treading the sidewalks between bus stops. They're all black. There are old men, with their chiseled faces and crooked postures, and women shepherding three, sometimes four children, and small groups of young men walking slowly along, wearing ball caps and khaki cargo pants with the waists cinched just above their knees. These are the poorest zip codes in the city. In the neighborhoods around Central High, the unemployment rate is 42 percent. One out of four workers earns less than $10,000 a year, and more than a third of the families with children live under the poverty line. The median income in the area is $22,000, compared with $46,992 for the Kansas City metro area.

A couple miles later my journey ended at a broad building of sturdy gray brick and painted steel, sitting back from the road, beyond a rolling lawn with middle-aged trees. Entering the parking lot, I marveled at the grand symmetry of the edifice, the hulking wings fanning out from a circular atrium of mirrored glass. It seemed out of place, like a mighty ark that set sail from somewhere in suburbia and washed up on a ghetto shore.

On first inspection, Central was worse than I imagined. Each morning at seven I passed through the school's metal detectors to meet Bryan or one of his friends. For the better part of a month, I followed them from class to class, where more than half the desks sat empty. Most of the student body had been purged from the rolls after months of absences, or they had already failed their classes and saw no point in coming, or they were simply off enjoying the springtime, knowing a parent would write an excuse. In each classroom I found dozens of computers, part of a twelve-hundred-unit network that was once acclaimed on national TV but has since stopped working. Only a couple of the machines in each room were equipped with a mouse. ("Kids keep stealing them," one teacher told me.) Most of the "lessons" I sat in on felt like babysitting sessions, with the teacher reading a magazine or visiting with a handful of students while the rest of the class chatted or, at best, copied answers from a textbook onto fill-in-the-blank Xeroxes. At one point, a teacher in an algebra class told me, "I hate math." And then she stuck out her tongue to blow a raspberry. Bryan and his friends enjoyed a privileged status because they were smart and well behaved. Teachers let them come and go at will, so I often roamed the colorless hallways with them or watched as they surfed the Web. It became clear that Bryan was sailing through high school on a false sense of accomplishment.

While I was there, ten adults bearing yellow name tags took a two-day tour of Central High. They arrived each day before the morning bell rang, emptied their pockets of keys and cell phones, and passed through the school's metal detectors. "They look like they're armed," one student said as she watched them stride by in their suits and ties.

They came from all corners of Missouri, some from as far away as St. Louis. Half were teachers. One was a school superintendent. They were appointed by the state's top education officials to find out why Central's numbers were so bad: only one out of three kids who come in as freshmen wind up wearing a cap and gown at the end of their senior year; just seventeen out of more than three thousand students who took achievement tests over the last five years were proficient in math, English, social studies, and science; only one scored at the advanced level, and, in that instance, only in math.

The visitors spent their days observing classes, jotting notes, and referring to lists of questions they carried in green folders: "What kinds of instructional strategies did you observe most commonly in the classes?" "What kinds of interactions did you observe?" "What kinds of interruptions or disruptions were present that interrupted the learning process?" They saw few strategies and a whole lot of disruptions. The lectures they witnessed were painfully slow, halted every minute or so by protests and outbursts from a handful of rowdy kids. The observers pulled students and teachers out of classes and took them to the school's library for long interviews. The students were blunt: "Most of the teachers here don't even know what they're teaching." "They're just babysitting us." "We don't learn nothin'." The teachers, in turn, blamed the kids, their parents, and the world: "We get all the bad kids in the district." "How can we teach kids when they don't have a home or don't have enough to eat?" "Test scores will never be up to state expectation levels, and that's because of poverty."

Months later, in the fall of 2001, when Ebony's high school career was just three weeks old, Missouri education officials compiled the visitors' notes into a thin report that was so alarming one member of the state board of education cited it as evidence of "educational malpractice." Released to the public and widely reported in the media, it accused Central's teachers and administrators of having such low expectations for the students that they had essentially abandoned the curriculum. When asked what Central's mission is, these teachers were at a loss for words. State officials found the school's planning and learning processes, its management and organization, its instructional leadership, its programs to aid struggling students, and its efforts to monitor academic progress to be "inadequate." Amid this "lack of a shared vision" and direction, the observers noted, the students were "making *no* academic progress."

After reviewing this report, the state's education commissioner officially declared Central "academically deficient." It was one of the first schools in the state to earn this dubious honor. Incredibly, the commissioner told reporters he viewed the distinction as a positive. It meant that Central would get additional assistance from the state in the form of a management team (another group of educators from around the state who would visit the school periodically) and more money to help improve the school. Though the school did win a $91,000 grant for staff development and a few computers and books, the principal later told me, "I've gotten no help from the state. None whatsoever."

The management team visited the school on two occasions, holding meetings in the library from which came lists of recommendations that were full of the sort of bureaucratic jargon the school's leaders had tossed around for years: "Core Department Instructional Leaders"; "Small Learning Communities"; "Job Embedded Staff Development." It offered suggestions that were never implemented, such as a later start time for the school day and the creation of a "vertical curriculum team" with officials from Central and the three middle schools that feed into it. The school's staff lounge was littered with documents such as these, stacks of school improvement plans stuffed in the corner and gathering dust. Like many of her colleagues, Coach Rinehart has served on the committees and special project teams that devised these schemes to save the school. Every year there seemed to be a new plan. The year before the auditors arrived, she was involved with the school's "cluster" initiative, in which a group of teachers who specialize in different subject areas were teamed up and assigned to a group of incoming freshmen. This, the reasoning went, would allow teachers to meet regularly to coordinate their study plans and share information. Rinehart's bosses in the main office had high hopes for this plan. They started with a small group of students, but a week or so into the fall semester the teachers discovered they were not, in fact, teaching the same kids. A scheduling snafu had to be undone, and a bunch of students were shuffled nearly a month into the school year.

That plan was tossed into the pile of previous plans in the staff lounge and essentially forgotten, as were the recommendations from the state management team. But the "academically deficient" label stuck. Now the school carried an easy-to-remember slogan for its pitifulness. Students and teachers alike felt demoralized. "I spent two hours with those people," Rinehart said of her interview with the state's audit team, "and *this* is what I get for it? My kids are making *no* academic progress? Thanks a lot."

Rinehart caught my attention immediately. On the first day I was there, Bryan showed me the fruits of her labor: the school's trophy cases, filled with plaques, medals, and awards that Central's debate team had won against schools with national reputations for greatness, such as New Trier on the North Shore of Chicago, Montgomery Bell Academy in Nashville, and the Blake School in Minneapolis. I was momentarily stunned. Before I'd even set foot in Central, I'd formed an idea of how it would be: bleak, violent, hopeless. This perception came, truth be told, from the work of other journalists who'd ventured before me into schools like Central. I was prepared to follow their lead, to give an unflinching account of America's miserable underside. I expected to find an anomaly or two, a gifted child (Bryan, perhaps) to play the role of the victim in my exposé. But these trophies shattered my preconceptions. They suggested a systemic force—a small one, yes, but not so tiny and insignificant as to be an aberration. Instantly, I understood Central's debate program to be a sort of anti-public-education system, a positive charge to counter the negative of segregated schools. These shelves of shiny metal documented several cycles of high school students who had, in a game of fast-talking, wit, and sheer brilliance, closed the academic achievement gap between black and white students—something educators and policy makers across the country have been grappling with for years. This, I thought, is the sort of success story that should be told and retold until it takes root in every urban school across America.

I learned immediately, however, that Rinehart's program wasn't spreading into other schools. In fact, it was struggling just to survive.

Almost as soon as she began taking her students to tournaments at predominantly white schools in suburban Kansas City, she received calls from officials at the Missouri State High School Activities Association accusing her of breaking rules. MSHSAA oversees high school extracurricular activities across the state. They threatened to ban Central from competing—not only in debate, but in other activities as well, such as football and basketball. Often the allegations were false, and were reported by anonymous coaches elsewhere in the state. In response, Rinehart had taken her kids to the more challenging national debate circuit, winning more debate rounds but drawing more intense scrutiny from the activities association as well.

Listening to Rinehart's pained accounts of this conflict, I began to see the sketchy outlines of what I came to Central hoping to find, though it was far uglier and more immense than I could possibly have imagined. It became instantly clear to me that I might find in this small but strong debate program, in the story of its struggles and triumphs, the whole of racism as it exists in America today.

So a year later I embarked on what I thought would be a season-long adventure with the team. I'd be a detached observer, hanging quietly on the periphery with my notebook and cassette recorder. I had no idea that the journey would change my life, that I would break my boundaries as an objective journalist and become deeply involved with the team, first as a friendly adult with good advice, then as a relatively well-connected advocate, lobbying against absurd limits imposed by downstate bureaucrats, then as an assistant coach, spending my own money and forsaking my social life to give them more opportunities to compete. I came in thinking this game of debate, with its recorded history dating back to 500 B.C. with Protagoras, Socrates, and Plato, might well be the ultimate savior for forgotten inner-city teens. By the end, I would be on a campaign to change the game itself, believing wholeheartedly that these black kids from the East Side of Kansas City are the real saviors, with their own plan to save a game so intrinsic to democracy—a game that is, by all appearances, dying out in America.

THREE

EBONY ROSE

ON HIS FIRST DAY back in Rinehart's class, Ebony claimed a desk next to the bookshelves near the far end of the room. He dropped his backpack on the floor with a thud and sank into his seat, drumming his thumbs on his desktop. He was lanky, with large hands and elbows he had not yet grown into. His shorn head peaked at its crown, and his ears jutted out in nearly perfect half circles. Acne and a thin frost of whiskers covered his chin, and his brows stuck out from his forehead like crooked roots. He fidgeted constantly, as though he were waging a war of mind and body. He'd cock his head back and to the side in a pose of cool detachment. Then he'd suddenly rub his nose with manic ferocity or grab a sheet of paper and crumple it into a ball. Then he'd catch himself and lay his hands on his desk to resume his "just chillin'" stare. His eyes were soft, though, so he never looked too tough.

If it weren't for the debate squad, Ebony wouldn't be at Central. His aunt Shavelle Christian, with whom he had lived since sixth grade, knew it was a bad school. To her, the "academically deficient" label was just administratese for what she already knew. Like most black Kansas Citians, she had relatives who went to Central, one of the first schools in the city to be integrated in the mid-1950s after the Supreme Court struck down forced segregation in its ruling on *Brown v. Board of Education*. By 1960 it had become nearly 100 percent black and has remained so almost every year since.

Shavelle's uncles and aunts told her it was a tough school, plagued with fights. The teachers, they said, assigned little homework. To hear them describe it, one would think Central was little more than a dangerous day care for teens.

Then there was the stuff she heard from friends who worked there. One, who worked in the school's cafeteria, told her that a lot of the students don't even know how to count change. They'd hand over a ten-dollar bill for a six-dollar order and demand five in return. Sometimes Shavelle's friend purposely shortchanged the kids just to test them. They often took whatever she gave them, stuffed it in their pockets, and started to leave before she stopped them to explain what she'd done. "They just can't count," Shavelle's friend told her.

Shavelle was dumbfounded. How could *teenagers* not know how to count money? "At some point," she later told me, "somebody's got to say, 'Hey! This is not good enough!'"

Teachers at Central told her pretty much the same thing. "You've got to get Ebony out of here," they said.

In Shavelle's mind, the Kansas City School District wasn't good enough for any kid, much less her nephew Ebony. Ever since he was an infant, he had amazed her with his curiosity and intelligence. He was a quiet child, withdrawn, always reading. He devoured everything from encyclopedias to novels to how-to manuals. His mother started him on Dr. Seuss books not long after he began walking. His grandmother supplied him with a Bible and stacks of religious books. He loved the stories—Noah's ark, Daniel and the lion's den. In Shavelle's mind, Ebony read because he wanted to be smart. But Ebony told me he read because he "didn't have shit else to do." When he did talk, it was often to cite some fact he'd picked up somewhere—how birds and animals go silent during eclipses, how you can tell east from west by gauging the position of the sun, how the earth once had one giant continent that slowly broke apart and formed the landmasses we live on today.

It astounded Shavelle the things Ebony knew. "You're too young to know stuff like that," she'd say to him. When he was no more than five months old, he'd group his blocks and toys by color and shape, sorting them into neat piles. Before he was even a year old, she says, he learned to relieve himself on a toddler toilet. "What's wrong with you?" Shavelle asked her sister Tina Marie when she saw Ebony doing this. "He's too young. It's too early."

"Trust me," Ebony's mom replied. "I know my baby can do it."

Shavelle was just ten years old when the call came in at three in the morning—the police saying her young nephews had been abandoned at a seedy motel on Independence Avenue, Kansas City's best-known red-light district. Tina Marie was addicted to crack and had simply vanished on that cold December night. Shavelle listened in shock when her mother told the police that they couldn't bring the boys to her home. Shavelle told me her mother was an alcoholic who slipped in and out of recovery, who could barely take care of the kids she had, much less two more boys. But the boys had nowhere else to go. Their father, Curtis Moore, was uninvolved; he lived and worked in Kansas City, but he wouldn't have anything to do with his sons. (Tina Marie also had a third son, Enoch, by a different father, who raised him.) The thought of those kids being set adrift without family tore at Shavelle's conscience. She vowed then and there that she would one day take care of them. As soon as she graduated from high school, she began dealing with the red tape. Years later, Ebony and Isaiah moved in with her and her husband, Eddy, and their two kids, Duran and Tiarra. Shavelle and Eddy were both very young, in their early twenties, and each had a full-time job. They were living in a cramped rental a few blocks north of Central High, and their lease was month to month, so their home was not yet secured. When Ebony and Isaiah moved in, ages thirteen and eleven, respectively, they were unsure whether or not they could trust her, because so many promises made to them had been broken.

Before Ebony even reached kindergarten, he and his brother had become wards of the state, shuffling back and forth between just about every homeless shelter and foster home on Kansas City's East Side, while their mother fell deeper and deeper into drug addiction. The facilities were always too small for the number of people living there, shelters with bunk beds all lined up in one tile-floored room, the foster homes just your average turn-of-the-century bungalows or two-story four-squares, creaking with age and often in need of new paint. Typically, Ebony and his brother would stay in these places for just a month or two before being uprooted and carted somewhere else. With no real space to claim as his own, Ebony found the stories he read to be oases. School was one of the few constants in his life, and he always excelled there. He was most fond of the "mean" teachers, the ones who cared enough to discipline him when he goofed off. He'd do his best to impress them, racing to the front of the room to scribble an answer on the chalkboard, helping explain the lessons to classmates. During sixth grade, right after Ebony moved in with Shavelle and Eddy, one of his teachers called his aunt several times to complain about his cockiness. "I continually ask him not to interrupt me in my class," the teacher said. "He wants to tell me how to teach my class."

Back then it was still cool to be smart. Ebony felt important and valued when he'd offer the right answers in class or when teachers would hand back his homework assignments with A's printed on them in red ink. When he reached middle school, though, his status shifted. The kids started to pick on him because of his name. "Your mom thought you was a girl," they'd tease. (A few got it, though. "Ebony means black," they'd say. "Damn right!" he'd reply proudly.)

His classmates were gaining a different notion of what it meant to be black. Some of his friends who had gotten good grades through elementary school began skipping school to smoke weed and fight and steal cars. One day he asked one of his school-yard buddies why he sold drugs. "I been knowing this for, like, a long time," the boy replied. "My daddy did it. And his dad before him did it."

Ebony saw the cycle. All his life he had stayed off to the side, studying the machinery of his world. "I just, like, take notes of everything around me," he later told me. "So I, like, notice everything around me and try to see why it is and why it isn't. Why they do the things they do." He called it "natural adaption." When I asked him once about his middle school classmates, he complained, "Everybody have to be hard. It's like everybody had to be the toughest. But, like, it can't go like that. Somebody have to be soft. Somebody got to be medium. Everybody just can't be tough. That's how I view it. I ain't no punk, but I ain't gonna be like a thug. I know I'm not going to get no $100,000-a-year job with my pants sagging, with braids in my hair, with gold teeth and a cell phone, walkin' in and sayin', 'Deez nuts, nigga!'"

He felt pressure to fail. When his peers grew tired of razzing him about his name, they tore into his studiousness, teasing him for raising his hand and turning in his assignments on time. In middle school the teachers no longer had the time or energy to praise his good work. They were too busy maintaining order. Their lessons became painfully slow, remedial, and Ebony was bored out of his mind. "Math, seventh grade, I didn't learn nothing," he told me. "I got tired. Fourth quarter in eighth and seventh grade, I didn't do shit. I'm like, fuck it. I quit." For the first time ever, Shavelle spotted Ds on his report card.

The kids were worse when he got to Central High. Again he endured taunts about his name. Fights broke out in the hallways almost daily, and sometimes in the classrooms. Each afternoon no fewer than ten school district cop cars parked outside the school to ensure safe passage to the buses. During his first month at Central, right about the time state officials declared the school "academically deficient," Ebony took an assessment test. When the results came in showing that his math skills were at the twelfth-grade level and that he could read as well as a college student, teachers started calling Shavelle. They urged her to transfer him to Lincoln College Prep, the lone high-performing high school in the Kansas City School District. To get in, students have to score well on tests. To stay in, they have to maintain a high grade point average.

Ebony wasn't hot on the idea. He was sick of being shuffled around. He was finally starting to feel at home at Shavelle's. Shortly after she took him and Isaiah in, they had moved yet again, to a big house a mile or so north of Central. He thought Shavelle and Eddy had bought it. In fact, they were on a month-to-month lease. Unbeknownst to Ebony, his aunt and uncle were worried that they might have to move again, perhaps even outside of Central's boundaries.

In truth, Ebony had always wanted to go to Central. The school's alumni are scattered everywhere in Kansas City, from clerks at corner stores to state senators. There was a time when Central couldn't be beat on a basketball court or track. And though years of academic failure had given the school a horrible reputation across the metro area, it still maintained some of its legendary pride. *It may be a bad place,* black Kansas Citians seemed to say, *but it's* our *bad place.*

EBONY'S TEST SCORES caught Coach Rinehart's attention. She made a habit of perusing the results every year, searching for new recruits for her team. A handful of freshmen had tested as high as Ebony. Not all would make good debaters. Her colleagues were always sending kids her way, but these were usually the well-behaved ones, the ones who did all their homework and sat quietly in the back of the class, not asking a lot of questions. But a few of Rinehart's fellow teachers understood what she was looking for: kids who buck authority, who are too smart for their own good. Even before she saw the test scores, some of Rinehart's trusted scouts were telling her about Ebony. "He talks so fast," they said, "half the time his family can't even understand him." Rinehart thought, *Wow. I've got to meet this kid.*

She and Brandon Dial, a junior and one of her top debaters, tracked Ebony down early in the second semester of his freshman year, finding him in a health class, where he was suffering through a slow lecture about muscles. They pulled him out into the hall. "We've heard good things about you," she told him.

Ebony shrugged and looked down at the floor. He was surprised. It wasn't the first time he'd been complimented by a teacher, but he'd never been sought after for his talents. Rinehart nudged Brandon, and he gave the sales pitch—trophies, out-of-state trips, the college scholarships, humiliated opponents from white suburban schools. Ebony responded the way most kids do. "I didn't even know we had a debate team," he said.

Rinehart invited him to visit room 109, headquarters for the squad. A few days later he showed up. He slipped quietly through the door and instantly fell in love with the mess of the place, the desks scattered every which way, the paper strewn across the desktops and the floors, and the stacks and stacks of books and paper on the shelf-desks that lined the perimeter of the room. There was freedom here. A dozen or so kids moved about the room at will, chatting among themselves, cutting blocks of text out of photocopied pages, or reading out loud about subjects he'd never heard in school—social realism, political capital, weapons of mass destruction. The kids seemed confident, cocky even, but not because they were hard. "Like, they knew it was cool to be smart," he told me. "That's the first I ever experienced that at school."

A few minutes later Rinehart arrived from a staff meeting. She spotted him and said, "You're the kid who reads fast. Let's hear you read."

"Now?" he asked.

"Why not?" She grabbed a random document bearing a gray box of fine print and handed it to him. He read it cold, with rhythm and force. Some of the other kids in the class stopped what they were doing to listen to him. They looked at one another, eyes widening.

That night Ebony went home and told his aunt, "I don't think I want to leave Central yet."

RINEHART FOUND SOME scholarship money to send Ebony to summer debate camp at the University of Missouri–Kansas City. It was like a fantasy come true. College had always loomed large in his life goals, and here he was on a vast campus in the middle of the city, staying in a dorm room for three weeks with his buddy Ray, whom he'd known since sixth grade. They'd trek across campus every morning to spend their days in lecture halls with rows of theater-style seats with collapsible desks, listening to college kids explain a game that seemed like a dress rehearsal for the real world. Ebony's goal in life, he has often told me, in almost complete seriousness, is "total world domination." And in debate he saw a chance to acquire the tools he'd need for his quest. He soaked up lessons about things he never learned in school— the various branches of government, economics, psychology. But what he really got into were all the peculiar aspects of the game, the jargon, the myriad strategies, the rings of status among debaters. Here was an exclusive subculture of power, and he had been invited to join. The instructors walked with the swagger of decorated warriors. They had weapons—file boxes full of documents gleaned from academic texts and government studies and newspapers—and they had their own terms of engagement, manly, power-ful words like "counterplan" and "disad" and "kritik" and "cross-x." Ebony mastered this new language quickly, and by the end of camp he was laying his opponents to rest in practice rounds.

He came into the 2002–2003 school year less a sophomore than a neo-phyte ruler eager to expand his conquest. His goal in life was to become as cool and important as the top seniors on the squad—Brandon Dial and, above all, the legendary Marcus Leach, who had competed at the National Forensic League's national championship and qualified for the prestigious Tournament of Champions.

But when he got his schedule, debate wasn't on it. He'd been enrolled in aerobics. So for the first few days of school he spent his mornings in the crowded counseling office, trying to get his schedule changed. Then school shut down for a few days when a heat wave hit Kansas City, sending temper-atures into the low 100s. The heat wave wound up being one of the longest in Kansas City history, so nearly two weeks passed before Ebony found him-self sitting in a full debate class, fully enrolled, ready to learn what he'd stuck around Central to learn.

Ebony claimed a desk and looked on as roughly two dozen kids filled the room. He sat up and hummed, bobbing his head as if to a low hip-hop groove. He knew they'd be no match for him.

FOUR

ANTOINE LEWIS

A FULL TWO WEEKS into the semester Rinehart was starting over. For the second time she went through her "welcome to debate" routine. She handed out copies of the season's schedule, with its list of tournaments as far away as Chicago and Washington, D.C. She told the students that in one week they would head off for Kansas City, Kansas, to compete in a practice tournament at Washington High School. It took a second or two for this fact to register.

"We go to Washington?" one girl asked. "Are we going to be debating?"

Rinehart nodded.

"Next week?!"

Rinehart laughed. "Okay," she said. "You'll be fine."

There was no time to debate Humpty Dumpty again. Rinehart dove right in. "Find someone you can work with," she said as the kids looked around at one another. "And if you need to move, move."

A few kids stood up. Most were slow to move. Ebony stayed in his seat, tapping his desk. "I'm working with who?" he asked nobody in particular. "I'm working with Shadow Man. No, I'm just playin'. I'm working with myself. Shit, I don't know."

He shot a glance at me and said something like, "My partner is Joe"—I can't be sure, because I didn't write it in my notes. I immediately edited the comment from the experience. This story would be Ebony's, not mine, I had decided, not realizing that I had become part of Ebony's story, whether I wanted to or not. Much later, after he and I had grown as close as family, Ebony told me how honored he'd felt when I'd introduced myself and told him I would be writing a book about him. In his mind, I became his partner at the first handshake. In this way, he rationalized my awkward, out-of-place presence in his world. He cast me in the role of his chronicler and, in all honesty, his ticket to possible fame and immortality. The same would be true for the other members of the squad, Rinehart included, though I would be the last to realize and understand.

ACROSS THE ROOM, Rinehart grabbed a slender kid by the wrist and pulled him over to Ebony. Stringy dreadlocks dangled around the kid's eyes.

"Eb, this is Antoine," she said. "Antoine, this is Eb." And she walked away.

"What's up, Antoine?"

Antoine dropped himself into the desk next to Ebony's and slumped so far down his chin nearly touched his chest. "Sup, man?" he said, raising his hand to cup his chin. He spied Ebony out of the corner of his eye. Ebony sat up straight and shuffled a stack of photocopied documents.

"Okay," Rinehart said, leaning against her desk at the front of the room, "everybody got a partner?"

"Yep," Ebony said, drawing it out long and slow.

"Here's the deal about partners," Rinehart said, holding up her hand to quiet a few kids who were still talking. "You're not marrying your partner. It's somebody you debate with. End of story. I've had partners who don't even talk to each other, they hate each other so much. But they debate together like dynamite. It's just a working relationship that you use to be successful in a debate round. No more, no less."

"So we're just using each other," Antoine scoffed.

"Exactly," Rinehart said.

Antoine laughed and looked at Ebony.

"You're exploiting the other person to the best of your ability."

"Don't give up, dude," Ebony told Antoine.

"Yeah, and don't give up, dude," Rinehart said. "Those are great words."

Ebony crossed his arms and looked down at Antoine. "My son, Antoine," he said. "You be my prodigy. I teach you how to debate."

"You gonna teach me?" Antoine asked, perking up out of his thinker pose.

"Yeah."

"How you teach me? It's all strategy."

"I'm gonna teach you how to debate," Ebony said, opening a folder and closing it. "And you become good like me."

"Not if I beat you. I probably could."

"No, you can't beat me," Ebony said, bringing a brief silence to the conversation.

"My son, Antoine," he continued. "My prodigy."

"If you say so."

Ebony grabbed a copy of the schedule with a quick jerk, clicked his pen, and drew a circle around the DEBATE–Kansas City championship, scheduled for mid-December. Then he drew a long curving arrow toward the bottom of the list to Urban Debate Leagues' Novice Nationals, set for late April. There were thirteen urban debate leagues across the nation, from New York to Seattle, and for Ebony their championship was the big show, a giant step on his march toward world domination, toward a life that matters. "Win this takes you here," he wrote in big letters in the margins of the page. He handed the note to me, to document in history.

Then he looked again at Antoine. "Yes, my son," he said, bobbing his head slowly like some Mafia don. "You stick with me and I will take you places. You my prodigy. I take you places you never seen."

ONE WEEK LATER Ebony rolled into class with a pair of glasses hanging down around his chin. His eyes were a little weak, but he hated to bother with specs, so he rarely wore them. He grabbed a gray plastic file box in the back of the room and set it on a desk. He opened it and peeked into one of the accordion files stuffed inside, thumbing through sheets of evidence he'd acquired at camp and from varsity debaters at after-school practice. A girl stepped up to him and asked, "Where's Antoine?"

Ebony shrugged. For a week Ebony had attended every after-school practice—"boot camp," Rinehart called it. Antoine hadn't shown up for a single session. And here it was, the day of the Washington High tournament, the first challenge of the year, and Ebony wasn't even sure if Antoine would show up. Ebony was ready to tear up the competition. But a good debater can carry a team only so far. Each round is divided into eight speeches—four for the affirmative team, four for the negative. Each partner has to deliver two speeches—one constructive, where the case for or against the resolution is laid out, and one rebuttal, where the opponents' arguments are refuted. When it's your turn to speak, you've got to carry your own.

Antoine finally arrived fifteen minutes after the bell rang, wearing a blue LAS VEGAS T-shirt with a white tiger printed on it—a violation of Central's dress code. He took a couple steps inside the classroom and leaned against the shelf-desk where Rinehart had set out bulky jars of generic peanut butter and jelly and a loaf of bread for the kids who stay after school for boot camp. He lingered there for a moment, eyeing Ebony, before sheepishly sauntering over to his partner.

Ebony sat backward on a desk, his feet on the chair, reading their negative case. He gave Antoine a sideways glance. He could tell Antoine was poor, the way his khakis were always stained and frayed at the cuff. Antoine wore bottom-of-the-line black Nikes. His shirts lacked the sheen of newness, were often rubbed thin at the shoulders. He was skinny, too, the kind of skinny that made Ebony wonder if he ate enough. He moved like a marionette with a few broken strings, a sagging posture tossed about by occasional bursts of energy. Antoine flopped down into a desk beside Ebony and idly rubbed the stubble on his chin. He didn't yet have enough whiskers to form a goatee, much less a beard. His narrow, uneven dreadlocks hung down to his eyes, almost obscuring his best feature. He had round, gleaming eyes like the characters in the Japanese comics he and his posse of misfit friends admired, with long, delicate lashes.

"Why weren't you at boot camp?" Ebony asked curtly.

Antoine told him that his mom wouldn't let him go. He had forgotten to ask her in time, he said. It wasn't true. He'd actually been at his friend Donyell's house, playing video games and listening to Linkin Park and John Mayer CDs. In truth, Antoine wasn't sure yet about this debate thing.

As she had with Ebony, Coach Rinehart had sought him out the previous school year. She tracked him down in a computer class, pulled him out into the hall, and said, "Your grades are kind of in the toilet, aren't they?"

"Yeah," he said, taken aback.

"That's a shame," she continued. "Because you're smarter than that. I can tell. Your test scores are really good."

Antoine thought, *Who is this woman? How does she know my grades and test scores?*

"I'm Jane Rinehart," she said, extending her hand. "I teach debate and English. I'd love for you to join our team."

Antoine responded the way Ebony did. "Wow," he said, "I didn't even know we had a debate team."

He reluctantly shook her hand. For months after that, he'd bump into her in the hall now and then, and she'd say, "When are you coming to debate?"

"I'm thinking about it," he told her.

Antoine's motto is: *I'll try everything once. And if I like it, I'll try it again.* But the prospect of joining debate seriously challenged this philosophy. The mere word "debate" conjured images of kids with taped-up glasses and pocket protectors, a life with no hope of ever getting laid. He imagined it as school to the tenth power, and by then Antoine had little interest in school. To him school was conformity, an institution of meaningless routines far removed from the real world and the many things that fascinated him: space, philosophy, religion, and the endless varieties of music and art. He wanted to learn everything he could, and in his experience school only impeded his curiosity. This became clear in sixth grade, the same stage when Ebony watched his peers fall off and turn hard. Being thin and small, Antoine wasn't much of a fighter, and the thug life was even less interesting to him than his history lessons. Not that he didn't like history. He loved it. But not the kind they doled out at his middle school in Kansas City, Kansas. There the story of how Antoine's world came to be was reduced to an endless procession of meaningless dates and fill-in-the-blank worksheets. The teachers rewarded the ability to be quiet and follow directions, not the eagerness to ask questions and understand.

So Antoine sought knowledge other places. He read unassigned books by J.R.R. Tolkien. He'd watch the Discovery Channel with his mother, Lisa Lewis, and they'd talk late into the night. He'd always been a bit of an odd-ball at Central, partly because he was from Kansas. His first year he made the mistake of telling a new acquaintance that they'd been "crowed"—a Kansas term for being put down. The kid looked at him funny and said, "Kansas, right?" From then on, Antoine's nickname was Cro. The name suited him. It sounded like a comic book character, one with black clothes and a prefer-ence for nighttime. He sought like-minded friends who were always on the hunt for new things—obscure comics and movies, any music other than hip-hop. Not that he didn't like hip-hop. He just wanted more. He got a skateboard long before the trend had hit the black side of town, and he and his crew rode all over the city, checking out the funky stores and coffee shops in the art district and talking to bums.

Antoine's "try anything" credo got the best of him, though, in the late spring of his sophomore year. Rinehart urged him to attend a debate orien-tation at the University of Missouri–Kansas City. He agreed to go as much to get out of class as anything else. He filed into a spacious auditorium on the midtown campus with kids from all over the city, from both sides of the state line. They started by watching the most boring video Antoine had ever seen. In it two pairs of black teens in suits and ties took turns at a podium, read-ing monotonously from dull texts about weapons of mass destruction. They spoke in image-less debate terms Antoine couldn't begin to understand.

Then the emcee, Linda Collier, director of debate at UMKC, told the students to divide into two groups. Each group then had to come up with ar-guments about locker searches, one side for, the other against. After a half hour or so, they reconvened and took turns making their cases. Antoine thought his peers' arguments were shallow. He started scribbling furiously into his journal. Then he got up to speak, even though he'd sworn he wouldn't do so when the exercise began. His leg shook, he was so nervous. But a few words into his speech, his ideas began flowing out of him. He spoke so quickly and for so long that he had to stop and gulp for air, at which point Collier thanked him and asked for the next speaker to step forward.

"Wait a minute," Antoine said curtly. "I'm not done."

The crowd whooped as if he were a badass, cutting off an adult like that. When he finished, they erupted in applause.

When he filed out of the auditorium with the other kids on the way to their buses, Collier pulled him aside. "If I don't see you debating next year," she said, pointing a finger at his chest, "I will come to your school and hunt you down like a dog."

And now here he was, a couple weeks into debate class, about to embark on his first competition, ready or not. *So what?* The class was all right, he supposed. Better than ROTC, that's for sure. He'd signed up for debate in the spring, but when he picked up his class schedule in late August, he was alarmed to instead find the military training class printed at the top of the list of courses. Central's administrators loved ROTC. For them, the lack of discipline at Central was the biggest challenge, and they believed the "hup-two" rigidity of Army rules eased the lawlessness. Its hierarchy provided goals. And the pseudo military unit took on various community projects, such as fixing up run-down homes in the surrounding neighborhood. Sometimes reporters from the daily paper and nightly newscasts came by to do glowing puff pieces about these projects, which offset the negative coverage that came every fall when the state's test scores were released. If the counselors' screwup had dealt him a class other than ROTC, gym perhaps, he probably wouldn't have bothered having it changed back to debate. But the last thing he wanted was some sophomore bossing him around, making him do push-ups. So he braved the mob scene in the counselors' office and got debate put back on his schedule.

Actually, debate class was better than any of his other classes. Its disorder pleased him. The desks were strewn about rather than arranged in the standard straight rows facing the teacher. And Rinehart's lessons seemed to jump all over the place. If he got bored, he knew she would change course in a minute or two. Or digress. Rinehart was always stopping to let the class go off on some fact or idea that caught their attention. All through his school career, Antoine loved it when his teachers got sidetracked and started talking about things that would never wind up on a test, such as politics or pop culture. These were the only times when he felt like he was learning. Debate, he quickly discovered, was all about this kind of exploration. Nothing was absolute. Anything Rinehart or one of his fellow students said could be turned over and disproved. And these refutations, in turn, could be countered as well. When the discussions got really good, he found himself peeling layers off ideas in his mind without a sense that he'd arrive at a core of truth. It was as if the more he learned, the less he knew, and that made him feel very much alive.

But there were also rules to the game, and these bored him. In a debate round he'd only be able to speak for thirteen minutes—eight for his constructive speech, five for his rebuttal. He'd have three minutes to grill his opponent during cross-examination, or cross-x, and another three minutes to be grilled. And during his speeches he'd have to read from evidence—"cards," Rinehart called them—photocopied paragraphs of text in teeny type. It seemed so limiting. Some of these cards were intriguing—the one that said forty-six million people in the United States suffer from some sort of mental illness, for instance, or another that claimed that "psychiatrists have labeled everything as a mental illness, from nose picking to altruism, lottery and playing with action dolls." But a lot of these cards seemed as pointless as the worksheets he filled out in social studies class. Like the ones dealing with "topicality."

When Rinehart started talking about T—that's what she called it, T—Ebony had pulled out a folder. As he flipped it open, he splayed the fingers on his hands and hummed as if to suggest the file contained the light of God. "I won a lot of rounds at camp with this," he bragged.

T, Rinehart explained, addresses whether or not the affirmative team is dealing with the subject of the resolution. "What if the affirmative stands up and runs a case that says we have to give after-school snacks because kids get hungry after school and then they can vomit and throw up and it's really bad and they get sick headaches and they're miserable?" she asked the class. She went on to explain that this wouldn't be fair. Without topicality, teams could run cases about anything, and their opponents would be at a loss for ways to counter them because it's impossible to research every subject on earth. Topicality is the core of debate, the first question addressed in just about every debate round: *Are we discussing what we agreed to discuss?* Debaters must be prepared to justify every position they take in the face of this question.

"Topicality is the playing field of debate," Rinehart had said. "T is your boundary lines."

This Antoine could understand. But Rinehart was proposing they argue that the subject of equal insurance benefits for mental illness cases was not topical, which seemed absurd. Of course it was topical. "Mental health" was written on practically every card. But apparently this didn't matter.

Rinehart handed them a folder with cards full of text that drilled into every minute, boring detail about the most boring words in the resolution: "significantly"; "services"; and "public." Antoine didn't want to nitpick over boring details; he wanted to get into the ideas and issues that really matter. He wondered, *Why not just let us argue?*

Worse still was "flow," debate jargon for note taking. To stay competitive in a debate round, Rinehart explained, teams had to answer every argument, every piece of evidence their opponents put forward. To keep track of all these lines of attack, she told them, they'd need to know how to flow. She used a deck of cards to teach them how to do this. She gave Antoine and his classmates long sheets of blank paper. Then she laid cards one by one faceup on the desk in front of her and read them off—queen of diamonds, two of clubs, ten of hearts, and so on. She instructed the students to write abbreviations—QD, 2C, 10H—for these cards in a column on the left side of the page (she told lefties to write on the right side of the page). She read very quickly.

"Okay," she said after laying down five cards, "those were the affirmative team's first arguments. Now I'm going to lay out the negative team's arguments. Write these down next to your first column."

Then she laid down eight cards in a row beside the first row, calling out both the name of the new card and the one she set it down beside. She kept doing this, going back and forth between affirmative and negative, until her desktop was full of cards. A couple of times she purposely skipped cards, not laying new ones next to ones in the previous row. When the students caught this aberration in the pattern, they protested.

Rinehart looked up at them and smiled.

"Those are dropped arguments!" she exclaimed. "Your opponents will sometimes not answer your arguments. And when that happens, you need to tell the judge that they dropped an argument and they should vote for your team. You'll be amazed how often this happens. And when it does, and you point it out to the judge, you win."

It didn't take long for Antoine to get sick of this exercise. It was like algebra—too much process, not enough payoff. He laid down his pen midway through and looked over at Ebony, who was hunched over, furiously scribbling down the meaningless abbreviations. *At least he's into it*, Antoine thought. Antoine found it amusing how cocky Ebony was, always going on and on about "my son" and "my prodigy," as if he were a Jedi knight.

Antoine's no-shows at boot camp showed he wasn't thrilled about being a disciple, especially to a sophomore like Ebony. Antoine was a junior, after all. He had no idea how much desperation lay beneath his partner's posturing. For Antoine debate was the least of many evils. But for Ebony debate was a way out of obscurity. Winning the city championship would mean much more to him than a free trip to Atlanta. It would give his life a meaning it didn't have when he was moving from homeless shelter to foster home and back again. Antoine could tell that Ebony was annoyed by his lack of commitment. But Ebony was good at hiding his true feelings. Antoine had no idea how much his partner had already come to depend on him.

FIVE

ACROSS THE DIVIDE

THEY BOARDED THE BUS and it lurched out of the parking lot onto Indiana Avenue, heading north toward the highway. Antoine rested his chin on his hand and stared out the window at the neighborhoods surrounding his school. Decades ago, the busy intersections near Central High were home to dozens of thriving businesses—restaurants, dime stores, even a bookstore. Many of them burned to the ground during the riots of 1968, which had begun with a mass demonstration at Central after the assassination of Martin Luther King, Jr. The few storefronts still standing either were boarded shut or housed tiny churches, their names hand-painted on warped wood in crooked letters. From some angles, in some spots, the residential side streets could look as quaint and homey as those in other parts of the city, boasting rows of sturdy three-story shirtwaists with stone porches and tidy lawns. But on every block Antoine saw one or more abandoned or deteriorating houses, often surrounded by groups of men standing on grassless patches of lawn, doing nothing.

His house was like that—not surrounded by loiterers, but in disrepair. The Lewises lived half a block east of Troost on Thirty-fourth Street in an old, cramped ranch house with a small add-on second floor. It was by far the most decrepit domicile I ever visited in the United States. The front door was boarded shut, and the back door had no knob; when I'd stop by there, I'd have to hook my fingers into the hole where the knob should have been to steady the door, lest it fly open from the force of my knocking. This was the only way I could contact Antoine after school, because the family had no phone. It was the middle of winter by the time I would finally visit Antoine's house, and for heat they'd turned on all the burners on the stove full blast and set the oven at five hundred with the door left open. The previous winter, after a rate hike established by Missouri Gas Energy, they'd gotten a bill for more than $1,000, which they couldn't afford, so their gas was turned off. The house was full of kids. Antoine had four younger brothers and a sister who wasn't yet four. Full of energy at the sight of a visitor, they were bounding in and out of the kitchen, ducking back and forth past the searing-hot range.

Lisa didn't work, choosing instead to stay at home until the youngest, Haley, was old enough for school. And despite all the obvious signs of poverty—the toilet that had to be flushed with a pair of pliers, the broken front window covered with secondhand blankets to fend off the cold, the exposed electrical sockets, and the walls and ceilings shot through with cracks and mottled with water stains—Lisa's presence gave the home a sort of richness. Within minutes of our talking, I found her to be as articulate as a published author. Indeed she did dabble in writing, spinning stories about romance or fantasy in longhand on whatever paper there was to be found, writing during whatever hours she could steal while her boys were at school and Haley was napping. She loved to read, always had, and she lived for a good debate. Evenings, the family often gathered around the TV, a good-sized set with a full cable package and an Xbox attached, by far the biggest luxury in the house, and watched low-budget documentaries on the high-numbered cable channels such as TLC, National Geographic, and sometimes CNN. These sparked long, deep conversations that probably kept the kids up longer than they should have been.

Antoine's friends loved his mom. They called her Aunt Lisa. Despite its shabbiness, his pad was the preferred hangout for his crew. They were there almost every hour they weren't in school or out exploring the urban wilderness. Or when Antoine's dad, Jay Lewis, wasn't there, which was most of the time. On paper, Jay appeared to have a good job. He managed the office of a day-labor shop downtown. But his salary was a mere $28,000, which placed the Lewises just below the federal poverty line. For a family of eight living in Kansas City, Lisa figured you'd need to make about $90,000 to really get a taste of American abundance—two cars, a decent home, vacations, a monthly day of fun for the whole family. It would cost the Lewises more than $100 to go to a movie and McDonald's, and they never seemed to have that kind of cash. And it wasn't just the usual life expenses that ate up all their paycheck-to-paycheck cash flow. Their financial life had been a constant run of rip-offs and bad luck.

For instance, Lisa still owed more than $7,000 on a $6,000 student loan she'd taken out more than fifteen years earlier to become a certified travel agent. The college went bankrupt almost as soon as she graduated, and her degree was essentially worthless. Her loan, on the other hand, was bought up by a bank somewhere in Nebraska, and it was every bit as valuable as the day she'd signed the papers. Interest continues to pile on the premium while she's unemployed and not paying. When she's worked, the minimum payments, which go almost entirely toward interest, have been garnished from her check.

Lisa had seasonal work with the IRS for a while, before her youngest, Haley, was born. It was pretty good money, so she set out to buy a car, stopping at a used lot on the south end of Troost. It was a 1990 Cavalier, a few years old but not in bad shape. The dealer wanted $5,000, and he was willing to offer credit, even though her credit had been shot by her school loan fiasco. The payments would be $250, which is almost as much as I pay for a 2003 Pontiac I bought off the lot for $19,000. They shook hands, and she started reading over the paperwork, despite the salesman's urging her to just sign and look it over later.

Then she noticed that the payments were specified for every two weeks, not per month like she'd been led to believe. She was only clearing about $600 every other week at the IRS, so this payment schedule—stretched out over two years for a total of $12,000—would bankrupt her.

She told the man no way. He got flustered, flipped through the stack of forms he'd handed her, found her signature, and pointed to it. "Too late," he said. "You've already signed." He pointed over her shoulder. "See that sign there? NO REFUND. You can't renege."

"What are you gonna do?" she barked back at him. "I just can't pay it. You're just gonna repossess it next week. Give me my eight hundred back."

He offered to cut 25 percent off the payment. She refused. And back and forth they went until she threatened to take him to court and he dropped the payments to monthly, stretching the term of the loan out a bit.

A few months later she got laid off from the IRS. She couldn't find another job immediately, so she drove the car back to the lot and walked away from it, along with the nearly two thousand she'd already paid. Two weeks later she got a telemarketing job at *The Kansas City Star.*

Jay had his financial mishaps, too, but he tried to keep those secret from her. One time she'd learned that he'd taken out a payday loan that, with its biweekly fee system, worked out to have roughly 500 percent interest. She needled him and found he'd taken out a number of these loans over the years. *No wonder we're always broke*, she thought.

Then there was the house, with its outrageous rent of $600 a month. They'd been in a great situation in Kansas City, Kansas, a few years earlier, living in a paid-for house Lisa had inherited from her grandmother. But some jealous relatives sicced the city inspectors on them. The bureaucrats spotted a few hazards and mandated repairs that, at $8,000, they couldn't afford. They learned of a grant program offered by the city. But they didn't qualify, because the deed was still in her grandmother's name. She tried to get it changed, but her relatives stymied her efforts.

Having been sprung into action, the city officials bore down on the Lewises. Lisa and Jay left with the kids one weekend to visit relatives and returned to find an UNFIT FOR HABITATION sign affixed to the front door. They had to leave immediately.

They tried to get something through the federal government's Section 8 housing-subsidy program, but they couldn't find a house that met all the government's requirements for a family as big as theirs, namely one with five bedrooms. There are many such homes in Kansas City, of course, but few in the poorer areas, where slumlords fatten their pockets with government checks. Friends told her to lie on the application form, but she couldn't bring herself to do it.

Desperate, Jay seized on an opportunity offered by a distant friend who was just getting into the real estate business. The friend had warned them that the four-bedroom house wasn't quite fixed up yet, but he promised to make the changes. The man did put on a new roof, but he left off the gutters, so water spread freely along the outside walls, seeping into cracks and rotting the wood on the inside.

Before the Lewises moved in, the house had been the lair of drug dealers, who'd trashed the place. The water had been shut off, and when a worker from the city came by to turn it on, they discovered that rags had been stuffed down the pipes, clogging them. It cost them $100 to fix, and their landlord didn't reimburse them. The fix didn't really solve the problem, though. During hard rains their pipes would back up, spilling sewage into their backyard and their neighbor's as well. Lisa would sometimes pester Jay to call their landlord and get the problem fixed, but he never would. He'd always say, "Let me get stuff straight on the job first."

Jay would go into work at about five in the morning and not return until eight at night, so exhausted that all he could do was gulp down a few bites of food and collapse on the bed. He worked six days a week, and when he wasn't in the office, his pager rang almost nonstop. Time was when Jay had as vibrant a personality as his wife. He devoured books about Black Power. He was the consummate family man. "He used to be the kick-ball daddy," Lisa told me. "And the walk-down-to-the-store-and-buy-a-grocery-bag-full-of-penny-candy daddy. And pass it out on the way back from the store to the little kids. 'Oooh! It's candy man!' That was him."

He had dreams of being a big-time concert promoter and was on his way there when a teenager was shot and killed in a nightclub he was helping to run. After that happened, he was desperate for work, any work. He scored a temp job and quickly moved up in the company—in title, not so much in income.

"Now he goes straight out to that car and straight to work," Lisa said. "He rarely speaks. He's like a machine."

THE BUS TURNED WEST on the highway and careened through the downtown loop and across the rail yards that separate Kansas and Missouri.

Antoine stared hard at the limestone bluffs overlooking the confluence of the Missouri and Kansas rivers, the tufts of trees that broke up the urban sprawl. He and his mother often fantasized about living in a more bucolic place, and these small aberrations of nature that dot Kansas City's landscape gave him a sense of what such a life might be like. He had only left the Kansas City metro area twice in his sixteen years, both times to St. Louis.

Antoine knew his mother saw debate as an opportunity for him to find the freedom she wanted. She described the program to me once, and to him often, as a "lotus flower, like something beautiful growing out of the muck." And maybe she was right, Antoine thought as the bus rumbled westward. All along, Rinehart had been promising chances to travel, and here they were, cruising across the state line. Never mind that it was to a state he was born and raised in. He had never seen the border's wooded hillocks on this particular day, under the sunlight of this unique moment.

In many ways, he was already a traveler. In his mind, he'd taken the first step of a journey by freeing himself from the conformity of his school and neighborhood. His imagination took him places. Half the time he was at school he'd tune out the teachers' lessons to conjure an epic fantasy novel he planned to write. It takes place on a distant planet named Mira, or, he told me, "some weird, mystical-sounding name I haven't set yet." Mira has one sun and two moons, and the trees and grass are a purplish blue, and some plants glow at night. It's inhabited by various species of people. "You got your weird lizardy-alien-type people," he explained. "Your cliché alien-looking people. And the weird humanoid, closest to what we look like."

The book's main character would be from a species of warriors. These beings start life with pale skin of slightly warm hue and blue eyes. Their lives would be gauged not by years or earthly notions of aging, but rather in the way of a video game, where there's a set quantity of life force that depletes with each injury in battle. With each hit, their skin grows redder, darker. Their eyes shift from blue to auburn, then deep black. The darker these beings become, the more respect they enjoy—though they're also visibly closer to death. "By the end they'd be a deep mahogany color," Antoine told me. "When they get down to a certain point, instead of dying, they cease to be. They're gone. They get blacker and blacker, and then disappear."

SIX

NEW LEADERS RISING

THE BUS PULLED in to Washington High's parking lot. The building was older than Central's, but not ancient—a no-frills 1950s-style cluster of brick, painted steel, and glass rectangles. Antoine followed his classmates into the school's cafeteria. The place was filling up with kids, some of them dressed up, but most casually attired in baggy jeans or khakis and T-shirts like Antoine and Ebony. The team from Paseo Academy, another school from the Missouri side, filed in, clear winners of the fashion show—the boys sporting thigh-length, six-button blazers with flashy stripes, the girls in snug skirt suits, their hair sculpted in festive curls. Antoine's eyes followed a couple of the Paseo girls. A few white kids milled about the scene, but most were black, hailing from the Kansas City, Missouri, and Kansas City, Kansas, school districts, which were 85 percent and 75 percent minority, respectively. Five years earlier this scene couldn't be found in Kansas City. A few inner-city schools had maintained speech and debate teams, but for the most part the activity had died in central Kansas City. This afternoon affair was sponsored by DEBATE–Kansas City, a league founded by Linda Collier, director of debate at University of Missouri–Kansas City, in 1998.

Collier had been coaching college debate at UMKC since the mid-1980s. She thought it was a great activity, but it bugged her that it was dominated by white men. She tried recruiting women and African-Americans on campus, with little success. Then, at a college tournament in the mid-1990s, she got to talking with Melissa Maxcy Wade, director of debate at Emory University in Atlanta. Both had built powerhouses in the male-driven game. Emory's and UMKC's teams were routinely ranked among the nation's top ten. In 1994 Collier won a national championship. Wade won in 1998. Wade was on her own quest to diversify the game. In 1985 Emory founded a small debate program among high schools in inner-city Atlanta. She invited Collier to attend an upcoming meeting at Emory with the Open Society Institute, a philanthropic venture funded by the billionaire George Soros. In the late 1980s the OSI had established high school debate programs in Eastern European nations—countries newly formed after the fall of the Soviet Union—as a way of fostering the principles of democracy. Those efforts had been successful, so the OSI hoped to expand into America's struggling urban communities. Within months, Collier had about $97,000 to fund a program for one year. (The OSI has spent a total of $9.3 million on the National Association of Urban Debate Leagues—commonly referred to as the UDL.) Soon DEBATE–Kansas City started holding regular afternoon tournaments at schools across the urban core, as did partner leagues in New York; Washington, D.C.; Baltimore; Providence; Atlanta; Detroit; Chicago; St. Louis; Newark; Los Angeles; San Francisco; Seattle; and Tuscaloosa, Alabama (the Tuscaloosa and San Francisco programs have since folded). In its first five years, more than twelve thousand city kids have participated nationwide, more than a thousand of them from Kansas City.

Antoine sat down at a long lunch table with circle-shaped plastic seats attached to it, a few of which were broken or missing. Ebony set down their file box and took a seat on the tabletop. Antoine opened the file and pulled out the folder containing evidence they'd have to read when they'd be the negative team in a debate round. At a debate tournament, all teams alternate each round between affirmative and negative. This tournament would offer two rounds. Antoine had gone over their affirmative case several times during class. He felt fairly comfortable with it. He wasn't so sure about the negative side of things. He opened the file and started reading it. Ebony yanked it out of his hand. "You second speaker," he said. "You don't gotta read that." He air-smacked at Antoine's face.

Holly Reiss, DEBATE–Kansas City's top administrator, a woman in her early thirties with shoulder-length blond hair, climbed atop a table on the other side of the cafeteria. "Can I have your attention?" she yelled, raising a hand. "We're about to hand out the schedules for the first round. But before I do that, I want you all to know and understand that this is not a tournament. This is a workshop. You'll be debating against teams from your own school. There will not be a winning team."

She apologized about these low stakes. During DEBATE–Kansas City's first year, they'd hosted afternoon tournaments almost every week. Collier figured there's no such thing as too much debate. But as the school year was drawing to a close, Coach Rinehart received a call from an official at the Missouri State High School Activities Association. He told her she had broken the association's rules by taking her team to too many tournaments. In Missouri kids can only compete ten times a year. The administrator threatened to suspend her squad from competition for a season. Distraught, Rinehart called Collier, who called the activities association. She asked to meet with the association's board of directors. In June 1998 she drove to the Tan-Tar-A resort on the Lake of the Ozarks and pleaded with them not to punish the school. She took the blame, saying she had started this league without even knowing about the activities association and its rules. The board members forgave the transgression, but warned her not to let it happen again.

Collier was relieved but miffed. She couldn't understand the logic of a rule that limited debate. The game could succeed, she reasoned, in the very schools that are academic and social failures. She'd seen it inspire kids who couldn't care less about school to dive into their studies simply to avoid losing an hour-long battle of the minds with someone their own age. Even during the first year of the UDL's existence, recruiters at colleges across the country were taking notice. They were finding that debate builds the skills kids need to make it in college. With affirmative action under attack, some schools, such as Marist College in upstate New York, began blindly offering scholarships to urban debaters, knowing they had a seven-in-ten chance of recruiting a minority.

Collier asked how she might go about getting the rule changed. They told her that she wouldn't be able to. The association's bylaws were crafted by its voting members, high school administrators from across the state. As a college official, she had no authority to make such a proposal. Principals at her member schools could propose new rules, which would then have to be voted into place by all the members—several hundred schools across the state. Collier did the math and quickly surmised that the four Missouri schools in her league wouldn't have the political clout to have their way. So she scaled back the schedule to four tournaments a year to allow teams opportunities to compete outside the league. She refashioned the first tournament of the year as a workshop. Without victors and interschool competition, the bureaucrats at the activities association were satisfied that it wasn't an official tournament.

EBONY GRABBED THEIR file box and bolted off. Antoine pushed his way through the crowd to grab a schedule. He scanned the sheet's columns of type, finding his name and his room number. He stepped out into the hall. The corridor was dimly lit, but more festive than Central's. Student artwork and motivational posters were plastered on the walls. Growing up, he'd heard plenty about Washington High—his mom's alma mater. Lisa Lewis often told tales about Monsieur Morris, her French teacher. A well-traveled black man, he re-created his trips to Europe for the class, passing out imported cheeses for the students to munch on while he flipped through slides and told stories about all the people he'd met. Lisa told her son that Morris "opened up the ghetto" for her. He taught her that just because she's black, it doesn't mean she has to be a certain way, or only listen to certain kinds of music, or eat certain kinds of food. "You can be whatever you want to be," he'd told her.

At sixteen, Antoine was poised to head down this path. He was brilliant, obviously ideal for college. But he was nonetheless at risk of being one of the first debaters in the history of Rinehart's program to not graduate on time. And he was only a junior.

WHEN ANTOINE got to the room, Ebony was already there. It overlooked a courtyard, and afternoon light sifted in through a shaggy bush outside the window. Algebraic equations covered the chalkboard, above which hung a sign that read, THOU SHALT NOT WHINE. The school had no air-conditioning. Though the city's heat wave had broken days earlier, the room felt hot and muggy. Antoine pulled a desk over beside Ebony's and grabbed the affirmative case file. He would deliver the first speech. Their opponents came in the room—Phillip, the kid who had broken out of his tough-guy pose during the Humpty Dumpty debate on the first day of school, and Shantel Hair, a shy freshman with a closely cropped Afro. Ebony leaned back and stared them down. "Rinehart told me to go easy on you guys," he said.

Antoine moved to the front of the room, shrugged his shoulders to loosen up, and began reading.

"As the nation's baby-boomer generation ages and life expectations and life expectancy grows," he read, "the number of Americans with mental disorders likely will rise, confronting our society with unprecedented challenges, a landmark U.S. surgeon general's report has concluded."

His head was lowered and he was almost mumbling. I could barely hear him above the echoing clamor of kids roaming the hall. But after a minute or so, he slid into a groove. He lifted his hands and thrust them emphatically. When the judge called out that there were fifteen seconds remaining, he lowered his evidence and looked directly at his small audience.

"We can't afford to wait," he said in a voice full of force. "Waiting means . . ."—he paused to draw out the drama—"*death.*"

Ebony dropped his pen, leaned back, and waved his arms in a smooth dance move.

Shantel slowly rose from her seat. Antoine stood at attention, rigid, staring straight forward, ready for cross-x. "I have no clue what he just said," Shantel said as she cupped a hand to her mouth to cover a nervous giggle. She took two tentative steps toward Antoine. "I'm confused. Can I sit back down?"

"What are you confused about?" the judge asked.

"*Everything.*" She bit at a fingernail. "Um," she began, "in your own words, what does your plan do?"

"We allow people with mental illness to receive the same benefits as people with physical illness," Antoine answered bluntly, his eyes locked on the judge.

After a long pause she tried again: "So how would your plan actually—"

Then she spun on her heels, laughed, and stomped back to her seat. Ebony flashed Antoine a thumbs-up.

Phillip strutted to the front of the room, rolling his shoulders coolly with each deliberate step. He tapped his stack of evidence against the desk, cocked his head back, and scowled down at the judge. When he began reading, though, his voice came out high-pitched and soft. His head down now, he shuffled his feet back and forth as if he had to pee. But when he concluded his speech, he resumed his intimidating stance, which he kept up while Antoine interrogated him for cross-x.

Then it was Ebony's turn. He didn't use any preparation time. He was ready to go. He tapped his evidence cards against the desk and dove in. Bent at the waist, he rocked on his feet and chopped at the desk with his hand. He looked like a singer, brows arched and eyes softened, as if every syllable flowing from his lips were sublime, full of color. His tone was even and calm, though the words came out mangled. Ever since he was a toddler, he had trouble talking, mushing his syllables together and confusing consonant sounds. The family never had the problem diagnosed; they merely assumed it was hereditary. The problem worsened during his motherless years adrift in the social services system. At one point, his speech impediment was so severe that a social worker told his family he'd never succeed in school, and on several occasions he simply stopped talking altogether for weeks and months at a time. Since moving in with Shavelle, he'd improved considerably. But he was still hard to understand. The judge leaned forward, trying to decipher the speech, catching enough recognizable syllables to get the gist. Phillip and Shantel laid down their pens, looking past him, their eyes glazed. When he finished, Ebony broke into another dance.

As the round progressed, the debaters grew more uncertain, their speeches broken with awkward silences and "um"s. They fidgeted as if covered with a rash. But Ebony kept up his pimp pose. He closed the round by filling his allotted five minutes with a thumping beat of facts and counterpoints. When the judge's timer beeped, he jabbed his forefinger at the desk and said, with power, "Vote affirmative!"

"I felt the force," he said as Antoine helped him pack up the file box. "I felt the vibe."

ON THE WAY to the next round Ebony swayed back and forth as they cruised down the hallway and sang, "Let my people go." "I'm in bondage!" he shouted, and shook his fists in the air. He stepped into the room and took a look at his opponents, one of whom was dancing, and said, "We about to whup on these people up in here."

He and Antoine were on the negative this time. While one of his opponents delivered his speech, Ebony pulled out his topicality file, the one he'd opened in class a few days earlier in a dramatic way, as if it were imbued with the light of God. He tapped his fingers on his desk as he silently read it to himself.

Later, during his cross-examination of the kid who'd been dancing, Ebony asked, "How are you all topical?"

The kid silently shifted his eyes. Ebony asked again.

"We're not," the kid replied, and looked down at his feet.

Ebony's eyes widened. "No further questions," he said, and then he raced over to me, barely able to contain his excitement. "They just admitted they're not topical," he whispered.

When Antoine got up to deliver the final negative speech, he reached for a stack of cards. The judge stopped him. "You don't need to have any paper," he said.

Antoine looked at him, confused.

"Get your ass over here," Ebony said, delivering an air slap as Antoine approached. Ebony tried to explain that their opponent had basically given them the win by admitting during cross-x that their case was not topical, but he was hyper with excitement and his words came out in a jumbled rush. Antoine rubbed the stubble on his chin.

"You only have to make one argument," the judge explained. "Just get up there and say that they concede that they're not topical. That's it."

"Okay," Antoine said dubiously. He sauntered up to the front of the room. "Um, the affirmative team admits that their case is not topical," he began. "And that's bad because, uh, topicality is, like, the playing field. It's not fair. We can't be expected to prepare for every argument out there, like cookies or picking your nose or stuff like that."

He wasn't convinced. It seemed too easy, anti-intellectual. He tried to fill up the rest of his speech time with the analytical arguments he'd worked out in his mind during the round, how forcing insurance companies to apply parity to mental health and physical health coverage would cause economic repercussions. But the judge had stopped taking notes and was sitting with his arms crossed behind his head. So Antoine stopped with a minute and a half to spare. Ebony slapped him on the back when he sat down. Antoine shook his head and smiled. It was a hollow victory, but he'd take it.

They packed up their file boxes and moved to the school's auditorium, where debaters were gathering by school into separate encampments. Antoine and Ebony sat down among their Central teammates. Asked how it went by a couple of girls on the varsity squad, Antoine shook his head. He still wasn't sure what had just happened.

Ebony sat alone, a few rows toward the front. All he cared about was winning a speaker award. He figured he had to win one. If he wasn't named one of the top speakers from his school, how could he expect to contend for the city championship? He leaned forward, his eyes trained on the tournament's director, Reiss, the blond woman who had handed out schedules earlier in the afternoon. He smacked the seat in front of him, raised his head, and scanned the crowd, nodding a couple times, as if to say, *A'ight. A'ight. I could beat you all.* Then he focused again on the blond woman. The wait was maddening.

Finally she began calling out the schools' names one by one. Everyone received a participation award certificate, so entire squads rushed to the edge of the stage. For most of them, the rounds had been confusing, even embarrassing, this being their first venture into the game. But that was no reason not to celebrate. They hooted and danced down the aisles. The woman handed out medallions to the top two speakers from each school, their rankings based on an average of the speaker points they'd been

awarded in both rounds. She called Central last; they were the league's powerhouse. Ebony moved to the stage with his peers. She passed out the certifi-
cates. When she announced the second-place speaker, the girl who won was
so surprised she doubled over and covered her face. The director paused before reading the winner's name, playing up the tension. Ebony lowered his
head and looked the other way. When she read his name, he just rubbed
his nose and reached out for his medal. He was too cool to even smile when
his teammates mobbed him and slapped his back.

On his way to the bus, he glanced at me a few times to gauge my reaction to this victorious turn of events. He stopped, squinted into the low sunlight, and said to me, the chronicler of his rise to power, "This is just a taste.
The real test comes October 15."

SEVEN

BRANDON DIAL

BRANDON DIAL POPPED a CD in the jam box and cued track five. He hooted. "This here's my theme song, boy!" he said. There were a half-dozen kids in room 109, staying after school, cutting cards for the first varsity debate tournament of the year, just four days away. They could work all they wanted, Brandon didn't care. He had better things to do, lyrics to memorize. Tech N9ne's new album, *Absolute Power*, was out. Not officially—it wouldn't hit the shelves until midnight. But Brandon had already bootlegged a copy off the Internet and burned it onto a twenty-cent Maxell CD. "Slacker," Brandon's new theme song, had the makings of an anthem, with a plodding syntho-string pulse and lyrics to inspire even the most disaffected teen to rise and shake his fist:

> *I don't do enough, I just fool around*
> *Y'all can go to hell, how does that sound?*

Brandon paced the room, his XXL Eckō shirt hanging midway down his thighs. He bobbed his head and tried to sneer, but his puffy cheeks and long lashes still made him look like a doll. From a distance, you could faintly see the trim patches of whiskers on his upper lip and the tip of his chin. A thin frost of curls capped his crown and faded neatly to smooth skin above his ears. His eyes were half-shut, like usual, his head angled back as if he were regarding a fool. The anthem suited him. Brandon had come down with chronic senioritis way back in the sixth grade. Now that he was a senior, the symptoms had turned near fatal. He'd done hardly any work during the first few weeks of school and had already missed a few classes. At Central, if you skip four, you flunk—unless you could get an excuse, and Brandon always could. Still, he missed lessons and was falling behind in algebra and English, two credits he'd need to graduate. He was four assignments behind in AP English, and Mrs. Rinehart was threatening to kick him out. He read just a few pages of Chinua Achebe's *Things Fall Apart* before giving up. "It's dull," he explained to me. "If she had given me some, like, Malcolm X to read, I read that no problem."

He showed up for practice every day, but only because it was his routine. After four years on the squad, room 109 had become an annex of his home. It had high-speed Internet access and a steady stream of friends coming and going. Even food—when he was hungry enough to brave the warm, generic grape jelly Rinehart left out on a desk near the door. "Rinehart," he said to his coach as she came in the room, "when you gonna put that jelly in the fridge? It's nasty."

She walked past him, to the jam box, and silenced Tech N9ne.

"Seriously," he continued, picking up the jar. "It says on the top, 'Refrigerate After Opening.'"

"You believe everything you read?" she replied. "When are *you* going to do some work? I'm beginning to think I shouldn't even bother taking you guys to Iowa. You're not ready."

"Shit, I'm always ready."

"Mouth!"

He laughed. It was so easy to push Rinehart's buttons. She was like a mom. He joined the team on day one of his freshman year. His older brother, Bryan, had debated. As a middle schooler, Brandon grew jealous as Bryan traveled on weekends to Iowa, Omaha, and Chicago. He wanted to go, too. At the time, his dreams of nabbing a basketball scholarship to the University of Kansas and becoming a first-round draft pick in the NBA were drying up. When he was younger, his goal was to succeed where his father had failed. Bryan senior was a top player in high school, and he received a scholarship to play ball for the University of Colorado. But then he got Brandon's mom pregnant with Bryan, and he had to give it up. By the time Brandon reached his early teens, it had become clear that he wouldn't get the chance his father had. He grew to five and a half feet tall and stopped there. His metabolism slowed, and his legs and belly bulged. His grandfather, with whom he and his brother and his younger sister, Brittany, had lived since their mother, Joyce Ferguson, died when Brandon was eight, was always on him to set aside the ball and focus on his education. Early on, his grandpa wouldn't tolerate low grades. If Brandon came home with so much as a C on his report card, his grandfather would force him to sit at the kitchen table and study from the minute he got home from school until dinner was served.

Alonzo Dial, or Bapa, as Brandon called him, was a cantankerous old man. He was retired, having spent almost all his working years as a mechanic at a Firestone shop in Lee's Summit, an eastern suburb. Before settling down, he lived on the streets for a while in New York City, and the experience tempered his worldview. "He was always like, 'Whatever you do, I did it before, so you can't get nothing past me,'" Brandon told me. "He used to tell me how he had holes in his shoes. He used to wrap his feet up in newspapers and stuff just to keep warm. He used to teach me how not to get beat by people, how to pay attention to things. Like, 'Keep your money. Don't trust a lot of people. Because friends really aren't friends. They'll turn their back on you. Quick.'"

Brandon had already experienced this, not from friends, but from family. With just a high school diploma, Bryan senior drifted through a series of low-paying service jobs, barely earning enough to care for himself, let alone three kids. After their mother's death, the Dial kids drew monthly Social Security checks. But Brandon's older brother, Bryan, told me these checks came to their legal guardian, their father, and he would cash them and pocket the money. One of Brandon's aunts eventually took Bryan senior to court to make sure the money would go to its rightful recipients, Bryan explained.

Brandon could count on Bapa, though. All through grade school and middle school, his grandpa would be waiting every afternoon in the same parking spot in the back row of the school's lot. Having braved the uncertain streets, Alonzo was a disciple of routine. He woke up at the same time every day, cooked the same breakfast of eggs and bacon or sausage, ate it in the same spot at the kitchen table, and watched the same morning news show for the exact same amount of time before retreating to his bed, which was in a corner of the living room because his emphysema made it too difficult to climb the stairs. At ten he was awake again for *The Price Is Right*, then *The Young and the Restless*, followed by the twelve o'clock news on KCTV.

When the kids got home from school, he'd spice things up with a good debate—less about political matters than about the orneriness of today's youth, namely Brandon. But as the old man grew more feeble, Brandon got more wily. He learned to argue around bad grades and lie about homework. Not that there was much anyway. By sixth grade, school wasn't so much about education as about socializing. His friends were there, so he went, too. He was more interested in learning about fashion and trends and new music on BlackPlanet.com or BET than about the stuff printed on the worksheets he was given. He did the minimum necessary to move with his friends to the next grade. All he had to do was scratch out a few correct answers now and then, and stay relatively well behaved, and he kept moving along.

For a while debate was an antidote. He wanted to win trophies like his brother—he envied those even more than the travel—so he worked at it. Besides, the game was fun. He didn't really think of it as education, even though it forced him to read stuff he would never have considered reading, stuff about the government and society and philosophy, with words as long as his forefinger. The summer after his freshman year Rinehart sent him to debate camp at the University of Missouri–Kansas City, which should have been boring as hell, but wasn't. It was just classes all day every day, but there were girls there, and they were cute, and they seemed to have a thing for good debaters. Like school, it was a social scene. Unlike school, learning was cool. He went to camp every summer during high school—at Wake Forest, then at Catholic University in Washington, D.C. He debated dozens of after-school practice rounds during his underclassman years. And he filled the shelf above his bed with trophies. Now that he was a senior, though, the thought of practicing made him want to puke. He could only compete if a real win was on the line. If a judge wasn't sitting in the back of the room, it wasn't debate—it was a bore.

Still, Brandon had high expectations. Marcus Leach was his new partner. A fellow senior, Marcus was one of the best debaters Rinehart had ever
coached. As a sophomore, he competed at the National Forensic League's
national championship in Norman, Oklahoma. As a junior, he won a bid to
the Tournament of Champions, the most prestigious event for teams that
compete on the national debate circuit. That's what Brandon wanted: a TOC
bid. You can't get more pimp than that, he thought. It meant you were
among the best of the best in the nation. To get there, he and Marcus would
have to win in the high trophy rounds at one or more of a select number
of tournaments—each chosen because of its high level of competitive-
ness, based on the number of schools that fly in from around the country to
compete.

Rinehart headed off to a meeting. Brandon surveyed the room, his head
still jerking to the beat. Everyone else was quiet, still working. He walked
over to the jam box, tracked forward to the final song, and cranked it. He
grabbed a stack of evidence and a pair of scissors and—a full month into the
school year—sat down to cut his cards for the season. As he worked, he
rapped along with Tech N9ne:

I'm a playa, I'm a playa, oh, oh, I'm a playa.

"Yeah, boy!" Brandon howled. "I'm a player. That's my other theme
song. When I don't feel like working, it's 'Slacker' and shit. When I'm rollin',
I'm a player."

EIGHT

MARCUS LEACH

"**HEY! YO!** Brandon's a ho!" Marcus called out from the other side of the room. "We all know it. So let's show it."

Brandon let out a yelp.

"So, like, who's a bigger player?" Marcus asked Mike Sobek, a skinny, curly-haired debater from the University of Missouri–Kansas City who worked part-time at Central as an assistant coach. "Me or Brandon?"

"Brandon," Sobek said flatly.

"Than *me*?!" Marcus dropped his highlighter pen on the desk and stared at Sobek incredulously.

"Oh yeah." Sobek nodded, grinning.

"Man, you done lost your . . . ," Marcus sputtered. "Brandon's not even . . . He don't even have no girlfriend." At least Marcus had one of those, a skinny girl from Notre Dame de Sion High whom he'd met at UMKC's camp. They were both into debate and Counter-Strike, a computer game in which mercenaries hunt and kill terrorists. She even knew how to program in C++, which was way ahead of him.

"That's why he's a bigger player," Sobek said.

Marcus looked genuinely dumbfounded. "Doesn't make sense," he said.

"If you have a girlfriend," Sobek explained in a slow, patronizing tone, "you can't be a player."

"All we gotta do is compare numbers," Brandon shouted, standing up.

"Let's compare numbers. Let's get it crackin'." He pulled a cell phone from his pocket and held it out toward Marcus. "I don't work with paper."

"Brandon's a whore then," Marcus said quietly, picking his highlighter back up, pulling off its cap. He set it back down and leaned forward. "Sobek, how many girls do you have? How many girls have you had?" He jabbed his finger at Sobek's bony chest. "Huh? Huh?"

"I don't talk about that stuff." Sobek was the prototypical debate nerd: white, frumpily dressed in T-shirts and tan cargo pants, with a slightly sagging posture that suggested something between confidence in all things debate and insecurity in almost all else—above all, females.

"What about that Kim chick from camp?" Marcus asked, rubbing his hands together. "Man, that girl was sexy, man."

"Kim?" Brandon joined in. "Where's Kim? I wanna see this shit."

"She was sexy," Marcus said.

"A'ight, a'ight. Sobek, you didn't tell me about Kim."

"I don't tell anyone about anything," Sobek said, not looking up from the evidence card he was working on.

"Brandon, she had body. She was like a slut, too. Sobek, you'd be lying to me if you told me you didn't sleep with her."

"She *liked* you, Sobek?" Brandon acted as if this were the most shocking news he'd heard in a month.

"YO, UH, SOBEK," Marcus said, his mood suddenly serious. "Give me, give me, uh. I don't remember what the fuck *The Hollow Hope* was about, Sobek"— referring to a book by the University of Chicago professor Gerald Rosenberg about how the federal court system can spark sweeping changes in America, even more effectively, in some cases, than any other branch of government.

"I really don't remember, either," Sobek said.

"I just remember arguments, like, empirically, *Brown v. Board*, 'courts can create great social change.'"

"Yeah?"

"Is there any mental health literature like that? Courts can create social change?"

Sobek shrugged. Marcus reached into the tub that sat on the floor beside him and pulled out his "courts" file. He flipped through pages photocopied from Rosenberg's book, his brow crumpled with concentration, his eyes focused hard on the words. They were lean dark brown eyes, and when he was in his element like this, honing his debate skills, they made him look too confident and smart to be a teen. He was almost sexy, despite his standard-issue beige plaid button-down shirt. A no-frills clipper cut made his head appear bigger than it was, as though he were wearing an old-fashioned leather football helmet. A dark, hairy mole marred his cheek. Marcus stood out among his senior class at Central, not as a player but as someone like Steve Urkel, the squeaky-voiced nerd from the TV show *Family Matters*. As a freshman, he was almost as skinny as Urkel, too, though not as frail. He played hoops—better than Brandon, he often told me. Debate had kept him off the court, though, as did Counter-Strike. Add a steady diet of chicken strips slathered in cheese sauce and forty-nine-cent hamburgers, and you get seventeen-year-old Marcus: five eight with arms and neck starting to go doughy, and a belly bulging beneath his loose shirt.

Like Brandon, Marcus cared little for school, though he had, in fact, read *Things Fall Apart*. He got off on the book's violence, the patriarchal West African culture it revealed. But he ignored most of the other assignments. He told Rinehart one morning that her reading list was elitist and oppressive. On the second day of class he ripped a page out of a spiral notebook and, in less than a minute, dashed off the class's first writing assignment. Rinehart had asked for a short essay about an early learning experience. He wrote about the first book he ever read: a selection from the Goosebumps mystery series for kids. He coveted the book because of its cover, all spooky-looking with a bug-eyed kid surrounded by colorful ghouls. The book cost $4.50. "I begged my mother for one," he wrote, "but like many children in my class living in poverty I was told 'Maybe some other time.'" He went to the library, and the librarian gave him one. "I guess there's a lesson here but I'm sure many teachers would disagree," he continued. "Yes, disagree. That lesson: stop creating elitist standards and rewarding stickers to 'superior' students because all you're doing is making sure normal kids like me don't get anywhere in life."

The assignment complemented a selection from *The Autobiography of Malcolm X*, which Rinehart asked Marcus and his classmates to read on the first day. It was the part where Malcolm taught himself to read in prison by going word by word through a dictionary. While Marcus cranked out his screed, Rinehart asked the class what they got out of the reading.

"Malcolm said prison was even better than school," one kid said.

"Keep that in mind, guys," Rinehart replied, shooting Marcus and Brandon a look. They sat by fellow debater Leo Muhammad, near the bookshelves on the far wall, leaning way back in their chairs, knees spread to take up maximum space. "I like the movie better," Leo said, oblivious to Rinehart's jab.

She forged on. "This reading shows you—at least I hope it shows you—how important education is. It's the one thing that can never be stripped away from you."

"Yes, they can!" Leo smacked his desk.

His classmates groaned.

"They can," he insisted. "Listen up. This is for real. Before we were slaves, right?"

Kids shifted in their seats, shook their heads, waved shoo, rolled their eyes. "Shut *up*," one said.

"No, listen," he said, sitting up and grabbing at the air in front of him. "Before we were slaves, we were building pyramids, you know what I'm sayin'? And they made us give all that up, you know what I'm sayin'? So they could make us how they wanted us to be. So we have been stripped of education."

He smacked the desk again, harder this time, closed his mouth tightly, and scanned his audience. They blinked back at him.

"You know what book had an effect on me?" he asked.

No answer.

"The biography of Carter G. Woodson." The book, subtitled *The Man Who Put "Black" in American History*, was about the author of the classic treatise *The Mis-education of the Negro*, published in the 1930s, which indicted America's public school system as a factory for white supremacy. It disempowers blacks, Woodson argues, by championing Western civilization and eschewing the African diaspora.

But Leo didn't explain any of this. He just let Woodson's name hang there, as if its mere mention would fire up his comrades and spark a revolt.

They just laughed.

Rinehart perched on her desk and crossed her legs. "What is the purpose of education?" she pressed on, ignoring Leo's indignation.

"To give you the chance to be what you want to be," a kid answered.

"Knowledge is the key to the future," another said. "Where did I hear that? From a movie or something?"

"To make money."

"Make money?!" Rinehart gasped. "You go to *Central* to learn how to *make money*? It must be from drugs."

"You're a racist!" Brandon barked. He turned to Leo and said it again. Leo nodded and scowled. Marcus leaned forward and pulled his arms into his T-shirt. The air-conditioning was cranked too high, the room cold.

"Why do we bother to educate the youth?" Rinehart asked again.

Marcus reached up through his shirt collar and rubbed his eyes.

"You're being educated to replace your *parental units*," she answered herself, mixing a note of derision into those last two words.

She paused and swept her gaze across their faces.

"Think about it," she went on. "Look around. Look at Central. Then look at the suburbs. Look at the private schools." Another pause. "Now look at who runs the country."

"We do," one kid said defensively.

"Who rules America?" Rinehart asked again.

"The people."

"One hundred families control 80 percent of the wealth," Rinehart said. "Do you think those hundred families went to Central?"

"I'm sick of being compared to other schools," Leo scoffed.

"Think about it," Rinehart persisted. "Who's going to grow up to be president of UMB Bank?"

"Anybody can."

"Wake up," she said. "The *Kempers* run UMB Bank"—referring to one of the handful of wealthy white families that control Kansas City. "You think someone other than a Kemper is going to be president of their bank?"

The class went silent. This message was coming out a bit harsher than she intended; such were Rinehart's blunt ways. She'd call it "tough love." Her point focused on a specific concept she'd learned as a graduate student at UMKC and had confirmed in her years as a teacher—that the public education system isn't designed to empower future leaders with knowledge so much as to perpetuate the status quo: uplift, by way of private schools, the privileged few to the highest (and wealthiest) seats of authority; make managers of the middle class; and leave the hard work to the poor.

"Look at Maurice Greene," Leo said, offering the world's fastest man, the Olympic champion sprinter. "He came out of KCK!"—local slang for Kansas City, Kansas. "He went to Schlagle"—another predominantly black school like Central.

"How many Maurice Greenes are there?" Rinehart asked.

"One," Leo replied. "But he came out of Schlagle."

The students offered more names of blacks who had risen to fame and wealth, all athletes and musicians. Rinehart listened with her arms folded, mouth crimped in a smirk. "You need to think about it," she said when they ran out of names. "I don't mean to put you down. But if you've never thought about this stuff before, you need to start thinking about it. You're seniors."

AFTER WRITING his diatribe against public education, Marcus became unusually quiet that morning. Rinehart's words resonated with him. Though he hated school, he'd never lost sight of his dream of one day being "somebody important," as he once put it to me. Even when he was a little kid, he imagined himself eventually doing "some sort of federal or international enforcement," a CIA agent, perhaps, or FBI. He always had a fascination with power. He'd see campaign signs blossom around the city during election seasons and think, *Wow. That's cool. They're changing things.* He longed to somehow peel away the campaign posters, to see the political mechanisms they represented. He wanted to learn, just not at school.

At first, school satisfied his voracious curiosity. There were field trips and lessons that felt more like playtime than chores. Marcus entered first grade in the early 1990s, during the halcyon days of Kansas City's $2 billion desegregation effort. Part of the scheme was to create dazzling magnet schools to lure whites into the inner city from the suburbs. At his school the magnet theme was science and math. Often his teacher would take the class outside to conduct experiments, such as launching rockets and calculating the arc of the blasts. For math lessons, his teacher would call out problems, and Marcus would leap from his seat and race his peers to solve them on the board. This was when schools were saturated with Apple computers. He played Oregon Trail for hours, picking up history lessons and boosting his math skills by calculating the rations he'd need to win the digital survival game.

But in third grade the fun started to disappear. Photocopied worksheets replaced the interactive lessons. He began catching glimpses of the bureau-cratic machinery in which he was ensnared. Once a month, it seemed, an ob-server in a suit would come to his class and quietly sit in the back of the room, jotting notes on a yellow notepad. His teachers would always act strange on those days. They'd hand out candy the day before. Marcus knew what the candy was for. The motive wasn't the teaching, he thought. It was just a pose. Marcus started to drift before he reached middle school. He would cut up in class, razzing the other kids and blowing off lessons, though he was always crafty enough to avoid getting into serious trouble.

Rinehart invited him to join the debate team after she substituted for his freshman computer class. Because of a typical scheduling snafu, the class had no teacher. Rinehart didn't know anything about computer program-ming, so she divided the kids up and had them play a game of charades. Right away, she noticed how Marcus caught on to the nuances of the game. After an hour or so, when the students' zeal started to wane, Rinehart sidled up beside him. "You seem pretty bright," she said. "Would you be interested in our debate team?"

He wasn't. "When I hear debate," he later told me, "I think boring shit." But he played along, asking questions and listening as Rinehart gave him her full sales pitch. Eventually she told him that if he joined the team, he'd have to transfer out of his music-appreciation class. That sold him.

And now here he was, the top senior on the team. And, having earned a bid to the Tournament of Champions as a junior, he could be counted among the top debaters in the country. But with the season's first national-circuit tournament just a few days away, he didn't feel like one of the best. As he cut cards with Sobek, I asked him if he was ready.

"Hell no," he said, guffawing.

Across the room Brandon began laughing, too. "Sobek, we ready for Valley? Hell naw!"

"We're never ready," Sobek said.

Marcus laughed, shaking spastically. "I mean, teams of like ten people started working like three months ago, Sobek! You know that?!"

"Yeah."

"We got two people." Marcus shook two fingers in Sobek's face. "We start the week before." He slapped his hands against his chest and elbows as if he were fighting back his inner dork. "Oh, shit. That's elite. That's nice."

Sobek ignored him and kept working. Marcus sat back down, calmed as quickly as he'd been riled. He highlighted a few more lines of Rosenberg's observations about the judicial branch. He looked up at Sobek. "Wait," he said. "If *Brown v. Board* didn't pass, would I be debating?"

"Ahhhh," Sobek said, raising a finger to his chin and drawing out the syllable as if he were giving the question a lot of thought. "No."

NINE

DEBATE CRIMINALS

RINEHART PULLED the school's fifteen-passenger van to a stop in front of a squat gray duplex on the hilly edge of Kansas City's East Side. Marcus lived there with his mom, Evaline Lumpkin, and her husband, Glen Mitchem (his father, a white man Evaline had never married, lived in a nursing home because a brain tumor had left him unable to care for himself). Marcus's younger brother, Jason Lumpkin, also lived there, as did, off and on, other siblings. Evaline had nine children, aged thirty-two on down. Marcus was the second youngest. Most of his siblings were getting along well, working and raising families in Kansas City. One of his older brothers was in an up-state prison, though, for shooting a cop in a drug deal that got out of hand, Marcus's mother told me.

A couple of young men stood in the barren, sloping front yard, one talking on a cordless phone. Both wore baggy baseball jerseys, one red, the other blue. As Kansas City neighborhoods go, Marcus's was about as tough as any. It was close to a highway off-ramp, so the drug trade was robust. When Marcus and Jason were young, Evaline spent more than she could afford with her salary as an upholstery seamstress to keep the boys supplied with the latest and best video games, so as to keep them off the street. Marcus spent a lot of his waking hours in his tiny room, with the door shut, eyes glued to a seventeen-inch computer screen, but she didn't mind. "Most of the little kids he used to run around with are out selling drugs now or caught up in jail," she told me.

She loved that he'd gotten into debate. It surprised her that he did. He hadn't liked school much, not like her youngest, Jason, did. Jason couldn't wait to get to school every day, mostly because that's where his friends were. Jason's problem was how he spent his time *after* school. As a freshman, in the fall of 2001, Jason had signed up for the debate team, hoping, along with his mother, that it would keep him out of trouble; just a week before the start of that school year, he and a friend stole a car and got into a high-speed chase with police, which ended with them crashing into a tree. By joining debate, he believed he was turning over a new leaf and the game would keep him out of trouble. But he didn't much like it, not like Marcus did, and he decided not to enroll in debate again for his sophomore year.

Marcus, on the other hand, really took to the game. He'd come home from a long day at school and spend hours in his room reading out loud from his stacks of evidence cards. And he'd walk around the house repeating tongue twisters like "rubber baby buggy bumpers" over and over to get his pronunciation skills in shape. Evaline wished he'd share a little bit more about his adventures with her, though. When he'd come home from tournaments, she'd ask him how he did, and he'd say he won this trophy or that. But he always left them at school for the trophy case. If he'd returned with just one for her to put on the shelf, between the cutesy figurines of black country kids she collected, it would've made her so happy. But Marcus never thought to do so. He figured his mom wouldn't be into all that. To him, debate was a world completely separate from his home life. Evaline sensed this, and she respected his boundaries. There was enough satisfaction in knowing that he was following this path rather than the hundred other more dangerous ones that might open up to him once he walked out her front door. She'd only met Rinehart once, but she felt profound gratitude for her interest in her son. On their lone, brief exchange, through the window of Evaline's car one afternoon when she was picking Marcus up after a tournament, Rinehart told her how talented her son is. "He just loves debate so much," Evaline had replied. "That's one thing I'll never take away from him when I ground him, because I know it's so important to him it'd just tear him up."

———

RINEHART BLEATED the van's horn twice, and Marcus's face appeared in a window. He held up an index finger and mouthed, "One second."

"He ain't even ready yet," Brandon said, sitting in the front passenger seat. "He on the phone in his mama's room."

Marcus emerged through the front door a minute or so later, huffing a big black bag. "Oh, look at him," Leo said, exasperated by the sight of the bag. "He should have come to school." Leo had meticulously packed the van, stuffing the file tubs and overnight bags in the cargo area and below seats to make room for the eleven passengers who would be making the three-hour trip to West Des Moines.

Marcus threw open the van's side door and assessed the seating arrangement. The first row was full. He hesitated. "Get in," Rinehart yelled.

"Come on," he said to DiAnna Saffold, Leo's partner, who sat in the middle of the front row playing with the ring tones on her cell phone. "Get up. Me and Brandon gotta work."

She didn't look up. She was an ROTC officer; she didn't take much guff. Having watched her a few times at practice, I could tell she was one of the best debaters on the squad, certainly better than her partner Leo, though, in the boy-dominated hierarchy of the squad, he called the shots.

The boy wasn't going to win *this* fight, though. "Marcus!" Rinehart shouted.

He crammed his bag into the space beside the wheel well and sat down in the second row. Rinehart headed out, traversing neighborhood side streets en route to the UMKC campus, where we would pick up Sobek. As we moved westward, the houses grew larger and older, from shoe-box ranches like Marcus's to the stone-porch four-squares that surround Kansas City's busiest commercial corridors, Main Street and Broadway. Until the 1960s, these stately homes were owned almost exclusively by whites. Now the neighborhood we drove through was almost entirely black. Rinehart stopped at a light, and Marcus tried to climb into the front seat, tugging on DiAnna's coat. "Come on," he whined. "Let's switch."

"No!" she said, not looking up from her cell phone.

"Come on!" he cried. He leaned forward, pushing DiAnna to the side.

"Excuse me," he said, pointing to a package of brownies that sat on the console between Brandon and Rinehart. "Give me those."

Brandon grabbed the brownies and caressed their package lovingly. "We're not opening those until we have some paper towels," Rinehart said.

Marcus reached out and grabbed an umbrella, the only thing in reach. He pressed the button and flung it open toward Brandon.

"Damn, Marcus!" Brandon said, flinching. "Why you so hyper today?"

Marcus giggled. He closed the umbrella and flipped it open again. One of its pointy tips grazed DiAnna's cheek.

"Damn, Marcus," she said. "You seventeen years old!"

He dropped the umbrella. "Brandon," he yelled, still leaning over DiAnna's shoulder. "I saw this movie today. *Monster's Ball.* Man. Halle Berry. She gets banged for like an hour and a half! That shit is sexy!"

"Mouth!" Rinehart yelled, turning the van onto Bruce R. Watkins Drive, a newly opened four-laner that rolls through the middle of Kansas City's predominantly black side of town. It's named after the city's first African-American councilman, who had lobbied hard against the road because it split the mostly black East Side in two. Hundreds of homes were razed for its construction. A light rain glazed the pavement.

"That shit is like porno to me," Marcus said, disregarding her scold. He sat back and flailed his hands like a toddler knocking down a stack of blocks.

I asked him why he didn't go to school that day.

"I couldn't go to school today," he said. "I was sick."

"You weren't sick," DiAnna said.

"I was stressed out. I was too stressed to go. I had to relax."

He and Brandon had gotten into a fight the day before. Marcus was pissed because Brandon wouldn't help cut cards for their affirmative case. He snapped at Brandon, called him lazy. Brandon knocked a chair over and got in Marcus's face. Rinehart had to pull them both out into the hall and talk them down. She later told me that it was nerves, especially on Brandon's part. Brandon felt a lot of pressure as Marcus's new partner. By winning bids to the Tournament of Champions and the National Forensic League national championship, Marcus and his previous teammate, Donnell Minton, who was now at college in north Iowa, had been the most successful debate team of Central's post-desegregation era. Brandon, on the other hand, had lost most of his rounds his junior year. He blamed his partner, a senior with more ego than wits. But Brandon also doubted himself, though he masked these doubts with cockiness. His attitude seemed to say, *I'm too good to trifle with busywork*. In truth, it gave him an out. If he lost, he could blame it on unpreparedness, not a lack of talent or smarts.

Brandon turned on the van's radio, flipped to Hot 103 Jamz, and spun the volume knob hard to the right. The deep rhythm of Ludacris's "Move Bitch" boomed fuzzily from the cheap, overtaxed speakers. All the debaters on board bobbed to the beat and sang along, adding the FCC-deleted cuss words back into the song: "Move, bitch, get out the way!"

RINEHART WHEELED the van into a parking lot just east of Troost Avenue and pulled to a stop by the front door of the UMKC administrative building that houses the school's debate squad room. Marcus slid open the side door and ran in to get Sobek. Rinehart stepped out into the drizzle and reached back into the van. She pulled out two signs that read, RINEHART FOR CONGRESS. Her sister, Cathy, was running as a Democrat for Missouri's Sixth District, which stretched from the north banks of the Missouri River in Kansas City up to the Iowa border. Her opponent was Sam Graves, an incumbent conservative known for intimidating campaign tactics. The signs were printed on a floppy magnetic material. Rinehart tried to cover the Central eagle logos on the sides of the van with them, but they weren't quite big enough. Wings stuck up from the top, words from the bottom.

It was against district policy to use school property for personal purposes, much less political ones. If Graves's camp were to catch wind of it, they'd no doubt let the press know, and get Rinehart and her sister into deep trouble. But here Rinehart was breaking one rule to hide her disregard of another. The Missouri State High School Activities Association, the same quasi-public body that had put the clamp on DEBATE–Kansas City's afternoon tournaments four years earlier, had rules forbidding her from taking her squad to this tournament in Iowa because it was being held one week be-

fore the official start of Missouri's debate season. To skirt the rules, she'd entered the Central squad as the Kansas City Debate Club (the first year they
competed there, they were the Mickey Mouse Club), and she was paying for
the whole trip out of her own pocket. The only problem, then, was the van,
which was very obviously the school's. So she hung the signs to prevent the
possibility, however unlikely, that a debate coach from the hinterlands of
northeast Missouri would pass them on the highway, deduce that they were
heading to an illegal tournament, and rat them out to the association's bureaucrats in Columbia. She'd been tattled on before, several times, always
anonymously. Once she was even accused of taking kids to the Harvard Invitational, the biggest high school debate competition in the country, even
though she hadn't. The Ivy League event was off-limits to her and all other
Missouri squads, which were restricted by association rules to tournaments
within 250 miles of the state's border. Most people would have been thrilled
to learn of a bunch of inner-city kids competing at the nation's top university. But to the folks at the activities association, it was a punishable
offense.

Rinehart stepped back and looked at the sign on the passenger side. She
readjusted it, but you could still plainly see it was Central's van. "I don't
know why I even bother," she said. "Everyone knows we're going. I'll probably get a letter Monday morning. It's ridiculous."

She looked at me and propped her hands on her hips. "But I refuse to
obey rules that harm children," she said. "And that's what these rules do.
They harm children."

AS THE VAN BARRELED along I-35, across rail yards and past smokestacks into wooded suburbs with box stores huddled around the off-ramps,
Brandon slid an adapter into the cassette player and plugged it into a
portable CD player. He popped in Tech N9ne's new CD. A few seconds into
the first song, the rapper rhymed: "Punk shit daily on, industry's a shady
one." But it sounded as if he were saying, "Fuck shit."

"Mouth!" Rinehart yelled, reaching for the stereo's controls.

Brandon knocked her hand away.

"Turn it off!" she protested. "I'm not playing! For real!"

Marcus, having won the front seat from DiAnna at the UMKC stop, leaned forward. "That's 'shoot'!" he shouted. "They're saying 'shoot'!"

The lyrics turned clean again, and Rinehart put her hands back on the wheel. Then Tech N9ne yelled, "Motherfucking" something or other.

"Hey!" Rinehart groped again for the stereo. Tech N9ne jumped back into the chorus, which, to Rinehart's ears, was a relentless chant of "fuck shit."

"Why is it such a big deal?" Brandon pushed her hand away.

"Because, you know the rules." Her fingers found the eject button and the adapter slid out. The van went quiet; wind and drizzle whistled against the windshield.

"Like you don't hear that every day." Brandon pouted and slumped back into his seat.

Music was like a life force for these kids, the urban beats setting the pace for their journeys, the lyrics, even the most obnoxious gangsta rap, like tribal folklore. From the back row, Leo offered a compromise. He passed forward a disc of oldies he'd jacked from the Internet. And suddenly we were sailing in the love van. Al Green and Barry White seduced us into singing along. The kids swayed to the slow, funky beats. Even Rinehart raised her chin and softly shook her head as she sang, "I can't get enough of your love, babe." Leo balled his fists and wailed the chorus for "Let's Get It On."

"Man, I'm so into that song," he said, "I got a headache."

Marcus was the first to let his head roll back and fall asleep. One by one, the debaters closed their eyes and nodded off, until Rinehart was the only one left singing as she veered down a ramp into the suburban sprawl of West Des Moines. The clouds broke to the west and were washed over with pink, fading sunlight.

RINEHART DROPPED THE CREW off at Valley West Mall, to spend an hour shopping while she went to West Des Moines's Valley High School to register for the tournament. Marcus and Sobek broke off from the group and headed down the long concourse. Marcus squeaked his sneakers against the faux-marble floor. Having napped, he was hyper again. "Butter pecan ice cream is elitist food," he said as he shuffled along beside Sobek, throwing jabs at his coach's shoulder. "No one actually likes that nasty crap. They just like to eat it because it makes them elite."

They wandered into a Waldenbooks and stopped in front of the self-help section. Marcus frowned at the face of Christopher Reeve staring back at him from a hardcover. "Man, I'm tired of seeing this," he said and smacked Reeve's face. "See all five of these?" he continued, sweeping his hand across a rack of bestsellers—*The Right Words at the Right Time* by Marlo Thomas, *A Child Called "It": One Child's Courage to Survive* by Dave Pelzer, *The Lost Boy* by the same author, Dr. Phil with his hand cupped around his chin. "These all should be burned."

"Why?" Sobek asked.

"They're all 'feel sorry for somebody else' books."

As they moved about the aisles, Marcus kept up his critic act. He pointed to *The Best-Loved Poems of Jacqueline Kennedy Onassis* and deemed it "crap." He picked up a copy of *Frankenstein* and waved it in my face, on its cover a dark, spooky hollow with a path winding through it. "I can't read this book," he said. "It's crap." Then he picked up the book sitting next to it, another copy of *Frankenstein*, this one with a maniacal man on the front. "Now, I could read *this*," he said.

He paused at a rack of Cliffs Notes and sneered at their yellow-and-black covers. "I see this and I think, 'Education,'" he said, making quotation marks with his fingers. "I think, 'Stuff I have to read.' No way am I reading that." He turned on his heels and waved his arm across an entire rack of foreign-language dictionaries and phrase books. "Crap."

Sobek wandered through the stacks, earnestly scanning the titles on the books' spines. An English major with an emphasis in rhetoric, Sobek loved books. He grew up in the suburbs of Phoenix. Skinny and shy, he didn't fit in with the jocks and popular crowd, and he didn't much care. Debate and church formed his social universe. He'd done fairly well on the national circuit as a high schooler, picking up a couple of bids to the Tournament of Champions. He'd attended debate camp at UMKC the summer before his junior year, where he caught Linda Collier's attention. She offered him a generous scholarship to compete on her squad. After college, he planned to go into teaching, so the assistant-coaching gig at Central was perfect. Rinehart even paid him out of the squad's budget. And he was good at it, though he devoted almost all of his attention to the guys on the squad; DiAnna, Day Brown, and Dionne Holt often complained that they were being ignored, but their protests had no effect.

Sobek pulled a fat textbook off a shelf and flipped to the index. "This has stuff about mental health in here," he said to Marcus.

"Man, Sobek, you're always working," Marcus said. "You need to get yourself a girlfriend."

On the way out of the store, Marcus zeroed in on a photo of a woman with her bare back turned to the camera, her head craned over her shoulder, her glossy lips pursed. *Bitch*, the book was called. "Now, *this*," Marcus said, "this is a book I can *read*." He snapped his middle finger against it. "Sobek, you need to get you some of that."

AFTER AN HOUR meandering in and out of shops, not buying anything, Marcus and Sobek sauntered into the food court, where they found Rinehart picking through a plate of chili-cheese fries. Brandon, Leo, DiAnna, and the other debaters were gathered around her. Marcus stepped up to her and crowded her space.

"What time is it?" he asked Sobek.

Sobek extended his arm to show Marcus his watch, but Marcus didn't look. "Rinehart, we were supposed to leave two minutes ago," he said. He tugged at the back of her chair. She looked straight ahead and raised a gooey fry to her mouth.

"Rinehart, we were supposed to leave three minutes ago," he said thirty seconds later. And fifteen seconds after that: "Rinehart, we were supposed to leave four minutes ago."

She said nothing. She chewed slowly. Marcus sighed and sat down. He stared at her. He got up. "Come on, J.R.," he whined. He dealt a weak kick to one of her chair's legs. He sat back down and stared at her some more.

She swallowed the last fry, took a sip of root beer, and dabbed at the corners of her mouth with a paper napkin. "Okay," she said, folding the napkin and laying it down neatly on the empty tray. "Are we ready?"

And Marcus was off. He marched swiftly toward the exit, Brandon and Leo and the rest of the team in pursuit. They were almost jogging as they reached the end of the corridor. They burst through the doors and broke into a sprint for the van, the girls racing behind. A driver tapped his brakes to avoid Marcus, who zagged and kept going.

As they darted between the parked cars, a red "Parking Safety" SUV accelerated and circled around to catch up with them. The window lowered on the driver's side and a white face emerged. "Are there any adults with your group?" the man asked curtly.

"Yeah, we're all eighteen," Marcus lied.

"Well, you know, you shouldn't be running," the man said, "because it's very dangerous. You could have been seriously injured by that car."

"Yeah, I know," Marcus said, not looking at him. The rest of the team had arrived. They climbed one by one into the van, hoping the man would leave them alone.

"Are there any adults in your group?" he asked again.

Sobek and I both said nothing, waiting for our turn to board.

"Anyone over eighteen?"

"Yeah, I'm eighteen," Marcus lied again.

"Can I speak with the over-eighteen-year-olds?"

"No, we've got to go," Marcus replied calmly.

"You're from Kansas City?" the guard asked, noticing the school's insignia. "What brings you here?"

"A debate tournament," Marcus replied as he stepped in, sliding the door shut behind him.

The guard jerked his truck in reverse and wheeled around behind the van, blocking it in. He got out and walked to the driver's side. Rinehart rolled down her window. "How can I help you?" she asked with forced courteousness.

"I noticed all your group was mouthy and all that," he began. "But I just want you to know they could have been hurt running across the parking lot like that. It's very dangerous. And I don't appreciate them being mouthy and having a bad attitude."

Up to this point, Marcus had kept calm. But he suddenly lurched forward. "Ms. Rinehart, I—"

"Marcus," she cut him off, displaying the back of her hand.

"But, Ms. Rinehart—"

"Shut it."

"But—"

"Shut up, Marcus." She turned and glared at him.

She turned to the security guard once again, mouth pinched tightly, brows arched. He had a buzz cut and a big overbite. His cotton-knit shirt bearing the mall's logo stretched snugly across his biceps and broad shoulders. "Like I said," he continued, "I just want you to know that I don't think it's a good idea for your group to be running through the parking lot."

DiAnna leaned over and whispered to me, "Especially an African-American group."

She wanted to be sure that I, in the role of squad documentarian that she and her teammates had silently assigned to me, was getting a proper read on the situation: this was about race, plain and simple.

"And I also want you to know that if I see this group here again," he added, "I'm going to ask them to leave. Simply because they're mouthy and disrespectful."

"And we black," DiAnna said.

"Especially that one there," the guard said, nodding in Marcus's direction. "He's got a real attitude problem."

"Okay," Rinehart said, and the guard retreated to his truck and released us from custody. As we made our way out of the parking lot and onto a broad parkway, Brandon pounded the dashboard. "Boy, I wish I had a gun," he said. "I'd a shot him right in his face."

"Brandon, that doesn't help," Rinehart said. Her voice was soft.

"I don't care," he barked. "What the fuck was wrong with him?"

"Brandon, mouth," she said, still calm and quiet.

"We can run through the parking lot if we want to. That shit pisses me off."

"Well, Joe," DiAnna said to me. "You just witnessed your first racist experience."

I had—my first overt one, anyway. I'd been acutely aware of race issues from the moment I'd walked into Central a year and a half earlier, but this instance of profiling by a mall rent-a-cop marked a tipping point of sorts, and I began to see the world as these students do: a place where everything boils down to race.

"Yeah," I replied. "Running while black."

TEN

FAST TIMES ON THE NATIONAL CIRCUIT

THE CENTRAL DEBATERS spent the night in the homes of families from the tournament's host school, Valley High. It saved Rinehart money and gave the kids a chance to see how the other half lives. Brandon, Marcus, and Leo had an entire finished basement to themselves, complete with big-screen TV and Xbox ("I walk in my room, first thing I see is a Jacuzzi," Marcus bragged). Rinehart, Sobek, and I checked into rooms at the Clarion Hotel, which offered a discount rate for tournament participants. When we arrived, the place was overrun with teens in untucked plaid shirts and cargo pants. They filled all the chairs in the lobby and sat along the walls and in small circles on the floor. The next morning they were all dressed in suits and skirts, waiting for a bus to shuttle them to the school. Teams had come from as far away as Oakland, California, and Lexington, Massachusetts. "These are the Cadillacs of schools," Rinehart said as we made our way to the van.

We followed a tree-lined parkway past subdivisions full of split-level homes, each with broad signs bearing bucolic names—Glen Oaks, Wistful Vista, Woodland Park. A light fog hugged the ground. When Rinehart turned onto Valley High's circular drive, she remarked, "This is another top, top school. They've got AP classes out the ying-yang."

The campus spread across several acres of lush landscape, with a baseball and football stadium, rows of tennis courts, and two wide parking lots surrounded by low trees. As we entered the school, we faced a large, silken banner adorned with a presidential seal, which the school won in 1985 when White House officials recognized its science and math teachers as among the best in the nation. In addition to advanced courses in chemistry, physics, and two levels of calculus, Valley students may take college-level courses in European and American history and computer science, as well as architectural drawing, accounting, business law, entrepreneurship, and four years of Latin, German, Russian, and Japanese—none of which are offered at Central.

Brandon and Marcus were already at the school, sleepy-eyed and dressed in blue blazers, light blue oxfords, and matching yellow ties. The first-round schedule had already been handed out, and dozens of debaters scuttled about the hall wheeling dolly carts stacked with Rubbermaid tubs, most of them dressed up like Brandon and Marcus. Marcus helped Leo unload the van, and Brandon followed him as he wheeled their evidence to room 235. The room was small and windowless, with posters of geometric art covering the walls. Their opponents, from Blaine High, located in the outer reaches of the Minneapolis metro area, had already set up camp in one corner of the room. They sat at a pair of desks pushed together with debate tubs on the floor beside them and folders of documents spread in front of them. Brandon and Marcus scooted a couple desks together and started unpacking.

After a few minutes the judge slinked in, wearing a flannel shirt, unbuttoned to reveal a Colorado T-shirt. He sunk into a desk and turned another sideways to prop up his feet. Blaine's first speaker moved to stand behind the teacher's desk, facing the judge. She was skinny but not lanky, with pale skin and red hair pulled back tightly in a long ponytail. She cleared her throat. "ObservationOne," she began in a sudden burst of words: "TheIndianHealth CareImprovementActPrecludesTraditionalHealersBecauseoftheOnerous IHS BureaucracyHaworth99." She hunched down, gulped for air, and continued even more rapidly.

"TheexclusionoftraditionalmedicinefromtheIHCIAisparticularlyproblematicinlightofthelackofsourcesandalternativesavailabletoNativeAmericans whowishtoreceivetraditionalIndianhealthcare." She gasped, her head jerking back.

"BecauseIHScontractservicesarebasedonapayeroflastresortsystemand medicalprioritydeterminations." She gasped again.

"NativeAmericanswhowishtousethemareleftwithveryfewalternatives."
Gasp.

"Mostalternativehealthcareproviders." Gasp. "SuchasMedicareandMed-
icaid." Gasp. "DonotprovidefortraditionalIndianmedicine."

Her shoulders were tensed up, and tendons stretched the skin of her neck,
as if they were rubber bands that had been wound nearly to the breaking
point and then released to send her jaw into a spastic flutter. She pounded
her fist rhythmically against the podium, not so much for emphasis as to
churn out more information. I could only understand every fourth or fifth
word. Brandon and Marcus appeared to be unconcerned, though. Brandon
casually jotted shorthand notes on a blank sheet of paper. Marcus strolled to
the front of the room, glancing over the speaker's shoulder. When she finished reading through a sheet of evidence, she handed it to him, not looking
up from her stack of documents. In all, it totaled thirteen pages, an average
of two hundred words per page. She had eight minutes to read them all.

This was nothing like how I had imagined debate before I started following the Central squad. My image of the game came from movies like *Listen to Me* and *Clueless*, where young Republicans strike statue poses and sell
ideas with huffy declarations and a smattering of sixty-five-dollar words. I
assumed that crowds would come to watch the rounds. But it hadn't been
that way for more than thirty years, at least not on the national circuit. The
game began to change in the 1930s, on the college scene, where budget con-
straints of the Depression forced universities to move away from the tradition of schools traveling to face each other one on one in front of packed
audiences in favor of tournaments where numerous schools competed. As a
result, arguments became more generic, so as to fit unexpected approaches
brought by many different teams. Judges began to emphasize evidence more
and more in their decisions. So, as legend has it, in the late 1960s the Harvard squad, figuring more was better, decided to pack their speeches with as
much evidence as possible, which they read faster than auctioneers. The gambit worked. They blew their opponents away, and soon it seemed everyone
was doing it. Within a couple of years, the trend caught on among the high
school squads that travel to tournaments from coast to coast.

At the same time, though, the activity underwent a precipitous decline.

Colleges and high schools alike began dropping their programs. In some states—Illinois and Nebraska, for instance, where the speedier style had become the norm—there were so few remaining high school squads that by the end of the century their state championship tournaments were in jeopardy. Speed has been a flash point of discord on the American debate scene ever since, with fierce loyalists for and against. Those in favor of it argue that it's a supreme exercise for logic and critical thinking skills. The prospect of a win compels students to dive with hypersonic abandon into the stuff of a Great American Education—reading, writing, history, civics, and even math and science, what with all the statistics and evidence needed for topics such as mental health. "The students become like human computers," I've heard several coaches crow, with apparent obliviousness to the Orwellian connotations. On the other side were those who argued that speed made debate too specialized a skill. To win, students have to attend costly summer camps to quickly build the base of knowledge and volumes of evidence needed. This, many believed, skewed the playing field in favor of more privileged schools. Plus, it became a lot harder to coach. And with politically driven, test-based standards of accountability demanding more and more of teachers' time, it had become harder to lure new coaches into the game, much less persuade them to stay.

For the kids at many of the schools still active in the game, though, speed debate is just about the coolest thing on earth. The Blaine girl's blur of words told a story: Native Americans tend to get depressed and commit suicide more often than other folks. Though their cultures have traditional ways of dealing with these problems, federal policy prevents them from getting this kind of treatment. So they get worse and drink a lot and become—en masse, I suppose—"The Drunken Indian." And this is exactly where white leaders in Washington want them. They use this racist identity "as a tool of cultural conquest and domination," the ultimate outcome of which is genocide. And if this genocide is allowed to continue unabated, as one piece of evidence from the outspoken University of Colorado professor Ward Churchill insisted, the entire human race will soon perish. Fortunately, the students from Blaine had a plan to stave off the bloodshed. They proposed directing the Indian Health Service, a division of the U.S. Department of

Health and Human Services, to create hundreds of health centers on Indian reservations. Native Americans would run these clinics, and, the Blaine debaters presumed, they would naturally return to their roots by treating their depressed brethren with herbs and sweat lodges and peyote ceremonies.

The judge's timer sounded, and the girl stopped mid-sentence, straightened, and stared blankly at the judge. Marcus moved to stand beside her. "Who's going to carry out this plan?" he asked.

"IHS."

"So those are executive agencies? The IHS?"

"Yeah."

"Okay. Now. What type of authority does the executive branch have to fully fund the program without Congress?"

Marcus's opponent shrugged. "Well, I suppose it'll have a budget," she replied.

Marcus grinned. He kept asking questions, but he could have stopped right there. With just three questions, he had set a trap that would make his and Brandon's negative case tough to beat.

After Marcus finished cross-x, Brandon used none of the allotted eight minutes of preparation time. He moved to the podium, calmly asked the judge if he was ready, then the Blaine kids, who sat poised with their pens. With a jerk of his wrist, he set off his timer and began reading at breakneck speed. He didn't contort himself like his counterpart from Blaine. His head bowed to read the cards, but his back was straight, his left arm raised outward, fanning gently to the pulse of his speech. Marcus may have been the best overall debater at Central, but no one could speed-read like Brandon. As a freshman and as a sophomore, he spent hours perfecting the skill by reciting tongue twisters over and over and reading evidence aloud with a pen jammed sideways in his mouth. He blazed through a couple of topicality arguments (standard procedure), then began rattling off excerpts from a series of news reports, all published within the previous five days.

From the *Arkansas Democrat-Gazette*: news that Senator Jean Carnahan of Missouri was holding on to a slim lead in a race against her Republican challenger, Jim Talent. From *The Kansas City Star*: this lead was disappearing because Carnahan wasn't standing up and claiming ownership of Democratic issues, most notably domestic concerns like health care. By acting on Blaine's plan as a member of Congress, Brandon argued, Carnahan could appease her left-leaning critics and squeak into office. This would be tragic because, according to *The Christian Science Monitor*, it would prevent the immediate creation of a one-vote Republican majority in the Senate. Reason: Carnahan was appointed to the Senate after her husband, Mel Carnahan, won the 2000 election as a dead man. Such appointees must, according to Senate rules, step down immediately after a midterm loss at the polls. With the Senate exactly half Democrat and half Republican, Vice President Dick Cheney would have, in the middle of November, regardless of how the other states' elections turned out, the power to break a tie. And with the support of this tiny majority, President George W. Bush would be able to launch an immediate unilateral attack against Iraq. And this would be a good thing, because it would spare the lives of millions of Americans, if not the entire human race. According to a report published in *Time* just four days earlier, Iraq already had the makings of a nuclear weapon.

Neither Brandon nor Marcus had unearthed all this evidence, which Brandon had laid out in less than eight minutes. Right before they left for Iowa, they had purchased the entire negative case file for eight dollars from Cross-X.com, an online forum for high school debaters. During debate season, the site's owner, Phil Kerpen, a researcher for the Washington-based Reagan-adoring lobby group the Club for Growth, sells upwards of eighty such cases each week to debaters nationwide, apparently oblivious to the possible copyright violations this entails. But here, in the first round of the Mid-America Cup at Valley High School, it didn't matter how Central had come by its evidence. Blaine had to answer it. Besides, the Blaine kids hadn't dug up the evidence for their case, either. It was put together at a summer debate camp by high schoolers under the tutelage of college debaters and coaches. Cases made entirely by high school debaters are incredibly rare; I saw only a handful all season. The rest were ready-made. Indeed, the "Natives" case, or "Drunken Indians," as it came to be known, was one of the most popular during the 2002–2003 season. Even Leo and DiAnna ran it.

After Brandon's speech and cross-x, the Blaine duo squandered all but one minute of their prep time. As the minutes ticked away, Marcus smiled at me and rubbed his hands together maniacally. With six speeches left to go in the round, sixty seconds wouldn't be nearly enough time for his opponents to prepare their rebuttals.

The Blaine kids looked pained as they struggled to keep up. During the final speech, Blaine's second speaker tugged at his bangs. "Health care, uh, mandates and statutes, uh, uh, and laws are passed, uh, all the time," he stammered, trying to speak quickly despite a lack of words.

The judge took just a few minutes to consider his decision. "I think you won the argument cold," he said to Marcus and Brandon. "This round proves why I love judging varsity debate."

THE WIN PERKED Marcus and Brandon up, and they snagged wins the next two rounds. They strutted through the hall, high as could be. "Shit, man," Marcus said, bouncing up and down as he moved along. "We elite! I thought we was gonna get smoked here, but these teams are even more behind than we are."

The hallway was filling with other debaters, who now had an hour or so to kill while the tournament's hosts tabulated the round-three results and matched teams for round four, the last of the day. Through an open classroom door, Marcus and Brandon spotted James Holley, a senior from Morgan Park High School on the South Side of Chicago. They'd all been friends since their freshman year. ("Us black folks gotta stick together," James told me.) James had just finished his round. "How'd you do?" Marcus asked him.

"We dropped," James said.

"We three-oh, playa!" Marcus smacked James's shoulder with a rolled-up round-three schedule.

Brandon slipped on his headphones and leaned against a wall, nodding to the beat. James snapped the lid shut on one of his tubs and hefted it onto a dolly. "No, no, James," Marcus said, tugging at his friend's sleeve. "That's three hundred years of slavery. He better be picking that up for you." He pointed to James's partner, David Beer, who was white.

"He'll pay me my slave wages," James said, stuffing evidence into another tub.

Marcus turned to David. "I'll forgive three hundred years of slavery if you pay me fifty bucks," he said.

"Hey, nobody in my family owned slaves," David replied.

Like Central, Morgan Park is predominantly black—about 90 percent for the 2002–2003 school year. But it's not quite as poor, with half its students qualifying for free or reduced-price lunches, a key indicator of poverty, as opposed to Central's 63 percent. And by all measures Morgan Park is a successful school. Its dropout rate is a mere 5.6 percent, and its students score well above the state average on standardized tests in all subject areas. It routinely ranks among Chicago's top five high schools, outpacing even magnet schools, which can screen applicants. But James didn't let on that he came from a better school. Over the years he and Marcus had worked up an escapees-from-the-'hood routine where they'd step up to random white debaters and heap blame on them for the oppression of blacks and demand reparations (which, by Marcus's standards, could be made for the price of a candy bar). They ogled asses, too, and whispered to each other about which girls they'd like to bed. In the hallway at Valley, they barged in on a group of girls who were talking, and while James flirted with them, Marcus stood off to the side, water bottle at his crotch, slowly stroking it. "Marcus doesn't like black women," James told me.

Half the debate life, it seemed, was spent whiling away hours like this, waiting for the next-round schedules to come out. In the right company, it could be the best part of being a debater, next to winning trophies. This was especially true on the first day of tournaments, when, until the first loss, wins aren't crucial, when there's still plenty of opportunities to bounce back and make it to the trophy rounds. As at most tournaments, every team at the 2002 Mid-America Cup was guaranteed six rounds of debate, after which the sixteen teams with the best records would move into single-elimination rounds, better known as "elims" or "out rounds." To make the cut at Valley, Marcus and Brandon would have to go at least four-two, though a win in one of their next three rounds didn't guarantee them a place among the trophy winners. With two losses, they'd be tied with at least a dozen other teams, the best of which would be selected based on speaker points and opponent records. And though they seemed carefree during this mid-afternoon downtime, both Marcus and Brandon knew their challenge was about to get a lot tougher. After two rounds, teams were matched against opponents with identical records so as to prevent a lucky pair from having an undeservedly easy path to the elimination rounds. Being undefeated, Marcus and Brandon could expect a more formidable foe, more than likely one of the best teams in the tournament.

"SO WHAT HAPPENED to your partner?" Brandon asked the kid who was unpacking files.

"Working at Dairy Queen, I guess," the kid said.

They were on opposite ends of a social studies classroom. Campaign political posters and an artificially aged copy of the Declaration of Independence hung on the walls, and red, white, and blue paper stars dangled from the ceiling.

"So you're just, like, debating by yourself?"

"Yeah."

"And you're three-oh?"

The kid wore the casual garb of a judge: wrinkly cargo pants and a loose flannel shirt. His thick, kinky hair poufed in all directions, nearly obscuring his rectangular glasses. But his cheeks were smooth, still too soft with baby fat for him to pass as a college kid. He introduced himself as Andrew Berg. If his winning streak as a maverick (that's what debaters call debaters who debate alone) had gotten to his head, he wasn't letting on. He was almost deferential. He smiled a lot and softened his statements with upturned endings, like questions.

Brandon moved an AV cart to a spot a few steps away from the dry-erase board. He laid a stack of blue pages on the overhead projector. "We begin observation one by highlighting that pervasive evidence shows that our health care system has emerged as a system based on race," he said quickly, after gulping down some air, "causing blacks to be denied basic medical care such as mental health."

With his hand raised to his side, he sped through thirteen pages, squeezing more than twenty-five hundred words into an eight-minute speech. At this three-hundred-words-a-minute clip, Brandon offered a slew of statistics and called for an extension of the 1964 Civil Rights Act to ensure "equitable and culturally sensitive" mental health care. Doing so, he argued, would push the nation toward freedom from racial divisions. "The walls of racism can be dismantled," he exclaimed, quoting Joseph Barndt, a white minister who wrote a book called *Dismantling Racism*. And if racial inequalities were not obliterated, he warned, citing the Canadian scholar Clarence Munford, their underlying hatred would continue to grow until it exploded into "the ultimate catastrophe . . . nuclear conflict in the coming century."

Brandon was calm as he cautioned us of our impending doom. Nuclear holocausts, genocide, mass dehumanization, the extinction of all life on Earth—they're all common in the debate world. Cases are all about impact. Whose plan would kill more? Whose would cause less harm? But mostly they're about saying cool things like "total thermal-nuclear meltdown," "utter annihilation," and, in one obscure case I heard, "flesh-eating aliens." In the mid-nineteenth century, when competitive debate between students is believed to have begun in the United States, the game meant putting on a tie and acting like a politician. But tradition appears to have met its match with the onset of video games. Now debaters are tensing up and flapping their jaws faster than they could work a joystick, escaping reality, slaying political and social demons exaggerated to ten times the size of the electric cyborg in War of the Monsters. Brandon and Marcus picked up this particular doom scenario at debate camp in Washington, D.C., the previous summer. They planned to use it all season, solely because they were black. During one after-school practice, Marcus bragged that they wouldn't lose with the case because judges wouldn't dare vote against two black kids who argued to end racism. At this, Sobek laughed. "If you were a big Native American with long hair and a feather," he asked, "would you run 'Natives'?"

"Absolutely," Marcus said.

Berg remained seated during cross-x and his first speech. This was the trend on the down-with-formalities college circuit, and it was just beginning to seep into the high school level. He began his first speech with the basics, a customary topicality argument, before jumping into what he really wanted to talk about: Michel Foucault. He'd first become acquainted with Foucault's work at a debate camp two summers earlier, and he'd since supplemented his public school curriculum with the philosopher's writings. Foucault was an iconoclast on many levels, not least of which was his examination of sexual repression and his taste for gay meat markets (he died of AIDS in the early 1980s and is believed to have infected many anonymous lovers). Berg was fascinated by Foucault's concept of bio-power, which he developed in probing examinations of the history of modernization. Focusing on nineteenth-century changes in the penal system, treatment of mental illness, education, and literature, Foucault perceived systems that actually dominate bodies and souls, mold humans into beings that live, almost naturally, according to the desires of those who control the systems. To him, the world looked like a factory farm where institutional structures ensure that the population, like pigs or cows, lives and dies in an orderly and economical way. This is bio-power at its most dangerous. On the other hand, individuals also possess bio-power, and it can be used for good. People can claim control of their own bodies, subscribe to their own truths, and live according to them, even, at times, in the face of oppressive regimes. In doing so, these freethinking types can set examples for others and thus exert power. Society can be changed from the bottom up, Foucault suggested, though it rarely is. In these writings, Berg saw his own high school. To him, Fargo North was a production line that churned out obedient, unquestioning young adults. Those who didn't fit into the school's narrow mold were, in essence, chucked to the discard pile with bad grades and suspensions. Berg fancied himself a rebel, and many of the kids being left behind were his friends. He hated seeing them become disempowered.

Berg argued that Marcus and Brandon's plan would feed into bio-power's dark side by using Congress to end racism through mental health care. If mental health is defined and controlled by those in power, he explained, it becomes a weapon against individuality. Treatment forces people to toe the line in a capitalist system, to become chattel whose lives feed the bounty of the oppressors. Worse, it breeds racism, because racism is a necessary component of capitalism, where, by definition, there are winners and losers, and the system works best when the losers are easy to spot. So, he insisted, the judge should "resist capitalism" by voting against Marcus and Brandon's plan.

My ears had become attuned to the fast speeches, and I was grasping the content. The three debaters ceased to be teens in my eyes. And it didn't feel like a game anymore; it seemed serious, as if real issues were on the line. It was like being transported to a college campus in the late 1960s, Berkeley perhaps, where Foucault taught during the last year of his life, and these were young radicals arguing into the wee morning hours over the best course of action for their revolution. All that was missing, it seemed, were the half-eaten takeout cartons of Chinese food. During Berg's late-round rebuttal speeches, Marcus sprawled out on the floor scribbling notes while Brandon rooted through their file boxes and covered a half-dozen school desks with dog-eared documents. During a break in the action the judge said, "This is great. This is probably the best round I've seen so far." I was so captivated, in fact, that I missed the crucial turning point, when Brandon pulled a novice mistake and lost the round for Central.

During the first affirmative rebuttal, or 1AR, as it's commonly called, Brandon stacked the front end of his speech with arguments against Foucault, laying his boilerplate topicality cards on the bottom of the pile. Just as he got to these cards, the timer sounded, and he looked up to find that the judge had stopped taking notes. Everyone in the room but me knew that he had blown it. Berg pounced on the dropped argument, spending almost all his final speech on an elementary T argument. The irony of this wasn't lost on him: he was calling on the powers that be—the judge—to confine the debate to a narrow path leading straight to the resolution, which is quite un-Foucauldian.

Marcus did his best to cover for Brandon in the last speech of the round. "I know Brandon didn't do, like, the best job covering T," he said, bent at the waist, squeezing his diaphragm as hard as possible. "But still, it was there, and you shouldn't penalize us for that."

But it was too late. "If you'd spent just one minute in the 1AR on T, you guys would have won," the judge said shortly after the round ended. "That's why I was sitting there shaking my head. I was like, 'What are you doing?'"

Brandon lowered his head and nodded.

"And, Marcus," the judge continued, "I respect you so much for standing up there and, you know, actually giving a speech. Most kids, like, when that happens, they're like, 'Shit, I don't even care anymore.'"

BRANDON LEFT MARCUS to pack up the tubs. He bumped into Rinehart in the hall. "Well?" she said, spreading her arms inquisitively.

"We went down. On T."

"You dropped T?"

"I don't know what I was thinking about," Brandon said, head bowed. "I think we would have won that debate hands down. Just. I don't know." He kicked at the carpet. "It's my fault. I accept it."

Rinehart planted her hands on her hips and scanned the crowd of debaters filling the hall. "Okay," she said finally. "What did you learn?"

"I shoulda put it on top."

"Put what on top?"

"Topicality."

"Didn't you know that? Debate 101?"

He raised his tie to his mouth, folded it, and bit down. Rinehart slapped it away from his lips. "Y'all need to quit with the ties in your face," she said.

"Why?"

"Because you're gonna get it all grody."

"I'm just smelling it."

"Well, quit smelling it."

"It smells good."

"No."

Brandon left Rinehart and roamed the halls. He walked slowly, running his finger along the lockers, his eyes focused a few steps ahead. I asked him how he felt, and he shrugged. "Man, we would have had an easy four-oh," he said. "Kinda sucks." A few other debaters said hi as he passed, and he meekly raised his hand and continued on. He told me he wouldn't be going out with Marcus and his camp friends that night. "I don't really like those people anyway," he said.

ELEVEN

THE HIGH FASHION OF MURDER
AND OPPRESSION

"**YOU EVER SEE SOMEBODY** get shot?" Marcus asked, ducking and swinging fake punches at a boy with a long neck and a bad case of acne. "I have."

It was true. The previous school year Marcus had heard shots just as Rinehart was dropping him off at home after practice. He'd looked over his shoulder and spotted one of his neighbors running and another neighbor lying on the ground, bleeding. Marcus sprinted into the house and Rinehart stepped on the gas. The next day the incident merited a short article in *The Kansas City Star*, primarily because the shooting arose out of a conflict over a gold tooth. The men were brothers. A local country station picked up on the story and wove it into its rush-hour broadcast, its deejays shouting to each other, "Gimme back my toof!" During the station's traffic report that day, a reporter announced an accident on Prospect Avenue, a busy road that bisects Kansas City's predominantly black East Side. "Where was that again?" one of the deejays asked. "Prospect," the reporter replied, then the deejay played the sound of gunshots. The incident was tragic for Marcus's neighbors. And Marcus was shaken by it. He spent that evening in his room with the door shut. But among this crowd of suburban white kids who had gathered at a Mexican chain restaurant in central Iowa, the tragedy was now a fashion statement.

Marcus was in hyper mode again. Having come straight from the tournament, he hadn't changed out of his debate uniform, though his shirttail dangled and his tie hung loosely. He looked like a frat pledge, despite his insinuations that he was a ghetto tough. One of the girls in his party lifted a camera to her eye, and Marcus and James crowded into the picture, trying to spell B-L-O-O-D with their fingers like gang members. "Can I make this thug-affiliated?" Marcus asked.

It was homecoming night in West Des Moines, and a few groups of boys in suits and girls wearing shiny black and red dresses crowded into the restaurant. Marcus and his friends from debate camp, a party of ten, were told they'd have to wait forty-five minutes for a table. They hailed from all parts of the United States: Billy and Kevin from Fayette County, Georgia; James, David, and Brittany from Chicago; Jacob from Evanston; Jessy and Allison from West Des Moines. Most had attended the Capital Classic debate camp sponsored by Catholic University in Washington, D.C., the previous summer. The camp, like many such camps held at universities across the country, cost several thousand dollars, though Marcus attended on a scholarship, one of a handful given to Urban Debate League members like him and James. They were the only blacks in the group. "Is it true that because you're black you have to run fast?" Jessy asked them. They looked at each other in mock shock and said in unison, "You're a racist!"

The shtick was a continuation of their antics at camp, where whites were the overwhelming majority, though Catholic's campus was located in a black neighborhood. Marcus and James had sized up the camp's culture and determined that they could fill a niche as resident gangstas, something neither could do in their home neighborhoods. They'd stepped up to random kids, crowded their personal space, and barked, "What you lookin' at?!" Whenever they tried to act tough at their own schools, though, kids would usually laugh. Sometimes in room 109, Marcus would succumb to a jolt of energy and flail his arms, smack his elbows, and shout, "I'm gonna unload a two-piece of Church's fried chicken and a biscuit!"—emphasizing "biscuit" with a groin-high kick. "Marcus," the girls would say, "you ain't no thug!"

Truth is, Marcus was quite comfortable around whites, perhaps even more so than around blacks. He was half-white himself, his father being Anglo. His mom felt it was important that he get to know white people. Whites run the country, she reasoned. If he was going to do anything with his life, he'd have to deal with them. When he was in grade school, Kansas City was undergoing a massive desegregation effort. She enrolled him in a magnet elementary school, one of the more reputable ones, a math and science school located near the Country Club Plaza shopping district, an outdoor mall made up to look like a European village. While there, he befriended a white kid named Richard who would become, as he put it, his "hetero life mate." Richard's parents looked on Marcus as another son. He spent half or more of his time with their family, taking trips with them, learning chess, stuff like that. At Christmas, they'd lavish him with gifts as nice as the ones they'd given to Richard.

James was similarly soft. A short teen with a widening frame, he favored button-down shirts and off-brand khakis, like Marcus. He spoke with the affect of a North Shore snob, his head always cocked back slightly as if everything and everyone were beneath him. Both had attended debate camps every summer during high school and had spent many of their weekends at debate tournaments hanging out with kids who rarely, if ever, visited neighborhoods like theirs. Far from being ostracized for their race and backgrounds, they'd attained an elite status because of them. Though Marcus and James weren't tough, their neighborhoods were, and their experience made them unique. What other debate camper could brag, as Marcus could, that his next-door neighbor was a drug dealer who was trying to go straight, that if he weren't debating he'd probably do as his younger brother, Jason, was doing, working for the criminal as he built a new empire as a slumlord?

At one point a car alarm went off in the parking lot. "Come on, Marcus," James said, spreading his arms and feet and leaning against a wall as if to be frisked, "assume the position."

"I almost got arrested in the first two hours in this state," Marcus bragged, taking the perfect cue for another yarn in his African-American-life routine. And suddenly the incident that had so infuriated him and his teammates the night before became social currency, and he regaled his fellow debaters with a hyped-up, laugh-filled version.

All through dinner he and James commanded the conversation, slapping the table and jumping out of their seats to punch up their tales. Every subject seemed to dovetail into a race issue. At the end of the night Marcus shouted, "Jessy, I'll forgive you for two hundred years of slavery if you'll pick up the bill!"

TWELVE

RUN FOR THE TOC, TAKE 1

OF ALL THE DEBATERS at the dinner party, Marcus laid claim to the best record for the Saturday rounds. Starting off the next day at three-one, he and Brandon knew they'd only need to pick up one win to advance to the elimination rounds. If that happened, they'd be just one win away from a bid to the Tournament of Champions, which would go to the top eight finishers. And at mid-morning Sunday, Marcus was beaming as he listened to his opponent deliver the final speech in round five. He had no doubt he and Brandon would pick up the win.

They were running negative against a team from College Preparatory Academy of Oakland, California, a team he and Donnell had defeated in a matchup the previous year. This time around it felt like an all-out rout. During the 1AR, College Prep failed to answer almost all of Brandon's arguments about the political repercussions of the California team's plan, and Marcus spent a full four minutes of his final speech pointing this out to the judge. "They strategically screwed up," he yelled. "That means *game over*. Better luck next time."

The timer sounded and the judge studied his notes. He filled out the ballot and folded it in half. "This was a pretty good debate," he said. "I, uh . . ." He drummed the table with his thumbs. "What do I want to say?"

Brandon stood facing the judge, his arms crossed. Marcus sat in a desk, leaning over the chair back, chewing on a pen.

"I vote affirmative," the judge said.

Marcus pulled the pen out of his mouth. He looked at Brandon, then at me.

"You've got to be kidding me!" he said. "Were you even listening? They conceded that we solve!"

"Just chill out," Brandon said, sensing a big fight. He stepped out into the hall. When he returned five minutes later, Marcus and the judge were still going at it.

"What *is* your plan?" the judge asked, clearly exasperated. "Telling me after the round is not your argument."

"What else am I supposed to do when it's conceded and I explain it?" Marcus said.

On and on they went. Brandon straightened a loose pile of documents and stuffed them into a tub. He sat down and listened for a while. He shook his head. Marcus finally realized his arguing would get him nowhere. The judge got up to leave. Brandon politely thanked him, and then turned to me and said, "Garbage."

Marcus was still fuming as they moved into the hall. "'Did you expect me to vote for the text of the counterplan?'" he asked, mockingly. "Yes, we expect you to vote on the text of the counterplan!"

He spotted Jane and marched up to her. "That was the dumbest judge I've ever had," he said, and stormed off. Around the corner he bumped into James. He laid the story out for his friend. James shook his head.

"Who was it to?"

"College Prep," Marcus said. "That team is bad. We beat them last year."

He turned to stare off into the distance of the hall. "We're about to lose the next round," he said.

"Why?" I asked.

"No prep," he said. "I'm ready to go home anyway. After that shit."

But they picked up an easy win the next round. Marcus breezed through the hall afterward, bouncing on his heels and swinging his arms. "You pick up?" Jessy asked him.

"We're four-two," he said.

"Cool," she said. "You'll break."

He found James. "Sup, pimp?" he asked.

James raised his fists to his chest and gave two thumbs up. "How'd you do?"

"Smokin' good," Marcus said.

They lazed around in the hall for the better part of an hour, waiting for the out-round pairings to come out. Suddenly the crowd shifted toward the cafeteria entryway, where a pair of Valley students were handing out elimination-round schedules. Jessy and James pushed through the maw while Marcus and Brandon stayed put, playing it cool. Jessy ran back to them. "You broke!" she said. "You're going against Highland Park."

"That means we're gonna lose," Marcus said. "They're one of the top teams in the nation right now."

"That means nothing," said Sobek, who stood nearby, eavesdropping.

MARCUS AND BRANDON had gone to camp with Highland Park's first speaker, Andrea. And the number two, the team's quarterback, was something of a legend on the national circuit. He had advanced to the quarterfinals at the TOC a year earlier—a stellar achievement for a junior. On one of his tubs was a sticker that read, I'M NOT PERFECT, BUT I'M SO CLOSE I'M SCARY.

Brandon got up and belted out Central's appeal to end racism with mental health reform. After cross-x, Highland Park took no prep time before launching their counterattack. Remaining seated, Andrea laid out a scenario similar to the one Marcus and Brandon had used earlier against other opponents, stating that passage of the plan would affect the midterm elections, resulting in a Republican majority on Capitol Hill. This would be an unfortunate turn of events, she argued, because the Republicans would then approve oil drilling in the Arctic National Wildlife Refuge in Alaska. This would disrupt the earth's delicate balance and trigger mass ecological extinction. She read in a high-pitched tone, and every dozen or so words she gasped for air such that her head kicked back violently.

Marcus and Brandon burned through more than half of their prep time. The room was quiet as they searched their tubs for good cards and frantically wrote out new ones. The younger debaters in the audience spun pens between their fingertips. A few were lying across the floor, asleep.

Marcus ripped through his speech, hunched over slightly, slapping the sides of a pair of tubs he'd stacked on a desk to make a podium. But Brandon spoke haltingly when it was his turn. At one point he stopped his speech cold. "Oh, God," he said, looking up at the judges. "Marcus wrote this." He spied his timer. "Damn, I only have a minute left."

Marcus waved his hand frantically in a circle. "Go! Go! Go!" he hissed.

Highland Park's top debater had a full seven minutes and forty seconds to prepare for his final speech, which he delivered quickly and cleanly from his seat. Marcus, on the other hand, had just forty-five seconds to get ready for Central's last argument. As he spoke, he drove his fists into the makeshift podium and bent deeply at the knees to squeeze urgency from his words.

The timer sounded and the debaters shook hands. Brandon stepped out into the hall. He sagged against a row of lockers next to Rinehart, who had stayed outside during the round. Brandon looked at her and shook his head. She nodded and went into the room.

The judges were scanning their notes. *A positive sign*, Rinehart thought. *At least it wasn't a blowout.* She helped Marcus gather evidence to file back in the tubs, and then took a seat, crossing her legs and resting her chin on the palm of her hand. This waiting part drove her crazy, especially when a bid to the TOC was on the line.

One by one, the judges set down their pens and folded their ballots. One judge collected them and tallied the votes. "It's two-one for the negative," he said.

Rinehart sighed and let her head drop.

ON THE RIDE HOME the Central crew was so rambunctious that Rinehart twice pulled onto the berm and slowed to a near stop, threatening to not move any farther until the kids settled down or at least quit cussing. It didn't work. A few miles north of the Missouri line, Dionne, with her headphones on, started singing along to Khia: "My neck, my back, lick my pussy and my crack." And just about everyone else joined in.

"Mouth!" Rinehart shouted.

"What does my cussing have to do with you getting past these semis?" Brandon asked as a tractor trailer rumbled past. "You the one 'bout to get us killed."

"Man, I ain't going to no school tomorrow," Marcus declared. "It's too damn hard. Doing debate work. Going to class. I'm sick of it."

"Shit, you got that right," Brandon said.

"Stuff," Rinehart corrected him.

Brandon ignored her, slipping his headphones over his ears. He clicked forward to track five, cranked it up, and started rapping along:

Y'all can go to hell, how does that sound?

THIRTEEN

WRONG LIFE

WHEN I SHOWED UP at Central for afternoon practice two days after the Valley tournament, there were ten school district cop cars lined up out front. During the first week of the semester, only one or two of the silver cruisers had been assigned to the school. But more and more kept showing up throughout September. It seemed like overkill; the truancy officers just stood around their cars chatting. I asked around and found out that a number of fights in the cafeteria and during passing periods had spurred the protective measures. It was mostly freshmen who were causing the problems. One of the rowdiest instigators was a kid called Porky, a childhood friend of Marcus's younger brother, Jason. Porky gave Jason a ride to school every day during the 2002–2003 school year, and Jason witnessed Porky spin deeper and deeper into violence. By the end of the year, Porky would graduate from fistfights to guns.

Like fresh meat at a penitentiary, the freshmen seemed to be out to prove themselves and claim their turf. Even without all the cop cars parked outside, without the armed officer assigned to the cafeteria, without the metal detectors at the front door or the security guards who patrolled the halls with bullhorns, Central would seem more like a prison than a school. A broad guard station confronted all who entered the building, beyond which stretched long corridors of cinder blocks painted dull gray. No posters adorned the walls, no student art, not a bit of color. In the classrooms, teachers had hung a few decorations, but they did little to warm the place. Nor did the tiny windows, set a foot or so above eye level so all you could see through them were roofs, treetops, and an occasional bird streaking by.

To a native Kansas Citian, the security measures would probably seem appropriate. Since the late 1950s the school had been the scene of several violent crimes that made the morning paper. In the early 1970s, a few years after riots had erupted around the school in the wake of the assassination of Martin Luther King, Jr., the school made national news when its security guards started packing pistols. From the late 1980s on, shootings on or near the campus occurred almost every year. During the first two weeks of the 2002–2003 school year, Central's principal, William McClendon, played Aretha Franklin's "Respect" on the PA system each day before the morning bell rang. It blared through the halls and out into the parking lot from conical speakers that stuck out from the edge of the roof. One day I spotted a teen dancing to it as the morning sun glinted off the rows of cars, his arms and legs moving slowly and his eyes nearly closed as if he were completely stoned. Each day McClendon added mini sermons to the morning announcements about the school's "zero tolerance for violence policy" and the virtues of education. "As long as there are people on earth," he said one morning, "there will never be another you. The question is, what kind of *you* will you be?" The kids in the class I was observing talked right over him. "This weekend we lost two individuals from our school," he said a few days later. Then he clicked off the microphone without saying anything else.

As I pulled in to the parking lot on my way to afternoon practice, I stopped beside a cruiser parked by the entrance. A couple cops were leaning against the hood. The school's head security guard approached and peeked through my open window. Seeing that I was a white adult, he waved me through without a word. Once inside the school, I bypassed the metal detectors with no hassle, as I usually did. In room 109 I found Marcus and Sobek seated near each other, working on debate cards. A few other debaters were there—DiAnna, Leo, and Day, a salty-mouthed junior who was on track to be valedictorian—and they were cutting cards, too. Discarded scraps of paper had fallen on the floor around them, and dollies full of debate tubs crowded the room's corners, right where they'd been abandoned after the

Valley tournament. Brandon was asleep, his head and arms resting on a desktop.

Rinehart sat at her desk and surfed the Internet for low airfares. She hadn't planned to take Sobek to the next varsity tournament, another Tournament of Champions qualifier at New Trier High School, in the suburbs north of Chicago. But Marcus whined and whined until she agreed to look into the possibility. Her research wasn't turning up any good news. A few weeks earlier she'd scored tickets for her and her debaters for $168. But since then the prices had gone up to over $350.

I sat down near Marcus and watched him read through a stack of documents. After a few minutes he started tapping a frantic beat with his highlighter. He spun it between his fingers like a helicopter blade. He looked up and rubbed his nose. He thumbed through his pages and sighed. Dozens more to go.

Then he abruptly bolted from his seat and started circling the room. He opened a debate tub and closed it. He kicked a dolly tire. Then he flopped down on one of the shelf-desks that line the room and sprawled out across it. His gaze fixed on the ceiling tiles, he picked up a disconnected computer wire and instinctively put it in his mouth. He looped it over his nose. Glancing at a small American flag that jutted out from the wall above the dry-erase board, he said, "Man, that flag is stupid. They could buy me a pencil and paper with what they spent on that."

His upright knees fanned together and apart and together again.

"I want to break that damn flag," he said.

He looked over at Brandon, who was now sitting up, blurry-eyed from his nap.

"Brandon, you ever go to sleep at night with no food?" he asked. "Not by choice, but because there's no food."

"Nah," Brandon said, laughing. "I've always had food."

"I'm so poor," Marcus said, "I've never had a birthday present."

"Shut up, man," Brandon said.

"I've been poor for so long," Marcus went on, "I begin to think it feels normal. Man, that's messed up. When you actually notice rich people you sleep with over the weekend, then you notice the difference."

He pictured the palatial house where he had stayed in West Des Moines, its spacious rooms with plush carpet and sturdy, clean furniture, its big-screen TV and Jacuzzi. It made his home seem like a shack. He lived a mile east of Central, in the southern half of a duplex on a street with no sidewalks overlooking the VA hospital. His home was barely nine hundred square feet, with the living room, dining room, and kitchen all crowded into one open area. The aging furniture carved up the space—the dining room table made of particleboard covered with a thin wood-grain sticker that was peeling at the edges and surrounded by brown vinyl-covered chairs, the puffy couch and love seat pushed next to each other to face the TV. In the corner stood a chrome-and-glass shelf filled with his mother's collection of figurines of black kids in overalls holding fishing poles and fresh-baked pies or bending over to kiss each other. Marcus's room was just off the kitchen, a ten-by-nine space with a twin bed, a dresser, a nightstand with a twelve-inch TV on it, and, incongruously, a tall computer tower with a hulking monitor perched on a desk not much bigger than a TV tray. The walls were beige and bore just one poster, an ad for the Grand Theft Auto video game, and a dry-erase calendar that hadn't been updated for months. His home was clean, and it had everything Marcus and his family needed, but you could fit the whole thing in the living room of the house he'd stayed at two days earlier.

"They tell you to be oppressed for eighteen years, and then they tell you to go be something," Marcus said.

"What are you *on* today?" DiAnna asked.

Marcus stared at the ceiling with a faraway look in his eyes. "I wish I could just have one dollar an hour," he said. "I'd be satisfied."

He calculated his needs on his fingertips—a couple McDonald's Value Meals a day, high-speed Internet access, bus fare.

"No," he corrected himself. "Fifty cents. No. Seventy-five cents. Yeah. Seventy-five cents. Twenty-four hours. Perfect. I could just be in my room. Eat fast food."

DiAnna looked at me and shook her head.

"No," Marcus went on, "I need to rob a bank or something. I need to do something to go to jail, something to get me arrested."

"You talkin' crazy," DiAnna said.

"Think about it," Marcus said. "You have everything. Social services. Health care. Food. Weight room. Think about it, Brandon."

Brandon had laid his head back down and closed his eyes.

"It's a shame," Marcus said. "I'm gonna be in jail in five years."

He sat up, his eyes narrow, hawkish. If he'd been kidding before, he wasn't anymore. He had followed the links of his bored musings and found a startling reality.

"Hey," he said. "Let me ask everybody something. When you lose in debate, do you punch someone or hold your head low?"

"I hold my head high," Day replied.

"That's the thing with debate," Marcus said, ignoring her answer. "Unless you're the number-one team in the nation, you're gonna end up a loser. I think I'm in the wrong activity. For real. I think I'm in the wrong life."

I looked at Rinehart and smiled warily, trying to gauge from her some sort of meaning in Marcus's monologue. She scowled.

"Marcus," she said. "Why don't you get up and do some work?"

FOURTEEN

JANE RINEHART

JANE RINEHART SOMETIMES PICTURED her life as a movie. Holly Hunter would play her. The actress was more slender, sure, but her red hair, pale skin, and slight southern accent made up for it. Crop her hair and perm some waves neatly around her ears, wrap her in a prim skirt suit with a seasonal brooch, put in some blue contacts, and have her purse her lips and widen her eyes a bit, and you'd be almost there. Hunter's attitude would do the rest, the kind she showed as a criminal profiler in *Copycat* mixed with some of the blossoming divorcée in *Living Out Loud*. It would be such a great Hollywood story: a white woman born in Jim Crow Louisiana comes to a ghetto school, takes no guff, and builds a champion debate squad. "I really think things happen for a reason," Rinehart said to me as she drove a rented cargo van down a tree-lined parkway in the suburbs north of Chicago. "For some reason I was meant to be at Central."

We moved southward through neighborhoods of stately homes and lush trees. Every couple miles, clusters of storefronts appeared, fashioned in stucco and dark wood trim like theme-park copies of quaint European villages. Rinehart gazed wistfully at a street-side café, its tables and chairs dappled with shade from the low trees that rose out of the sidewalk. "What a perfect Chicago day," she said to me. "On days like this I wish I wasn't a debate coach. Fall is my favorite season." For a moment she imagined herself spending the day shopping and having a glass of wine in the afternoon sun.

Instead, she was heading for a day under fluorescent lights, sipping stale coffee and listening to kids speed-read the words of scholars. To me, her life
seemed to be a series of sacrifices. She got up every morning at 4:30 to make
it to school on time, and it was almost 7:00 at night by the time she got
home, after practice and delivering debaters to houses scattered around the
East Side. On road trips she did all the driving. Hip-hop—not her first
choice in music—was almost always cranked from the van's shoddy speakers.
And she spent a lot of her own money on her students. Before the start of the
2002–2003 school year, she bought a used copy machine for her room for a
couple hundred bucks. When I told her once that I'd heard teachers spend
on average more than $400 on stuff to supplement their lessons, she
laughed. "I wish I spent that little."

During warm months she volunteered with a dozen or so kids to work
at Worlds of Fun amusement park in Kansas City's northern suburbs or at
Chiefs and Royals games. Usually, they worked eight-hour shifts, with their
minimum-wage earnings going into the debate account. I joined them on
one of these ventures at Worlds of Fun, and it was among the worst work
experiences I'd had since high school. Teens half my age ordered me to
keep constantly busy wiping down tables and mopping up grease from behind fryers and ovens. Rinehart grabbed a broom and dug in, just like
everybody else.

The only thing that ever made her consider giving it up was her students. The week before the New Trier tournament had been particularly trying. Just a few days before they were set to leave, after she'd already bought
the plane tickets, Brandon announced he wouldn't be going. He was pissed
off at Marcus, who said he wouldn't go to the Iowa Caucus, another TOC
qualifier in Cedar Rapids scheduled for late October. Marcus's reason: He
had a Counter-Strike tournament to attend. He planned to spend that weekend connected to the Internet, roaming a virtual war zone with an AK-47.
He stood a chance of winning a share of a $500 prize. Rinehart tried to
talk him out of it, but she gave up. Then Sobek jumped in, saying he might
as well quit as assistant coach if they weren't going to compete at the few
TOC qualifiers that fit under Missouri travel limitations. But Marcus coolly
rebuffed him. Finally I pulled Marcus aside and reminded him that I was

writing a book about him. "Years from now," I told him, "people will go to the library, read about Marcus Leach, and say, 'What an idiot.'" He blinked at me a couple times and abruptly changed his mind. Brandon quickly followed suit.

Rinehart turned left at the village of Winnetka, toward Lake Michigan, and pulled in to a parking space outside New Trier High School. The original structure was built in the boom years before the Depression, and it appeared to have been frozen in prosperity; it was so impeccable and regal, with its various bond-issue annexes spreading out in three-stories-high shoots from an art deco core of brick and terra-cotta. Ivy crept up its sides. This, or something like it, is, more often than not, the setting for high school movies, the ones where dorky boys make bets about who'll lose their virginity first and shy girls snare the captain of the football team. In the distance, a runner trotted around a red all-weather track, and tennis players shuffled back and forth on a row of courts. A boy rolled by in a red Sebring convertible with the top down and Jay-Z cranked. Flowers bloomed along the sidewalks. Tucked among them were benches where kids could read or chat. "Look at this landscaping," Rinehart said as she made her way to the front door. "Why can't we have landscaping?"

Seeing this, I couldn't help but feel embarrassed for Central High, with its front lawn of cracked parking lot and sidewalks pocked with hardened black wads of gum. Whenever Rinehart took her kids to a school like New Trier, or even ones in the suburbs of Kansas City, the first thing they always said was, "My God, look at how clean this place is!"

I followed Rinehart into the school's entryway, where there stood a guard station that was much smaller than Central's and unmanned. On the walls beyond it were display cases full of themed dioramas. Rinehart paused at one full of fake yellow and brown birds perched on tree limbs. Each was labeled with its common name and its scientific one in parentheses and information about its habitat, diet, and mating patterns. "This is how you can tell this is a good school," Rinehart said, tapping the glass. "When they have stuff like this. Students probably made this." No such thing existed at Central. Principal McClendon forbade hanging posters and art because, it seemed, whenever anyone did, rowdy kids tore them down.

Rinehart pushed open the door to the lounge and laughed. "Oh, jeez," she said, "look at this."

The place was done up like a Swiss chalet, with dark wainscoting and rustic wood beams bracing the gabled ceiling. Burgundy leather chairs were tucked neatly under the tables, and a brick fireplace stood at the far end, surrounded by sumptuous couches and armchairs. The room smelled of coffee, and trays of melon and Danishes and pitchers of orange juice were lined up on a banquet table along the far wall.

"See," Rinehart said. "This is what I gave up."

In 1979 she was offered the head coach position at New Trier, but she declined. The baby boom had passed, and it was a time of slow economic growth in the nation; New Trier's budget and enrollment were on the decline. Its school board was considering a consolidation of school programs, so she couldn't be guaranteed a job for more than a year. At the time she was a debate coach and an English teacher at Illinois's Pekin Community High School. A town of thirty thousand south of Peoria, Pekin is referred to by locals as "The Marigold Capital of the World." It's a farm and factory community, nestled in the bluffs and woods around the Illinois River. Historically, downstate schools such as Rinehart's had been dog meat on the Illinois debate circuit, where teams from Chicago's suburbs have long ruled. But Rinehart, a debater from way back, was oblivious to the status quo. She worked her teams hard, and soon they were beating giants like Glenbrook North, located a few miles west of New Trier, which was honored in 2000 as having "the best high school debate program of the century." One year Rinehart's team won the novice division of Glenbrook's annual tournament, which, outside of the Harvard Invitational, is the biggest high school tournament in the country.

After turning down the job, Rinehart moved back to Kansas City, where she'd spent most of her adolescence. Her parents still lived there, in the suburbs north of the Missouri River. She got out of teaching for a while, trying stints as a gate and reservation agent for Eastern and America West airlines before returning to the classroom. More than twenty years later, the woman who took the New Trier job after Rinehart declined was still there, earning $94,545 per year. At Central, Rinehart earned $54,000. Doug Springer, who hired Rinehart at Pekin in the early 1970s, also worked at New Trier as an assistant coach. When he was hired in 1994, he told Rinehart that his salary was higher than Pekin's superintendent's. Springer once bragged to Rinehart that the staff at New Trier were so capable and dedicated that they could go anywhere in the country and make a successful school. The school's budget for speech and debate in 2002–2003 was $207,294, compared with Central's $15,000. Any student or teacher with an idea for a new club or activity is eligible for $1,500 to cover expenses. There are more than a hundred such clubs, from the AIDS Coalition and a group of anime fanatics to Russian, synchronized swimming, and ultimate Frisbee. During the 2001–2002 school year, some kids decided they wanted to take up rowing, so the school board almost immediately agreed to buy a boat for $30,000. The school has a cable TV station and a 100-watt radio station run by students. There are courses in Spanish, French, German, Latin, Japanese, Chinese, and Hebrew. New Trier offers six full-time post-high-school counselors and has separate departments for multicultural studies, social work, and business, in which ambitious teens may take American Business, a class that, according to the school's catalog, will introduce them to the "development and functioning of the free enterprise system" through lessons on "stock market operations, business organization, marketing practices and taxes." In 2001 a New Trier alumnus, the physicist Jack Steinberger, donated to his alma mater the Nobel Prize he'd won in 1988 to show appreciation for his education.

When Rinehart first arrived at Central, on the other hand, one of her colleagues told her that some of the students didn't even know that there were twelve inches in a foot, three feet in a yard. The school offered only three advanced-placement courses, in English, American history, and algebra. For foreign languages, there was just Spanish and Japanese (now all that's offered is Spanish). The racial dynamic of this disparity wasn't lost on her: at New Trier, the black population was 0.6 percent, while Central's was 95 percent. The contrast in wealth was as distinct as the contrast in skin tone. In New Trier Township, the median household income was $122,641, according to the 2000 census. At Central, 63 percent of the students qualified for free or reduced-price lunches. When I asked Rinehart if she regretted passing on the New Trier job, she said it was only because she couldn't give her current students the benefit of such abundance. "They shouldn't have to be of a privileged class to be able to have things available to them," she complained to me once. "I really find that philosophically unacceptable, that there are certain haves and have-nots." Which is what made it all the more satisfying when her have-nots beat the snot out of the haves at debate tournaments.

It was in Rinehart's blood. Her parents were teachers. Fred Rinehart worked concessions at Friday night football games to raise money for his students to put on plays. Her mom, Catherine, known to her friends as Kitty, was a grade school teacher and had a soft spot for underdogs. Once, the sixth-grade softball team she coached beat the mighty Holy Family parochial school squad. "Here they had on their uniforms, and they thought they were so much," her mom bragged when she came home, "and we beat 'em."

That was about when the Supreme Court's decision in *Brown v. Board of Education* came down. Rinehart confided to me that her parents were segregationists. Though she was rarely at a loss for words, she would clam up whenever I pressed her for more information about this. That was the way things were around Baton Rouge, where they lived, she explained. Yet she said her parents gave her a keen sense of justice. "We were big as a family that things should be just," she told me. "They should be right, though the world wasn't, necessarily. But you certainly didn't mess it up yourself by not being fair."

Rinehart's parents were always teaching her and her sister—at the dinner table, during chores, and on their drives along the country roads that wound into town. They read the newspaper together every afternoon, and any tidbit of information could spark a lesson. Plus, they treated her like an equal, even though she was a girl. Her dad told her she could do anything. She shot BB guns, fished, rowed boats, and helped out with house projects. When she was a teenager and got into debate, it never occurred to her that the game was the domain of boys. For her, the game was a rare oasis of fairness. You worked hard, you argued hard, and, if you were the best team, you won. Her dad pushed her to succeed. He helped her build arguments. He had a keen eye for the economics of politics. When she'd explain to him one of her opponents' plans, he'd say, "Well, it's gonna cost money. If you spend money, you have to take it from somewhere else. Or raise taxes. And we don't want to do that."

And so Rinehart came to Central with a democratic attitude. It was obvious that her students were poor and hampered by a lousy school. But debate was still debate. Anyone can argue, she figured. Indeed, these students seemed to take to debate better than any other educational activity. It was as if it were written into their genetic codes. And within a few years her teams were routinely advancing to trophy rounds at national-circuit tournaments. They qualified for the Catholic Forensic League's national championship several times, as well as the NFL championship and the Tournament of Champions—the first Missouri team ever to have done so, so she could forgive her colleagues for thinking hers was a school for gifted children.

FIFTEEN

BLACK BOYS AND GIRLS

MORE THAN ANYTHING, Brandon wanted to be on the second team in Missouri history to qualify for the TOC, though he wasn't letting on this morning. Sleepy-eyed and sullen, he let Marcus unload the tubs from the rental van and followed his partner through New Trier's crowded halls, dragging his feet. When he got to the room where their first round was to be held, it was locked. He leaned against a wall and scowled. A few paces away, his opponents huddled with their coach. His headphones covered his ears, but no music was playing. "They're from Kansas City," he heard the coach tell her team. "They're UDL. This should be an easy win."

Brandon and I looked at each other in disbelief. He grabbed my shirt, pulled me a few steps away, and whispered, "Did you hear that? That's like the most racist thing I've ever heard."

For all the hoopla about the formation of the Urban Debate Leagues among folks in the debate community, their debaters were privately given little respect. A study conducted by a graduate student at California State University–Fullerton found that when debaters at schools affiliated with Urban Debate Leagues compete at invitational tournaments such as New Trier's, they lose more often and get lower speaker points than any other debaters, including poor minority kids from non-UDL schools. The study's author, Casey Arbenz, a debater himself, suggested that the UDLs carried a stigma.

Down the hall Marcus was busy wrestling a dolly off of the elevator. When Brandon told him what the other team's coach had said, he stopped in his tracks.

"Are you serious?" he asked.

He rubbed his hands together in a spasm and grinned broadly. "That's *sooo* racist!" he said, genuinely thrilled.

Sometimes Marcus loved prejudice, as if it helped define him. He often manufactured it, like when he had branded his debate camp friends as racist at dinner in West Des Moines, or a few days before the New Trier tournament, when he tried to persuade Rinehart to take him to a fast-food joint by accusing her of having a book called *How to Control Black People* in the trunk of her car. ("Didn't you read chapter 3?" he'd asked her. "'Give Them Fried Chicken.'") But blatantly racist comments were best, especially when he had the power to meet them head-on. "Man," he said to Brandon, literally shaking with excitement. "We gon' make them *pay* for that!"

The opposing team hailed from Eisenhower High, a school in the northern exurbs of Detroit. They seemed a mismatched pair—a thin, fidgety boy with thick, wavy hair pushed to one side in a greasy hold, and a fair-skinned girl in a prim skirt suit who moved with the poise of a lunchroom goddess. Clearly she was in charge, the way she barked orders at her doting partner. She started out confidently, cockily even. But by the final speech, she was sputtering "um," "like," and "uh" with a bit of debate jargon and "save the world" rhetoric sprinkled here and there.

"Game over," Marcus said as he began the round's final speech.

BRANDON WAS IN BETTER form this morning. Unlike at the earlier tournament in West Des Moines, he didn't need Marcus to answer so many of his questions during cross-x. His speeches were smooth, forceful. For a moment he looked to me like a leader, with his tie loosened and his outstretched hand.

But in the hall after the round, he resumed his mope. He followed Marcus into an elevator and slumped against a handrail. "I'm not into debating," he said.

"Sucks to be you," Marcus replied, not looking at him.

"No. Sucks to be *you*." Brandon looked up at the elevator's light fixture. "It's boring," he said.

On the first floor they crossed paths with Rinehart. Marcus told her about the "easy" comment and how they'd clobbered them. Brandon sulked off to the side. Rinehart glanced at him. "We need to pump you up," she said.

"Whatever."

"What's the deal?" she asked. "Sounds like you destroyed them in that round."

"I'm bored." He slipped on his earphones and sauntered off down the hall.

Watching him go, Rinehart said to me, "It's a front. He's just doing it to get attention."

RINEHART WAS MORE WORRIED about the other team she'd brought to the tournament, Day and Dionne, both juniors. They'd lost their first round. And their second round. And the one after that. While Brandon and Marcus finished the day three-one, on track for a place in out rounds and a chance at a TOC bid, the girls lost all their debates.

Rinehart sat in on one of their rounds and was appalled. They didn't understand basic terms, such as "liberal" and "conservative" and "political capital." It was ridiculous, she thought. These were brilliant girls. Day was ranked at the top of the junior class. How could they get this far without knowing what a liberal is? In the round Rinehart watched, their opponents ran a case for transcendental meditation programs in prisons. It was clear her students had no clue what transcendental meditation was. Rinehart didn't necessarily have a problem with that. But they never *asked* what it was. It was as if they were afraid to.

They made their way to the van at the end of the day, past the rosebushes and ivy cast in orange streetlight glow. "We're going to read the newspaper," Rinehart said to her students, who were slumping along behind her. "We're going to practice. We're going to take basic grammar."

"I feel like crying," Day said.

"You don't cry," Rinehart said, stopping to unlock the van. "You make other teams cry. Real women don't cry. We have to be more assertive."

"She don't do that," Dionne said of Day as she climbed into the front seat. Day slammed the side door shut behind her.

"She doesn't do that, does she?" Rinehart corrected Dionne, in a smooth sophisticated voice. "No, she doesn't."

"Our lessons have started," Dionne said, rolling her eyes.

"That is correct, they have," Rinehart said, still sounding prissy as she fired the engine.

We were off in search of a restaurant still open at ten at night. The van lurched forward and turned slowly onto a side street lined with houses as big as office buildings. The average price of a house in Winnetka was $756,500 in 2002, and over a third were worth more than a million. The property tax levy for New Trier Township was just under $2, less than half the rate in the middle of Chicago, but because the properties are worth so much, the school district could spend almost $14,000 per student per year.

"We might have to sit down and watch *My Fair Lady*," Rinehart said.

"Oh no," Day exclaimed. "What is . . . What? I don't understand that."

"Well, if Henry Higgins can do it, then, by golly, so can I."

The girls sat silently. They had no idea what she was talking about.

"He changes—" Rinehart began. "He takes this woman. This cockney flower girl." She switched into an accent less like a British tramp than like an old lady who's put her dentures in backward. "Ya know wha a Cah-ney is?"

"No," Day and Dionne said in unison.

"Aw-rye," Rinehart replied, still in character. "T'sa, t'sa groo uh pee-pul in a sur-en air-ya uh Lon-don 'n day tawk la daat." She made her voice sound even less human. "Cuz day raw-en. Ya know Ma-ee Poh-pens?"

The girls laughed.

"Yeah," Rinehart continued. She changed back into a Midwesterner. "Okay, that's a cockney accent. They drop the *h*'s and all kinds of stuff like that. So it's cockney. So he takes her, she's a cockney flower girl." Rinehart's voice went silky and full of pompous wonder: "And he transforms her into this lady who can pass herself off as a *duchess* at the *embassy* ball."

Day and Dionne watched the houses go by.

"It's possible," Rinehart said after a long pause. "You think?"

"Man, they got two houses," Day said, craning to take in a broad estate with white columns. Its living room lights glowed warmly through lush curtains.

"Man, I want a house like that one day," Dionne said.

"Well," Rinehart said, "you have to get it by talking properly."

"Rinehart, man," Dionne scoffed. "I just need to do my, my doctor's degree."

Rinehart turned right, onto a one-way street. Trees spread a canopy of leaves across it, and through the branches Dionne could see more mansions, their windows full of cozy light. "Oh, Lord, these houses," she said. "I'm gonna be sick."

"I'm gonna be sick if I don't get out of here," Rinehart said, confused by all the one-way streets.

"I envy them and their houses," Dionne said.

"Why?" Day asked.

"Because I don't have a house like this."

"Well, it's not your job to have a house."

"But I want a house."

"It's your parents' job," Day said. "I'm fine where I am." She thought about this for a second. "No. Actually, not. As far as, like, house, yeah. But, like, school, no."

"House, no," Dionne said. "School, no."

"No, she don't," Day said, laughing.

"No, she doesn't," Rinehart corrected her, resuming her lady-of-the-ball elegance. "Does she? No. I don't think so."

SIXTEEN

RUN FOR THE TOC, TAKE 2

ON THE SECOND DAY of the tournament Marcus swiped a disconnected light switch from a teacher's desk. As he wandered the halls between rounds, he flipped its toggle back and forth. "My brain is on," he said. "My brain is off."

It was only ten in the morning and his tie was already off, his sleeves rolled up, his shirttail pulled free from his roomy trousers. He moved aimlessly, in slow, shuffling steps, ducking between clusters of gabbing kids. He wore a blank expression, somewhere between bored and pissed off. In the cafeteria he'd spotted Rinehart with Brandon. Her face was all twisted up; from twenty paces away he could tell she was in one of her moods. He approached just as she was concluding a rant. "We might as well cancel the season," she said, and then walked away in a huff.

Marcus and Brandon watched her go. "Man, fuck her," Marcus said when she was out of earshot. "She's always saying wack shit like that."

Marcus was upset enough as it was. As at Valley, they'd lost round five. Now down two, they had to pick up a win in round six in order to clear to out rounds. Another loss and they'd be off having dinner somewhere with Rinehart instead of debating in the trophy rounds and pushing for a Tournament of Champions bid. And if they went home without a bid, he'd have to peddle hot dogs at a Royals game next spring. That was the deal he'd struck. He'd begged Rinehart to bring Sobek to the tournament. She told him the only way she could afford it was if Sobek agreed to forgo his pay. Sobek offered to do so only if Marcus and Brandon picked up a bid. If not, he'd demand his pay, and Marcus would have to work a fund-raiser to cover it.

But there was no way he would let that happen. If they lost, it would be Brandon's fault, not his. That's the way he saw it, anyway. His partner was turning out to be a dud this season. He kept mishandling arguments in his rebuttal speeches. After round three, against one of Glenbrook North's top teams, Marcus had stormed into the hall and told Sobek, "Man, we need to work with Brandon on that 1AR. We just lost that round because of him."

ALL AT ONCE the kids who were scattered in groups about the hall converged on the entrance of the cafeteria like iron fillings to a magnet. At the doorway a handful of New Trier students dealt round-five schedules to outstretched hands as quickly as they could. Marcus pushed his way through, but when he got there, the schedules were all gone, so he looked over a kid's shoulder and traced his finger down the columns of text. Glenbrook North. Affirmative. "Shit," he said. GBN was a dynamo on the circuit. He and Brandon had lost to a different GBN team on the affirmative the night before.

It was a boy-girl team. They pushed a dolly stacked with four tubs—one more than Brandon and Marcus—into the room and set up camp near bookshelves full of business textbooks. They were dressed up like corporate salespeople, he in a charcoal gray suit with a royal blue shirt and shiny print tie, she in a black blazer and black skirt, her blond bobbed hair curled in around her neck. Marcus asked what their record was. Three-two, the guy said. At that, Marcus's posture softened. This certainly wasn't GBN's top team. But they were also on the brink of elimination. They'd be giving it their all.

After Brandon laid out their case in the first speech and was interrogated for cross-x, the girl immediately took her place behind the teacher's desk. No prep time, Marcus observed. No doubt they'd been told what to expect. The girl's words rushed out in a frantic blur, her shoulders tensed up, her eyes widened, her head moving back and forth as if to shake syllables free. She hadn't quite mastered the breathing. Every ten seconds or so, she stiffened and gulped down two quick breaths, as if someone had doused her with icy water. The main gist of her argument, so far as I could decipher, was that Brandon and Marcus's plan would actually worsen racism; by equalizing mental health care between blacks and whites, it would somehow deepen entrenched racial divisions.

During cross-x Brandon asked warily, "So by me saying I'm a black male, I'm making racism worse?"

"It's the sense that those in power," she replied, "the white male, you know, the white male in Congress, can decide what is good for the black man because they classify people as black just because that's the color of their skin."

Brandon scrunched up his face as if this were the most absurd thing he'd ever heard.

Late in the round the judge leaned over and whispered to Sobek, who, on Marcus's urging, had agreed to watch the round. "This case is so . . . ," she said, clutching at the air with her hands as though the right word were hanging there. "It just makes sense. With these schools. It's just real interesting."

Sobek grinned shyly and nodded. She turned to face him. "Like this idea of people, like, sitting up in their offices talking about race," she continued. "You know, like, I was in my English class the other day and we were talking about being at Columbia during the Harlem Renaissance, and what it would have been like at, like, an Ivy League school looking down on Harlem. Like trying to figure out how to help them. Kind of like they can't do it on their own."

She glanced over at Marcus and Brandon. Marcus hurriedly wrote a card for his 2AR. Brandon leaned back with his fingers laced behind his head. She leaned closer to Sobek and whispered some more. "It's an interesting debate to go down. And it's hard to judge, to look at it based on better debating or, like, on some kind of card, because, you know, like, I think a lot of . . . arguments are actually, like, racial politicking. It's an interesting round.

"It's also hard," she continued after a thoughtful pause, "because they don't have the rep that Glenbrook North or New Trier have. It's harder to win here. Not impossible. But it's harder to attract the good coaching and stuff. It's an underdog in every sense. The debate-rep thing."

After Marcus belted out the final speech, the judge spent a long time poring over her notes. Finally she looked up and said, "Why did you guys have to make it so hard for me?" Then she embarked on a long criticism of each debater's performance in the round. Marcus and Brandon gave a show like they were listening intently, but to them it was all just blather. They wished she'd shut up and tell them who won.

OUTSIDE THE CAFETERIA the masses swarmed the New Trier kids who were handing out elimination-round schedules. Central had won their last round, but Brandon and Marcus weren't sure if they'd gotten high enough speaker points to make the cut. Brandon snagged a sheet and found Central listed with the thirty-one other teams that made it to out rounds. He took it to Rinehart and held it in front of her face. "You broke!" she exclaimed and flapped her hands at the air.

They were matched against a team from nearby Evanston who were known for running arguments based on the work of Foucault. After Brandon's first speech, Evanston's first speaker, a lanky kid in a light blue pullover sweatshirt, read a couple of standard topicality arguments before moving on to Foucault. "Debate is the production of truth," he said. "We're not real policy makers. We're intellectuals."

He spoke quickly but smoothly, with an air of cockiness. The judges' job, he said, "is not to pretend that the affirmative plan really happens, but instead to challenge the assumptions that are presented as natural in the 1AC"—short for "first affirmative constructive," the first speech in a debate round. "The 1AC buys into the concept of bio-power. Bio-power is the idea that life is a garden that should be cared for by the state. That mentality entails the fostering of life; it also necessitates the extermination of anything that threatens the beauty of the garden."

Central's case, he continued, "classifies racial minorities in those same groups that have their bio-power removed in order to exterminate them. You can't be racist against a group unless you define them as other and a threat to the people. Our alternative is pointing out how their truths are a function of power."

Marcus got up to cross-examine him. "Okay, my question is, first of all, the racism you refer to in our plan text is institutional, not individual, right?"

"No," he replied, remaining seated. "It's not institutional racism."

"So what's the root cause of racism in our 1AC in your opinion?"

"Our argument is that your 1AC buys into the idea that races can be categorized separate from each other. And that people have stable racial identities. That mind-set is—"

"Okay, okay," Marcus cut him off. "Here's a better question. At the end of the round, why should the, why should the judges vote for Foucault at the end of the round?"

"Because it calls, it, it, it casts out the assumption of categorization of bio-power . . ."

"So . . ."

". . . of universal humanism."

Brandon sat watching them, clearly lost. When it was his turn to speak, he stammered uncharacteristically. "We don't lead," he shouted. "We give blacks control over their health. And we're, uh . . . We're . . . Well. Uh. Um. Our conceding moral obligation sets up standards for us. And, straight to the line-by-line debate. I guess." He chuckled nervously.

As the round progressed, the topicality arguments fell away, and it all boiled down to the words of Foucault, the scholar's notions about race, or rather the Evanston debaters' notions of Foucault's notions about race. Like the GBN team a few hours earlier, these white kids from the Chicago suburbs were saying that two black kids from Kansas City were making racism worse by pointing out problems that blacks face in a society where institutions are rigged against them. And while I understood that debate is a game where pretty much any idea can be tested, I couldn't help but feel uneasy about the dynamics. Color blindness, which these smart kids from Evanston were suggesting we embrace, seemed to me a luxury of whiteness and a mask hiding the very real issues Brandon and Marcus were raising in the round and, indeed, facing every day. If policy makers dare not mention race, I wondered, how can racism be addressed?

Marcus got up for the final speech, grabbed a box of tissues off a file cabinet, and blew his nose loudly. He leaned over the podium and stretched his cheeks and jaw to loosen them up. "Game over!" he began, and proceeded to pack his speech with bluster, clutching his hands toward the judges like a beggar.

"We uphold Barndt," he shouted, referring to Joseph Barndt, whose book *Dismantling Racism* provided the poetic core of Marcus and Brandon's case: "Brick by brick, stone by stone, the prison of individual, institutional and cultural racism can be destroyed."

"Take one brick out of the wall," Marcus said, "sure the wall might still be there, but we're still the step in the right direction against it."

He glanced at the egg timer in his right hand, crouched over, and picked up the pace. "They say we should ignore the brick and leave it in the wall," he spouted. "Until we figure out how to take down the whole wall. That's silly. The wall's still gonna exist.

"We tell you that by using race as a way to break down the wall, we can actually take a stance against it because we bring people back together. Like the Barndt evidence says, as long as the people of color and people of white are separated in their own prisons, they can't choose, uh, uh, achieve the actual intellectual steps needed to solve racism."

After the round the judges asked for some of Central's evidence—a good sign. Marcus went into the hall. I asked him how he felt about the round. He thought it could go either way. Aimlessly, he moved back and forth, in and out of the room. He picked up some evidence, packed it, then resumed pacing. He cinched his tie around his neck, then loosened it, then took it off and threw it on the table. Dionne came in and quietly sat down on a file cabinet. Rinehart perched daintily on a chair near the wall. She sat stiffly, betraying her anxiety. She pulled a book out of her purse, Michael Moore's *Stupid White Men*, and read, her brows forced upward as if to show she hadn't a care in the world. Brandon sat beside her, spinning a pen. While the judges scanned their notes, he and his coach glanced at the clock every minute or so. The red second hand spun: 6:25, 6:30, 6:35. Hardly anyone in the room spoke.

One of the judges folded her ballot and got up to go into the hall. At twenty till, another judge sat back, giving his ballot one last look over. Brandon craned his neck, hoping to catch a peek. The judge folded it over and sat quietly with his hands covering it. Five minutes later the last judge signed his.

"Okay, she voted," he said. "Let's go."

Marcus immediately sat down, leaned forward, and stared at the judge.

The judge casually opened the ballots one by one, held them out in front of him like a hand of cards, and nodded.

"Okay," he said. "On a three-oh decision. The negative team. Evanston. Wins."

Rinehart's shoulders slumped. Marcus and Brandon got up and slapped hands weakly. In the hallway Sobek spotted Marcus and flashed his thumb, pointing it up, then down, then up again. "We lost," Marcus replied. "We need to work with Brandon."

SEVENTEEN

LITTLE GIRLS CRY

THE FIRST TEARS of the season were shed, and Ebony Rose wasn't happy about it.

"Who cry?" he demanded. "Y'all made somebody cry before I did?!"

That was Rinehart's promise: *We make little girls cry*. It hadn't taken long. Here it was, the first official UDL tournament of the year—at Central no less—and the mighty Eagle debate squad had once again forced tears from some debater from a lowly crosstown school. Except Ebony wasn't the one who made it happen, and he was bummed.

The varsity kids had made two treks out onto the national circuit. Now it was Ebony's turn. This was a day he'd been waiting for, his chance to begin his march through the competition in DEBATE–Kansas City, en route to a free trip to Atlanta for the National Association of Urban Debate Leagues's Novice Nationals.

He stood in Central's cafeteria, eavesdropping on his teammates. The place was noisy with the excited chitchat of a hundred kids, their voices echoing off the hard walls.

"Hold up," Ebony said, trying to break into the conversation. "Shut up. I shoulda been the first. My teams was pitiful. Okay. First round, they run on affirmative. And then Eb gets up." He tugged at his shirt, cocked his head back. "Two disadvantages. And three topicalities. I was like, 'A'ight.'" He bobbed his head.

The girls shot him a glance and went on talking among themselves. He rubbed his nose, looked down at his shoes.

"See my little bear?" he said, raising a yellow teddy bear he had attached to his belt loop.

The girls ignored him.

He sauntered off and sat down at one of the cafeteria's tables. The room was the hub of Central High, its high ceilings laced with ductwork painted a dull burgundy. As in the rest of the school, its cinder-block walls were light gray. On one far wall, above a row of soda machines, hung a digital message display system, across which scrolled test patterns and information about the model and the company that made it. It had been there for several years, but no one had ever programmed it. It would remain that way for as long as it hung on the wall; someone had misplaced the instructions.

Ebony sat back and scoped the scene. So this was it. His first official tournament. He gazed at all the kids milling around, as if looking down from above. He figured he could beat everyone in the room.

Rinehart quieted the crowd and began reading off the list of winners. She called out Antoine's name at sixteenth place, and Antoine jumped up, dreads bouncing, and darted toward Marcus to snag his yellow ribbon. *A good sign*, Ebony thought. She got all the way to second place without reading Ebony's name. *A really good sign.* He thought for sure he would win this thing. They'd call his name, and the whole place would just go crazy with applause, and he'd strut up there to receive his award from none other than the mighty Marcus Leach.

But then Rinehart called out for Shanee, the girl who had spilled the first tears of the season.

Ebony let his head fall back on his shoulders and slid down in his seat.

Shanee jumped up and screamed and pranced to the front of the crowd, flailing her arms. She danced back, holding her trophy high, showing off.

Ebony averted his eyes.

Seeing him look so down, Shanee grew serious for a moment. "How did you go from being the top speaker to not placing?" she asked.

He just looked away.

EIGHTEEN

ALL DELIBERATE SPEED

THERE HAD BEEN a buzz leading up to the Central tournament. In class Rinehart had mentioned several times that a *60 Minutes* crew might be flying in to film it. Lesley Stahl was working on a report about the UDLs. She was set to interview Linda Collier, the director of debate at the University of Missouri–Kansas City who had helped establish the UDLs and had founded the Kansas City league. It seemed only natural that Stahl would want to come to Collier's hometown to talk with debaters from Central, one of the most successful UDL squads in the nation. But the show's producers never called back, so the debate tournament went on without CBS. It seemed like a missed opportunity, less for Kansas City than for CBS.

Almost ten years earlier, Stahl came to Kansas City for a story about its desegregation case. Much of her report focused on Central, and its new $32 million building, the centerpiece of the $2 billion integration effort. Stahl had come to town at the tail end of a national flurry surrounding the case, and Central in particular. Reporters from *The New York Times, The Wall Street Journal, The Washington Post, The Boston Globe, The Chicago Tribune, MacNeil/Lehrer NewsHour,* and *The Economist* had all passed through the school's hallways before her. Titled "On the Money," Stahl's report, which offered comments from just two main sources, wasn't as thorough as the preceding ones. But Stahl raised pretty much the same question her predecessors had: Can money save our failing inner-city schools?

The piece ended on an upbeat note; it seemed to suggest that Kansas City just might pull it off. But later, when Collier sat down for an interview with Stahl, she learned that the 1994 report had been one of the biggest embarrassments of Stahl's career. She was new to *60 Minutes*, and she spent a bit of political capital to air the piece with its cautiously optimistic spin. Five years later the district lost its accreditation. Shortly after that, Central was deemed academically deficient.

Now the question was answered: money can't save our schools, or, deeper still and unspoken, *nothing* can. But the reporters were asking the wrong question. The money was just the glitter on top. Kansas City could have spent $12 billion or a measly dime; the effort would have failed either way. A better question would have been: Does America really want integration? Or, tougher still: Is integration really what's best for blacks? If so, on whose terms?

After *Brown v. Board of Education*, Kansas City's desegregation case is believed to be the most significant case in desegregation law. It reached the Supreme Court three times, and the Court's decision on the third hearing essentially killed all the desegregation efforts that had preoccupied the courts for the latter half of the twentieth century. It's impossible to point to one cause for the failure, one key adversary or devastating turning point in the twenty-five-year saga, because there are so many and they're all intertwined. But together, they point to a legal term that has puzzled litigators and scholars ever since it was codified in the Supreme Court's second decision in *Brown II*, in 1955. Schools shall be integrated, the justices had agreed, "with all deliberate speed."

Thurgood Marshall joked that this meant "slow." Kansas City's case shows that it meant "never."

THE DESEGREGATION CASE was filed in 1977 by the school district itself (the first odd twist on this strange journey). The plaintiffs shot for the moon, naming as defendants both Missouri and Kansas, more than a dozen school districts on both sides of the state line, and several federal agencies. It was as if they wanted to eradicate racism itself, which, after the legal changes borne on the civil rights movement, had gone into hiding in the nation's institutions. It wasn't the first desegregation case to surface in Kansas City. The district had been sued on two previous occasions, once by the local chapter of Martin Luther King, Jr.'s Southern Christian Leadership Conference, the other by Kansas City's only integrated neighborhood. The district had also been under pressure since the late 1960s from the U.S. Department of Health, Education, and Welfare to integrate, lest they lose millions in federal funds. But by the late 1970s, white flight had already left the district more than 65 percent black, and it seemed no amount of student reshuffling could bring about the kind of integration that was being called for. Recent history had shown that such moves would only push more whites away. So district officials decided to aim right for the source.

Kansas City is as American as any metropolis in the nation. Situated near the very center of the Lower 48, it's part East, part West, a little North, and a lot South. Missouri was a slave state, bordering Free State Kansas, though it was never officially a member of the Confederacy (which only meant that slavery lasted longer there, because the Emancipation Proclamation didn't apply). It was a Jim Crow state, with enforced segregation in schools and many public places. When the *Brown* decision came down, though, Missouri quickly complied, unlike its stubborn counterparts down south. And Central was one of the first schools to integrate, in 1955, because of its proximity to the growing black part of town.

Legend has it that Central is the oldest public school in the city. In reality, it shares that distinction with Lincoln, the city's original all-black school. The newly formed Kansas City Board of Education established both schools in 1867. But Central *was* the first high school—back then, blacks weren't offered a secondary education at Lincoln or any other Kansas City school. Central held classes in a nine-room brick schoolhouse downtown. Lincoln operated in a building that, according to one historian, was located in an "unsightly gully and resembled anything but a place of learning."

Twenty years later the district started providing a high school education to blacks. And as the student populations at Central and Lincoln grew, both schools moved into bigger buildings, south and east of downtown. They built separate legacies, too. At Lincoln, Major N. Clark Smith's music class became a talent mill for Kansas City's jazz scene, turning out the bandleader Harlan Leonard; Bennie Moten's cornet player, Lamar Wright; and Walter Page, whom one critic deemed "the greatest jazz counterbass." Charlie Parker attended classes at Lincoln, though "mostly he was an absentee and truant," writes Ross Russell in *Jazz Style in Kansas City and the Southwest*. Meanwhile, a mile or so to the southeast, Central reigned as the city's premier white high school. Its graduates included the baseball Hall of Famer Casey Stengel, the movie star William Powell, the opera singer Gladys Swarthout, and Robert Heinlein, the author of *Stranger in a Strange Land*.

Until the middle of the twentieth century, most blacks were confined by zoning restrictions to the area northeast of Troost Avenue and Twenty-seventh Street. Because Central was just a few blocks south of the area, it was one of the earliest schools to feel the impact of *Brown*. And because of Central's storied history as the leading white school in town, observers predicted riots. During the first days of school, police officers parked nearby. *The Kansas City Star* reported that "white and Negro students began living by gangland rule. Bullies of both races extorted nickels and dimes from younger students; when arguments started, the races closed ranks."

The school's most prestigious extracurricular activity was Intersociety, a group of boys' and girls' clubs that resembled academic fraternities and sororities. In a tradition dating back to 1886, the Minervas, Delphians, Websters, Violets, and others competed each spring in the prestigious Intersociety Contest. The winner was heralded with a banner headline in the final edition of *The Central Luminary*. Blacks were not allowed in the Intersociety, even as Central's white population rapidly decreased during the late 1950s and the Intersociety's pool of eligible students declined. "Rather than dwindle to nothing, each of the clubs voted . . . to disband in a final blaze of glory," reads an article in Central's 1959 yearbook.

That was the last year whites made up the majority at Central. The next year its student body was 70 percent black. By 1962 it was 99 percent, partly because district officials altered their integration policies to allow whites to attend different, all-white schools. After some black students beat up two white teachers, dozens of white faculty members quit or requested transfers.

In January 1959, Superintendent James A. Hazlett visited the school and was met by a student who threw a long butcher knife on the ground in front of him. The superintendent blamed the unrest on the racial mix at the school, and the school board responded by allowing the transfers. It was an obvious violation of the *Brown* decision. But it drew praise nationally. In 1961 *Time* magazine quoted the school's principal, a white man named James Boyd, in an article ironically titled "Central Sets Example in Integration": "You have most of the problem when you have no definite [racial] majority. When you have a definite majority, it reduces friction."

But afterward, Central improved academically. Many of the teachers stayed on, and they kept their standards high. In the *Time* article, one teacher was quoted as saying, "We've fought against letting our expectations drop. We are not willing to accept the idea that because a child comes from a less favorable environment he can't make it." Another said, "I am very frank with my Negro boys and girls. When I get someone who isn't doing the work he could do, I say to him, 'You wanted integration. Now you got it. What are you going to do with it?'"

Before *Brown*, Central had sent fewer than 15 percent of its graduates to college, according to another 1961 report by the economics scholar Martin Mayer. But in its first years as a predominantly black school, Mayer wrote, Central saw "150 out of 350 graduates go on to college, 50 of them with scholarships." And he didn't mean junior colleges. Centralites gained admittance to Yale, Vassar, Smith, Oberlin, Northwestern, and the University of Chicago.

The school's principal during the 2002–2003 season, William McClendon, attended the school during those years. He told me that the community around Central was strong and closely knit back then, and that helped facilitate the success. "We had a high quality of living," he told me. "There was still a feeling of neighborhood connection. There was a strong sense of pride from the standpoint of strong academic standards."

That "feeling of neighborhood connection" remained strong through the early 1970s. If the weather was good, all the kids would be out playing, and, come evening, one could hear mothers holler for dinner all up and down the blocks. Folks looked out for one another. And Central, perhaps even more than the many churches in the area, was the focal point of the community. The school was a sports powerhouse. Throughout the 1960s the track team rarely lost a meet. In basketball they often finished among Missouri's top four, bringing home the state trophy on several occasions. On game nights the school district's field house would be packed with people, all getting fired up as the Eagles ran their infamous slam-dunk drill.

But the school and the community were eroding. After becoming nearly all black, the school's student population mushroomed. Each day the building was packed with a thousand more students than it had been designed to hold. Student bodies at all-white Northeast and Van Horn high schools—both of which were adjacent to Central's boundaries—remained level because the school board continually tweaked the district's boundaries to maintain segregation. Resources tended to follow the white students, so Central deteriorated. Cracks spread across the walls, holes opened up between floors. Students studied with books that had been used years earlier at whiter schools like Southwest. Worst of all, academics began to slide. When McClendon returned as a student teacher in 1969, he noticed that "a lot of the expectations [students had been held to] in the early '60s had gone . . . The neighborhood had changed." The results of standardized tests from the time, for whatever they're worth, show that academic achievement had dropped precipitously.

People started getting fed up. Central yearbooks from the time are scattered with indications of social unrest, quotations from Frederick Douglass, Malcolm X, and Stokely Carmichael. Some of the teachers who initially heeded Principal Boyd's call for high academic standards retired or sought transfers because they were frustrated by the changing attitudes of their students.

During this period Kansas City saw the first serious pushes for a comprehensive desegregation plan. These initially arose from the black community's response to overcrowding at Central. The district bused about a hundred kids from Central to other schools that were already trending black, though that was hardly enough to ease the problem. Meanwhile, the all-white populations at Northeast, Van Horn, and Southwest remained level. In 1968, Superintendent Hazlett released a long-awaited master plan for integrating the district that proposed busing kids out of overcrowded schools. But the school board issued a statement that read, "We do not advocate 'bussing' for the sole purpose of integration."

ON APRIL 9, 1968, the day of Martin Luther King, Jr.'s funeral, some Central students—upset that students in Kansas City, Kansas, had been given the day off while those in Missouri had not—gathered outside the school, shouting, "Let's go! Come on!"

Students inside the school ran through the halls shouting, pushing teachers aside, setting trash cans on fire, and throwing books and desks through windows. The principal announced over the intercom that classes were dismissed. Students poured out of the building, and cop cars swarmed the scene. Black officers were ordered to roam the crowd on foot and urge calmness, according to an eyewitness account published in the *Kansas City Call*, a newspaper serving the black community. White officers sat watching from their cars in the distance. With the exception of a few bottles lobbed here and there, the crowd remained peaceful at first—partly due to the presence of a cadre of black clergy and a pair of Kansas City Chiefs players.

The students, now more than one thousand strong, moved toward downtown until they reached a police barricade, then turned around and headed back toward the school. But when a student staggered back from a cop car, writhing in pain from a chemical sprayed in his eyes, the crowd erupted and surged northward. A few agitators smashed windows, hurled bricks, and overturned cars. When they reached I-70, they leaped over the embankment and forced traffic to a standstill before moving on to city hall.

In an attempt to calm the mob, KPRS, the city's black-owned radio station, announced a party at a nearby church. A lot of the protesters opted to go there. But as the crowd was dispersing, cops fired tear gas. Violence engulfed the streets and continued for three days, much of it within a block or two of Central. Entire blocks of stores and apartment buildings burned. One witness told me he watched massive troop carriers full of soldiers roll down his street, "fire coming out of their guns."

THE COMMUNITY never fully recovered. Some of the lots where once stood stores remain vacant and weedy to this day.

And Central High continued to struggle with unrest. The next fall a few students attacked two teachers, injuring one severely enough to require plastic surgery. The following spring others broke into the school and destroyed records, trophies, and typewriters, showered offices with fire-extinguisher foam, and ripped phones out of walls. The damage totaled $10,000.

At the beginning of the 1970 school year, Central's security guards came to school wearing guns. When school board members learned of this, they called an emergency meeting. Classes dismissed early so that teachers could show their support for the drastic protection measures. Some threatened to quit if the guards couldn't remain armed. But after weeks of community outcry, the guards agreed to disarm.

Then, in 1972, a mass brawl erupted after a basketball game between Central and Raytown South. There had long been bad blood between the two schools. Known as the Rebels, Raytown South always paraded a giant confederate flag before games and during intermission—a tradition Central didn't appreciate. The two schools were to meet in a state quarterfinals matchup. State activities officials hoped to avert trouble by holding the game in Maryville, a small town an hour to the north.

The game was excruciatingly close. It ended with a goal-tending call in favor of Raytown. Central fans cried, "Bad call!" while Raytown fans unfurled the Stars and Bars and shouted racist epithets. Central fans stormed the floor, throwing chairs and swinging fists. Though Central's coach and his players tried to stop the fight, the state activities association suspended Central for a year. The stiff penalty brought national attention, and state officials lifted the ban after the NAACP threatened to sue.

A 1971 *Star* article headlined "Chicken as Morale Builder" demanded, "Will fried chicken in the cafeteria prevent student uprisings at Central high school?" It closed with an obviously out-of-context quotation from a black board member: "Is there an expert here who can tell us whether fried chicken is soul food?" Days later black leaders picketed the *Star*'s office to protest the article. But Central's negative image, it seemed, had been sealed.

IN 1973 the Southern Christian Leadership Conference filed a lawsuit to desegregate Kansas City's high schools. Federal officials applied pressure, threatening to sever funds. So the school board came up with "Plan 6C," having devised and scrapped a half dozen before. The plan emerged after two years of contentious board meetings at which parents and residents— most of them from the areas around all-white Van Horn and Northeast high schools—brandished signs saying, NO BUSING! and INTEGRATION SHOULD BE A CHOICE! Plan 6C proposed to limit minority enrollment at Southwest and several other schools in the area to 30 percent.

The plan enraged blacks and whites alike. "This is probably the weakest desegregation effort in the country," the Reverend Emanuel Cleaver, then president of the SCLC, who would later become mayor of Kansas City, complained to reporters.

And whites left the district in greater numbers than before.

The media were ready for a fight on the first day of school in 1977. Amid threats of a Ku Klux Klan rally, black students arrived at Van Horn wearing their Central letter jackets. "The tension was very thick," David Griffin, Van Horn's principal, told the *Star* at the time. "That first year there were a lot of rumors, uncertainties and fights."

The plan actually made matters worse for Central. The federal government increased funding for schools such as Van Horn and Northeast, which, despite their vicious protestations, became more mixed than all-black schools like Central. So Central continued to deteriorate. Students there went on studying with outdated, hand-me-down books. Classes remained overcrowded, sometimes meeting in utility closets.

In the late 1970s, the civil rights leader Bernard Powell, a Central graduate, grew dismayed by the decay at his alma mater. He formed a coalition of alumni and neighbors to repair the floor-to-ceiling cracks, the window casings perforated with wide gaps, the dangerous old light fixtures with bare wires, and the dingy walls and chipped tiles. The group embraced Jesse Jackson's national inner-city education-reform movement, which sought to rally communities around their schoolchildren, and Jackson himself visited Central several times. But the community revival began to fizzle after Powell was murdered by drug dealers in 1979 at Papa Doc's East Side Social Club, a favorite watering hole for Kansas City's black politicos, just a few blocks away from Central.

JESSE JACKSON SPOKE at Central on May 25, 1977, the same day the school board directed its lawyers to file its wide-reaching desegregation lawsuit. The case officially began the next day. The suit proposed either consolidating metro school districts or cross-district busing. But the day's top story was the abrupt resignation of the school board's president, James Lyddon. Throughout his tenure, Lyddon had fought to maintain "the delicate balance" in the district and had warned against an integration plan that would make the district virtually all black. "I no longer feel I can go to groups both black and white to try to justify why living cooperatively together will benefit us all," he wrote in his resignation letter. "Neither has wanted to hear."

The case went to Russell G. Clark, a new Democratic appointee to the federal bench who had grown up in small-town Missouri and lived in Springfield, the most conservative part of the state. He was initially hostile to the case, using as his guide the Supreme Court's 1974 ruling in Detroit's desegregation case *Milliken v. Bradley*. Integration proponents point to this decision as the beginning of the end of desegregation. It was one of the first major decisions of a court that had changed drastically during Richard Nixon's presidency. Nixon's ascent to the White House signified a dramatic shift in American politics, when Southerners switched their alliance from the Democratic to the Republican Party following Lyndon Baines Johnson's push for civil rights legislation. Nixon had campaigned on his opposition to recent decisions by the Supreme Court, which was then, under the leadership of Earl Warren, one of the most liberal in American history. His campaign director openly said Nixon wanted to end Court-ordered desegregation. Nixon had the privilege of appointing four justices, including William Rehnquist, who, as a Supreme Court clerk in the early 1950s, had written a brief to the justices arguing that the "separate but equal" provisions of the 1896 *Plessy v. Ferguson* decision were good policy. In *Milliken*, this new conservative-heavy Court agreed that Detroit didn't have the constitutional right to require suburban school districts to participate in a busing program unless it could be proven that those districts were guilty of overt segregation in the past. This was so difficult to prove that Detroit opted for a remedy providing for budgetary parity between districts.

Obviously, the precedent set a high hurdle for Kansas City to clear. Nearly seven years passed before the case went to trial. One of the first things Judge Clark did was release the Kansas districts from the case and name the Missouri school district defendant, after which Arthur A. Benson II, an attorney with the American Civil Liberties Union, stepped in to represent the plaintiffs. Benson grew up in Kansas City, having attended Pembroke Hill, an expensive private school on the city's southwest side. He was married to Karen McCarthy, a rising Democrat who was then a state representative and would later serve in Congress. Benson was known as a champion of tough causes, a true liberal. With the help of the NAACP's Legal Defense and Educational Fund, he and a team of lawyers set out to make the case. They worked almost around the clock, documenting housing patterns and transportation and school policies, to prove that all the municipalities in the fractured metro area had, with the help of the state and federal governments, conspired to keep blacks and whites in separate classrooms.

After a sixty-seven-day trial, which generated seventeen thousand pages of testimony from one hundred and forty witnesses and two thousand exhibits, Clark delivered a mixed verdict: he found the district and the state guilty, but he exonerated suburban districts and federal agencies, leaving Kansas City in a position similar to Detroit's. By then, the district was nearly 70 percent black, so it would have been futile to bus kids for the sake of racial balance. But that was the goal—the *Brown* decision of 1954 offered only the right to a desegregated education. Clark ordered both the state and the school district to come back with plans to integrate the schools. His hope was that they would work together.

This had already been tried and failed. Before the trial began, several state and district officials sought a settlement. Bob Bartman, then second in command at the state's Education Department, told me in an interview that they had met at a Holiday Inn in Warrensburg, southwest of Kansas City, and had agreed that they might be able to get the matter settled if the state would spend some money to improve the district's facilities and restore its credit rating. They all went home and crunched the numbers and agreed that it could be worked out for about $8 million. When Bartman and his colleagues floated the idea at the state capital, though, they couldn't get any representatives or senators to stand behind it. "Everybody thought it was outrageous," he told me. "The attorney general's office. The governor's office. They all thought it was outrageous."

School officials wanted to spend as much money as possible, while the state preferred not to spend any. "The state's position was, 'Argue everything, appeal everything,'" Bartman told me. "The position was the state did nothing wrong." Yet Missouri had already been found guilty in two other desegregation cases. Indeed, until 1976, its constitution contained a provision making it illegal for black and white kids to go to school together.

The oppositional mind-set was put in place by a rising star on the Missouri political scene, John Ashcroft, who was Missouri's newly elected attorney general when the Kansas City case was filed and had just taken the oath as governor when the guilty verdict came down. In his inauguration address, Governor Ashcroft had told a story about a boy from a small town in northwest Missouri who had gotten lost on a winter afternoon. It was getting late, Ashcroft told his fellow citizens, and a snowstorm was moving in, and the townsfolk futilely combed the area, walking every which way. "Then the school master," Ashcroft intoned, "said, 'Let's join hands, and together—hand in hand—we will find the child.' And they did." The moral, he said, was that "it's not the government's duty to solve our problems. But the government can lead us to work together—hand in hand—to solve our problems and to meet the challenges of the future." Then he got to work as governor and said, in essence, of kids who'd inherited the dregs of enforced segregation, Let 'em freeze.

Diane Vaughan, former director of desegregation services for Missouri's Education Department, told the authors of *Dismantling Desegregation: The Quiet Reversal of Brown v. Board of Education* that her office did almost nothing to help Kansas City's school district solve the problem of separate and unequal education. "In the late 1980s," the book states, "the governor and attorney general discouraged . . . taking an active role in monitoring the plan and chose to appeal even those components of the remedy that [the Education Department] favored. Committed to a policy of blanket opposition, therefore, the state executive branch not only failed to monitor the district's execution of the remedy, but also barred the state educational leaders from doing so."

Bartman agrees. "We were third in the power structure" behind the attorney general and the governor, he told me. "We wanted to find educational solutions. But we were shut out."

When the state and the district came back with their proposed solutions to the problem, they were almost $200 million apart in their estimates. In his response, Clark lambasted the state's lowball response, pointing out, for instance, how they'd allocated a mere $5,000 to fix the crumbling walls of a high school that would ultimately be condemned and razed.

So began the nation's most expensive desegregation remedy—as much out of stubbornness and spite as anything. Clark had become emotionally involved. Obstinate in the early days of the case, he'd been moved by the injustices revealed during the trial. In an interview with PBS, he said that he had "visited at least six different federal prisons, and the conditions of federal prisons are far, far superior to the condition of these schools."

Ashcroft, on the other hand, invariably used high-pitched and scathing rhetoric when referring to the case in public. The case was "bleeding revenue" from the state budget, he often said. Judge Clark was just "tossing a fist full of dollars" at the problem. The remedy plan was a "tragedy" and a "disastrous, debilitating delusion." In one major speech he said, "This ludicrous court order does nothing more than rob Peter to pay Paul when Paul doesn't need the money and Peter doesn't have it."

———

IN HONESTY, the desegregation plan *was* ludicrous. Because of his adherence to *Milliken*, Clark had put the district in a tough position. The U.S. Constitution, as it was interpreted at the time, only guaranteed an integrated school system. Everything else—the school buildings, teacher pay, quality of education—only mattered inasmuch as it could draw blacks and whites into classrooms together. Having declared the suburbs not guilty, Clark couldn't mandate that white kids be bused in or black kids be bused out. So he ordered a plan that would facilitate voluntary busing. This, Clark hoped, would go both ways. Suburban schools would open their doors to blacks and, with money from the state, offer them a ride to school. And whites would choose to send their kids to school in the heart of the city if the schools were made more attractive.

Clark had hoped that the state would step in to make the first part happen. With a new law or two, and a generous appropriations bill, state legislators could make it happen in one session. The demand was there. Ever since the late 1960s, inner-city residents had been illegally enrolling their kids in outlying schools, which they believed to be superior. The practice continues today, and some districts even employ private investigators to track these scofflaws down and kick their kids out.

A few bills surfaced in Jefferson City, but they didn't go anywhere. And all but one suburban district refused to allow so much as one black kid from the urban core to attend their schools. They all denied that race was an issue; publicly they blamed logistics and money, and at least in news reports these excuses rarely seemed unreasonable. The only district that didn't balk, though, was arguably the poorest and most challenging logistically: tiny Missouri City, a one-school town of fewer than three hundred residents, located on the far northern edge of the metro area.

To lure whites into the city, Clark approved the creation of the most magnificent school system imaginable. Eventually, all of the schools would be refashioned into magnet schools, each offering a unique curriculum that couldn't be found anywhere else. On Clark's order, a small group of lawyers and education experts—one set hired by the longtime plaintiff attorney Benson, the other by the school district—devised a plan. They came up with it in a series of meetings over a couple of weeks, Benson told me. They started big, reconfiguring all the high schools and middle schools and more than half the elementary schools into themed magnets—foreign languages, fine arts, business, science, law enforcement, and agriculture. The public had no access to these meetings, in which the lawyers and "experts" compiled a long list of academic themes they imagined might be attractive to suburban whites. While the consultants wrote in one room, Benson and the others examined the printed drafts in another room, fine-tuning the plan.

At the end of it all, Central High School emerged as the proposed site for two magnet themes: Computers Unlimited and Classical Greek. For the former, they planned a state-of-the-art network, offering a computer for each of the thousand kids who would attend. The Greek theme was a bit more esoteric. Benson and his fellow planners included a brief essay by Sir Richard Livingstone in the school's plan, presumably to offer poetic insight. "And what is a complete human being?" Livingstone asked in the 1940s. "I shall take the Greek answer to this question. Human beings have bodies, minds and characters . . . This trinity of body, mind and character is man; man's aim, besides earning his living, is to make the most of all three."

To house this program, they proposed athletic facilities that would be the envy of a private college: racquetball and handball courts; a huge, well-stocked weight room; a gymnastic center; a large indoor track (complete with indoor long-jump pit); and, to top it all off, an Olympic-size indoor pool with two high dives and an underwater observation booth.

They proposed bestowing equally generous facilities on the other district schools: two fully equipped theaters for the arts magnet; a model courtroom for the law magnet; a working farm. Politically, Ashcroft and his similarly conservative attorney general, William Webster, couldn't have asked for a better foe. It wasn't tough to foment dissent among the populace. These were lean years, the end of the Reagan era and the height of a recession. Clark was making the state pay, but the coffers were shrinking. So Ashcroft cut. He took money from departments across the board, but he made sure everyone knew about the hit the state's schools would take.

After a particularly expensive order, laid down in the middle of the fiscal year in 1991, Ashcroft shifted $71 million from the education budget. Soon newspapers across the state were carrying tallies of the dollar amount their local districts had lost. They sent reporters to Kansas City to tour Central—the "Taj Mahal," in Webster's words—and come home to file stories under such headlines as "Your Tax Dollars at Work" and "More Dollars Down the Desegregation Rat Hole."

The same year Ashcroft cut the education budget, he also asked legislators to allocate a million dollars to fight the case in court. They quickly obliged.

The price tag for the desegregation plan soon grew so steep that the district couldn't afford its 25 percent. And they couldn't raise any more money on their own. The state constitution required a three-fourths majority at the polls for a tax increase, and Kansas Citians hadn't garnered that much voter support since 1969, the last year the district was majority white. Clark urged the state to amend the constitution, but legislators balked—although a couple of top lawyers in the Republican attorney general's office contemplated in internal memos I later uncovered that it might be in the best interest of the state if Clark were made to raise taxes himself, so as to reduce the state's burden.

And that's exactly what Clark did.

"As a matter of fact, I hand-carried [the order] to Kansas City myself," Clark later told PBS. "And I filed it myself. And when I filed it, I don't mind telling you, I had tears in my eyes because I knew it would be controversial."

Many Kansas Citians were enraged. The judge acquired the name "King Clark." A group of taxpayers hired a lawyer and tried to enjoin the suit. The head of Jackson County (who would, a few years later, become a paid lobbyist for the district) refused to collect the tax. And the attorney general, despite earlier deliberations in favor of the court-imposed tax, appealed the matter all the way to the Supreme Court. The justices agreed in 1990 that Clark couldn't raise taxes himself, but they allowed him to order the district to do so without a vote.

ON TOP OF all this, the plan didn't work. The schools failed to attract anywhere near the number of white students Clark had outlined in his order's goals, not even with a multimillion-dollar marketing scheme. For a while in the late 1980s and early '90s, Kansas City TV stations were inundated with ads showing kids, most of them white, happily learning to the accompaniment of Whitney Houston's sappy "Greatest Love of All." In another, an announcer said of Central, "There's a school where Olympic hopefuls are coached by champion athletes, where students master the discipline and self-control essential to maximum effort and achievement, where rigorous training of the body is second only to rigorous training of the mind. Math. Science. English. History. Philosophy. Debate. Where is this remarkable school? Right here in Kansas City." A phone number—842-KIDS—would flash on the screen. The district employed telemarketers and, in some areas, door-to-door salespeople. But few were buying. A 1989 survey of suburban parents revealed that less than 10 percent had ever even considered sending their children to a magnet school. The overwhelming majority said that they would do so under "no set of circumstances."

Indeed, white enrollment went down initially. "Most magnet programs across the country have achieved whatever success they have in the first year," observed Michael Fields, the state's lead attorney on the case. "To have actually lost more whites in the first year of the most expensive program in the country does not bode well."

Again, race was never publicly cited as a reason. And here it was easier to believe. The district had long been a mess, and the influx of cash appeared to have only made it messier. There were missing textbooks, instances of embezzlement, extravagant purchases by board members. Buses ran off schedule, leaving kids stranded on street corners. The district's newly hired comptroller, a former Army officer, told reporters that he'd arrived to find a check-signing machine just sitting on the floor in district offices, waiting for anyone to misuse it, as well as tens of thousands of dollars' worth of unpaid bills and piles of out-of-balance ledgers. His first day on the job he was paid a visit by cops investigating the embezzlement of a few hundred thousand dollars.

And, most alarming to politicians, test scores were still going down. Few of the teachers really knew how to teach the new curriculums, so the few whites who did try the schools often pulled their children out after a year. Even Benson, the white attorney for the plaintiffs, took his own daughter out of Kansas City schools and enrolled her in his alma mater, Pembroke.

TO MAKE MATTERS WORSE, a great many blacks in Kansas City opposed the desegregation effort.

In late October 1988, a group of protesters gathered on the front steps of the old Central High School carrying signs reading, FLUNK THE SCHOOL BOARD! and END EDUCATIONAL AND ECONOMIC APARTHEID!

"We're fired up!" they shouted. "We want our share!"

"This is the beginning of a movement," said Ajamu Webster, president of the local chapter of the National Black United Front.

Webster and his fellow activists pointed out that most of the $200 million the district had spent up to that point in the desegregation case had gone to white-owned firms. Shortly after the costly desegregation order, the Civic Council of Greater Kansas City, a secretive consortium of the city's top CEOs, offered to supply the district with a chief financial officer to help oversee the process. Though the group had been in existence since 1964, the predominantly white organization had not offered any public support of earlier desegregation efforts. But as money began flowing into the district, these leaders, apparently, wanted to become involved.

Central's new building was the most costly project. A local black-owned firm called By Design Architects drew the plans for the building at a cost of $1.2 million, but a white-owned firm from Johnson County won the $32 million contract to build it. That company, Midwest Titan, also won the contract for another massive project at Paseo Academy. In its bid for Central, Midwest Titan had promised to subcontract more than 20 percent of the work to minority- and woman-owned businesses. But the firm later faced allegations of unfair business practices from some of those minority-owned firms. In response, a district official admitted, "There have been instances when we have hired minority contractors and they have not hired minorities. There's no way for us to tell who the minority contractors are hiring."

Black leaders also raised concerns about the educational side of the desegregation scheme. In the summer of 1989, members of the Coalition for Educational and Economic Justice and other civic and political groups such as Freedom Inc. passed a petition decrying the use of racial quotas to fill the district's classrooms. At the time, the district was abiding by a federal court order mandating that minority enrollment in magnet schools be limited to 60 percent. So when some schools reached their limit, they stopped enrolling blacks in order to keep desks empty and waiting for white kids.

Eventually Clark agreed to ease the quotas, but it did not appease the more vocal members of the black community. On a Saturday in April 1992, members of the coalition once again gathered at Central, this time in a Greek theater inside the brand-new $32 million building, and lambasted the desegregation plan's curriculum mandates. Classical Greek, Latin, Spanish, French—all of them were Eurocentric. They believed a district with a majority of African-American students should offer African-centered education as well. Despite Benson's repeated protests, based on his opinion that Kansas City teachers wouldn't be qualified for such a program—as if they *were* qualified to teach classical Greek—the district did establish several African-centered schools, most of which still operate today.

DURING THE 1992 RACE for governor, Kansas City's costly program became a central issue. In TV markets outside Kansas City, Mel Carnahan and his Republican opponent, Attorney General William Webster, aired ads attacking each other's position on the case. On the campaign trail, Webster often referred to Central as "the gold-plated school." All this, even though Ashcroft was crowing at the same time about how he'd left the state with a $125 million surplus. He'd also been able to restore all of the budget cuts he'd made to accommodate Clark's orders—all except education, Bartman would learn after he'd been named the state's education commissioner. Throughout his two terms, Ashcroft had championed himself as "the education governor." His favorite quotation for speeches: "My dream for this state is that it would be a place where every person, every man and every woman and every boy and every girl, would have the opportunity to meet the maximum of their God-given potential."

Carnahan rode into office thanks in part to his promise to settle the case and free the state from the burden of paying for it, and he soon got a major break from the U.S. Supreme Court. By the mid-1990s the balance of the high court had tipped completely toward the conservative—Thurgood Marshall, the lead attorney for *Brown*, had been replaced on the bench by Clarence Thomas.

Thomas was no stranger to discrimination. He'd grown up in the Deep South. Later in life, on a visit to the Kansas City area, he was refused service at a pizza parlor, according to a biography. At a conference prior to deciding the Kansas City case, Thomas looked at his white peers and reminded them of his experiences with racism. "I'm the only one at this table who attended a segregated school," he reportedly said. "And the problem with segregation was not that we didn't have white people in our class. The problem was that we didn't have equal facilities, we didn't have heating, we didn't have books and we had rickety chairs."

On June 12, 1995, Thomas joined four other justices in striking down the underlying premise of Kansas City's desegregation case, ruling that Judge Clark had overstepped his constitutional authority. "It never ceases to amaze me that the courts are so willing to assume that anything that is predominately black must be inferior," Thomas famously began his concurring opinion. At one point in his long written opinion, he could easily have been talking about the old Central: "Black schools might actually benefit blacks because they can function as the center and symbol of black communities, and provide examples of independent black leadership, success and achievement."

In actuality, it was a political decision. Its scope reached beyond the matter before the Court. In debate terms, it was a topicality violation.

"The Court's process of orderly adjudication has broken down in this case," Justice David Souter wrote in his dissent. The decision

> resolves a foundational issue . . . that we did not accept for review in this case, that we did not reach in order to consider when it was presented in a prior petition . . . [U]nder these circumstances, the respondent school district and pupils naturally came to the Court

without expecting that a foundational premise . . . would become the focus of the case, the essence of the Court's misjudgment in reviewing and repudiating that central premise lies in its failure to have warned the respondents of what was really at stake. This failure lulled the respondents into addressing the case without sufficient attention to the foundational issue, and their lack of attention has now infected the Court's decision.

Three years later, after a long settlement process in which the state bought its freedom for $320 million, Central reverted to being a neighborhood school. Again, blacks didn't have a seat at the table; the matter was decided by attorneys, the governor, and the all-white Civic Council. During its ten years as a magnet, it had made some strides toward integration. Before becoming a magnet in 1988, Central had just one white student; by 1993, it was 20 percent white, though that number began to decline the following year.

After the district drafted its settlement with the state in 1996, the matter went before Judge Clark. On March 25, 1997, Clark didn't hide his bitterness over the district's failure when he wrote his final order before retiring from the case: "This court warns not only the citizens of Kansas City, but also the entire country, that while this court may be powerless to remedy social ills, some action must come soon to give hope to these disenfranchised [black] citizens before the chasm in America becomes so wide that it cannot be crossed." Clark approved the agreement, noting that the school district had assumed an "awkward posture" in its motion to bring about a gradual end to the case. On the one hand, the district argued that it had done all it could to desegregate its classrooms, which were now more segregated than they'd been when the case was filed. On the other, it argued that it had not done enough to reduce the achievement gap between black and white students.

The district did this for one reason: to avoid bankruptcy. The magnet plan had bloated the district, which was operating on funds generated by a court-ordered levy increase that would disappear upon the case's closure. To keep the money flowing, the district needed to keep the case going. It worked, but it was a devil's gambit. In 1999 voters approved a statewide referendum (heavily advertised outside the city as a stick-it-to-KC plan, but barely promoted where the taxes would be collected) freezing the court-ordered tax rate that Judge Clark had imposed.

So now the money flow was in place, but the case, with its costly legal fees, kept on going. By the time Ebony entered Central as a freshman, the only matter left to resolve was the achievement gap, which Clark had defined using scores from a multiple-choice test the district no longer gives.

NINETEEN

DEBATE HELL

MARCUS PRESSED HIS PALMS against his eyes and rubbed hard. He looked up, blinked, and laid his head back down on the desk. A few paces away Ebony Rose, his partner for the day, held a podium with a cliff-hanger's grip and struggled through a speech about the righteous mightiness of the federal courts system.

"They don't have enough money, or, states doesn't have enough money because they can't even, like, support highways and stuff like that," Ebony said, sweat beading on his brow. "They need a courts to help 'em widdit. Cuz, the courts can't. Or the state. They can't, like, even keep education and them in order because, cuz, the courts have, like, the right to do all that. And, like. I mean. And."

Marcus shifted his arms, tried to make a better pillow out of them, turned his head, adjusted his arms again. Finally he gave in and sat up, his red eyes barely open. He couldn't believe he was here at 8:15 on a Saturday morning. Here in the Bed Bath & Beyond heart of Johnson County, Kansas. At Shawnee Mission South High School, where debate was cryogenically frozen in the 1960s. With a novice who was scared of his own necktie. He'd been up until four in the morning killing terrorists in cyberspace, and he'd still gotten up at 6:30 to be ferried here, to the seventh ring of debate hell. Why had he promised Rinehart he'd team up with Ebony and show him the ropes? His foggy mind couldn't recall exactly. Must've been trying to get something out of her, a deal they'd brokered. Whatever it was, it wasn't worth it. That much he knew.

Four minutes into his speech, Ebony abruptly stopped and mumbled, "So vote negative." He lowered his head and started back toward Marcus before realizing he still had to stand for cross-x. His opponent, a black kid from the selective Sumner Academy in Kansas City, Kansas (one of *Newsweek*'s top five hundred schools in America), took his place beside him. "What is your counterplan saying?" the kid asked.

Ebony stiffened, wiggled his mouth. "Um," he said, "states can't solve, because, like, they get all their money from the courts."

He glanced at Marcus, who was shaking his head. "I mean, um," he muttered, dropping his gaze down to his shoes. "I don't know."

And in this way he answered all the kid's questions, his eyes shifting from the floor to Marcus to me and back to the floor, his expression becoming more and more pained, his fists at his sides clenched tighter and tighter. *I don't know. I don't know. I don't know.* When the timer finally sounded, releasing him from his torture, he stormed back to his seat. "Fuck!" he said to himself.

As Ebony sat down, shaking his head, Marcus leaned over and whispered, "You're cool." Ebony allowed the shadow of a grin to creep across his face.

Marcus resumed his show of sleepless agony. His head wobbled slightly, as though he were a drunk hiding his condition. When the other Sumner debater, a white kid dressed in a black silk shirt and a Three Stooges tie, took his place at the podium, Marcus tried to focus, but he kept dropping his pen and pressing his fingers against his puffy eye sockets.

Then the kid said, "Congress and courts are both under the judicial branch."

Suddenly Marcus perked up and looked at me, beaming. He rubbed his hands together conspiratorially. Marcus was so competitive that even if he were in the throes of illness or death, he'd still perk up at a sign of weakness in an opponent. His hawk eyes returned when he stood at the podium and belted out a long, forceful invective, much of it spontaneous. Ebony turned to me and mouthed "fuck!" again, this time in amazement.

Afterward, in the hall outside, Marcus slid back into exhaustion, his brow crisscrossed with grumpy lines. "I hate this," he told me. "It's just whining back and forth."

He sauntered over to Rinehart and told her about their opponent's judicial-branch flub, and the recollection sent a quick wave of energy through him.

"And we're an academically deficient school," she said sourly. "I guess that means we're going to lose."

MARCUS DRAGGED HIS FEET down the halls of Shawnee Mission South, eventually running out of steam in a lonely stretch of hall, and hunkered down with his back propped against a wall. He reached to his right and grabbed a piece of paper someone had dropped on the floor. "Judge's Instructions," it read. Marcus scanned the list of pointers, his eyes zeroing in on four items under the subcategory "Delivery":

1. General Appearance
2. Voice
3. Gestures
4. Courtesy

"I have to have 'general appearance' to be a good debater," he scoffed. He pulled a pen from behind his ear, circled the offending pointers, and wrote, "The reason I don't debate around here—too many idiots running shit."

Rinehart approached. "I just realized this type of debate makes people dumb," he said to her. "I don't think this type of debate helps novices at all."

She nodded in agreement. She hated coming to the Kansas City suburbs as much as he did. The problem, in their opinion, was the judging pool at these tournaments. Instead of hiring college kids with debate experience to decide who would win or lose, tournament directors in Kansas and Missouri enlisted parents (many of whom had never watched a debate) to serve as judges. There were reasonable arguments for doing things this way. For one, volunteers would save money. It got parents more involved with the schools, which most education experts agree is key to schools' success. And, in most people's minds, debate is democratic. Anyone with a brain ought to be able to watch a debate and get the gist of it, like when one watches pundit shows on TV. It's about the power of persuasion. It's about building the skills necessary to make it in life: stand tall; speak clearly and with confidence; be assertive but polite; dress sharp; smile.

But Marcus and Rinehart thought this notion was absurd. It was like having someone who couldn't tell the difference between a backboard and a free-throw line officiate a basketball game. Ignorant officials would tend to judge aesthetics, such as the way players looked as they dribbled down the court or even the color of their uniforms (think how many b-ball illiterates choose teams in their office's NCAA Tournament betting pool this way). And in debate, lay judges—or "Suzy's mom," as Rinehart derisively called them—often do make these kinds of subjective calls. They don't know topicality from counterplan, and they don't flow (debate jargon for taking notes). They politely watch the rounds with their arms folded or their fingers thoughtfully wrapped around their chins, and when the final buzzer sounds, they let their opinions serve as their guide. Having been on the losing end of this equation a few too many times, Marcus and Rinehart had become convinced that it opened the door to racism.

There was a time when Rinehart thought all the talk about "the vestiges of slavery" and "institutional racism" was just whiny ballyhoo. This is America, she reasoned; you work hard, you succeed. So the thought of having a ghetto debate team never occurred to her. She'd never be satisfied confining her kids to barely official matchups against other inner-city schools. From the start, she set her sights on the real deal: big weekend tournaments, packed with competition from across Missouri and Kansas, the teams that would be gunning for a state championship and a bid to the NFL nationals. And it wouldn't be "a learning experience" where she'd pat her kids on the head and say, "You did your best," or, "At least you tried." No. She hated to lose. She wanted her debaters to feel the thrill of hoisting trophies over their heads. She wanted to feel it, too. She had no doubt it would happen. All kids are teachable, she figured, no matter how poor they are, and certainly regardless of their skin color.

But during her first year at Central, her teams continually suffered beatings at the hands of their more experienced rivals from nearby suburban schools like Blue Springs and Lee's Summit. For a new squad, this seemed natural, so she managed to find some money for a few of her kids to travel to colleges for summer debate camps. They came back hyped and ready to nab some metal. But her teams quickly fell into a pattern of winning their first two rounds, then bowing out after losing the next two, no matter how hard they practiced. Puzzled, she sat in on a few rounds. In her opinion, her students should have been winning: their speeches were packed with substantiated arguments, which their opponents dropped left and right. She read the judges' ballots and was appalled by their justification for these losses. Her kids were losing because they'd opened their evidence tubs too loudly, or because they whispered to each other during the round. ("How are they supposed to work together if they can't communicate?" she complained.) The judges rarely paid attention to the evidence presented in the rounds, which, in Rinehart's mind, was the essence of debate—it's what made it a game of intellect, not a game of schmoozing. "If you're judging based on how kids talk and look, our kids are always going to lose," Rinehart told me.

She became convinced that it was racism, plain and simple. How else could you explain her squad's success on the national circuit and its failure close to home? Standing in front of middle-aged, middle-class white moms who hailed from the security-fence suburban sprawl, her kids weren't debaters; they were black kids with a whole lot of baggage. Anyone who read the daily newspaper or watched the evening news knew that Central was the school that, despite millions of taxpayers' dollars, was "academically deficient." (Often, when I talked with white longtime Kansas Citians about Central, they would shake their head and say, "What a waste.") It was the site of the riots that had chased the earliest white-flight settlers into their subdivisions. It was in the middle of a war zone, where gunshots rang out every night. It was from the unaccredited district. It never happened to her, but Rinehart had heard from some of her fellow coaches that suburban judges had even expressed surprise that the city kids could read.

WHEN I ASKED MARCUS how he thought he and Ebony were doing, he frowned and said, "We better be undefeated." Unlike in national-circuit tournaments, most of the judges here wouldn't reveal the winner at the end of a round, so he wasn't sure. This was another nod to the old way of doing things, a forced element of surprise that, from what I could tell, only served to drive kids crazy. After giving their all in a round, they wanted instant gratification. The adults who ran the tournament apparently felt it best to deny them. Good for their character, I suppose.

Still, Marcus had a strong hunch that he and Ebony weren't undefeated. The teams they were paired against kept getting worse as the tournament progressed. More than likely, they were being power-matched down into lower and lower brackets. So Marcus decided to shake things up.

Right before the last round of the day, he pulled Ebony to the side and whispered, "We're gonna run 'Pet Therapy.'"

"You bet," Ebony said with one quick nod of his head. He raised a hand to his mouth to suppress a giggle. "Pet Therapy," one of the most squirrelly cases on the national circuit.

"Fuck 'em," Marcus said.

"You bet," Ebony said, giving another emphatic nod.

Marcus loosened his tie and pulled his shirttail free. He rolled up his sleeves. Across the room their opponents, from Shawnee Mission West, unpacked their tub. They were done up in their Sunday suits. Both sported short bangs that were gelled up from their foreheads like ski ramps. When the judges came in, they moved across the room to shake hands and introduce themselves. Marcus and Ebony stayed put. On the national circuit, debaters rarely tried to glad-hand the judges, and the judges usually sneered at those who did and turned their noses up at the outstretched hands.

Ebony walked to the podium and, while the judges settled into their seats, flipped through the cards for the 1AC. *Man, this is some crazy shit*, he thought as he read the cards' titles: "Pet Therapy Alleviates Stress"; "Pet Therapy Solves Depression"; "Pet Therapy Is Not Just Dogs and Cuddly Animals." Marcus had picked up the case at camp and stuffed it in his designated files to use in "fuck 'em" situations like this.

Ebony scratched his head and dove in. The judges leaned forward and squinted, as if doing so made their hearing more acute. Only one of them took notes. The other two, both parent volunteers who appeared to be in their mid-forties, had no experience with debate.

One of the Shawnee Mission West debaters got up for cross-x when Ebony finished. He tugged at his hardened cowlick. "How are you going to have funding for this?" he asked.

"I don't know," Ebony replied, shifty-eyed.

"You don't have funding?" the kid asked, his voice heavy with disbelief.

"Yes, we have funding," Ebony blurted. "I don't know where it's from." He saw Marcus shaking his head again. "I mean, we don't."

"Okay," the kid said, widening his eyes. "So you're just going to take pets into places?"

"Yes," Ebony said. "Trained dogs with their trainers and everything." His posture was stiff, his tone mechanical. All day Ebony had moved with locked-muscle uncertainty, like he was surrounded by land mines wired to explode at mistakes. He knew this case was supposed to be fun, but he was too worried about what the great Marcus would think of him.

After cross-x the other Shawnee Mission West debater took his place at the front of the room. His face was slack with disbelief, but as he spoke, it hardened into anger. "This plan is so ridiculous," he said, "we shouldn't even be forced to debate it. I mean, pets are great. I love my dog. But it's a lot of work to take care of them. We can't expect people with mental illness to be able to do it." He leered in Marcus and Ebony's direction and shook his head. "All you do is give people a pet and hope that works."

Marcus then got up and put it all into perspective—for me, anyway. "We argue we aren't people of power," he said during his 2AC. "We're intellectuals who argue in debate." He paused and raised a hand thoughtfully. He was speaking slowly, old-school.

"What we're saying is that in every debate you've ever been to, you pass a policy. But it never actually passes. We just waste time saying we can wave a magic wand and make Congress pass something. Debate is an intellectual activity. We can change mind-sets."

The point of today's intellectual exercise? *Pets make people happy*. By voting for the affirmative's plan of encouraging mental health caregivers to offer their patients a little quality time with a Labrador or collie, the judges would affirm this basic truth. Their vote would acknowledge that everyone watching the round had learned something very important about pets and, being so enlightened, they would go home and tell their family and friends, who would, in turn, spread the good news, and soon depressed people nationwide would be petting doggies and smiling and feeling a whole lot better.

"We actually change the world," Marcus said. "Instead of offering cases that do wild things like make Congress sign a legislation, we solve for sadness with happiness."

I grinned at Marcus. This was the most logical case I'd heard. Silly, yes, but fundamentally true. And real. A pair of high school kids could never compel Congress or the Supreme Court to change, say, the way blacks and Native Americans are treated in public health policy. But they could, in an hour or so, enlighten a group of adults, encourage them to make a minor adjustment in the way they see the world and live in it. More than that, though, this "Pet Therapy" case gave the debaters a chance to be introspective, which, from my experience, is a rare state of mind among teens. Beneath all the funny stuff about dogs—and not very far beneath, either—was a simple, profound statement: knowledge is powerful.

Clearly, however, this realization wasn't dawning on the other adults in the room. They cringed at Marcus as if he'd just fouled the air. The mom among them looked at one of her colleagues, made her eyes go buggy, and let out a laugh.

Shawnee Mission West's first debater got up to interrogate Marcus.

"What's the point of debate?" he asked quickly, like an attorney on TV.

"To argue," Marcus replied. "To be intellectual. So it's just a game."

"Debate is a game," the kid agreed. "But you still have to set a policy up. You still have to vote on it."

Marcus tried to explain, but his opponent couldn't understand, so he changed course: "Okay, okay, okay. Can you recite the resolution to me?"

"Can I recite it?"

"Yeah."

The Shawnee Mission West kid rolled his eyes upward, as if to read text on the back of his lashes. "Um, resolved, the United States federal government will, uh, significantly increase, uh, mental health, uh, services. I don't know all the—"

"But you do know enough to see that there's not the word 'policy' in the resolution?"

"We're policy makers," the kid insisted.

"No, no. My job is to affirm the resolution. As the affirmative team. What I'm asking is, is there the word 'policy' in the resolution?"

"This is policy debate."

"Debate is about ideas!" Marcus said suddenly, after a minute of back and forth. He was bent slightly at the waist now. He shook a piece of evidence in his left hand. "Since we really can't make changes, our change is enlightening people through an intellectual activity. Why is that so hard to comprehend? That's how activism works! Why should debate be a game? Why can't debate be an activity which should be where people actually produce solutions to problems?"

"Then if you wanted to do that," the kid said, pouting, "go make up your own debate and say it's 'Idea Debate.'" He made quotation marks with his fingers.

"But there are no rules within this form of debate!" Marcus karate-chopped his hand.

"Well," the kid said, cocking his head back, "if you would like me to get the debate handbook . . . They have a debate handbook, and they state what you can and can't do."

Marcus let out a hard, forced laugh. "The only rule in debate is speech times, last time I checked, right?"

"No, there's rules to debate."

"If there's rules to debate," Marcus offered, "why would there be any debate?"

Just then, one of the judges barked, "Hey, let's just quit debating what debate is and just debate the debate."

"Yeah," said the mom judge.

Marcus looked genuinely shocked. In his four years of debate, no judge had ever stopped him mid-round for any reason, much less for—of all things—getting into an argument.

Marcus scowled through the rest of the round. As soon as it was over, he bolted out into the hall. I stuck around in the room and listened to the judges confer about their decision, which at every other tournament I've attended was a big unwritten no-no. The judges seemed flustered, as if the kids had worn clown suits and delivered their speeches backward. "I'm sitting here thinking this is pretty weird," the mom said. "That one kid," she added, "the lighter one," referring to Marcus, "I don't know what his deal was. That guy could be really good. He has all the tools to be great."

"Well, for me it was simple," said the dad judge, who, before the round, told me he'd never seen a debate round before that day. "They broke the rules. They committed the cardinal sin of debate."

The two of them looked at me in a way that indicated they wanted to know my thoughts. I was still trying to stay out of the action, to protect the fourth wall. But I couldn't resist, especially after the "that guy could be really good" remark. I felt compelled to jump in and defend Marcus and Ebony, who I believed had been wronged.

"You know the one guy you were talking about?" I asked. "The one with all the tools to be great? He's one of the top debaters in the country."

They looked at me in complete disbelief. "That guy?" the woman asked. "I find that hard to believe."

I tried telling them about his TOC bid, his trip to NFL nationals, his trophy finishes in West Des Moines and at New Trier, but they seemed to have stopped listening, so I went out into the hall to find Marcus. He was still hot, pacing back and forth.

I told him about the potential the judge saw in him. "They can blow me," he said. "I don't want to be good here."

MARCUS'S THORNY EXPRESSION stayed on his face for the rest of the afternoon, though it wilted a little under his exhaustion. He dragged his feet down the long hallways of Shawnee Mission South, weaving like a drunken sloth. Ebony followed him, saying nothing except "uh-huh" now and then to punctuate his mentor's relentless bitching about the tournament, about how he had vowed never to return to the land of the racist, the boring, and the dumb, about the precious sleep and computer games he was missing. Near the school's front door, with autumn sunlight angling in around their shoes, Marcus turned to Ebony and regarded him as if for the first time. "Well, it was nice working with you on your first debate," he said, after a long glance up and down. "It'll never happen again."

Ebony cast his eyes downward, revealing for a moment the sting of the remark, but quickly recovered and locked his gaze on Marcus's eyes.

"I know," he said.

Marcus looked away and resumed his aimless shuffle. Ebony lowered his head, wiggled his mouth as if to shoo away the self-pity, then raised his face back to a cockier angle, rearranging it into something close to confidence. He knew this was all part of it. Young warriors have to take their licks. It was an honor, really, especially coming from someone like Marcus. At that moment nobody, not even R. Kelly or Shaquille O'Neal or Malcolm X, was as mighty to Ebony as Marcus Leach was. During the rounds Ebony was blown away by the senior's debate prowess, the way he could stand up there with little more than a few words scribbled on a sheet of paper and fill the room with a thunderstorm of sheer brilliance. "Marcus is a god," he had told me several times that day.

While the master spoke during rounds, Ebony had occasionally looked at me with doughnut eyes and silently exclaimed, "Fuck!" It was intimidating. He so wanted to impress Marcus that his mind went into overdrive and he seemed to slip into survival mode, blood draining from his brain to protect his organs and extremities. His mind would tighten into such a narrow focus that it locked shut at the first mistake, silencing him. After he did this a couple of times, Marcus passed him a note that read, "Stop pussying out and being non-confident!" Then, as Rinehart drove the squad to Taco Bell for lunch, Marcus had sat in the front of the van and made Ebony the subject of a comedy routine. "His speech was like twenty seconds long!" Marcus had shouted. "You shoulda seen him! We was up against two totally dumb kids. They be like, 'How are you topical?' Eb be like, 'I'm done.' "

All their teammates had cracked up.

"You need to at least look like you got confidence to win some of these rounds," Marcus had said, shaking with laughter.

Ebony had sat there and taken it. He'd even forced a smile, though it struck his face like a slap, as if he were punishing himself for betraying the slightest inkling of pity. He had come a long way, really. A few years earlier, when he'd just moved into his auntie's house, he would wither under any razzing, good-natured or otherwise. There was a time when he'd stopped talking altogether, partly because of his speech impediment but mostly because his mother's abandonment had hurt him so much. Moving back and forth between shelters and foster homes, he had no real space of his own, no permanent environment in which to spread roots and grow. Everything and everyone around him carried a threat, overt or silent, so the only thing he knew how to do was pull himself inward and try to disappear. So he'd close his mouth and open books, and he'd lash back at anything remotely resembling an attack. But now a few years had gone by. His auntie hadn't told him to leave, hadn't drifted into a life of drugs. He was part of something that had been around for years and would be around for a few more. He was on the legendary Central debate team. He was new. He was paying his dues.

MARCUS AND EBONY eventually made their way to the school's auditorium, where trophies would be awarded and out-round matchups announced. Groups of debaters and coaches were forming separate school islands amid the sea of theater seats. The Central crew was near the back, gathered in a small pool of darkness cast by a burned-out bulb overhead. Marcus sank down into a seat, propped his legs on the row in front of him, closed his eyes, and fell asleep.

His teammates looked sleepy, too. They hardly spoke as they stared up at the stage, at the display of trophies gleaming in the spotlights. Rinehart sat off to the side of the encampment, lips pursed, legs crossed. Down front, a woman appeared on the stage and began reading off the teams that had broken to elimination rounds. When she finished the list without naming their school, the Central debaters flashed one another grins—they'd be going home soon. Marcus parted his eyelids for a split second and gave a thumbs-up. "If I get a speaker award, that would be an insult," he mumbled.

He didn't get one, nor did any of his teammates. As they filed out of the auditorium, Brandon ducked his head and shouted in a deep, solicitous Uncle Remus voice, "Y'all outdebated our asses!"

In the hallway Rinehart was handed a manila envelope stuffed with judges' ballots. She passed them out to her students, who clustered in pairs to read them. All but one of the duos went two-three. Marcus and Ebony went one-four. Ebony was dumbfounded. "Damn," he said, "Marcus shoulda won all them. Ain't nobody was good as him."

Marcus read one of the ballots, his brow clenched. "My decision," it read, "is based on: preparation, knowledge of materials, choice of words, courtesy, professionalism, speaking clearly, professional appearance, organization of facts, and delivery of material." Marcus threw the ballot on the floor. "Stupid-ass judges," he said. "Here's my answer to you." He raised his middle finger. "Fuck you."

All around Rinehart, cuss words rose, but she just stood with her hands on her hips and let them get it out of their systems.

"Look at this shit," one of the seniors said. "Bitch says, 'Way too fast! I couldn't follow anything you said.' What are you doin' judgin' debate, then?!"

"Too fast" was a common refrain, and the kids found it supremely annoying, because that's the style they liked best. Rinehart was ambivalent about this criticism. She liked speed, too, but in the days leading up to the tournament, she had implored her students to go slowly. "Why?" she asked. "Because you'll be debating for Suzy's mom, and Suzy's mom is dumb."

What irked Rinehart were the remarks about "reading too much evidence." In her mind, evidence was the name of the game, the stuff that made it a true test of intellect, not social appeal. Worst of all, though, were the instances where the judges voted against her kids because their plans "had holes" in them or were "outlandish," even though their opponents hadn't raised those arguments during the round.

"I'm like, 'Come on,'" she said to me. "It's hard enough to go up against two kids from another school. They expect these kids to argue against adults' thoughts, too?"

We headed for the van, the kids all glowering, ready for naps. Rinehart watched them climb in, then turned to me and said, "Magnify this by every weekend, and that shows how the first two years were for us. Finally I said enough is enough."

TWENTY

PRODICAL MOM

TWO DAYS before Halloween, Ebony sat on a desk near the front of room 109 with his backpack strapped on backward, swinging his legs off the edge and staring down at the floor. All around him, kids were filling plastic document boxes with debate evidence and straightening their ties and talking and shouting and laughing. A girl hopped up and broke into a quick dance in front of him. "Where your partner?" she asked.

"I dunno," he said. "Probably off massaging his dreads. I don't give a damn no more."

He turned his gaze back toward the floor. After a moment he looked up at me and twisted his lips as if to banish his gloom. Then he started to hum and bob his head to an R. Kelly song that only he could hear. Music had always been Ebony's favorite remedy for disappointment. When he was a young ward of the system, shuttled from crowded homeless shelters to foster homes and back again, his mom off smoking crack or trying to quit, he'd fall asleep to Magic 107.3, wrapping himself in the sounds of Marvin Gaye, the Temptations, and Barry White. When there was no radio, he'd hum.

Now sixteen years old, Ebony knew better than to expect anything from anyone, least of all another sixteen-year-old. For the past several weeks Antoine had been skipping practice and debate class. And here it was, fifteen minutes before the squad was to board the bus for an afternoon tournament at Paseo Academy, and Antoine was nowhere in sight.

Ebony wiggled out of his backpack and dropped it on the floor beside him. He grabbed his case file and went through the motions of getting ready for the tournament. If Antoine didn't show, Coach Rinehart would probably pair Ebony up with one of the kids who sit in the back of debate class and never say anything. "One of them kids that can't read," he told me. "I don't give a fuck."

He obviously did. Almost every day since the first day of school he'd bragged about how he was going to win the city championship and, with it, a trip to the Urban Debate Leagues's Novice Nationals in Atlanta. Though the championship was still six weeks away, the Paseo tournament was an important step in his journey, a rare opportunity to test the competition. DEBATE–Kansas City, the local UDL chapter, could only sponsor three events before its championship tournament because of rules created decades ago by the Missouri State High School Activities Association that limit how many debate tournaments kids can compete in.

But Ebony had even more riding on this afternoon tournament. Before he left for school that morning, his aunt told him that his mother would come watch him compete. Ebony kept this information to himself. If history were any indication, she probably wouldn't show up. Throughout his childhood he had waited for his mother to make good on her promises. "She kept on telling us she gonna get us back one day," Ebony once told me. "She gonna get us back. She gonna get us back. She gonna get us back. I was like, 'I'm gonna live with my mama one day.' After I got older, I know that she needed help and that, I guess, she probably wouldn't get us back anytime soon. And by the time she get help, I'll probably be gone, you know."

With about ten minutes to spare, Antoine finally strolled into the room. Ebony tried to hide his relief. Antoine plopped down into a chair next to Ebony and rested his chin in his hand. Ebony glanced at him a couple times, but mostly kept his eyes locked straight ahead, swinging his legs off the side of the desk.

"What's up with *you*?" Antoine asked.

"Where you been lately?" Ebony demanded.

"Been doin' work."

"What kind of work?"

Ebony knew better. Only a handful of Central kids did homework, and Antoine wasn't one of them. Antoine did hardly any homework and was a chronic truant. As a junior, he was carrying a 1.4 grade point average and behind on credits. Graduation was far from a certainty for him.

Antoine ignored him. He got up, hoisted a file box onto a desk, opened it, and rooted through the files.

"What are we running today?" Ebony asked.

"I was gonna ask *you*," Antoine snapped.

"You weren't in yesterday."

Antoine glared at him. He pulled out a file, looked at it for a second, and slapped it down. "I'm running 'Drunk African-Americans,'" he said.

"Crackheads!" Ebony exclaimed, breaking into his high-pitched cackle. "We can run that! Crackheads. It's a squirrelly case. Crack. Gotta help them crackheads."

Despite all he'd been through with his mother, Ebony looked on drug addicts the way most of his peers did: as clowns, goofy bit players in the urban drama they were all living.

He slapped hands with Antoine and got up to help organize their files.

NEAR THE DOOR, Coach Rinehart raised her hand. "All right, guys," she shouted. "There are going to be sixty-four teams there today. This isn't going to be a walk in the park."

"Rinehart trying to make us scared," Ebony hooted. "Like there's some sort of competition. Ain't no competition."

"Not from Paseo," another kid said.

"They a bunch of fags," Ebony said.

"Well," Rinehart said, throwing up her hands in mock exasperation, "I'm just saying these teams are going to be ready. And they're going to be coming after us."

The kids drowned her out with a flurry of trash talk. They felt invincible. Central had dominated DEBATE–Kansas City since its start in 1998.

With just a couple exceptions, the league's traveling sweepstakes trophy—awarded at each tournament to the squad with the best overall record—had been on display in Central's front hallway that entire time.

But Rinehart had reason for concern. At the season opener, hosted by Central in mid-October, Paseo had made a serious showing, placing several teams in the top ten. The school had a new coach who had debated in high school. And, more important, the coach was beginning to learn how to work the district's bureaucracy the way Rinehart had. The previous summer the coach had scored enough money to send several of her debaters to camp. And a summer of intense debate training is usually enough to separate the winners from the losers in the novice division, where Ebony and Antoine competed.

THE SQUAD piled their evidence tubs onto dollies, zipped up their jackets, and headed for the bus. On the short ride to Paseo, Ebony sat sideways with his back against the window and both arms resting high on the chair backs. He bobbed his head and sang to himself, "I got hos, I got hos, in different area codes."

When he stepped off the bus at Paseo, a woman in a long leather coat approached him. "Ebony!" she exclaimed, throwing her arms open.

"Hi, Mom," he said in a low monotone, sheepishly ducking into her hug.

She held him out at arm's length and looked him up and down. Ebony's eyes roamed past her toward the classmates who were filing into the school and staring at him as his mom pulled out a disposable camera. "Smile," she said, stretching the word out into two singsongy syllables.

"You know how long I been waiting for you?" she asked. "I got here more than an hour ago."

Ebony didn't reply. He knelt down, picked up his tub, and led his mother through Paseo's metal detectors. They found seats at a round table in the school's cafeteria. Sitting to his right, Ebony's mom kept gazing at him, holding her smile.

"I'm very excited," she said, after introducing herself to me as Tina Marie Harrison. "I've never been to a debate before." She leaned in closer and lowered her voice. "This is the first I've been involved with Ebony for nine years. See, I'm an addict. But I'm getting my life back together. I'm two weeks clean and sober."

Her hair was twisted into short, bleached dreads. Her eyebrows had been plucked and repainted in an exaggerated Egyptian curve. Thick layers of mascara and eyeliner stretched the corners of her eyes into fine points. I couldn't help but feel embarrassed for Ebony. Parents almost never come to debate tournaments. And when they do, they don't hover around their kids flashing sappy grins, snapping pictures every few minutes.

She told Ebony that while she was waiting for him to arrive, she'd struck up a conversation with a school administrator. "And he said if I talk to your principal, I can do something to get involved with kids."

Ebony shrugged.

"Don't worry," Tina said. "I won't do anything to embarrass you." She laid her hand on his arm. "But I got to do something. This quitting is too hard."

Ebony twisted a piece of paper tightly between his fingers and looked out over the cafeteria. Orange and black streamers were strewn along the walls, and in the center of each table someone had arranged pumpkins with jack-o'-lantern faces drawn on them in Magic Marker. In the spirit of the season, the Paseo hosts had named their tournament "Two Rounds of Terror." A few of them had come dressed in costumes—a witch, an angel, a girl in a poofy blue Afro wig.

Tina picked a piece of lint off her son's oversize sport coat and lightly brushed his lapel with her fingertips. "When's your next tournament?" she asked.

"I dunno," he whispered, not looking at her.

"I wish I could go out of town with you," she said. "But that's not possible."

TINA STARTED using drugs when she was twelve years old. At first it was just pot, she later told me in a series of interviews I had with her. Her first drug buddy was a girl named Vanessa, whom she met at the beginning of junior high. Vanessa was Tina's only friend during her teen years. They were loners, outsiders, and they often skipped school to smoke weed and roam the gritty streets downtown. Vanessa got pregnant soon after graduation, and Tina enrolled in a residential job-training program in Excelsior Springs, a small town north of Kansas City. Her dream was to become a welder, just like the main character in *Flashdance*. At first, things went well. She told me she could out-weld most of her fellow students, all of them male, and her teacher was trying to line up an apprenticeship for her in Atlanta, where she could learn underwater welding and move on to a career pulling in the big bucks.

But then she met Curtis Moore, a fellow student. He was tall, burly, and as black as rich coffee, "like a Mandingo warrior," she told me. Growing up, Tina didn't like blacks. As a young kid, she had lived with her family in the housing projects just northeast of downtown, isolated by the freeway, rows of train tracks, and the Missouri River. Almost all her neighbors were black, and they were mean to her. She was lighter than most of them, with a slight red tint to her hair, and the other kids called her "yellow bitch" and "bougie nigga," meaning she was bourgeois, uppity. Curtis called her bougie, too, but she didn't mind. Her lust for him was sudden and furious, and she quickly got pregnant. Curtis joked that he was going to take their baby to Africa so the child could learn more about its roots. Tina was torn. She thought she loved Curtis, but she didn't want to give up her dream of leaving Kansas City to become a wealthy, nightclub-hopping welder. Curtis pleaded with her not to have an abortion. He told her he loved her and that they would be a family. So she opted for motherhood, and she took on her new role with the same zeal she brought to her welding classes.

On the advice of a family friend, she switched to a health food diet. She checked out stacks of books about early childhood development from the library. Somewhere in her reading she discovered that babies start learning in the womb, so she started reading to her swelling belly, mostly from the Bible. While pregnant, she began attending services at the Worldwide Church of God in Lee's Summit, a suburb on Kansas City's eastern periphery. Started in 1934 as a branch of the Seventh-Day Adventists, this sect was very strict. Its adherents believed that theirs was the only true church, that other denominations preached a false Gospel.

After Ebony was born, she kept reading to him from the Bible, as well as books she brought home from the library about music and history. She bathed her son in love. By then, she had dropped out of welding school and had started a program to become a nurse. When she wasn't at school or some church function, she had Ebony in her arms. She'd spend hours smothering him in kisses, she told me, caressing him, or just gazing into his eyes. She never left him in a crib; the two shared her bed.

Despite Curtis's promises, he never married Tina. Filled with her church's preaching, she refused to have sex with him unless they said vows. Then, in a moment of weakness, she acquiesced—once, she claims—and she became pregnant with her second child, Isaiah. Curtis dumped her while she was pregnant (for a young white girl no less). For the rest of his sons' lives, he would remain almost completely detached. Occasionally he would shell out a few bucks for a pair of shoes or some clothes if he was pressed long and hard enough, but always with extreme bitterness and resentment.

After Curtis left, Tina fell into a deep depression. She stopped going to church as often and picked up a cigarette habit. She went through the motions of showering her newborn with affection, but her feelings were empty.

By and by she befriended a guy from church. They started dating, then lust kicked in. Against the church elders' advice, they stole off to get married. She immediately became pregnant with her third son, Enoch. After he was born, though, she grew melancholy again, even though she was with a caring man. She now claims it was postpartum depression. She became distant from her husband, then mean, until finally she left with her first two boys (Enoch went with his dad).

She and the boys were living in an apartment in the southeast part of the city when she first tried crack. She was at a party when a man handed her a cigarette and lit it. She took a couple of drags, and then he smiled and asked her, "How do you feel?"

That's the last thing she remembers. She didn't learn until later that he had laced her cigarette with crack. She stayed up until eleven the next morning pacing her apartment, wondering what was going on.

That incident, she said, planted the seeds of the addiction that would swallow more than a decade of her life and destroy her family.

SHE STAYED CLEAN for the next year, until Vanessa drifted back into her life and handed her a crack pipe. Tina's life spiraled out of control.

For a while she had a good job with the post office, clearing $645 a week, sometimes even $725. She and her boys moved into a big, beautiful house on Twenty-seventh Street, just off Prospect, the main drag on the black side of town. But her new neighborhood turned out to be the crack mecca of Kansas City (Twenty-seventh and Prospect was such a rough corner HBO filmed a bleak documentary about it).

It wasn't long before she was evicted. She lost her job at the post office and hauled her kids to a homeless shelter. She got on welfare. She went to Cocaine Anonymous meetings and curbed her addiction. She'd get clean for a couple of weeks, then go out on a jag that would last a day or two. These short blasts always seemed to make matters worse. They'd temporarily alleviate her loneliness, but after she'd come down, she'd feel not only lonelier but guilty.

After a while she met a guy she liked. He had a good job, and he loved her kids. He knew she had some problems with drugs, but she appeared to be working on them. One night he wanted to take her out, but she couldn't get her mom to babysit the kids. So he took them all to a motel on Independence Avenue, a long, seedy thoroughfare on Kansas City's northeast side that's known regionally as a red-light district. The boys were on one bed, she and her new man on the other.

He turned to her and said, "Tina, I think you're a good mother. I know you're going through some things. But I really want to be with you."

After he fell asleep, she grabbed his car keys and stole off into the night, not knowing where she was headed. A few blocks later she "rolled up on somebody who was looking," as she put it, and within an hour she was high again, all of her wants instantly and momentarily satisfied.

She went missing for several days, crashing on the floor of some apartment she'd never been in before, and lent her new man's car out to strangers to make drug runs.

Tina's mom got the call from the police in the middle of the night. The cops told her Ebony and his brothers had been abandoned at some no-tell motel on the Avenue. With Tina's younger sisters eavesdropping, their mom told the cops she couldn't accept the boys. And so Ebony and his brothers began their long run through the foster care system. With the exception of a few short-lived "Praise the Lord, I'm sober now!" periods, their mother would be away from that day forward.

TINA PICKED a bad day for a triumphant return. Nothing seemed to go right at the Paseo tournament. When the schedules came out, Ebony and Antoine raced with the other kids to grab a copy, only to find they weren't scheduled to compete.

"Oh, *man!*" Antoine complained. "I was all set to tear someone up."

Rinehart got them matched up against a couple kids from their own school, which hardly appeased Ebony. "We gotta debate *them*?!" he whined. "We come all the way to *Paseo* to debate our *own school*?!"

Tina insisted on helping carry Ebony's evidence files up the stairs to the room they'd be debating in. After a few steps she was out of breath. "Eb, what do you have in this?" she asked. "A side of beef?"

"Books," he said, bounding the stairs two at a time.

Ebony stepped into the room and flicked on the lights. The walls were covered from floor to ceiling with vocabulary words. "Valor." "Assail." "Jubilant." "Obsolescence." Tina handed Ebony his tub, and he put it on a table to make a podium. She headed off for the bathroom. While she was gone, a woman wearing a navy blue skirt suit came in. "Are you Ebony?" she asked. "Where's your mom?"

He shook his head just slightly and mumbled, "I dunno."

"She was just talking to me earlier," the woman said, trying to act cheery. "I'm not coming to take you away."

Ebony ignored her, though the comment touched nerves that had grown tender years ago. Ebony didn't like to revisit his past. When I told him early in my travels with the team that I would like to sit down with him and learn about his family history, he forcefully shook his head and said, "Uh-uh, not my family history." He and I would become close friends during the

2002–2003 season and after, and we could talk about almost anything. But whenever I asked him how it had felt to spend his childhood in foster homes and homeless shelters, he'd usually glance at his shoes, shrug, and whisper, "It was coo. For real."

Tina returned just as Antoine was beginning the first speech of the debate round. She took a seat next to me, placing her hands flat on the table and straightening her posture. But by the time Antoine finished, she was sagging, looking around the room. One of the opposing team's debaters got up to cross-examine Antoine, and when the exchange grew heated at one point, Tina perked up. "I would have been good at this," she whispered to me. "You can't shut me up."

But as the round progressed, she grew more bored. She grabbed a stack of magazines from a rack in the corner of the room and flipped through them noisily, stopping only when it was Ebony's turn to speak. A few words into his first speech, she raised her camera and loudly wound the film. Ebony looked up. He held his hand out flat to his side, subtly motioning for her to stop. But she clicked the shutter anyway. The other debaters laughed. One made a big show of blinking the glare of the flash out of his eyes. Ebony stuttered for a moment before catching his rhythm again.

"That's my boy," Tina whispered to me. "You definitely have to have a little bit of arrogance to do this. I see he's got some of his dad in him. But he's got an *awful* lot of *me* in him."

The judge looked over at her as a hint to stop talking. But Tina ignored her. "I only found out a month ago that he's in debate," she continued. "I was at a party with him and my sisters. I asked him what the topic was, and he said, 'Mental health.' I laughed for about a week. My sisters said, 'You can just do it on your mom and you'll go to Harvard.'"

FOR THE SECOND ROUND, Ebony and Antoine faced bona fide opponents from Schlagle High in Kansas City, Kansas. It took place in the same room, and when the judge arrived, she asked Tina, "Are you a coach?"

"No, I'm his mother," she replied, pointing at Ebony.

"I would just love it if parents would volunteer to go with me as sponsors," the opposing team's coach said as she sat down.

"Well, I don't have a car," Tina said. "And I don't know anybody."

"Don't they take a bus?" the coach asked. She and Tina looked at Ebony. Without glancing up, he let out a long, slow "*yyyyyyepp.*"

"In fact," Tina told the coach, "this is the first debate I've ever been to."

"I think Central, they always take buses," the coach said.

"Or vans," Ebony interrupted. "We mostly take vans. Early in the morning."

"But I would have to be at the school? Then I could ride with you?" Tina asked, getting excited. "Is that what you're saying?"

"I think," Ebony stammered. "I don't know. You ask Rinehart. Something."

"Who would I ask?"

"I dunno." Ebony lowered his head and continued preparing for the round.

"His coach?" Tina asked, turning to the judge. "I would. I would love to. I'd get up at four in the morning. I'm only, like, five blocks from the school."

The judge looked over at Ebony. "You can tell he's all embarrassed," she said gamely. "He doesn't want you to come."

"That's a'ight," Tina said, laughing. "I'll just get to talking about the stories how I breast-fed him. He be all right."

Soon after the round began, it became clear that the Schlagle team was ill prepared. They didn't even know their own case, and they withered under cross-examination.

"Could you please tell us what your plan does?" Ebony asked.

"Well," one of the Schlagle kids replied, scratching the back of his neck, "basically what the plan does is it, it helps, uh, everybody that, um, you know, has a mental disorder? And also helps, you know, uh, children and, you know—"

"What's stopping your plan from passing right now?" Ebony cut him off.

"Because the law states that . . . ," his voice trailed off.

Ebony's spirits lifted. Between speeches he bobbed his head to the imaginary sound of some driving hip-hop song. During his final speech he lightly tapped a beat on the makeshift podium as he rattled off the reasons to vote down the plan. His voice was soft, slightly high-pitched, as if he were singing along to R. Kelly. He kept looking up at me—not his mother—to see if I was paying attention, if I was grasping how on top of his game he was.

"They are not going to help the whole population," he declared, pointing toward the Schlagle guys as he drove his speech to its climax. "They do not go outside and say, 'Hey, more free public health insurance.' No. They only give it to the people who work, and this does not serve for everybody."

"This is so ironic," Tina whispered to me. "Because I was turned down for mental health care."

EBONY AND ANTOINE packed up their files, and Tina followed them down to one of Paseo's auditoriums. Ebony took a seat high on a chair back, so he could see all and be seen by all. He paid no attention as his mom settled into the row behind him. After a minute or so, he strolled down the aisle and squeezed himself in between rows of girls who sat along the edge of the stage, kicking their legs. He hunched his shoulders, looking shy and not saying much, but happy nonetheless to have such a prime seat.

His mother followed him down, handed her camera to one of the girls, and wrapped her arm around his neck. I cringed. All afternoon he had seemed leery of Tina's presence. The last thing he would want, I assumed, was for his mom to jump in the middle just as he was about to mack on some girls. But then, just before the flashbulb went off, Ebony briefly laid his head on her shoulder. She stayed beside him, and they chatted for a minute or two. Then Tina headed back up the aisle.

"I'm so excited," she told me. "I'm going to bake for him. I used to bake for him all the time." She told me she planned to go to their next tournament, scheduled for the following weekend. She offered to bring a treat, and when she asked what he would like her to make, he said strawberry cake.

The tournament's director took the stage and started handing out trophies. She read through the names of the top twenty speakers, raising hoots and hollers from the crowd as the winners came down to claim their prizes. Sitting beside me, Ebony leaned forward as the emcee moved up the rankings. He balled his fist when she paused dramatically before announcing the top speaker—from Southeast High.

Ebony sank back in his seat. Again he would come home from a UDL tournament with nothing.

It was a bad day for Central. They finished fourth in the sweepstakes category, which calculates the total score of all debaters on the squad. For only the third time in the program's history, the traveling trophy would go into another school's trophy case—Paseo's.

Ebony squeezed into the crowd heading for the buses parked outside the school without saying goodbye to his mom. He snatched the judges' ballots out of a teammate's hand and took a seat near the back of the bus.

"Oh, my God, Joe," he said to me after he'd read the scorecard for his second round, which, to his and my amazement, he had lost. "That Schlagle dude didn't even have a case! That motherfucker dropped four off case and they got a *26*! Aw, fuck! He got up there and read parity evidence through the whole thing. I read . . ." He shook his head and stared out the window at the car lights passing by in the rainy night.

The judge had a bad reputation among debaters of being old-school. She often scored against kids for petty infractions, such as looking at opponents during cross-x or showboating, neither of which Ebony could refrain from during what he and I both thought was a lopsided round.

Back in room 109, Brandon razzed the young squad. "You all lost to *Paseo*?!" he said, half-feigning incredulity. "Man, when I was a novice, Central *never* lost."

Ebony climbed up on a desk and lowered his head, the way he had earlier that afternoon when he wasn't sure if Antoine would show up. He'd been cold to his mother all evening. Still, he'd wanted to stride up on that stage and show her that despite the tattered childhood she had given him, he had become the best in Kansas City.

A few paces away, Rinehart frowned as she read through the tournament score sheets. She folded them up and handed them to me. "We were only a few points away from second place," she said, forcing a slight grin. "That doesn't feel quite as bad."

Then she spotted Ebony sitting there with his chin in his hands. She laid her hand on his back.

"It's gonna be okay," she told him. "There's always another debate round."

"I don't care no more."

TWENTY-ONE

SOUTHERN PRIDE

USUALLY, JANE RINEHART didn't even try to keep room 109 clean. Tidy rooms were for teachers who didn't teach. How else could one keep one's room neat? There just wasn't time to deal with messes, especially all the stuff she and her debaters amassed during a season. Once, the school's assistant principal came into her room for some reason or another, looked around at the stacks of file boxes, the piles of paper, the handcarts abandoned in the middle of the room, the clothes rack stuffed with wrinkled blazers and shirts, the beat-up, secondhand copy machine, and the cockeyed rows of books on the bookshelves, and said, "What is all this junk?"

Junk?! Rinehart felt like she'd been slapped. What did her assistant principal think this was? A glee club? Her kids were reading Michel Foucault and her boss thought it was *junk*.

Not that it didn't annoy her, too, sometimes, all this disorder. She was constantly on her kids to pick up the scraps they made when they cut cards. "See this?" she'd say, holding up a standard metal wastebasket. "This is a trash can. You put trash in it." Sometimes her kids even got on her about it: *Damn, Rinehart. This place is a sty!* They'd get bored and roam around the room, picking through the layers of detritus.

But on this day Rinehart was making a show of bringing order to the chaos. She moved between the desks with icy precision, bending to pick up curls of cut paper, straightening stacks of things, all with little effect on the overall disorder. She stopped and planted her hands on her hips, elbows out like a flared mane, and glared at Brandon, who was curled over a desk in a nap pose.

"Come on, you guys," she said. "You need to work."

Brandon bolted upright. "What are you upset about?!" he demanded.

She shook her head and resumed her futile assault on the mess.

Brandon stood up and puffed his chest out. "I'm talking to you!" he shouted in a deep, camped-up thug voice.

She slammed a stack of documents down on a desk. "Because you guys are screwing up. You're smart. You're capable. And you're screwing up!"

"What do you mean, screwing up?"

"You know what I mean. You're just sitting around, doing nothing."

It wasn't even two months into the school year, and already she'd dropped Brandon out of AP English, lest he wind up with an F. He'd only done a couple of the assignments, and halfheartedly at that. Marcus was next on the block. One more missed assignment, and she'd boot him, too. Worse, they were doing less than the minimum in debate. She almost regretted their respectable showings at Valley and New Trier. Maybe if they'd really tanked one of them, they'd have been shocked into working harder. By breaking at both tournaments, they saw that they could slack and still walk away with at least something to feel good about. But they could be so much better. She knew those other teams—Highland Park, Glenbrook North, Valley High from West Des Moines—were all working it hard, holding practice rounds every day after school, cutting cards with their legions of college-kid coaches. If Marcus and Brandon had put in half the effort of their suburban counterparts, they would have sewn up their TOC bid a month ago.

MARCUS WAS IN the back of the room, surfing the Web, shopping for parts for his home computer. Brandon pulled up a chair beside him and whispered, "The Southern Bell invite came in."

Marcus looked up, grinning. "Serious?" He rubbed his hands together. "Where? Go get 'em."

Brandon got up and strolled toward Rinehart's desk, saying, "That means we're still in the top seventy-two in the nation." He picked up the package, a big white envelope. "Rinehart, can I open this?"

She snatched it out of his hands and buried it in a pile of unopened letters. "I might have if you guys weren't being such jerks."

"Man, she is trippin'," Brandon said to Marcus. "Watch me. I'm about to jap out on her." He made a show of tearing off his hooded sweatshirt. But she ignored him, so he put it back on and sauntered over to Marcus, who was now sifting through his Hotmail in-box.

"Check this out," he said. "Juicy and Fruity are going to the Glenbrooks."

"Who are Juicy and Fruity?" I asked.

"Two chicks we banged at camp," Brandon said.

"We didn't bang them," Marcus said. "They like fourteen years old."

"R. Kelly," Brandon said, a smile creeping across his face.

"R. Kelly," Marcus echoed. They slapped hands.

"They're from the Meadows," Brandon offered. "Some private school in Las Vegas. It's like $62,000 a year."

"Yeah," Marcus said. "Isn't that bling-bling? 'The Meadows.'" He made quotation marks with his fingers.

His smile disappeared. "Brandon, seriously, go get it."

"I can't. Rinehart be trippin'."

Marcus looked crestfallen.

"I'll try," Brandon said.

He proceeded slowly across the room in a low crouch. He carefully raised his hand over the edge of Rinehart's desk, and just as his fingers lit on the prize, Marcus yelled, "Rinehart, can't I see that thing?"

Brandon stood up and stomped his foot. "You crazy! I'm 'bout to get it."

Rinehart grabbed the invite and set it on a tall file cabinet behind her.

Marcus shot up out of his chair and marched over to her.

"Rinehart, can I see it? *Good Lord!*"

He snagged it off the file cabinet. She swiped it from his hand. They stared each other down for a few seconds.

"Yes," Rinehart said finally. "I'll let you see it. If you just quit bothering me."

She stood there a while longer, holding the envelope behind her back. Marcus's hand was outstretched, his eyes soft, pleading.

"Rinehart, I just want to read it," he said, in the sweetest voice he could muster.

Slowly she presented it to him. He snatched it and ran over to Brandon. "I'm keeping this!"

They hunched over a desk. "Let's open this bling-bling!" Marcus said.

He hooked a finger under the flap, tore the envelope open, and pulled out a folder bearing a red etching of a southern mansion with high columns and lazy magnolia trees surrounding it and a silver inlay border that glimmered under the room's fluorescent lights. Brandon yelped and ripped it out of Marcus's hands and held it up in the light. He hummed the sound of angels singing.

Marcus reached out for the folder. "Seriously. We gonna read it together on the table."

"Don't cry about it."

Brandon set it down and opened it. Inside were info sheets about the nation's most elite debate tournament, hosted by Montgomery Bell Academy in Nashville. Only seventy-two teams were invited to attend. That's teams, not squads—only the top two debaters from each school. Brandon's claim that the invite meant they were among the top seventy-two in the country wasn't exactly true. Only schools that had competed there the previous year were invited to return. Others were put on a waiting list and were invited when other schools declined, so really, any school could go if they were patient. But still, the invitees were among the nation's best. A trip to Nashville for the benefit of just a pair of students is an extravagant expense, and only directors of the most competitive debate programs agree to pay it.

Marcus pulled out the cover letter, and they read through it.

"Look at this!" Marcus exclaimed. "'Southern hospitality!' You gotta dress up for this!" He tugged at his T-shirt. "Look at this dinner! Hors d'oeuvres! They don't have housing! You get to stay at the hotel! They set up a room with a bar! Snacks! PlayStation! We be just kickin' it! Stayin' up to midnight! Bling-blingin'!" He was jumping up and down, flailing his arms.

Brandon was beaming. He looked at Marcus. "I'm proud to go to this," he said. "Thanks to Marcus." He wrapped an arm around his partner's shoulder.

"We wouldn't have been able to go," Marcus said, ignorant of the facts, "if we didn't bling-bling at New Trier."

TWENTY-TWO

TRICKLE DOWN

WHEN THE CREW took a pit stop in Cameron, Missouri, en route to Cedar Rapids for the annual Iowa Caucus, Marcus bought three twenty-ounce cans of citrus-flavored 180 energy drink and, as we cruised across the rainy prairie, proceeded to fortify his hyper soul with this sugary gruel spiked with "guarana—a dried paste made from seeds of climbing evergreen shrubs native to the Amazon" that provide a "natural form of caffeine."

"Look at this," Marcus said, squinting at the label. "It's got guarana. This stuff called taurine. Orange flavor. Chemicals. Chemicals. Chemicals."

He chugged it like a factory worker swilling beer, leaned forward in his seat, and held forth about the problems in this here world. Rinehart had made the mistake of saying something about his poor work ethic, and it set him off.

"I don't see why I gotta earn my slave wages," he snapped. "I already gave you so much."

"What are you talking about?" Rinehart asked, her face crumpled. "You're not a slave."

"Well, you're white."

"I didn't own slaves."

"You benefited from it, though. You benefited from it."

"How?"

"You know how there's those white-only signs? In your lifetime. Those are jobs that we coulda had."

Rinehart shook her head.

"Yes. Yes. Yes," Marcus insisted.

"They weren't jobs," Rinehart tried to explain. "I don't know where you get the—"

"No, no, no!" He cut her off. "There's no competition for you, Ms. Rinehart. There wasn't competition for you. It's a *ivory road*. For us there was *competition*. I went up to a water fountain, I saw '*colored*.'"

"That's why I was the only female on my debate team," Rinehart retorted. DiAnna, Day, and Dionne all hooted in approval of the counterargument; Day and Dionne slapped five.

"And sexism was a problem, too." Marcus barreled on after gulping some of his 180. "But white women were the worst, though. They were the worst racists."

"*White women?*"

"Yeah. *White women.* They were the ultimate racists, Ms. Rinehart. They, they're like: 'Well, I have to cook dinner.' It sucks for them because they just looked at black people and worried about their dinner cooking over that. There's no 'Let's include their revolution with ours.' It was like: 'You shut up! I gotta get my rights first!'"

The girls were now laughing so hard they were falling all over each other. I chuckled, too, though I couldn't help but notice the irony. Central's debate squad was quite patriarchal. The lineup for the tournament we were heading to had a definite hierarchy, with the males occupying the top positions of privilege and prowess and the females pushed to the bottom. The boys ran the show and claimed first dibs on the perks, be it a choice seat in the van or control of the music selection or veto power over which restaurant the squad would eat in. The girls never protested, though. They seemed to accept the unfair division of power between the sexes as the natural order of things.

"What about the argument that the only thing the civil rights movement did was get black women out of white women's kitchens?" Rinehart asked.

Marcus paused for a second, lifted the skinny orange and silver can to his lip, and gulped hard.

"I don't even think it did that," he said, wiping off his mouth. "You know what it did? It tried to shut 'em up is all it did. We had all these beautiful, we have all these beautiful marches and revolts and all these gains."

"Right." Rinehart was nodding now.

"And then." Another chug. "And then it was shut us up. That's what the women's right to vote did." Big swig. He wiped his mouth with his shirt-sleeve. "You know I still don't have my rights."

"You got your right to vote," Rinehart said, mocking sternness. "Now go home and shut up."

"That's a gift!" Sobek piped in from the front passenger seat.

"Exactly," Marcus said. "It's like: 'Here's what you get, now go home and shut up.' It stops movements."

"The government co-opted the movement," Sobek said. "Shuts you all up. Puts you back in your place."

"They say it's crazy whining," Marcus went on. "They say, 'Quit whining and get a job.' And they don't realize that it trickles down. Trickle down. Trickle down. Trickle down." To these last words he added a bit of funky rhythm and shook a bent hand like a jokester rapper, which made everyone in the van howl with laughter.

"I didn't choose to live in poverty," he said, still in a funny voice, but with a note of real rage creeping in around the edges. "Poverty chose *my ass.*" He leaned forward. "Look, this is how recent slavery was, Ms. Rinehart." His voice was suddenly as steady and serious as it would be in a debate round. "My mother couldn't. She was a victim of slavery." Then funky voice again: "The trickle down."

"Your *mom*?" Rinehart asked, genuine shock in her voice. "Come on. She's not that old."

"See, you can, you can, you can mock slavery, but I say she was a victim of the trickle down," Marcus said, his voice serious again. "The slavery and its mind-set in business was still going on. Like, she couldn't get a fair job. That affects me. I can't get a fair job, hell, these days."

"Maybe you should go to Stanford and Sons Comedy Club and just spout off about some of this stuff," Rinehart said.

"I'm serious," Marcus protested, turning to the others for support. "She's telling me to shut up. That's racist."

"*I'm* serious," Rinehart replied. "You'd be a riot."

Marcus tilted the shiny can and downed the last of his hyper brew. If caffeine weren't making his blood race, kicking his brain into scrambling overdrive, he might have launched a poignant lecture about how the legacy of slavery had been passed down through his family tree. His mom, Evaline Lumpkin, was born in the Mississippi Delta, in a tiny town called Rome, just outside Clarksville. Starting when she was five years old, she worked twelve hours a day in cotton fields with her parents and siblings: from six in the morning until six in the evening, in the relentless sun, with a straw hat on and just an hour for lunch, and all she'd wind up contributing to her family at the end of the day was a measly $2.50. They worked Saturdays, too. Her great-grandparents had tended the same land as slaves: the Flowers Plantation, just off the highway heading to Glendale. Though free, Evaline and her relatives didn't earn much more than their ancestors, and they paid rent for the same one-room houses that had been provided less than a century earlier to those in bondage.

Evaline's first child had arrived shortly after she graduated from high school. She'd go on to bear another eight, Marcus being the second youngest. In her early twenties she moved to Kansas City, where the work was more plentiful, though, with her high school education, it didn't pay very much, and she had a lot of mouths to feed. Her first marriage fell apart, so she was doing it all on her own. Marcus's father, a white man who worked as a painter at the Kansas City housing project where the family lived, could offer little help. The relationship was pleasant but short. Gale Leach contracted brain cancer right around the time Marcus was born, which left him mentally disabled and unable to work. So Lumpkin turned her apartment into a nursery, taking in neighbors' kids for money to subsidize time spent with her own. When Marcus and his younger brother, Jason, were old enough to go to government-subsidized preschool, she got a job sewing upholstery, which paid a little better and didn't have as many liabilities.

Though money was tight, she tried to provide a stable home. She finally met a man who was kind and responsible, Glen Mitchem, who worked as a security guard at the tallest tower downtown. Marcus grew up considering Glen his father. When Glen first started coming around, he drove a black

Mustang, which Marcus thought was cool as could be. Glen tried to impart some fatherly wisdom to Marcus, but when I pressed Marcus for details, he couldn't remember much about it. He told me they were out fishing once and young Marcus had loaded his hook with a mass of wiggly worms, thinking, *Motherfuckers gonna eat this!* And Glen had stopped him and said, "If you're aiming for one fish, he's always gonna eat the one bait." And this message of moderation stuck with him, though in a twisted way: *Give only what is required*, his unspoken motto for school.

The van sailed along I-35, nearing the Iowa border, and Marcus quieted down, as if the 180 had metabolized in his system and brought a calming effect, like Ritalin.

"Sure," he muttered. "I have affirmative action and things to appease me, but, hell, it's still not a fifty-fifty split."

He looked out the window, which had fogged at the edges from his rant and the attendant laughter. With his finger he wrote "DEBATE 4 LIFE" in the condensation, and the words slowly faded with the steam of breath as drops of rain streaked in the wind on the other side of the glass.

RINEHART PULLED the van to a stop outside an entrance to Valley West Mall in West Des Moines. "Okay, I'm gonna go get some gas," she said as her debaters slid open the side door and started filing out. "Is forty-five minutes enough time for you to go say hello to your security guard friend?"

"If you see me come out in handcuffs," Leo replied, "you'll know why."

Marcus, Brandon, and Sobek headed straight for the Sam Goody store. Sobek wanted to buy a copy of *The Eminem Show* with all the cuss words censored out. On the ride up, they'd gotten into another big fight with Rinehart over the music, and they had to endure long stretches with nothing but whistling wind and Marcus's yammering. Marcus's eyes widened with genuine surprise when they walked into the store: a black man was working the counter.

"Man, I didn't think they even allowed black folks in here," Marcus said immediately to his new comrade. "Last time we was here, we almost got sent to jail just for runnin'."

"Yeah," the guy agreed. "I believe it. One time I came here at five in the morning just to open the place up for inventory, and a security guard came up and said, 'What are you doing?' I'm like: 'What do you think I'm doing?' I, like, had my shirt on and everything"—referring to the knit shirt with "Sam Goody" embroidered on it, which he was wearing as he talked to Marcus.

Marcus, Brandon, Sobek, and I went down to the main level and sauntered up to a jewelry kiosk in the middle of the concourse.

"Yo!" Marcus said to the woman working the counter. "You got any bling-bling?! I need some bling!" He stood with his head and shoulders cocked back, his hands splayed out chest high, like he was posing for the cover of a CD.

"You want some bling-bling?" the clerk replied, raising a brow knowingly. She appeared to be in her early twenties, with long, curly blond hair. "Well, we're *all about* bling-bling. Let's see."

She knelt and fished around below the counter, then stood to present a necklace with a rhinestone-encrusted dollar sign as big as a chocolate chip cookie.

Marcus was taken aback, both by the medallion's ostentatiousness and by the realization that this little piece of black slang had made it all the way to suburban Iowa, where even white girls could hear it and know what it means.

"A'ight! A'ight!" he said, nodding. "That's blingin'!"

She held it out to him, and he jumped back. "I don't want to touch it!"

"Why not?" she asked.

"Because I'm black. I'll get arrested." He took a tentative step forward. "Now, how much is it gonna cost me to be bling-blingin' with this?"

She turned it over and read the tag. A hundred and forty dollars.

"What about those minority achievement grants?" he said without skipping a beat. "So I can be, like, bling-bling. You got any financial assistance?"

She lowered her smile into a mock frown. "We're not a college," she said.

"Man, I can't bling-bling it," Marcus complained. "Man, I look poor."

And so he continued for the rest of the mall break, drifting from store to store, running his bling-bling game on every poor white worker he came across. By the fourth store, Brandon had become visibly peeved. "Man," he said to me, "he actin' such a fool."

"Who you callin' fool?" Marcus demanded, bumping Brandon with a puffed-out chest. "I'm just tryin' to get me some *bling-bling*. I gotta *get* what's *comin'* to me, *nigga*. Shit, that's four hundred years of oppression. Muthafucka *owe* me."

TWENTY-THREE

SPECIFIC INTELLECTUALS

IT WAS ALMOST TEN at night when we stopped at a Super 8 Motel off I-80, a little less than an hour west of Cedar Rapids. Marcus, Brandon, Leo, and Sobek shared a room, paired off on two queen-size beds. Leo promptly stripped to a wife-beater undershirt and boxers. When he wasn't debating, he played safety for the football team, and in the spring he was a sprinter for the track team, so his body was cut with handsome muscles. He and Marcus got to work cutting cards, Leo on one of the beds, Marcus kneeling at the small table provided for motel guests. Brandon stretched out on the other bed, working the buttons on his cell phone. The TV was turned on to CNN, where the top story was about the arrest of two black men accused of terrorizing the Washington, D.C., area with random sniper attacks.

Sobek sat in an armchair, dictating a card to Marcus. It related to a selection from the Clemson philosophy professor Todd May's 1993 book, *Between Genealogy and Epistemology: Psychology, Politics, and Knowledge in the Thought of Michel Foucault*. Sobek had pulled it out of UMKC's massive debate files before the New Trier tournament to fend off Foucault attacks. Marcus and Brandon had used it against Evanston, though not very well, because they lost and missed their TOC bid by inches. The card would ultimately become a cornerstone of Central's debate program for years to come as the squad—in large part owing to my urging—shifted its focus to confront the racial shortcomings of the debate community. In the book May pointed out that Foucault "sought to define a new form of intellectual work that would address particular strategies of oppression" and that the French philosopher shunned "'the indignity of speaking for others.' When it came to strategies for action, he preferred to listen to the oppressed rather than act as a standard-bearer for their 'liberation.'" People who do this become "specific intellectuals" who, "rather than standing above or outside their society," are "immersed within it. They cite, analyze, and engage in struggles not in the name of the oppressed, but alongside them, in solidarity with them."

At the end of the New Trier debate against Evanston, during their post-round critique, the judges told Marcus and Brandon that if they had carried this argument all the way through, they would have won their precious bid, because it was so damning. It was like the perfect race card, a hard-evidence basis for Marcus's theory that they couldn't lose by running a case against racism. Used correctly, it said, *We're black. We're the oppressed. You need to listen to us, to stand alongside us in our move to overthrow The Man.*

Now, in this motel room, on the eve of their third national-circuit tournament of the year, Marcus and Sobek were working on sharpening the point, paraphrasing it in an end-round card that would really drive the argument home.

"Don't dictate the revolution," Sobek said to Marcus slowly. He was stretched out on the bed, hands laced together behind his head, like the king of the boys' club.

"Okay," Marcus said, looking up for more.

"Your job as intellectuals," Sobek continued, "is not to dictate the movement from above but to stand alongside the people and their struggle. This means the counterplan will only work to perpetuate the institutional racism that exists in the status quo."

Marcus set down his pen and rubbed his hands together. "Don't dictate the revolution!" he crowed.

Then his face drained of energy. "I think I'm ready for bed," he said softly.

He glanced at Sobek, who was on the bed by the window—the prime spot, Marcus thought. "I'll arm wrestle you for that bed," he said.

Sobek smiled slyly and turned on his stomach, elbow against the mattress, fist raised.

"On the table, nigga!" Marcus said. "Not the bed."

"Look at him," Sobek said to the rest of us. "He's punkin' out!"

Marcus sighed, knelt at the edge of the bed, and clasped Sobek's hand. Sobek beat him in seconds.

Marcus bolted to his feet. "You cheated, nigga!" he said. "I'm about to wrestle you for this muthafuckin' bed!"

Sobek stretched out and clasped his hands behind his head. "Bring it on," he said confidently.

Marcus jumped on the bed and did his "Church's fried chicken and a biscuit" routine, his arms flailing spastically. Sobek didn't even flinch.

THE IOWA CAUCUS started out like the previous two national tournaments. Against a field of seventy-two schools from as far away as Lexington, Massachusetts, and Nashville, Tennessee, Marcus and Brandon went four-two, dropping an early round on what they thought was a bad decision and a later round against a more formidable foe. But by the time they filed into the auditorium at Cedar Rapids's Washington High for the awards ceremony on Saturday night, they were feeling confident. With their record, they were sure they'd break to the trophy rounds. A TOC bid would be harder to get here: they'd have to make it to semifinals, and to do that, they'd have to win twice.

But they were feeling a spark. Brandon especially. After screwing up on topicality a second time, he kicked into a higher gear rather than kicking himself. All the hours he'd spent at debate camp had locked a wealth of debate knowledge and skill into his brain matter, and he had finally figured out how to get at it. Unlike his outings at Valley and New Trier, he didn't have to lean so heavily on Marcus during cross-x. And Marcus didn't have to interrupt Brandon's speeches to remind him of the arguments he had to cover. He felt like a basketball player in the zone, when the basket is the size of a Dumpster. The words and ideas flowed from him with ease, as if speaking so fast were as natural as drinking water. And in the final prelim round, he could do no wrong. After that matchup, the judge gave him and Marcus both 29.5 speaker points—just shy of the highest possible score. The judge was apparently so moved that she abandoned decorum and praised it in orgasmic terms. "It was so good," she gushed, "I creamed my panties." The high from that comment alone could carry the two horny teens through at least one out-round win.

Out in the hall, as it was getting dark outside, Brandon spotted Andrew Berg, the kid from Fargo who had beaten them at Valley when Brandon dropped T. They gave each other five. "How'd you guys do?" Berg asked.

"Four-two. You?"

"Five-one," Berg said. "Cool, we'll probably both break."

"Yeah, then we'll probably hit you in out rounds. That would suck."

Berg smiled, trying to shuck off the compliment. "It's just fun, though. Isn't it? I mean, it's competitive, too. But it's supposed to be about fun."

"Yeah. I guess you're right."

Marcus strode up to them, rubbing his cheek. "I can't talk," he said. "My tooth hurts like a motherfucker." All through the weekend, a sharp pain had been building in his deepest molars.

They moved into the auditorium, where the rest of the Central squad sat near the back, off to the right. Marcus and Brandon were the only team that had done well. Marcus sat quietly, cringing as he rubbed his face. A bearded man, the tournament's director, took his place at the podium, faded velvet curtains dangling behind him. The man made a note of his grandmother's ninetieth birthday, which was that day, and the crowd clapped appropriately. Then he began reading off the speaker award winners. Starting at fifteen, he rattled off a list of familiar schools, the heavy hitters of the national circuit: Dowling, Montgomery Bell Academy, Lexington, Blake of Minneapolis, Valley High. As the numbers got smaller, ticking off toward number one, Rinehart shifted in her seat and began gazing around, figuring neither Brandon nor Marcus would be claiming an award. Brandon hadn't won one all season, and Marcus had only scored the eighteenth-place prize at Valley.

Then the man said, "Second place, from Kansas City Central, Marcus Leach," and she perked up, let out a little yelp, and started clapping wildly. Marcus stopped rubbing his cheek and strolled down to the stage, his head lowered shyly. He smiled broadly as he returned to his seat, giving his commemorative gavel to Rinehart to admire. He later told me he wasn't surprised by his high finish. Throughout the tournament, judges told him they'd given him high speaker points. And the creamed-panties comment seemed to confirm it.

ON THEIR WAY out of the auditorium, they were handed schedules for the octofinal round, where sixteen teams would go head-to-head in do-or-die rounds. Rinehart peeked over Brandon's shoulder at the list and saw that they were matched up against Dowling. "This is like a repeat of last year," she said warily.

At the previous Iowa Caucus, Marcus and Donnell hit Dowling in the first trophy round. They won it, and afterward one of the Dowling debaters laid into the judges for nearly a half hour, lambasting them for what he thought was a bad decision. That particular debater had graduated, but his then-partner, Mike Krantz, was anchoring the team Central was about to meet. One of the circuit's top debaters, he'd finished third among the speakers at this year's affair, just a half point behind Marcus.

Krantz was already at their assigned room with his partner, a younger fellow whom he didn't usually debate with; his regular partner was unable to make it that weekend. Krantz wore a dark gray shirt with a silver tie, but his chin was covered in several days' worth of stubble, and a tattered ball cap sat on his crown. He greeted Marcus and Brandon warmly; they'd all gotten to know one another pretty well over the previous four years at tournaments and debate camps. But Krantz was from a completely different world. His parents own Adventureland USA, the only amusement park in Iowa, a sprawling complex east of Des Moines with more than a hundred rides, including a roller coaster that they claim is ranked among the nation's top ten. It also boasts a campground and a full-service inn, which, at the time of the Iowa Caucus, was undergoing a $6 million expansion. Marcus once visited Krantz's house and was blown away. It was massive. Marcus was shocked to see his teenage friend's car: a sleek and sporty Mercedes SL500.

Brandon would be speaking first. After the three judges arrived, he moved to the front of the room and hoisted two debate tubs on top of the teacher's desk to make a podium. He spread out an expando folder and laid the cards of their case on it. With a click of his timer, he was off, chopping his hand at the air as he declared, "Brick by brick, stone by stone, the walls of institutional racism can be destroyed."

Krantz got up and casually collected the cards as Brandon finished them, rubbing the back of his neck as he studied the highlighted lines of text. His expression was calm, lips slightly pursed.

Brandon ripped through his pile of cards so quickly that he finished with more than thirty seconds to spare. He looked up at Marcus. "Anything else you want me to read?"

Marcus waved his hand meekly. "No. That's okay."

Krantz stood to Brandon's right, rocking lightly on his fight. "All right, cool," he said. "If your plan perpetuates a racist dichotomy, do you vote affirmative?"

Brandon scrunched his face in an "are you nuts?" look and said, "Well, we'll say that we don't evaluate the consequences because plan has an action that solves racism."

"What if I win that the way you frame your plan promotes racist dichotomy?"

"It doesn't. It ends institutional racism."

Krantz's partner immediately took his place at the front of the room, wasting no prep time. "Um," he said tentatively. "Nine off case."

Marcus guffawed. The judges sighed, shot one another weary glances, and sagged a couple of inches into their seats. "Nine off" meant Dowling would be laying out an ungodly number of arguments, each demanding its own sheet of notepaper, each read at blistering speed.

The kid commenced. He tensed his shoulders and clutched at the makeshift podium as if he were directing all of his muscle strength to his mouth and jaw. His words weren't said so much as buzzed, like a wounded locust flailing against the ground. I could only understand two words—"super volcano"—which apparently was one of the worst impacts of their case because it was the only part the kid found urgent enough to merit eye contact and a forceful jab at the podium.

Marcus and Brandon furiously took notes, Marcus with his tongue sticking out the side of his mouth. They had no trouble deciphering their opponent's formless hum. During cross-x I began to understand what Dowling was getting at. "What's the alternative in the kritik?" Brandon asked, referring to the jargony name for arguments that raise philosophical or ethical concerns about what's being said in the round.

"It's to give a wider instance of racism," Krantz answered for his partner. "I.e., Mexican-Americans, Japanese-Americans, the racist policies that affect those individuals, too." To do so, they would take Marcus and Brandon's plan text, add a few more inclusive words, and amend it into the Constitution. They also threw in a few of your standard topicality arguments, but they would kick out all of these by the end of the debate.

Marcus used several minutes of prep time before the next speech. He had pages spread everywhere, across two tables, on several chairs, on the floor, on a computer desk stuffed into the corner near the door. He frantically looked through all the pages, scratching his head, muttering to himself. Finally he went to the front of the room. "Okay," he said, and the timekeeping judge stopped her watch. He grabbed a Kleenex from a box on top of a file cabinet and bought some time by heartily blowing his nose. "Okay, road map," he started again, meaning a brief outline of where he'd go with his speech.

One of the judges rolled her eyes and laughed. "This is going to take a while."

Then Marcus was hunched over once again in his hyper-speech stance, bent at the knees and waist, his brow crumpled such that a sudden visitor wouldn't be sure if he was concentrating or in pain. Midway through, he slowed his words for a moment and yelled, "Don't let them dictate the revolution!" And he read through the May card he had worked on with Sobek in the motel room two nights before. Krantz started to get up to retrieve it, but thought better of it and sent his younger partner instead.

WHILE KRANTZ DELIVERED the final negative speech, Marcus had the distinct feeling he was going to lose. There had been so many arguments that had sucked up so much of him and Brandon's time that he feared their speeches were full of holes. Plus, Krantz had confidence. Unlike his partner's, Krantz's words came out smoothly and forcefully, despite their incredible speed.

"What they concede in the 1AR is that they only perpetuate racism against other cultures," Krantz declared. "Focusing on white racism against blacks excludes and legitimizes racism against other people of color. Only our broader scope of rethinking—i.e., our criticism—is the only way we're actually gonna be able to solve society's racism."

Near the end of his speech he looked up from his cards and addressed the judges directly. "Their revolution is racist because it perpetuates an otherization of other people which is always going to be a reason you reject them. That perpetuates worse racism post-plan, which is a reason you vote negative. We solve all their case *and* solve the revolution."

Marcus's feeling of impending doom only worsened after Krantz concluded his speech, solidly tying up all of Dowling's loose ends. Worse, Marcus had less than a minute to prepare his response. He quickly gathered up sheets of evidence, arranging them in a pile he hoped to coherently follow. Brandon sat at the desk, scribbling out a card. He finished, dropped his pen, and held it out to Marcus. Marcus regarded him with a look of sudden shock, as if he'd been snatched out of a dream. "All right," he said. "Cool. Cool. Just let me think." He rubbed his temples, sifted through a few more documents. Then he saw the May card, stuffed it in the pile, and moved to the front just as the buzzer sounded.

With time running out, he finally uncovered the May card and started riffing on it. "Our argument is pretty sweet," he said. "It tells you, 'Don't let them dictate our revolution.' Because we're telling you that as a minority group, the group of oppression, we're calling for change in the legislation. Your job as intellectuals is not to dictate the revolution or allow them to dictate it, but instead you should stand alongside the people in our struggle. They can't stand alongside us, because they dictate the way we should do it. Instead of, like, rejecting racism, they say we should reject plan and make it wider, which means that their only alternative will only perpetuate racism in the status quo. They're just silencing our voices."

The buzzer sounded, the debaters shook hands, and a long wait commenced.

All the judges asked for various pieces of evidence, and they spent what seemed like an hour poring over them.

The debaters moved out into the hall. Marcus slapped Krantz's chest with the back of his hand. "*Nine off*, Mike?"

"I gotta do something," Krantz said with a shrug. "How else am I supposed to argue against racism?"

They all went back into the room. Paper was strewn everywhere. The judges hunched over their notes, trying to figure it all out. Rinehart sat cross-legged in the back, book opened on her lap, trying to act as if she didn't care. If they won, they'd be one step away from a TOC bid. She could stay another night at the sumptuous Five Seasons in downtown Cedar Rapids, where the remaining trophy rounds would be held in the morning. If they lost, she'd be driving all night.

The debaters had the room cleaned up before one of the judges finally shifted in her seat and said, "Okay, everybody, we have a winner."

The room quieted, and all eyes were on her.

She looked through the three ballots one more time, as if she could somehow miscount such a small tally.

"The decision is a two-one," she said, "for the affirmative, Kansas City Central."

WE DROVE WEST on one of Cedar Rapids's main thoroughfares, looking for food, but every restaurant we passed was closed. It was nearly midnight. Everyone was ecstatic, especially Marcus.

"Who bling-blinged that final speech with just a minute of prep?" he shouted.

"Marcus!" the girls replied, charged by his enthusiasm and settling for the role of cheerleaders for the celebrated boys on the squad.

"Who bling-blinged that speech with a minute of prep and a sore tooth that felt like a broken mouth?"

"Marcus!"

He sat back and rubbed his cheek.

"Man, I thought we were gonna lose that round," he said. "Then I remembered the May evidence, and I was like, 'Nigga, you white! You can't dictate the revolution!'"

TWENTY-FOUR

RUN FOR THE TOC, TAKE 3

THE NEXT MORNING Rinehart sat in the lobby bar of the Five Seasons, sipping a cup of coffee. Marcus came in and took a seat at the table with her. He wore a blue sweater Rinehart had bought for him when they stopped at a factory outlet center off I-80 on their way to Cedar Rapids. He looked like he was dressed up for Christmas Eve or for church. His eyes were puffy, barely open. He gently stroked his cheek and jaw. "Man," he said, "my tooth is killing me."

"You want some orange juice?" Rinehart asked.

"I want some painkillers."

Rinehart dug through her purse and pulled out a bottle of Tylenol. She handed him two. He held them in his palm and glanced around the room for something to wash them down with.

"Get some orange juice," Rinehart said.

"I don't want orange juice."

Their exchange was quiet, tender, like that of a mother and son. Rinehart once told me that if she'd ever had a son, she would have prayed for him to be like Marcus. He's fun and funny, and when he gets excited about something, it's hard not to get caught up in his enthusiasm. He challenges authority, the way she would want a son to. He walks the edge, and though she'd like to strangle him sometimes, he's never boring. For her, the challenging kids are always easiest to be proud of, because they're the ones willing to take risks. And risks, it seems to her, bring the sweetest success.

In all her years of coaching, she'd never had a debater as brilliant as Marcus. On several occasions, she told me she thought that he had the mind of a great general. Even in the beginning, when he first started coming around room 109 as a freshman, he approached the game differently from his peers. While they fretted about the procedures, what to say and how to stand, his mind was busy sorting through the arguments, tracing their threads of logic until he got a big-picture understanding of them. He worked so hard those early years, staying after school every day to cut cards and run dozens of practice rounds. After he'd been on the team for a while, Rinehart learned that he was a master chess player, playing weekly with a club that met at a burger joint in Westport, Kansas City's main entertainment district. Among the club's members was the city auditor, whose job it was to study the complex mechanics of the local government and offer strategies to make it better. That a teen like Marcus could hold his own intellectually with a man like that only made Rinehart prouder.

Rinehart never wanted kids, didn't have any of her own, though she wound up with a daughter of sorts shortly after she took her job at Central. The girl's name was Shauntell Norton, one of Rinehart's early debate recruits. Shauntell was living at her great-aunt's house. But when her aunt was approved for Section 8 housing through the U.S. Department of Housing and Urban Development, they made it clear to the family that Shauntell could not continue living with them because of restrictions on the number of residents in such homes. Shauntell came to school in tears, worried that she'd be homeless or that she'd be forced to move to Topeka to live with her grandma. The latter would mean losing a lot of the credits she'd built up in school, and she wouldn't be able to graduate early as she had hoped. Rinehart told her not to worry about it. At first Shauntell stayed at Rinehart's place on weekends, so she could have an early-morning ride for tournaments. Then, when the HUD vouchers came through, Rinehart and her husband, Richard, decided to let her move in with them.

It wasn't a hassle in the least. Shauntell was a quiet kid who spent most of her time in her room doing homework. Shortly after she moved in, her estranged father tried to get involved in her life, but Shauntell wanted no part of it. After a few heated encounters, Rinehart asked Richard to intervene. In a phone conversation he told Shauntell's dad she didn't want to see him. The man threatened to sue. "Go for it," Richard said.

Shauntell went on to graduate early and attend Dillard University, a historically black school in New Orleans. She was set to graduate with a degree in accounting at the end of the 2002–2003 school year. Rinehart planned to attend the ceremony. Every summer during college Shauntell had returned to Kansas City to live with Rinehart and work at Kmart.

Rinehart didn't regret taking Shauntell in. She would probably do it again. Every year there was at least one student at Central who wound up with no place to stay, often because of the red tape of federal programs. "It's really hard," Rinehart once said to me. "I don't understand in a country that is as wealthy as this is—I've traveled abroad, I know, I see the wealth. What we do with our children is just terrible. There's no reason for children to come to school hungry in this country, but they do. And there's no reason for children to leave school hungry, but they do. It's just not right."

THE QUARTERFINAL ROUNDS were held in several of the hotel's conference rooms, each decorated with plush burgundy, green, and gold carpeting. The hotel staff had set up two long tables at one end of the room where Marcus and Brandon would be competing, each draped with forest green linen tablecloths. They'd also set out pitchers of ice water and glasses and arranged an audience section with conference chairs facing the tables where the debaters would compete. The whole setup seemed to raise the stakes a little, as if this were an actual policy confab where matters of life and death might be decided.

Central was matched against Rosemount High, a school from the suburbs of Minneapolis. Rosemount was the top seed, having gone undefeated during the prelim rounds. Marcus and Sobek had worked the lobby crowd before the round, and most of the other debaters they spoke with had downplayed Rosemount's success, saying they'd been lucky. It was hard for me to gauge if this was true or just sour grapes. After all, Rosemount *had* gone six-oh. One kid from Minneapolis's Blake School told Marcus that Rosemount was weak on critical arguments. "They don't understand how to debate kritiks," the kid had said. "Their strategy is: 'We want to be policy debaters. We debate policy.'"

So Marcus and Sobek quickly devised a plan. They'd run their wildest kritik, known among debaters as the K, based on the writings of the philosopher Slavoj Žižek. It was a gamble. Central's strength was politics. They'd only run one kritik all season, albeit with great success. At New Trier they'd pulled out the Žižek file against a team from Cedar Rapids and driven their opponents to tears. After the round Marcus admitted they'd never run the case before. Hearing this, one of the Iowa debaters rubbed her red eyes and said, "Oh, my God! That hurts!" Still, this was a national-circuit quarterfinals against a top seed, a whole other level entirely. To make matters worse, one of the judges for the round would be the kid from Dowling who had been upset a year earlier when Central beat them. Rinehart worried the guy might still hold a grudge and be looking for revenge.

Marcus wanted to blindside Rosemount with the Žižek stuff, so as they sat at one of the tables in the front of the room, with the Rosemount pair working just a few steps away, they made like they were going to run a standard political attack. In a voice loud enough for all to hear, Marcus asked Sobek to help him write speeches on political capital and peace in the Middle East. Then Brandon came in. Marcus whispered in his ear, and he quickly joined in the game of deception. As they prepared, Rinehart stood in the back of the room and raised a small camera to her eye. Marcus looked up at the flash and shot her an annoyed look.

By and by, the three judges filed in, and Rosemount's first speaker, Josh Oie, took his place at the center table. He was blond, with bushy sideburns running the length of his puffy cheeks. He belted out a souped-up version of the parity case that Central's novices had run at their first two DEBATE–Kansas City tournaments. Few teams on the national circuit ran the case, because it was believed to be too simple, too susceptible to topicality attacks. But this team had gotten a lot of mileage out of it. They had packed their 1AC with lots of cards to preempt the T, and impact cards warning of several doomsday scenarios, from nuclear war to genocide.

Remaining seated, Marcus began cross-x by asking, "Why should the judges vote for you after this round?"

"Well, because we win," Josh replied snidely. "Parity is the best option."

"So wait. Why is your case important?"

"Are you going for a K link?" Josh asked, meaning kritik. "Politics link? What are you going for here, man?"

"I'm asking you questions," Marcus said, smiling at the judges. "Is that such a problem?" He paused. "Yeah, it's politics."

"Yeah, that's what I thought," Josh said honestly.

THE ROSEMOUNT DEBATERS looked up aghast when Brandon started tearing through the Žižek material, going off at more than three hundred words a minute about how Rosemount's case was essentially "obscene pornography," that the young Minnesotans on the other side of the room had appropriated the suffering of real people, people with mental illnesses, for the sole purpose of winning a high school debate round. Brandon argued that his opponents had no power to effect policy change in the real world. When the round ended, there'd be no new legislation on Capitol Hill. All that would remain is the shared experience of those who had witnessed the round. Debate is an intellectual exercise, Brandon insisted. It's powerful only inasmuch as it can inform and enlighten. But the way Rosemount was going about it, he said, was harmful. If mentally ill people were sitting in the room watching, they would be deeply offended because their real trauma had been stolen and cheapened for the sake of a petty trophy. A better alternative, Brandon explained, would be to discuss the issue of mental illness using fictional characters, so as not to reduce real human beings to mere pawns in a game.

The Rosemount debaters furrowed their brows and furiously scribbled notes. Every so often they looked up and leered at Brandon, shook their heads, and resumed their note taking. Brandon got through his stack of evidence with forty-five seconds to spare. Marcus handed him a few more cards to read. The timer sounded, and Josh rose, pushing the sleeves of his wool sweater up over his elbows.

"What's the link?" he asked, meaning: *How does our case relate in any way to all this crap you've spewed?*

"The link is you use, like, the 1AC for your own personal enjoyment," Brandon replied.

"Our argument is," Marcus chimed in, "the way you outline your harms to dictate a solution, instead of just saying we need a solution, you go through obscene pornography, like, of suicide and things like people."

"So what would be a solution?"

"A solution?" Marcus asked.

"Yeah."

"You can base it on fictitious characters," Marcus answered in a calm voice, as if it were obvious. "You can't harm a fictitious character."

"What is a fictitious character?"

"Call it Superman if you like to."

"Okay, wait, wait, wait," Josh interrupted, waving a hand in the air. "So your alternative is that saying 'Superman has a mental illness' is a lot better than saying *real people* are committing suicide?" He asked this question slowly, as if dealing with someone deranged.

"You can't otherize Superman," Marcus said, shrugging.

"That's *it*?"

"Yeah."

"Okay. Thanks," Josh said. "I understand this now." He sucked in a deep breath and widened his eyes as he returned to his seat.

RINEHART SAT BESIDE ME in the audience section. Ordinarily, she stayed away from trophy rounds; she got too nervous. But after the win over Dowling the night before, she felt momentum in her team's favor. A TOC bid was so close she could almost feel the celebration, and she simply couldn't stay away. While Rosemount took prep time, I leaned over and asked what she thought of Marcus and Brandon's case. "We'll see," she said, primly raising her eyebrows. She was leery of these critical arguments; they just seemed so strange to her. As an adult sitting in the audience, she found herself poking all sorts of holes in them.

Right out the gate, Matt Little, Rosemount's second speaker, started calling Central's attack "crazy." He bent at the waist and drove his fist hard against the table as he insisted that they offer a real policy option that helps real people. He spoke very quickly, and the tendons in his neck tensed, stretching his skin. "There's no reason why we shouldn't be helping people," he said. "This is not for your pleasure. It's for your knowledge. I'm sure you don't want to be here on a Sunday morning listening to 'parity.' I'm sure you want to go home." Central's fiction alternative, he added, was "absolutely horrible" because "kritik debates do not apply to policy debate. It's not revolutionary. Don't vote for it just because it's cool."

His strongest argument was that Central offered no real link to their plan. Aside from one card about suicide, he said, the Rosemount case didn't commit the rhetorical atrocities Marcus and Brandon (and Žižek) claimed it did. He also made a strong case for the ineffectiveness of Central's plan, saying, "We address the atrocities with action. They answer with fiction. They don't do anything."

APPARENTLY, MARCUS HEARD SOMETHING in Rosemount's second speech that alarmed him, because he used up several minutes of prep time. He got up to speak, carrying with him a disordered mass of pages. A minute or so into his speech, he stopped cold and began riffling through his documents. He looked frantically to the table where Brandon was sitting, to the podium table, and back again. "I can't find my flow," he said.

Brandon sat up and rooted through the pages in front of him. He glanced down at his timer. "Time is ticking!" he said.

At last, Marcus found the missing page and resumed at breakneck speed. "Rosemount's case is not based on compassion," he said. "It's based on a continuation of otherization."

As he read, he flicked pages off to the side, and Josh retrieved them as they fell, sharing them with his partner.

"Their case is like *Entertainment Weekly* using Kurt Cobain's death to benefit itself," Marcus declared. At this, Brandon looked up and said, "Huh?"

When it was his turn to speak, Brandon was derailed by missing evidence as well. As he fumbled through his pages for the right card, it became clear how inexperienced Central was with this kritik. Brandon stammered through much of the speech, not speaking as clearly and forcefully as he had for the political arguments they ran earlier in the tournament.

AFTER ROSEMOUNT DELIVERED the final speech and the debaters shook hands, the judges asked for evidence from both sides. There was no telling which way they were leaning. And they took a long time deciding, quietly scanning their notes for flaws on both sides, trying to figure out which team had the fewest.

I went out into the hall and bumped into Sobek. We shook hands, after which Sobek rubbed his hand against his cargo pants; my palms were sweaty. Full of nervous energy, I returned to the room. Rinehart sat with her legs propped up on a chair, Michael Moore book open on her lap, her eyes staring at a low spot on the far wall. Leo stepped up to Marcus and asked for some paper. Marcus shook his head quickly, not looking at him, and walked away. He leaned against a wall and locked his eyes on the judges.

Fifteen minutes passed. Applause erupted in the next room—a decision had been made. The Iowa Caucus field of nearly seventy-two teams was narrowing to four, each of which would earn a TOC bid. Brandon stood and crumpled up a few sheets of notepaper into a ball, tossed it toward a trash bin in the corner, and sighed when he missed a basket.

Finally the judges folded up their ballots. The one seated in the center slowly opened them one by one.

Marcus leaned forward in a chair, gnawing on a pen.

Brandon chewed on the rim of a Styrofoam coffee cup.

Rinehart shifted in her seat, recrossed her legs.

"And the decision is . . ." the judge said. He looked through the ballots again. "Let me make sure," he said slowly.

"The decision is," he continued, "a two-one for the negative from KC Central. Congratulations."

Rinehart jumped up from her chair, both fists pumping.

Marcus and Brandon simultaneously exhaled, smiled, patted each other's back. Brandon turned and high-fived Sobek.

Opposite them the Rosemount debaters sat, staring holes in the floor.

THE CELEBRATION DIDN'T LAST LONG. Brandon immediately discovered that they'd be going against Fargo North in the semifinals. Fargo had beaten them at Valley, even though they then had only one debater, Andrew Berg. Now Berg had a partner. Brandon stopped Berg in the hall as he was wheeling his dolly full of evidence into the room.

"I guess we're going up against you again," he said.

"I know," Berg said.

"See, I told you this was gonna happen," Brandon said, smiling and lightly smacking Berg's shoulder with a rolled-up stack of papers. "That sucks."

"At least we both got the TOC bid," Berg said.

"I know. That's sweet."

"Like, that was what was most important to me, getting that bid. Now that I've got it, it kind of ends the motivation."

TOC bids had become so coveted on the national circuit that they actually overshadowed tournament wins. In fact Evanston, the team that beat out Central for a bid at the New Trier tournament, failed to show up for its round the next day. After learning of this incident, the director of the prestigious TOC quickly changed the tournament's entry rules to rescind the bids of any teams that failed to continue competing after bids were earned.

"We've got a long ride home," Berg continued. "And I've got a lot of homework."

"Yeah," Brandon said halfheartedly. "I guess we can relax a little."

"That's right," Berg said, removing his thick sweater to reveal a House of Blues shirt. "Now the sweater comes off."

"Now the pants come off," joked Marcus, who was eavesdropping over Berg's shoulder. He started to undo his belt and they all laughed.

Brandon wandered off, to clear his thoughts. Berg could clown around all he wanted, but Brandon wanted to win. They were so close. Winning the Iowa Caucus would make Central debate history—indeed, Urban Debate League history. No UDL squad had ever won a major national-circuit tournament.

This was it for Brandon, the final lap of a four-year run that had given his teen years pretty much all their meaning. Outside of debate, Brandon didn't do much else. His dreams of sports superstardom had faded in his early teens, and his life away from the squad was a small cycle of comfortable routine: school, take care of Bapa, surf the Web, gab on the phone for hours. In debate, he'd become somebody. He could type his name on an Internet forum, and folks from California to Carolina would know who he was. And it was *so* addictive. He might be tired and cranky and homesick when he arrived at debate tournaments at eight in the morning, but once that round would start, he'd sizzle with energy, so engrossed that time would just disappear. He was most alive in these moments, filled with a sense of purpose, as though he suddenly had access to the American Dream folks would sometimes talk about on TV shows and, more often, commercials. After the victory over Krantz the night before, when we were in the parking lot of T.G.I. Friday's, Brandon had said, "This sucks. This is my last time coming to Caucus."

"I know," Rinehart had replied softly.

"My last time at Valley."

"I know."

"My first and last time at New Trier."

"I know."

"My last time at Shawnee Mission South."

"Thank God."

"I'm serious," Brandon had said. "You know what Donnell said? He said, 'I can't believe high school is over.' He cried like a bitch. I'm not gonna cry."

"I will," Rinehart had replied. "I cry every time."

ALONE IN A FAR END of the hall at the Five Seasons, Brandon closed his eyes and lowered his head. He said a prayer to his mother, Joyce Ferguson, who he believed was looking down on him from heaven. He tried to pray to her every time he debated, but he often forgot, which was dumb, he had to admit, because it seemed as though every time he did pray he won. He knew she would have been proud of his debate accomplishments, and he was sad she couldn't be around to celebrate with him. They had been so close during the first eight years of his life. Every morning she'd come into his room, turn on the light, and say sweetly, "Brandito, you mosquito, get up out the bed." That's the only thing that would rouse him from bed. She could lean over and scream his name in his ear and he wouldn't budge. But her soft words always got him moving.

She worked, so she often communicated with him through notes, which she always signed, "Love ya!" and decorated with a smiley face. They both loved music, and when new songs came on the radio, they'd get up and dance to them in the living room. That might be the thing he missed most about her, discovering new songs. Whenever new R&B artists became all the rage on Hot 103 Jamz, like Destiny's Child or Aaliyah or R. Kelly, he'd wonder what she would think of them, if the new tunes would move her to dance. Sometimes he'd be out around town and he'd swear he'd seen her. There was this woman who frequented the same stores and fast-food joints Brandon did who looked just like his mother. He never talked to her. He'd just stare at her, transfixed and sad.

It all happened so fast, and Brandon still doesn't know what caused his mom's death. In retrospect, though, it was like she expected it. During the last year of her life, she started showing Brandon's older brother, Bryan, who was then only nine years old, how to fend for the family, how to cook and clean, how to wash and iron clothes. Brandon's grandpa later told him his mom always said she was going to die young.

Brandon talked to her on the phone early, on the day it happened. He'd gotten into a fight with Bryan over who would get to talk to her last. Since Bryan was older, he got in trouble and lost the fight. So he had to talk to her first, and Brandon got the last words. Before he hung up, Brandon said, "I love you, I love you, I love you."

"I love you, too," she said.

The next morning a couple of aunties from his mama's side came over all dressed up, but he didn't think anything of it. "Come on," they said, "we're going to your grandma's house."

Cool, Brandon thought. He started jumping up and down because he knew he'd be able to play his cousins' new Sega Genesis game set.

Then he saw his dad come in and run up the steps. Brandon followed him up. He peeked in his grandpa's room and saw Bryan and his younger sister sitting on the bed, crying.

"What's wrong?" he asked. "Why is everybody crying?"

His dad took him into the other room and told him. For reasons Brandon still doesn't know, his mom's heart suddenly gave out on her. She was twenty-seven years old.

SOBEK TOSSED A COIN, Marcus called heads, and finally they won. Marcus asked Berg if he could read Fargo's plan before deciding. Berg handed it over. Marcus and Sobek stood off to the side, poring over it. It was long and convoluted, with clauses like, "specifically includes, but is not limited to." Sobek laughed. "I don't have my file that I would run against this crap," he said.

Marcus turned to Berg. "Do you guys have a preference?"

"Do you?" Berg replied.

"No, we honestly don't."

"Yeah, I don't care."

"Okay," Marcus said. "We'll affirm."

SAME NEGATIVE ATTACK, different part of Iowa. Berg and his partner dragged out Foucault and flavored him with a heavy dose of topicality. But Central shot down the dead bald philosopher with their May card ("Don't dictate the revolution!") and pulled out a different stop-topicality card from the one they'd run against Berg at Valley. In the speed of the speeches, though, Berg argued against the anti-T arguments he'd heard a month earlier. "They thought they were still at Valley," Marcus taunted in his 2AC. "That means: Ha, ha, you lose."

It was like an answer to Brandon's prayers, a chance to avenge his bone-headed loss at the first tournament of the year. For his final speech he stacked the topicality cards on top.

When he finished, Berg got up and made a passionate plea for a vote on T. "There's no way I can say racism is good," he told the judges. "They've made it impossible to answer their case because they've focused on one race and not the whole public."

Apparently, this held some traction, because after the round the judges spent a lot of time thinking about it, even though it seemed clear to me Central had slaughtered Fargo.

The debaters all moved into the hall. Sobek lightly punched Berg's shoulder and said, "How could you go for T on this case? It's *so* topical."

"I have a lot of homework," he said. "I want to get home."

I asked him if he actually threw the round, or if he was being self-deprecating, or just spewing sour grapes. He looked at me as if I'd asked if he wanted to sell his mother into bondage.

"No, I *want* to win," he insisted. "And we haven't lost yet. They haven't voted yet."

Indeed, it was closer than I expected. Central squeaked by on another two-one decision.

But a win is a win. And Marcus and Brandon were heading for the championship round.

I'LL NEVER PRESUME to know exactly how Brandon, Marcus, Rinehart, and Sobek felt in the moments leading up to the final round at the Caucus. When I asked them about it later, they were short on words, as if the emotions were too big to wrap words around. At the time, they betrayed few feelings. Marcus and Brandon were stone-faced as they sat at their table, working out strategies with Sobek. Rinehart hovered off to the side, waiting to jump in if called upon. Her arms were crossed, brows tensed. Meantime,

I was a wreck. My palms were sopping with sweat, and all my muscles and nerves felt twitchy from a lack of food and an overload of coffee and adrenaline. I honestly can't remember feeling more nervous and excited—not before my rare dates in high school, or for big job interviews, or when I was a student at the University of Colorado and the Golden Buffaloes won a nail-biter against Notre Dame in the Orange Bowl for the national championship. I desperately wanted Central to win.

I'd only been hanging out with these kids for two months, and I was already hopelessly attached to them. Though I went into the season planning to be a detached observer of the proceedings, I saw the lines of separation quickly blur. I had become part of the team. The kids had even given me a nickname: Slap-a-Ho Joe, which they shouted out every time I came into the room (though I've never hollered at a ho, much less slapped one). So, being one of them, I wanted the team to succeed, and I fudged the boundaries of journalism here and there. Not much. I wasn't doing research for them or writing out cards. I never scolded them for not practicing, and I didn't tell them how to live their lives. But when they asked for help, I gave it. Then, when I chastised Marcus for backing out of the Caucus, essentially talking him into it, I actually changed the course of their lives and affected the story I was reporting. After it happened, I beat myself up for days, thinking I'd committed the worst journalistic sin. Now that we were all gathered in a conference room at the Five Seasons in downtown Cedar Rapids, staring at a real chance to make debate history, I didn't regret it at all.

So there was more to my desire for a win than the wish to see a pair of kids succeed. This would be a victory for me, too. Obviously, Rinehart felt the same way. Otherwise, why would she go to such great lengths to get her students to tournaments? Why else would her moods spike and plummet so severely with wins and losses? The other coaches I met at tournaments seemed to be along for similar vicarious-thrill rides.

The Central journey seemed sweeter, though, because these kids were such underdogs, and I can't help but wince at the inherent racism of this sentiment. Marcus's and Brandon's brains work as well as any other teen's. *Of course* they were capable of winning a national-circuit tournament. Truly, when you get down to it, to assume otherwise amounts to the same lowering of expectations social scholars bemoan at inner-city public schools. One can go on and on about all the challenges these kids face, the poverty, the crime, the broken families, but when it's all boiled down to a rancid core, what's left is a pervasive belief in black inferiority. Say "inner city," and "black and broken" comes to mind. When blacks rise out of the ghetto intact, when they attain successes that are taken for granted on the white side of town, it's celebrated. Newspapers run front-page articles. Hollywood producers option film rights. And, as excited as I was to be in that hotel on a Sunday morning in late October, I was also disturbed that a win should feel so important to me. It should be common, I thought.

But then, a team like Central had never won such a competition. History is history, even if it comes more than a century late.

THERE WAS A BITTER IRONY to this championship round. Central would be going against Edina High, a wealthy public school from the suburbs of Minneapolis. During the previous school year the football team from Rockhurst High, a private Catholic school from the Missouri side of Kansas City, had traveled to Minnesota for a matchup against Edina. Because Minneapolis is more than 250 miles beyond the Missouri border, debate teams can't compete there, but football teams can. They can go anywhere in the country to play a game, as can basketball teams. During the Caucus one of the coaches from Minneapolis's Blake School judged a Central round and was so impressed that he invited them to their tournament in December. But Central wouldn't be able to go. Worse, the Missouri State High School Activities Association had forbidden Central from competing at Emory University in Atlanta the previous year. This was a painful blow because Emory's coach, Melissa Maxcy Wade, one of the founders of the UDL, was poised to offer Marcus's former partner Donnell a scholarship. ("I wanted Donnell real bad," she later told me.) To receive it, though, he would have had to compete at their tournament. He wound up going to the University of Northern Iowa instead—a decent school, but definitely not in the same league as Emory, an Ivy League–caliber school in a city known as the "Black Mecca" of the United States. Rinehart had even complained about this circumstance directly to Becky Oakes, executive director of the activities association. "Well, he got into a college, didn't he?" Oakes had replied, flippantly. *The gall*, Rinehart fumed. *Who the hell are these downstate hicks to decide what's good enough for my kids?!* Of all the run-ins Rinehart had with the activities association, this one angered her most. Every time she thought about it, she felt like a crime victim. Linda Collier at UMKC had on several occasions recommended that they sue the association over it, though they both knew such a case would likely go nowhere and would only make matters worse for Central's squad.

There wasn't much time to reflect on this, however, or even prepare for the round. No sooner had the Edina team wheeled their dollies into the room, with their ties still cinched to the top buttons of their oxford shirts, than the tournament director came in, clapped his hands together, and shouted, "Okay. Everybody ready? Let's debate!"

Brandon got up and called once more for an end to racism. If he was nervous, he wasn't showing it. Relaxed, confident, he tore through the stack of evidence without so much as a stutter, finishing with a good forty-five seconds to spare. Off to his left, Marcus calmly listened, leaning back in his chair with his fingers laced behind his head. Rinehart and I both sat bolt upright in the audience section. I'm sure I looked as desperate as she did, with her eyes narrowed and her face flexed, as if she were trying to conjure powers of psychic control. Leo sat beside us, hurriedly scribbling notes. There were few others in the audience, just the three judges and the other members of the Edina and Central squads, who were sprawled out on the floor in the back of the room. Some of them looked like they were about to fall asleep.

The debate boiled down to a kritik, which called on the judges to reject Central's case as a flawed, if well-intentioned, plea to the racist, capitalistic power-mongers of Congress.

"Okay, okay," Marcus said during cross-x, waving his hand as if to fan away a cloud of hot air. "What exactly does *rejecting* mean?"

The kid lowered his head and looked sideways at Marcus. "*Rejection*," he said slowly, like Mr. Rogers, "is the act of being *against*."

"Could you write that down?" Marcus asked.

Silence momentarily spread through the room, then everyone who was still awake laughed.

"What do you mean?" the kid asked. "As a *text*?"

"Whatever you want to call it. I just want something to have some way to attack this argument. I don't know what this argument is, so could you just write it out, like, what your alternative does."

"Essentially, all of our arguments are reasons why the judge should reject your case."

"Could you just *write* it?" Marcus held out his hands in a show of pleading.

"Okay, fine." The kid grabbed a piece of paper and leaned over the table to scribble something out.

"Okay, while you're writing that," Marcus said, "how exactly does, like, rejecting our plan solve for racism? Like, like, I understand the argument, but—"

His opponent looked up. "Do you want me to *write* it? Or you want me to—"

Marcus waved his question off.

"Okay."

The room remained quiet while he wrote. I looked at Rinehart, and she grinned approvingly. The buzzer sounded, and the debater hurriedly finished his text and handed it to Marcus. Marcus read it quickly.

"I think I got it," he said, grinning.

CENTRAL STILL HAD almost all their prep time left before Brandon gave his rebuttal speech. While Brandon prepared, Marcus got up and paced. He jabbed a finger deep into his mouth, pulled it out, and inspected it. "Damn," he said. "I'm bleeding."

During his speech Brandon lost his way a couple of times. All the adrenaline and lost sleep and lack of food was apparently getting to him. At one point he stammered for several seconds, desperately grasping for words. Marcus shot him a ferocious glance and shook a timer at him.

The second Edina speaker rose to the podium table, official-looking in his royal blue shirt and still-tight tie. He pounded the podium while laying out their "rejection" argument. While he spoke, the tournament director came in with George Washington busts, one bronze, the other white and slightly larger. Brandon's and Marcus's eyes locked on the bigger one, the champion prize, for several seconds before resuming their flow of the Edina speech.

Rinehart and I sat so rigidly in our seats we could have been shattered with a single blow. She had given up on taking notes. Her hands were clasped tightly in her lap. I felt as though electric currents were pulsing through my veins. At the front of the room, the Edina debater was sputtering and gulping for air as if he were drowning in the spaces between the words that just wouldn't come. A few forceful phrases came through here and there, such as "We spark a revolution!" and "They're inherently capitalist!" but mostly he said the same things over and over again: "grassroots"; "they make racism worse"; "capitalism, capitalism, capitalism."

I looked at Marcus, and he was trying hard to keep from grinning.

"I don't know much else to say," the Edina debater said quietly just before the buzzer sounded.

Marcus stood to deliver the final speech of the 2002 Iowa Caucus. He went straight into high gear. Rinehart watched him with soft eyes, her mouth curled up slightly at the corners, as if he were singing the most delicate cantata. Marcus's rebuttal speeches were marvels of performance. He relied almost entirely on notes taken during the round, spouting off cogent arguments at a speed nearly as fast as Brandon's well-practiced 1AR. Still, he managed to work into his machine-gun rhythm notes of urgency and emotion, like a barn-burning sermon sped up with the latest sound engineering software. Deep trenches formed across his forehead, and his eyebrows bent sharply under the force of concentration. He shook his head back and forth, bobbed his torso front and back, and slapped the table emphatically.

"The biggest mistake they make in this round is joking around in cross-x," he declared, waving the handwritten definition of "rejection" the Edina debater had hastily scribbled down during cross-x. He read it aloud, stammering through its grammatical errors and lack of coherence. "Don't give them any leeway," he told the judges. "Call for their text after the round."

"*Oh yeah*," Leo said quietly from the audience, smiling and bobbing his head.

The Edina debater who agreed to put it in writing looked down at his hands.

THE ROOM ERUPTED WITH APPLAUSE when Marcus finished. The judges asked for various pieces of evidence, including the impromptu definition Edina had devised during cross-x. Rinehart got up and started cleaning the room, picking up candy and chip wrappers, cramming them into overstuffed waste bins. The room was humid; it stank of stale clothes. The chairs had been turned every which way; the linen tablecloths were falling off the tables. I stood, took a step, looked at my notes, and sat back down. Then I stood up again. A win seemed so close. But there was no guarantee, and the suspense made my skin and bones feel foreign and uncomfortable.

After picking up all the debris she could see, Rinehart stopped to chat with the tournament director. He congratulated her on winning the TOC bid and on her team's great run, no matter which way the judges would decide. "Thanks," she said, looking down and smiling shyly. "Now if we can just get the state activities association to let them go to the TOC."

"I know," he said. "I can't believe all the stuff they make you go through."

She had almost been unable to bring her team to the Iowa Caucus. Ever since she and her school administrators pleaded for permission to attend the TOC the previous year, they had been cracking down on her for attending "unsanctioned" tournaments. Sanctioning is an old bureaucratic practice few state activities associations still uphold for debate. It was developed in the 1920s, when these activities associations were created, to prevent teens from competing in quasi-professional sporting events where cash prizes were handed out or where there were few safeguards against injury. All it entailed was for tournament directors to obtain an official sanction from their state activities association, and to submit that paperwork to officials at Missouri's activities association. They also had to fill out paperwork declaring how much would be spent on trophies. The Caucus's director had a hard time doing this because the Iowa association didn't sanction debate events anymore—its officials had long ago figured out that debating is more educational and less dangerous than football or wrestling.

Rinehart apologized again for making him deal with all the red tape, as she had numerous times before, but he waved her off. "I just hope you get to go to TOC this year," he said.

"Yeah," she said, frowning and looking away. "We'll see. Something tells me the Missouri State Activities Association isn't going to change its ways for our little debate team."

Just then, the judges announced that they had a decision. Rinehart moved for a better look.

"It's three-oh for the affirmative."

Rinehart let out a wail and jumped in the air. Never in her coaching career had a team of hers won a varsity national-circuit tournament. This was a first for her, and for the fledgling Urban Debate Leagues. I shook my fist in the air. Leo raced to the front of the room to high-five Brandon and Marcus and clutch them in burly man hugs.

The tournament director handed Marcus the big white trophy, and Marcus held it out in front of him, beaming. Brandon leaned over and whispered in his ear, "They had to give us the white one. Like we aren't good enough for the black one."

Marcus frowned and quickly shook his head at his partner, and a guilty look crept momentarily across Brandon's face, as if he were scolding himself for spoiling the moment by bringing race into it.

"**NOW I KNOW WHY** I didn't want to come," Marcus said as we arrived at the van in the parking garage, our bags and tubs in tow. Everyone stopped and looked at him, wondering how he could still find merit in missing out on such an experience.

"Too easy." He displayed a shit-eating grin. Sobek smacked the back of his head.

Marcus held up the trophy and gave it a little tap. "It feels like marble," he said proudly.

This was the highest point of his high school debate career. A few weeks earlier he had lolled lazily in Central's squad room, complaining about the inherent frustration in debate for someone as fiercely competitive as him. "That's the thing with debate," he had said. "Unless you're the number-one team in the nation, you're gonna end up a loser." Now there could be no doubt that he and Brandon were among the best debaters in the country.

We wound our way out of the parking lot and onto the rain-slick streets of Cedar Rapids. Rinehart was grinning widely as she took us over the river and the train yards, past the hulking Quaker Oats factory, and she was still smiling as she turned onto the highway. Gradually the rain turned to snow, and as dusk settled in, streaks of it collected on the plowed rows of the corn-fields. Sobek popped the cleaned-up Eminem disc in the portable player, and we barreled through the blizzard toward Missouri as the white rapper screamed over and over again, *"White America! White America!"*

TWENTY-FIVE

FUCKITY FUCK FUCK FUCK

AS SOON AS RINEHART arrived at Central on the Monday after the Iowa Caucus, she carted the handsome George Washington bust to the main office to show off to Principal McClendon. The office was buzzing with the usual morning chaos, teachers breezing in and out to collect their mail, students leaning on the counter and waiting for the secretaries to approve absence and tardy excuses. A security guard brought in a pair of frowning kids, clutching both by their arms. "That's outstanding," McClendon said when he saw the trophy, in a tone that struck Rinehart as distant, contrived.

This was his second year on the job. He had blazed in like a phoenix, talking about how he was on a mission to restore the school to its glory days in the late 1950s and early '60s, when the all-black institution was a beacon of the black community and many of its graduates went on to respectable colleges. He attended the school back then, he knew the neighborhood, and the story he told was that he'd been called by a higher force to set aside a lucrative business career to go into education and give back to the community.

In his early days on the job he had evoked the timeworn cliché of so many would-be reformers: "Think outside the box." He'd even bought a rug with the motto knit into it in blocky letters and laid it in his office in front of his desk, for all visitors to see. But other than the uniforms the kids wore every day, the school didn't seem much different. He'd sought partnerships with the business community, but all he seemed able to create was a sporadic schedule of meetings. His leadership had become an exercise in avoiding trouble, the guiding philosophy of ponderous institutions. To cope with an unruly freshman class and their propensity for fighting, he started canceling activities: dances, after-school clubs, even the homecoming football game.

The students didn't like him much. They thought he was clueless. He didn't seem to know any of their names, always calling them either "young man" or "young lady." Indeed, he didn't even know the valedictorian's name, or that of the girl who helped him read the announcements every morning and afternoon. He was the same with his teachers. He always called Rinehart Jan or Janet or Janice, never her real name, Jane, and she found that insulting.

After politely thanking her boss for his compliment, Rinehart informed him that the win in Iowa had put the team in the same position they'd been in the year before: they had a TOC bid, but the Missouri State High School Activities Association rules would once again prohibit them from going unless something drastic were done. When Marcus and Donnell were denied the same opportunity in the spring of 2002, McClendon was appropriately livid, and, still somewhat new to the job, he had vowed to fight to prevent such a thing from happening again. So had higher-ups in the district. After I wrote about the situation for *The Pitch*, several school board members met to discuss it. They agreed to direct the superintendent to try to have the rules changed. But so far this campaign to help Rinehart's squad had only made things worse.

After the superintendent received his orders from the board to amend the situation, he passed the job along to Phyllis Budesheim, a top district administrator who oversaw Central and all the other district high schools. Budesheim first contacted association officials. They were friendly enough, she later told me, and she was encouraged by their advice about how to appeal the rules. A bureaucrat through and through, Budesheim felt comfortable with procedure, and on this level she connected with her downstate counterparts. In the course of her conversations with them, though, she learned of their discomfort with the coach she was ostensibly trying to protect. They told Budesheim that Rinehart had a dangerous habit of taking her debaters to "unsanctioned" tournaments, a forbidden practice that association officials rarely cracked down on. The organization's policies didn't call for proactive investigations. Infractions were usually only looked into when association members filed complaints. But in Central's case, the school was being closely scrutinized for attendance at unsanctioned tournaments ever since activities association officials had learned that Central had competed at an unsanctioned event the year before, when Rinehart appealed to be allowed to attend the TOC. Now they were demanding regular updates on Central's schedule. And they were warning Budesheim that if Central broke the rules again, there could be serious consequences, such as banning the debate squad from competing for a year. Worse, they could ban the school from competing in *any* activities controlled by the activities association, such as football, basketball, or track. That struck fear in Budesheim's administrative bones, and she immediately started hounding Rinehart, refusing to allow the coach to access her budget unless her tournaments were sanctioned. All this sounds easy enough to deal with, except that none of the states Central was allowed to compete in officially sanctioned debate tournaments. So she had to beg tournament directors to conjure policies and paperwork where there were none. She hated doing this because she knew debate coaches and teachers already had to deal with too much paperwork as it was.

McClendon assured Rinehart that they were doing everything they could to allow Marcus and Brandon to compete at the TOC that coming spring. But, he added, Rinehart needed to be mindful of the association's sanctioning rules. "There are a lot of people that are willing to go to bat for you," he told her. "We don't want to go out there and have egg on our face."

So when Rinehart carried the trophy to her room to show off to her novice class, the thrill of victory had already been sullied. And when McClendon reported the win in the morning announcements, she could tell by the mounting din of kids gathering at their classroom doors down the lengths of the halls that hardly anyone would hear it anyway.

BRANDON, ON THE OTHER HAND, was ecstatic. After his customary ditch of school on the Monday after the tournament, he showed up on Tuesday with his head tilted back a little more than usual, his chest flexed. The news of their victory was all over the Internet. On Cross-X.com a debater from St. Louis posted, "Congrats to KCC for winning the tournament! It's nice to have a team from MO representing so well on the national circuit." Another wrote, "You guys KICK ASS!" No less than Phil Kerpen himself, owner of Cross-X.com and author of the popular weekly evidence packets known as Thursday Files, offered props. So did Daryl Burch, from duPont Manual in Louisville, Kentucky, a favorite coach and judge on the national circuit. Burch had written Brandon and Marcus's "End Racism" case while teaching at the Capital Classic debate camp in Washington, D.C., and he kept a running, informal top-twenty list of national-circuit teams. He called the victory "huge," though it wasn't enough for Central to crack his list.

Still, Brandon was thrilled when he clicked on the more formal national-rankings list, one compiled by a coach from Texas who employed a point system based on teams' performances at TOC-qualifying tournaments. By breaking to trophy rounds at these tournaments, teams picked up at least one point. As they moved up the brackets toward the finals, they earned more points. Central's win at Caucus, combined with the low points they'd earned by breaking at Valley and New Trier, suddenly catapulted Brandon and Marcus to twenty-sixth in the nation. Brandon showed the list to me and said, "Man, that is so *tight!*"

After school that day he was itching to work. "Let's go," he said as he paced the room, pushing chairs and desks out of his way. "Let's debate."

He wanted to run a practice round; it didn't matter with whom. But everyone else was slow to move. He tugged at the shirt of one of his team-mates, trying to pull her out of her desk, but she slapped his hand.

"Come on!" he yelled. "I can't just be sittin' around like this. I need to *debate!*"

Everyone just kept doing what they were doing, cutting cards, working on homework, staring off into space. Finally Brandon slumped down into the chair by the computer in the back of the room. "Fuckin' Marcus," he said to me. "I can't debate even if I wanted to. He's got our 1AC."

Marcus wasn't in school that day, nor would he be for the rest of the week. His toothache had worsened, and he had to make a hurried visit to the dentist to have a molar pulled. Such medical trauma was too much not to cash in on. While nursing himself back to health, he hung around his house sleeping and reading and lurking on Cross-X.com, checking up on everything that was being written about him. When Kerpen posted his note of congratulations, he'd closed with a note of suspense: "But will MSHSAA allow them to go to TOC this year?" That had sparked a rambling online debate, with other kids from across the state opining that the rules forbidding competition at the TOC were unjust or at least unwise. Marcus couldn't resist chiming in.

"Can anyone explain to me what hardship Rockhurst football players face in Missouri . . . ," he wrote in his usual ellipsis-heavy punctuation style, "that allowed them to travel over the 250 mile travel limit? It's funny— friends from Edina call me and say their school just lost to a football team from my area . . . named Rockhurst . . . I wonder if MSHSAA cares . . . oh wait . . . their parents are too powerful to mess with . . . we better pretend like we didn't notice this."

This was one of Marcus's favorite examples of the activities association's unfairness, that the most elite private school in Kansas City is continually allowed to travel the country for football and basketball contests. He assumed they were allowed to skirt the rules because the downstate bureaucrats favored the white, wealthy, and powerful. In fact, the association's rules allowed schools to send football and basketball teams anywhere in the country to compete. I never got a good reason why, though. Association officials simply said that these were the rules their member schools had agreed on. But my suspicion was that Missouri coaches were tired of being crushed by Rockhurst, which often ranks among the nation's top ten in football, so they agreed to allow the team to roam the country and take on other powerhouse squads.

The association's rules are written and voted on by coaches at schools across the state. Obviously, the football and basketball coaches had no problem with travel. But the debate coaches did. The coaches who were most involved with the activities association, those who served on its speech and debate subcommittee, were fiercely loyal to the old style of debate; they disliked the speed and complexity of arguments used at national-circuit tournaments. One way they kept this style at bay was to employ layperson judges, parent volunteers who were unfamiliar with the faster style and would award wins to teams that compete in a more traditional manner. Kids tend to prefer the faster style, and they seemed to slow down and simplify their arguments if they knew they would lose otherwise. The other way these coaches protected their old manner of doing things was to limit students' exposure to the national style, and the travel restrictions offered an effective means of doing this. With the 250-mile limit, schools were only eligible to compete in a half-dozen national-circuit tournaments, and the activities association's crackdown against competing at so-called unsanctioned tournaments threatened to reduce this number further still.

Marcus had been on a holy war against the activities association since the previous spring, when his request to compete at the TOC was denied at a terse, five-minute appeals committee meeting in Columbia. Almost as soon as he had returned from that four-hour round-trip, he got online and started blasting the organization. He copied a picture of the association's all-male, all-white board of directors and posted it on Cross-X.com with the caption "What's missing?" He fired off an angry e-mail to one of the association's top officials. "Since I, as Marcus Leach a member of the KC Central debate team have neither asked nor wished to be a part of the social community defined herein," he wrote, meaning the activities association, "I decline to be ruled by your said 'private' organization . . . By forcing me to join and be a part of a racist community to which I have been the butt of such racism and discrimination for several years, I was denied my personal rights to freedom protected by higher laws . . . I wish for your warrant-less resistance to my academic achievement to halt or I will be forced to take legal action to protect my civil rights."

Though Becky Oakes would later apparently be too busy to respond when four black state legislators wrote her an official appeal on Marcus's behalf, the association's executive director, who makes more than $100,000 per year, immediately wrote a letter to Principal McClendon demanding that Marcus be disciplined for his inappropriate behavior. Marcus was hauled into the office and ordered to write a letter of apology. When he protested that his First Amendment rights were being violated, McClendon threatened to suspend him. Only after Rinehart burst into tears and begged him to write the letter did Marcus acquiesce.

"It was certainly not my intent to incur the wrath of the Missouri State High School Activities Association," he wrote. "You may rest assured that I will be more reflective before exercising my first amendment rights in the future."

Oakes responded patronizingly, writing to McClendon that Marcus's "enthusiasm and passion shall serve him well with a few stopping points for guidance along the way."

But Marcus's rage hadn't abated. In the weeks leading up to the Iowa Caucus, he got on Cross-X.com and wrote, "Any MSHSAA officials caught on this network . . . will be banned. No questions asked." He signed this "Marcus L. Leach, Chief Technical Officer, Fiat Utopia Inc." And he wasn't kidding. As a friend of Kerpen's, he sometimes helped with the technical aspects of Cross-X.com, so he was able to block anyone from the mshsaa.org domain from surfing the site.

This power move, short-lived though it was, was in response to a resolution voted on at the activities association's most recent board meeting "to address," in the words of the official declaration, "a growing concern of inappropriate use of internet message boards by students, coaches and others involved in interscholastic programs." The association's officials had learned of incidents of trash talk on Cross-X.com, and presumably similar sites for other activities, and they wanted to officially instruct school administrators to "take an active role in the prevention of unsportsmanlike materials" showing up on such forums.

When this long, stuffy, toothless resolution was posted on Cross-X.com, Marcus logged on and wrote:

Fuck Fuck Fuck Fuck Fuck Fuck
Fuckity Fuck Fuck Fuck

Attention . . . Attention . . . To all you idiots out there who should be in class coaching instead of reading a private forum . . . GET A LIFE GET A LIFE EAT LESS FOOD GET A LIFE LOSE SOME WEIGHT YOU KNOW WHO ATTEN-

TION ATTENTION . . . ok, I'm bored, I'm sure someone will be notified that
I posted this and I'm sure I'll get another letter, well, tomorrow is a new day

Fueled by hate,
Loved by none,
Marcus

TWENTY-SIX

COMFORT ZONE

WHEN I ARRIVED AT ROOM 109 on Wednesday, Rinehart wasn't there. Ebony and Antoine were missing, too. Brandon, who was surfing the Web in the back of the room, told me to check the library. "They're meeting with the people from Russia," he said.

At the beginning of the year, Rinehart told me she had applied for a debate exchange program sponsored by the Soros Foundations. But she didn't make a big deal about it, so I'd forgotten. She habitually applied for stuff like this—scholarships, grants, unusual debate training programs—without expecting them to come through. Sometimes they did, though, and it pleased her to be able to provide more opportunities for her kids. The previous year she had signed up Donnell, Marcus's old partner, for a paper debate, in which contestants wrote out their constructive speeches and rebuttals and sent them to one another and to judges in the mail. By the end of the school year, Rinehart had forgotten all about it, until Donnell came in all excited one day, saying he'd won a free trip to San Francisco to compete in the finals.

I cautiously made my way to the school's library, which was just off the cavernous commons area where the students ate lunch every day. The principals' offices had windows overlooking the lunchroom, and I was worried about being seen. When I had first asked Principal McClendon if I could follow Central's debate squad through a season, he sternly denied my request. He did so because some members of his staff were upset about an article I'd written about the school for *The Pitch* in the spring of 2001. I had thought the piece was overwhelmingly positive; it followed several of the school's top students through their daily routines, and at a time when the school was getting a lot of ink about being named "academically deficient," it showed Kansas Citians that bright, college-bound kids attend the school, and that they have a few dedicated teachers who do a good job preparing them for their futures. But it wasn't a puff piece. I published all the school's dismal statistics, and I exposed instances where teachers were doing a poor job. McClendon's new colleagues were concerned less about the school's problems than that they'd been exposed to the community, to the parents and taxpayers whom the school ostensibly served. So they prevailed on McClendon to keep me away.

McClendon changed his mind, however, after I'd written a history of Kansas City's desegregation case, which focused on Central, and a story about Marcus and Donnell being denied their opportunity to compete at the TOC by the state activities association. In the late summer of 2002, I had called Rinehart just to see how things were going, and she told me McClendon was ecstatic about the articles. When I called him, he said, "I love you, man!" He readily allowed me to hang out with the team, with the caveat that I wouldn't get unfettered access to the school. As such, my time at the school was tainted with a fear that someone would spot me roaming the halls and complain to him and my project would be torpedoed. So I always headed straight for room 109 when I arrived at the school each day. Even my occasional treks to the bathroom felt like covert missions.

I found Rinehart, Ebony, Antoine, and a few other students in a conference room at the back of the library. James Franson, a special-education teacher and coach of the speech team, was with them. So was Assistant Principal Dorothy Phillips, and her presence raised my anxiety considerably. Rinehart had told me Phillips was the administrator who'd been most upset by my first article, the one who had pushed the hardest for me to be banned from the premises. She'd been at Central for decades, and under McClendon's unfocused leadership she basically called the shots. When I researched the desegregation case, trolling through its document archives, I found her name all over the memos and meeting notes associated with Central's transformation into a magnet school and back again into a neighborhood school. My experience with investigative reporting taught me long ago that if you want to find the problem in a problem institution, start with the people who've been there the longest. Rinehart and other teachers at the school confirmed my suspicions. In their opinion, Phillips was one of the main causes of the school's ineffectiveness.

An entrenched administrator, Phillips was skilled at maintaining the status quo, nixing innovative ideas so as to protect her own comfort level and her position in the hierarchy. She typically shot down Rinehart's ideas and requests. A master of institutional politics, she had a vindictive streak. I was told by several teachers that when they crossed her they'd often return the next year to find the worst schedule imaginable, with either a late or a ridiculously early lunch period and with the bulk of the school's most unruly students assigned to their classes. Phillips oversaw the school's scheduling process, and Rinehart believed that she was behind the beginning-of-the-year snafu that left not one of her recruits enrolled in her debate class. This happened every year, she told me, and it was getting worse each time around. One year, Phillips had made it so Rinehart hadn't gotten paid her coaching stipend, Rinehart told me: a mere $1,500 per year, far less than what the athletic coaches earn. She was only paid after she filed an official grievance through the teachers' union, a move that no doubt peeved Phillips even more. Once, when Rinehart was escorting me through the hallway, she spotted Phillips and quickened her pace. "Watch out," she said. "Here comes the gargoyle."

Most of the students I talked with couldn't stand Phillips, and, looking at her scowling from the end of the long conference table, I could easily understand why. With her flattop buzz cut and mannish face, she looked like the antagonist in a Hollywood high school movie. She sat with her arms crossed firmly over her midsection girth, and her head was cocked arrogantly, as if to imply that this whole meeting was just a charade, that there was no way these hard-luck kids would be chosen for a foreign exchange program, much less be allowed to go. In the late 1980s and early '90s, a lone Central student had traveled to Europe at great expense to compete in fencing tournaments. But that was in an effort to lure whites back to the inner-city school. When that scheme failed, the traveling ceased. Unlike many public school districts across the country, Kansas City's offered no opportunities for kids to study abroad.

Still, the atmosphere at the meeting was light and hopeful; Rinehart and Franson were bristling with enthusiasm, and it was rubbing off on the students, who peppered the Soros Foundations official with sweetly naive questions. Turns out, the exchange program wouldn't be with Russia, but with Azerbaijan, a former member of the Soviet Union located on the western edge of the Caspian Sea, which seemed all the more exotic to the kids.

"Do they got TVs?"

"What kind of food do they eat?"

"What are their houses like?"

Amrita Dhawan, the Soros official, answered all the questions with ease, as if she'd fielded them before. She'd flown in from New York specifically for this meeting. Central was among several dozen finalists for the exchange program. She told them the country's population was primarily Muslim, that its citizens were still getting used to freedom after the fall of the Soviet Union. The Central kids, she said, would be young ambassadors for democracy. The kids were thrilled by this prospect. And when she told them that the country was much poorer than the United States, even poorer than Kansas City's East Side, they were astonished.

"Man," one of the girls said, "I could move over there and be like a millionaire."

"TV is a big luxury over there," Franson said.

Phillips added, "Y'all are gonna find out how spoiled you really are."

"You live a very spoiled life, guys," Franson agreed. "You guys have heard in your history class that we are the richest country in the world. And we're also the most spoiled country in the world."

Ebony crossed his arms and frowned.

"What about minorities in Azerbaijan?" Franson asked. "Are there any racial things to consider?"

"Um, it's not really . . ." Dhawan answered slowly. "Um, it's not really diverse."

"Do they have, like, urban schools?" one of the girls asked. Before

Dhawan could answer, the girl turned to Rinehart with a look of distress. "They're not gonna pick no urban schools. How are they going to fit in with a bunch of black people?"

"There're no black people in that country," Phillips concurred, leaning back in her chair with an air of resignation, as if she'd thrown out a possible deal breaker. "You can count on that."

"I mean," the girl sputtered, "it's gonna be strange for them."

"*No!*" Franson said sarcastically. "Oh, *really*? Are you *sure*?"

"*Yes!*" she insisted.

"Think about it," Franson said with a chortle. "Ten white students *here*."

Ebony tapped the table nervously. He quickly rubbed his nose. Then he turned to Antoine. "I'm not so sure," he said. "Why Russia? I'm not goin' there, Ms. Rinehart."

Next to Ebony, Antoine stiffened in his seat. "Why not?!"

"Cuz I'm not."

"Yes, you are! Why not?!"

"Why do we gotta go to all them Third World countries for?" Ebony said, truly pained. "Why we can't go to a prosperous country? Like France?"

"Why do you want to go to a country where you're gonna be poor?" Rinehart replied.

"I got my own room," Ebony said, counting off his life's luxuries on his fingers. "My own space. Own TV. Own video games. I got a shower. New shoes. I can't do it. I like living here. I don't want some communist trying to get me, some Muslim trying to make me, um, a fundamentalist."

Even if they would have been heading for Paris, Ebony would still have had reservations about traveling. He'd never been outside of Kansas City. He was scared, especially of flying. He'd done enough moving around in his short life. He was finally at a place where he could settle in and start spreading roots. He was unaware how tenuously his aunt and uncle were holding on to his home. They had no long-term lease, and just a week before this meeting about the exchange program the landlord had told Shavelle and Eddy that he wanted to sell the property. He had promised them first dibs and gave them a little time to secure a loan. But the young couple's credit was far from clean, and they had serious doubts about their chances at a mortgage. But they couldn't bring themselves to tell Ebony. He was finally starting to come out of his shell. Bad news, they feared, might send him back into an emotional cocoon.

Rinehart wasn't surprised by Ebony's reluctance. Of all the things that disturbed her about teaching in the inner city, the worst was the way the kids limited their own experiences. It was as if they'd resigned themselves to a narrow cultural cell, beyond which lie bogeymen and perilous pitfalls. Since coming to Central, she'd read a number of books about teaching minority children, many of which explained that such kids often resist education because they have internalized racial stereotypes about themselves. One of the best of these was Paulo Freire's *Pedagogy of the Oppressed*. The book doesn't specifically mention African-Americans (Freire was from Brazil), but everything he wrote about perfectly described race dynamics in the United States. Freire observed that oppressed people often identify with their oppression. It had become their way of life, and they tended to shun experiences that might lift them out of it. Rinehart often complained that her students locked themselves in a "comfort zone." They would only listen to a small selection of music, watch just a handful of TV shows, read few if any books (they read their debate evidence in small pieces, just evidence cards they picked up at camp or from other debaters and coaches), and travel only to familiar haunts, usually ones frequented by other blacks. They were extremely picky about food. That drove her the most crazy. Sometimes she'd take her top debaters to a nice restaurant like Danny's Big Easy, a downtown New Orleans–style bistro, and they'd order the same things they ordered every day in the cafeteria: burgers or chicken strips smothered in cheese sauce. When the burger came out with a bright slice of red onion and a multigrain bun, or the chicken arrived mesquite-grilled and with tricolor cheese, they'd grimace and say, "Man, this restaurant is jacked up."

Which is why she kept foisting new experiences on them, why she fought to take her teams to Des Moines, Omaha, and suburban Chicago, places most would consider mundane but were wildly exotic to her kids. A trip to Azerbaijan would be out of this world.

She doubted it would ever happen.

TWENTY-SEVEN

CENTRAL HIGH PRISON

RINEHART SCORED TICKETS to an Angela Davis speech at UMKC for the Friday after the Caucus. A week had passed, and Marcus hadn't spent a minute in school, due to his toothache. He wouldn't return until the following Thursday, a day before UMKC's annual debate tournament. It wasn't a national-circuit event, but it was one of Marcus's favorites because college kids served as judges and it offered the only opportunity for Central kids to compete against local squads in the faster style. Rinehart begged him to go to the Angela Davis event. She figured he, more than anyone else on the squad, would be electrified by what the radical intellectual had to offer, because of his frequent rants about race and his love of all things revolutionary. But he couldn't be swayed, so she offered his ticket to someone else.

Brandon commandeered the front passenger seat of the van, and we rolled southwestward, toward the opulent heart of the city. Rinehart took her usual route, zigzagging through East Side backstreets until she got to Thirty-ninth and cut west. When they passed Brandon's street, Chestnut Avenue, catching a brief glimpse of his granddaddy's house, Brandon shouted out his usual refrain: "Chestnut U!" It had become his running joke; whenever anyone asked about his postgraduation plans, he brayed the name of this pretend college, giving panache to the notion of not continuing on in school.

Rinehart slowed to a stop at the intersection of Thirty-ninth and Prospect, still within shouting distance of Brandon's home. Decades ago, it was a thriving corner, with rows of two-story storefronts stretching north and south. Now vacant lots braced three corners of the intersection, and the fourth hosted a shabby mini-mart with painted signs advertising Newport cigarettes and malt liquor for a buck and a quarter. Supposedly, this corner was the focus of an earnest revitalization campaign, spearheaded by Troy Nash, the city councilman who represented much of Kansas City's mostly black East Side. When drug trafficking and violent crime were at their worst on the corner, he had camped out there in a tent for more than a week. This won him a lot of ink in the local paper and face time on the ten o'clock news, and soon he persuaded his colleagues on the council to back a modest expenditure for a Prospect Corridor redevelopment initiative. In three years, though, all the program had accomplished was the demolition of the last remaining vacant building and high salaries for several of Nash's close friends.

Before the 2002–2003 school year Brandon and Marcus briefly served as interns for Nash, which meant they went out for breakfast with the politician a few times and listened while he bragged about how he worked the system. He openly told them how he pulled publicity stunts (like the inner-city campout) to snag free advertising, and he used so-called new initiatives to access the city's postage budget. Under the guise of these programs, he could write open letters to constituents and crow about accomplishments, splashing his name all over the place. Not that campaign funding was tight for Nash. Other than the mayor, he pulled in more contributions than any of his colleagues, hundreds of thousands of dollars more. This money, Nash told the teens with a wink and a nudge, went toward "restaurant meetings with constituents," just like the ones he was having with Brandon and Marcus. When I checked Nash's campaign files as a reporter for The Pitch, I found receipts for common groceries such as Eggos, milk, and paper towels. In Missouri, politicians are not allowed to use campaign funds for personal purposes. I also found receipts for meals he had bought for his wife and five-year-old daughter, both of whom had looked on as I interviewed him in the Peachtree Bistro, Kansas City's upscale soul food restaurant (I paid for my own lunch). In some instances, he had turned in receipts to both his campaign trust and the city for reimbursement as office expenses. His would-be mentees had mixed feelings about these tricks. On the one hand, they admired the "Fuck The Man" quality of it all. On the other, they thought it was sleazy. When Nash finally gave them an internship project, asking them to input a yard-high stack of phone logs into a database, they balked. It was one thing to run a game on the system, they thought. But they'd be damned if they'd let themselves be exploited.

As she waited for the light to change, Rinehart shot Brandon a sideways glance. "By the way," she asked, "where are you applying for college?"

"I already *told* you," he said. "Right here. *Chestnut U!*"

RINEHART WHEELED THE VAN into a public parking lot near UMKC's student union. She circled around, growing frustrated as she saw all the empty spaces protected by RESERVED FOR FACULTY signs.

"You ain't gonna find nothing," Brandon said. "I think we need to go home."

Rinehart kept circling.

"What is she going to be talking about?" Brandon asked, his voice demanding, slightly irritated.

"I guess her life," Rinehart said.

"Her experiences with the Black Panthers?"

"Yeah."

Brandon yelped and pounded his fists against the dash. "The black militants!"

Rinehart parked, and we crossed the campus as the evening light was beginning to fade and the air turned nippy. In addition to tickets for the lecture, Rinehart had scored invites to a reception with Angela Davis in the sumptuous lobby of the university's alumni center. When we got to the door, Brandon peeked through the windows at the people milling about dressed in dark turtlenecks, five-button blazers, crisply pressed slacks, and austere skirt suits. He shook his head. "Uh-uh," he said. "I'm not going in there. I'm gonna stay out here and smoke a joint."

Aware that he was kidding, Rinehart pulled the door open and gestured for her entourage to enter. The room had high ceilings with ornately carved trim, and the floor and fireplace were done up in slick marble. Vines spread from broad planters up the iron railing of a staircase. At the far end of the room stood a long banquet table draped in white cloth, bearing silver trays of fussy hors d'oeuvres. The Central crew quickly claimed a spot along the edge of the scene and leaned against the wall.

"What are we doing here?" Brandon asked. "We don't know anybody."

"Well, go around and introduce yourselves," Rinehart said.

Brandon and Leo looked at each other, curling their lips in a show of supreme annoyance.

The guest of honor stood a few paces off. Davis was quite tall, with perfect posture. Her hair, a bouquet of curls somewhere between dreadlocks and Afro, rose above the other heads in the crowd. A line was forming around her, people waiting to shake her hand or take a picture with her or hand her a book to sign. Rinehart took a place at the end of it, and as she neared the star, she waved her students over.

"Hi, I'm Jane Rinehart," she said when finally face-to-face with Davis. She politely extended her hand, and Davis smiled and shook it. "I'm a teacher at Kansas City Central High School. These are my students. They're on the debate team."

Davis nodded approvingly and said, "Some of my students at the University of Louisville were on the debate team. It's an excellent activity."

Rinehart waved Brandon, Leo, and the other debaters in closer, had them stand around Davis, and then stepped back and snapped a picture. Davis grinned warmly, clutching a tall cup of Starbucks coffee in her left hand.

They moved on to the food. Brandon picked up a pair of tongs and jabbed at a cucumber slice covered with a ridged dollop of beige goo sprinkled with paprika. "What is this stuff?" he said.

Across the table ran a parade of kalamata olives, melba toasts slathered in hummus, an assortment of sliced wraps, cucumber wedges, and miniature quiches. The kids stuck with the familiar, loading their tiny plates with baby carrots and melon balls. Rinehart tried a little of everything. She glanced over at Day's austere selection. "Why don't you try one of these?" Rinehart asked, holding up one of the tiny bronze-colored pies.

Day cringed.

"Why not?!"

"Because," Day said, "it's outside my comfort zone."

"It's reception food," Rinehart said, trying to assure them that it was perfectly safe, affecting a snobbish tone. "This is what high-society people do. They come to places like this. They visit. They eat food."

"I don't like high society," Leo barked, his brow furrowed.

"I like olives," Day said gamely, and she popped a standard, pimento-stuffed green one in her mouth.

IT SEEMED THAT ALL of liberal Kansas City had come out for Davis's lecture. Nearly a thousand people crowded into a vast ballroom in the student union. I spotted several city council members and state representatives shaking hands with people as they moved slowly toward their reserved seats in front. We found a row of seats off to the left side of the stage. Leo and Brandon sat high in their seats, their necks outstretched to look over the crowd. Leo smacked Brandon's shoulder and pointed to a college-age woman with tight pants stretched across a spectacularly round behind.

"A'ight! A'ight!" Brandon said, nodding. The irony of his doing this at a lecture given by an outspoken, radical feminist was completely lost on him. Leo, too. On the walk from the alumni center to the student union, they had talked nonstop about girls. Leo scrolled through the numbers saved on his cell phone as he rolled on. When he got to the end, he crowed, "Forty-two! I got digits for forty-two chickadees."

"Man, I got one hundred and fifty-two in mine," Brandon bragged. "Females, mostly."

They rubbernecked as girls strode past. "Man, I have *got* to go here!" Brandon said after a particularly statuesque woman passed them.

"Marcus don't never have no girls," Leo blurted suddenly.

"I thought he said he had a girlfriend," I said.

Leo and Brandon laughed. "He might have *liked* her," Brandon said. "But he's never had a girlfriend."

"We called her Coffee Stains," Leo said, laughing. "Because she had jacked-up teeth."

Brandon cracked up, too. "Yeah," he said. "Marcus kept saying she was 'thick.' But she was, like, anorexic."

After a good five minutes of girl watching, Brandon settled down into his seat. He picked up a program and read the schedule. "Damn," he said. "This is going to last an *hour*?!"

Then he proceeded to read the program out loud at debate-round speed, finishing it in a couple of seconds. Leo grabbed it from him when he was done and did the same, gesturing with his hand as if he were in a championship round.

After a rousing poetry-slam introduction by a member of UMKC's African-American student group, Davis climbed up to the podium.

"I have to acknowledge the horror of the moment," she began. "It's difficult for me to imagine that George W. Bush is the president of the United States." At that, the crowd erupted in applause and hearty cheers. Brandon laughed, immediately won over by Davis's forcefulness.

"We need more radical politics," Davis declared. "We need an expanding movement."

Her lecture was about how gender structures the nation's prison-industrial complex, and how it should be immediately dismantled. Her basic thesis, so far as I could discern from the wide wander of the speech, was that prisons are a manifestation of a masculine desire for conquest and domination and that now, in a twisted reading of feminist ideology, more and more women are being plowed into a system of institutionalized bondage and outright rape. She peppered the lecture with statistics and anecdotes about cavity searches and so-called romantic affairs between female prisoners and their male guards. Her words flowed in a precise, assertive rhythm, each sentence punctuated with a short, upturned "uh," as if she were groaning from the exertion of lobbing such heavy thoughts into the crowd. Often she'd veer off into other, related subject matter, such as crime statistics and poverty and race, at which she'd catch herself and say, "But that deserves yet another entire lecture of its own."

She didn't ramble so much as stretch to suggest the vastness of America's many, interconnected ills. And her expansiveness gave me (and I presume most of my fellow listeners) a sense of fullness, as if I'd been briefly

ferried high above society to gain a better view of it all. The effect this perspective had on me was profound, if not immediate. Later, after I became an
assistant coach for Central's squad, I would turn time and time again to
Davis's lecture as a theoretical framework for my activism.

The thrust of her thesis jarred much of the audience at the outset.
"We must abolish prisons," she said early on, to tepid applause. "The prison-
industrial complex is a major detriment to a democratic society."

I looked around to gauge the reaction to this startling proposal. Most of
the black and white faces in the crowd gazed back at Davis with a look of
puzzled patience. In my years of reporting in Kansas City, focusing heavily
on its predominantly black East Side, I had learned that folks were troubled
by the obvious racism of the prison system, the way a disproportionate
number of blacks are locked away. But they were even more upset about
crime. I'd once spent a month in an almost entirely black neighborhood
barely a mile east of UMKC's campus, Blue Hills, where Leo's family lived,
and its residents told me that a key factor in turning the drug-infested war
zone into a thriving neighborhood was the reinstatement of the beat-cop
program, where a pair of officers was assigned to patrol the neighborhood
full-time and work closely with the residents and area church leaders to
squash crime. I rode along with these cops one day, and they told me they
had a "zero tolerance" policy for drug offenses; even teens with a joint or two
in their pocket would be cuffed and hauled away. I watched them arrest a
guy they saw purchase a package of bogus crack no bigger than a garbanzo
bean. As his neighbors looked on, he had knelt in handcuffs on the sidewalk,
wailing, "My life is ruined!"

Davis's proposal was like a high school debate case. As a policy option,
her suggestion was as realistic as Brandon and Marcus's affirmative plan,
which they boldly claimed would end institutional racism (and, as an added
bonus, avert the imminent nuclear holocaust). But at its core was a provoca-
tive point, effective to the extent that it challenged standard ways of thinking. By the end of Davis's lecture, I began to come around to her point of
view that the entire system is back assward, that it exacerbates the very problem of crime it purports to solve by perpetuating racist, sexist, and classist
structures in society. Soon the audience was responding to Davis with cho-

ruses of "Mmm hmm!" and "Amen!" I looked over at Brandon and saw that he was slowly nodding his head, transfixed.

"Racism hides from view within institutional structures," Davis said at one point, rousing an emphatic outburst from the crowd. "And its most reliable refuge is within the prison system."

At this, Brandon looked at me and said, *"Damn!"*

During the question-and-answer period, someone asked Davis, "Do you see any relation between the prison system and the public school system?"

Hearing this, Rinehart raised her fists a little and quietly said, "Yay!" She often told her colleagues on the national debate circuit that Central was designed much like a prison, with long wings fanning out from a central pod, which could quickly be closed off in the instance of a riot. Every year the school goes into lockdown at least once or twice as cops are brought in with hungry German shepherds trained to sniff out drugs and gunpowder. Soon after I first met her, she told me that truant students were routinely brought to the school in handcuffs, which were removed as soon as they stepped through the door. The disturbing nature of this didn't register until I witnessed it myself. When I saw a kid muscled into the school one autumn day, wincing at the dig of the cuffs, I dreaded the message it was sending to the kid or any of the others who were standing around watching: *You're just a prisoner, nigger. The only lesson you need to learn is how to obey.*

You can feel this the minute you enter the door before the first class bell rings at 7:15. Every morning the throng of students pushes toward the two unlocked front doors to pass single file through the metal detectors and be patted down by the half-dozen uniformed guards. The school's administrators stand nearby dressed in suits with their arms crossed, watching the procession like wardens. A few of them carry bullhorns, and as the time for the beginning of class nears, they begin barking at the students through amplified voices, chasing them off to their assigned rooms. The shrill sound of bullhorns accompanies lunch period, which is also patrolled by an armed city cop. And at the end of the day, as many as ten district police cars arrive, and the patrolmen pace the parking lot, shooing the kids off into the deteriorating neighborhoods around the school. The school's front doors are locked every afternoon promptly at 2:00 p.m., so as to keep kids away. Then, for the rest of the afternoon, the school's administrators repeatedly announce on the PA system that students not affiliated with an official activity, or accompanied by an adult, are to leave the premises immediately or face trespassing charges. The message seems clear: Students are tolerated for only the minimum amount of time required to count them as warm bodies in order to keep the state's per-pupil dollars flowing in. Beyond that, they're intruders.

Upon hearing the question, Davis clucked her tongue with a note of shame. "Why is it that schools in poor neighborhoods look more like prisons than schools?" she asked, as if she were reading Rinehart's mind. "With more emphasis on metal detectors and punishment than learning? This is the way the prison culture bleeds into our society."

"You know," she continued after a beat, "this is one of the reasons why prisons really need to be abolished. It's . . . It's . . . It's . . . It serves as a default solution for a whole range of social problems that really ought to be dealt with elsewhere. It's the default solution to illiteracy. The schools don't work. We don't talk about building better schools, schools that are designed to encourage students to develop a passion about learning. We simply penalize our children by sending them to prison."

TWENTY-EIGHT

SION GIRL

MARCUS GOT WELL JUST IN TIME for the Kansas City Classic. The annual UMKC tournament was a sentimental favorite of his. As a freshman, he'd been named top speaker there, and he and his partner had won the tournament, beating Johnson County's Shawnee Mission East. His junior year he and Donnell made it to the finals but lost on a two-one decision.

He came into the tournament more determined than he'd been all year. The win at the Caucus had given him a jolt of earnestness (though not enough to encourage him to attend school while his tooth hurt). Almost as soon as he got home from the trip to Cedar Rapids, he had rummaged through his computer's hard drive and deleted all the game files. Without a doubt, the Caucus victory was the highlight of his young life, and it frightened him to think he'd almost missed it because he had wanted to go to a Counter-Strike tournament instead. As he lay around the house, popping tablets of Tylenol 3 to keep the pain of his pulled tooth at bay, he thought about the course of his life. He reflected on his early dreams of "becoming someone important," of following an educational and career path that would lead him to a position of power, preferably something in politics.

With all his gaming software gone, he filled his time by reading Sun Tzu's *Art of War*, which the father of a friend of his had given him. The ancient text's message of focus and conciseness in the face of chaos and adversity resonated with him, and he imagined himself a fearless and effective warrior. It didn't provide an awakening so much as an affirmation that he was doing all the right things to win the war. The book echoed his stepdad Glen's early lesson about fishing, when Marcus learned he needed just one worm to catch a fish. "One hundred victories in one hundred battles is not skillful," Sun Tzu told him. "Subduing the other's military without battle is the most skillful."

He found a special connection with the chapter on spies, because it reminded him of debate, the way debaters and coaches formed a network in tournaments and on Internet forums to help one another out:

Foreknowledge cannot be grasped from ghosts and spirits.

And to grasp knowledge, one needs knowledgeable people: spies. Marcus realized he had an abundance of spies. Rinehart was a spy. As was Sobek, as well as the judges on the circuit. And his friends from debate camp. And his teammates. Marcus felt sly as he read this, as if he'd pulled off a great trick. As soon as he got into debate, he had been surrounded by people with the answers and tools he'd need to succeed. All he'd had to do was show up and avail himself of their foreknowledge. But the trick had been on him. He thought he was cheating somehow, but really he'd gotten an education from his spies, despite his distaste for school.

"Secret! Secret!" Sun Tzu told him. "There is nothing for which one cannot employ spies."

Throughout the rounds of the UMKC tournament, and even during the downtime between rounds, he maintained a determined look, displaying the narrowed-eyes expression he typically reserved only for the later rounds, when trophies were on the line. He wanted nothing less than a perfect record at this, his final Kansas City Classic. And he was furious when this goal was thwarted in the second-to-last preliminary round, when the judge voted him and Brandon down on what they both felt was a boneheaded decision.

After the round he and Brandon stormed across campus to the student union, where they found Rinehart eating lunch. Marcus marched up to her and barked, "That was the stupidest fucking judge I've ever had in my life!" He abruptly turned and walked away before she could even ask why, much less scold him for cussing. She looked at Brandon, who frowned and shook his head. "He voted us down on topicality," Brandon said, "even though the other team didn't even really argue it. They just said," he switched into the goofy tone of a dolt, " 'Duh, topicality.' And he voted on it."

Rinehart twisted her face into a smirk. "Well," she said, "it's just one loss. You'll still break."

"I know," Brandon said. "But Marcus is pissed. He really wanted to go undefeated."

We looked across the food court. Marcus was leaning against a wall, leering at the floor, his hands jammed in his pockets. On either side of him stood a blond girl, each dressed in men's navy pin-striped suits and bright-colored Converse All Stars. They both looked at Marcus with their eyes opened wide and their lower lips protruding slightly, as if they wished to cheer him but were at a loss for how to do so.

I had learned earlier in the day that one of them, the shorter and skinnier of the two, was his girlfriend. Marcus introduced her to me as Libby Wichman. Her friend's name was Katie Schaag. They both debated for Notre Dame de Sion, an all-girls Catholic school in the wealthier southwest part of Kansas City. Marcus met Libby at UMKC's debate camp the previous summer. I wouldn't have called her "Coffee Stains" or "anorexic" as Brandon and Leo had done a week earlier right before Angela Davis's lecture. She was thin, yes, with a narrow face that extended into a pointy jaw. But her blue eyes were big and welcoming, and her long hair shone softly. She didn't look sexy so much as smart.

Their relationship started as a friendship. At camp the two talked about their mutual love for debate, later learning that they both played Counter-Strike. Libby could even program computers, which Marcus thought was cool. After camp, they stayed in touch through e-mail and Instant Messenger, and soon they were going on weekly dates. Invariably, they'd meet up in Westport, Kansas City's main nightlife zone, where they'd have dinner and catch a flick at the Tivoli Theater, an art house. There they watched movies most of his Central classmates wouldn't see even if they were paid to do so, character-driven films such as *Bend It Like Beckham*, *The Pianist*, and *Lovely and Amazing*. Afterward, they'd go to the Broadway Café, a popular nightspot for the city's teenage bohemians, and talk about the films. Marcus knew what guys like Brandon and Leo thought of Libby. They razzed him about her plain looks and her geeky interests. Sometimes he even bowed to their hazing and downplayed the romance. Inside, though, he felt proud of having won the affections of a girl like Libby. She was from the other side of the tracks, so to speak, a Sion girl, cultured, wealthy, sharp. In his mind, a ghetto kid like him dating a girl like her was a social coup.

She was white, but Marcus shrugged this off. He told me he didn't consider race when it came to women, though I never heard him talk fondly of any girls from his school. Marcus was hardly a Don Juan, and a brainy girl like Libby seemed a perfect match for him. At Central, pretty much all of the really sharp girls, at least the ones who weren't shy about displaying their intelligence, were on the debate squad, and debate was too important to Marcus for him to mix it up with an affair.

Before I officially met Libby, I was standing with Brandon, Sobek, and DeAndre Tolbert, a former Central debater who had come to the UMKC tournament to volunteer as a judge, in a commons area outside the classrooms where rounds were being held. It was a between time, and the place was crowded with kids and coaches standing around waiting for schedules to come out. Sobek spotted Marcus on the other side of the room with two girls. "Is that them?" he asked, pointing.

"Yep," Brandon said, smiling as if he were about to crack up.

"Which one is Libby?" Sobek asked.

"The shorter one."

"Oh, Marcus," DeAndre said, shaking his head. "Man, his body language is all wrong."

We watched the scene for a few minutes. Marcus was stooped slightly at the waist as he talked to the girls, as if he were subconsciously trying to keep his crotch away from them. His eyes darted around while Libby's were locked right in on his.

MARCUS EVENTUALLY COOLED DOWN from his anger over the defeat. When the schedule for the final preliminary round came out, he grabbed one, and he and Libby looked at it together. Libby's partner, Katie, looked over their shoulders. "Oh, my God!" she exclaimed, throwing her head back in exasperation. "We're debating you!"

Marcus tried to give the friendliest smile he could, saying, "Don't worry about it."

But his eyes betrayed a hint of his bloodlust, his eagerness to show his girlfriend what he could do. He added, "You guys'll probably win."

"Yeah, right," Libby said.

They made their way up to a classroom on the fourth floor. The Sion girls ran the health insurance parity case, not as simple a version as the novice debaters did in DEBATE–Kansas City, of course, but not as complicated as the one Brandon and Marcus had faced when they beat Rosemount at the Caucus. The Central guys ran a political argument against it, saying passage of a bill forcing insurance companies to provide the same benefits for mental illness as for physical maladies would cost President Bush political capital and he wouldn't be able to pass tax cuts, on which the health of America's economy depends, according to the evidence Rinehart bought for them from Cross-X.com, much of it culled from the shrill conservative voice of *The Wall Street Journal*'s editorial board.

Marcus was extremely polite as he laid out his arguments and interrogated his girlfriend during cross-x, speaking in a gentle voice and peppering everything with pleases and thank yous and gratuitous compliments. But he and Brandon still went all out, spinning a web of arguments that the girls found impossible to untangle. By the end of the round, Libby and Katie had sunk far down in their seats with their hands over their mouths to stifle embarrassed giggles.

When the round ended, they rushed into the hall and burst out laughing. Marcus came out with a contrite smile stretched across his face.

"We didn't have any, like, evidence for your counterplan," Katie said, "so I just, like, picked, like, cards at random to read."

Marcus gave a guilty shrug, and the girls collapsed into each other, laughing. He reached out and gently grabbed Libby's shoulder. "You looked like you were comfortable," he offered.

"That's good," she said, suppressing her laughter for a moment.

"Definitely." He nodded affirmingly. "The next thing you have to do is, like, completely forget about that round now."

Libby tilted her head and gave a classic "you've got to be kidding" nod.

"Like, forget about it," he insisted. "Okay?"

"All right," she said meekly. Their chuckles returned.

"Never happened," Marcus said, waving a hand across the space between them to shoo the experience away.

MARCUS WANDERED THE HALLS with Libby and Katie while they waited for the elimination-round pairings to come out. The matchups arrived as bittersweet news: two Central teams—Marcus and Brandon, as well as Francesca Menes and Kerra McCorkle—had broken, but owing to the ranking system they were paired against each other. Rinehart hated when that happened. It meant she'd have to decide which team would go on competing and which would be done for the weekend.

Rinehart called a quick conference between the victorious debaters. "I want all four of you at one time, please," she said, waving them toward her.

"Okay, here's my decision," Marcus blurted, pointing at Fran. "Whatever you wanna do."

Rinehart turned to Fran and Kerra. Like Day and Dionne, they were far down on the Central squad's pecking order. While Marcus and Brandon had traveled to every tournament that season, the girl teams traded off. All of the females got very little coaching from Sobek.

"Okay, what Marcus is saying," she began slowly before Marcus cut her off.

"I've been through it all before," he said, meaning trophy rounds. "Whatever you wanna do."

"He wants another team to advance," Rinehart continued. "But Brandon hasn't advanced in all these rounds," meaning he hadn't ever made it to the latter stages of the Kansas City Classic, as Marcus had. The comment undercut her show of neutrality; it was clear that she would prefer for Marcus and Brandon to continue on, because, of the two teams, they had the best chance of winning it all. In her entire coaching career, Rinehart had never had a varsity team win two tournaments in a single season, much less in a two-week span. "It's a decision between the four of you all," she added.

"I have a coin," Marcus said impatiently. "Call it heads or tails."

"No, y'all can *go*," Fran insisted.

"No!" Brandon yelled. "No 'heads or tails.' Look. Come here." He pulled Marcus over to him. He looked as though he wanted to tell Marcus that they should keep going, that he'd caught the winning buzz and he didn't want to come down. The Caucus win had lit a fire in him. All through the UMKC tournament, judges were telling him how much he'd improved over the previous years when they'd judged his rounds. But instead he said, "I mean, whatever you wanna do."

"I mean . . ." Marcus said. He looked at Brandon, and his partner's longing seemed to register with him. "Okay, we'll debate."

"You sure?" Rinehart asked, bending slightly so she could look in his down-turned eyes. He nodded silently. His eyes had narrowed again. The game was on.

THEY MOVED EASILY through the trophy rounds, dispensing with the suburban Kansas City teams with rapid-fire, byzantine political and philosophical arguments. As they advanced, the crowds watching their rounds grew larger and larger until the final round, where all the desks were quickly claimed and people had to sit on the floor. Most of the onlookers were there to watch Marcus and Brandon: the Sion girls, a few Central teammates, some kids from other Kansas City School District schools. Much of the chatting I eavesdropped on was about the Central duo. One kid from a suburban school on the Missouri side of the metro area told a friend that Marcus and Brandon were the best debaters in the state, if you were judging based on the faster national-circuit style. "Missouri debate is bad," he added. He called out to Marcus, mentioning the state's high school activities association. "They can suck it, right, Marcus?" he asked.

"I won't even give them the pleasure," Marcus said, looking up, his expression dead serious.

The final-round opponents, from Blue Valley High, a school on the southwestern frontier of the Kansas City metro area, argued on the negative side. They launched a political disadvantage argument. When they did, Leo let out a short, quiet whistle. "They shouldn't run politics," he whispered to me. "Marcus is a politics debater."

During cross-x, Dionne leaned over and whispered to me, "Marcus is so smart. He's a genius." She would have liked to be as good as Marcus, but she didn't believe she ever could be. Truth be told, she didn't really like debate, even though she was naturally argumentative and, judging from her nearly perfect grades, very smart. She only participated on the squad because it was the only viable option at Central for brainy kids. Sure, she liked the culture of the team and didn't really mind her lowly status. It seemed just to her. The boys *were* better, though she knew this was due to their getting the lion's share of help from Sobek. But the game itself, she just couldn't click with it. The speed-reading was awkward and weird. And all the arguments seemed ridiculous, all that nuclear war and genocide. *Why can't we debate stuff that's real?* she often thought—like poverty issues and crime, the stuff she dealt with in her life. This year's topic, mental health care, seemed perfect for that. It was an issue with real substance in her little corner of American society, what with all the broken souls wandering day and night along the busy streets that crisscross her neighborhood. But, no, all that these white boys in debate seemed to want to argue about was Democrats hating Republicans and genocide and nuclear war. It was bullshit, if you asked her.

Still, she could appreciate talent when she saw it. And Marcus was all that. Being a member of the debate squad, even one of those always sitting in the back of the room during the trophy rounds, or relegated to the least-coveted seats in the squad van, she could claim a little piece of his glory. Hierarchies or no, they were all comrades in the same cause. They were family.

AFTERWARD, WHEN Marcus and Brandon were given the championship trophy, well-wishers crowded around them. A debater from Lincoln College Prep bowed and wailed playfully, "You guys are awesome! I'm not worthy!"

Rinehart ran up and hugged Brandon. "Way to go, baby!" she yelled.

Marcus cowered away from her. "What is that crap?" he said. "Don't do that to me!"

Marcus went out into the hall with Libby and Katie.

"You were awesome," Libby said, reaching out for his shoulder. For a second it looked as though they might embrace, but she just gave him a light tap.

He lowered his head and smiled shyly.

"Thanks," he said. "You guys were great, too. You should have won it."

Then she and Katie were off, having stayed out long past the hour they'd told their parents they'd be home.

We all loaded into the school van and went to Winstead's, a 1950s-style hamburger joint near the Country Club Plaza. It was nearly midnight.

Rinehart beamed as her debaters plowed through their burgers, onion rings, and tall, creamy shakes.

"I never thought I'd see the day," she said. "Two wins in two weeks."

"Now," she added, suddenly twisting her smile into a smirk, "if we can just pull off a win against MSHSAA"—she pronounced it "Mee-sha"—"this season will be a *total* success."

TWENTY-NINE

POLITICAL CAPITAL

IF RINEHART WAS SURPRISED when Antoine sauntered into her class on a drizzly afternoon in early November, she didn't show it. She had harangued him almost every day about his no-shows for after-school practice, but she got sick of it and gave up. She had even gone so far as to ponder possible new partners for Ebony, which killed her because she knew Antoine could be one of the squad's best debaters. Not since Marcus had she had a novice debater who caught on so quickly. And Ebony couldn't stand the thought of a switch. But he was getting desperate. That seemed the only way he'd have a chance of winning the city championship and a free trip to the UDL national championship in Atlanta.

Antoine settled into a desk near the bookshelves and cupped his fingers thoughtfully around his chin, glancing casually across the room through the gaps between his spindly dreads as if he'd never been gone. He wouldn't admit it, but Rinehart's nagging had gotten to him. So had his relatives. Every time he went to a family gathering, his mom would start bragging about his being on the debate squad, and his relatives would brighten and slap him on the shoulder and say, "You stick with that debatin'. It'll take you places." The mixed message wasn't lost on him. The words were part compliment, part threat: *You're smart as hell, so don't fuck it up and let your people down.*

In truth, he came back for the perks. Like Ebony, he didn't have shit else to do. Debate wasn't that bad. The tournaments weren't overrun with pimply punks with pocket protectors, like he'd imagined. There were girls there, and fine-looking ones at that. He'd felt like a pimp at the Paseo tournament, sitting on the edge of the stage before the awards ceremony with Ebony and a couple of girls from the host school. One was Principal McClendon's granddaughter, and she looked good in her snug jeans and smart, lacy blouse. They'd been just hanging out there, talking about nothing in particular, when she'd suddenly blurted, "You have pretty eyes." He'd blushed and whispered, "Thanks." And then he shyly walked away. Later, Ebony had smacked him on the shoulder. "Dude!" Antoine's partner had scolded him. "Why you walk off like that?! They want your jungle snake!" That botched opportunity alone was enough to bring him back.

And then there was Chicago. A few days after the Paseo tournament, in class, Rinehart laid out details about their upcoming trip to the Windy City to compete at the Glenbrooks, a big national tournament that Ebony, judging from the way he leaned back in his seat and tugged at his collar like a badass, seemed to regard as bigger than the Super Bowl. For a week straight, Ebony kept saying "Mothereffin' Glenbrooks" over and over again. Antoine had to laugh at this; more of Ebony's wanksta posturing. He figured that no debate tournament, no matter how cool, could be *that* cool. But then Rinehart said, in a phony show of disappointment, that they'd have to skip two days of school to go there, that they'd be boarding a big charter bus with kids from all over the city (including the Paseo girls), and that they'd be staying in a motel, in rooms with no adults. Upon hearing this, Antoine rubbed his chin whiskers pensively. "Hmmm," he said. "I get to skip school *and* go to Chicago. I'm gonna have to think about this." He laughed so hard his body shook. "Mothereffin' Glenbrooks," he said.

So now it was Antoine Lewis: bona fide no-life debater. As if he had a life anyway. If he weren't here, he'd be . . . "What *would* I be doing?" he replied when I asked him one afternoon. "I dunno. Hang out." He scratched his head and said, "Damn. It's kind of bothering me that I can't think of anything we really do."

He was always with his crew—Donyell, Brandon, Ronnell, Alana, sometimes Isabelle. They all carted around backpacks stuffed with changes of clothes, CDs, comic books, book books, a dictionary (they all carried dictionaries). They *did* things. It just wasn't ever anything really worth remembering. They'd play video games. They'd walk all over town. Sometimes they'd hop a bus and go to Westport, "the hippie part of town," he called it, where all they could do was browse in the skateboard and clothing shops because they didn't have any money. Sometimes they'd get into deep conversations about God and the universe, but he couldn't recite any conclusions they'd reached. Sometimes they'd share their half-finished writing with each other. Sometimes they'd fight. One time they got into it ("I mean, *really* got into it," Antoine explained, "like almost hitting each other") over who was the sexiest in the bunch. Their arguments always seemed so important at the time. But when he'd wake up the next day, he'd forget what they'd said. He often thought that most of his fellow students were trapped in a prison of sorts, a mental cage, one of their own making. But when he took the time to honestly look at where he was, what he had to show for his days, he had to admit he was in one, too.

It was a good day to come back to debate practice. The first chills of winter were moving in, and the sun was setting earlier each night, so his limited nonschool options were dwindling further still. And Rinehart's lessons had finally advanced to some real issues. No sooner had he found his seat than she went to the dry-erase board, uncapped a marker, and wrote "Political Capital" in big orange letters.

"Okay," she said. "You know we have a two-party system in this country. Basically. What are those two parties?"

"Democrats and Republicans," Antoine answered.

"Who are considered the liberals?" Rinehart asked. "What party?"

"I thought it was, um, the Republicans," Antoine said.

"No," said Fran, the varsity debater. "Democrats are the liberals."

"So what are the issues?" Rinehart continued. "What are some liberal issues? Things that liberals think are good?"

"Like welfare and stuff like that?" Antoine asked.

"Okay," Rinehart allowed. "Not welfare so much, but social services."

She wrote "social services" on the board in angled cursive.

"What's another thing that they would be supportive of?"

"Who?" Ebony asked, suddenly coming to attention. He had been humming a tune to himself, affecting an air of cool, as if he hadn't noticed the return of his prodigal son, much less cared about it.

"Health care," Fran shouted over him.

"Health care," Rinehart concurred. "Women's issues. Children's issues. The environment."

She wrote these down, too, her handwriting getting messier with speed. She capped her pen and tapped the board. "These are all what you would consider liberal issues. Liberal *ideas*. And pretty much, we've associated the Democratic Party with them."

After a deliberate scan of their faces, she began again. "Okay. What kind of issues would the conservatives be in favor of?"

There was a long silence.

"Money, basically," Antoine said with a laugh, straightening in his chair. "Money."

"Okay." Rinehart nodded. "Um, yeah. Balanced budget." And as she wrote that down, she muttered, "Supposedly."

"Improving the economy for their country," Antoine added.

"Um, oil," Rinehart said, and she put that on the list. "Drilling anyplace they want to. Making more money. You know, cutting down trees."

"So basically what, Ms. Rinehart?" Ebony stammered. "So the Democrats are poor and the Republicans are rich?"

Rinehart nodded emphatically and smiled. "Right," she said. "And they're very much anti–women's rights. I mean, they're not in favor of any kind of abortion issues."

"They don't really care for minorities," Antoine suggested.

"That's right," Rinehart agreed. "They really don't like the poor."

These were hellish times for a liberal like Rinehart. President George W. Bush was pushing for his third tax cut in two years; this one—aimed at the capital gains tax on investment—would almost exclusively benefit the nation's wealthy. The budget surplus that had blossomed during the Clinton years had disappeared, and the deficit was growing. Rinehart feared this would eventually lead to cuts in education and the scant social services her students depend on. And Bush was pushing for an attack on Iraq—too eagerly, she thought. All the talk was about weapons of mass destruction that were hidden somewhere in the country, but, it seemed to her, the president wasn't giving UN inspectors enough time to snoop around and find them, if, in fact, they were even there.

"Okay." Rinehart set her marker down. "Now, as long as there's a balance in this two-party system, as long as we've got fifty Democrats in the Senate and fifty Republicans in the Senate, things are gonna pretty much, you know, we get in that gridlock situation. Now, political capital is when . . . Bush wants something, he wants a bill passed. How does he get stuff done?"

"Well," Antoine said tentatively, "he takes it to the Senate a lot of times."

"'Cause they're his buddy," Fran agreed. "Now he has them."

"Yeah," Antoine said.

"He picks up the phone!" Rinehart said, waving her arms excitedly.

"Yeah," Antoine said, "because they control the Senate now and they can get it passed."

"Right," Rinehart agreed. "So when he wants something, he uses what they call political capital. He can call up and say things like, 'You know, my brother's got a company over here; we can hire your little brother. We can get your cousin on the board. We can do a lot of things for you. Not give him money per se, because that would be a bribe, and that would be really bad. But we could get you a job somewhere. Maybe I could appoint your sister to the council of something or other and give her $75,000 a year just to be the assistant secretary of nothing."

"I wouldn't say no," Ebony said, stretching back, lacing his fingers behind his neck.

"So he uses *political capital*," Rinehart said. "He uses *favors* to get what he wants passed."

"Bush is evil," Antoine said as if he were spitting.

"Well, all politicians do it," Rinehart said. "It's not just . . . In fairness, everybody does it. All right? So the argument is, to get this passed, or to get . . . If the affirmative plan gets passed, Bush has to use a lot of political capital."

"It's trade-offs," Antoine said.

"Bush is just so fuckin' stupid," one of the varsity debaters said, and Rinehart didn't scold her.

"And cash on the side." Antoine finished his point, laughing.

"It's complicated," Rinehart said, drawing the discussion toward its conclusion. "And it's hard. And I know you won't understand it until you run it for a while. Truly."

"It sounds pretty cool, though," Antoine said. He leaned back, looking as though he'd been sufficiently entertained. "I wanna run one of these political capital arguments Wednesday night."

"What's Wednesday night?" I asked.

"Practice," he said.

Rinehart raised her eyebrows at me and allowed a glimpse of her smile.

How great would it be to be a kid again? Rinehart found herself wondering that from time to time. Wouldn't it be nice to be so young that a concept like political capital wasn't yet real, was actually fun? For her, the whole notion of favor trading hit too close to home. It reminded her of how power-poor she was as an urban schoolteacher. Hers was a vicious, hierarchical world, and, unfortunately, she knew exactly where she stood in it: next to the bottom, right above the students.

RINEHART HATED THIS PLACE. She stepped into the auditorium where the Kansas City school board meets every other Wednesday night, paused at the top of the aisle, and looked around until she spotted me, sitting down near the front. She descended into the dimly lit room, with its light blue walls all dingy with age. The brightest spot in the whole place was the stage, which displayed a long curving banquet table draped in plush maroon fabric, surrounded by high-back leather executive chairs, each empty, awaiting the arrival of the members of the Kansas City school board. The elected officials were running late, as usual. They were all in a sumptuous boardroom ten stories above, conducting their weekly "executive," or secret, meeting. That's where the real decisions were made. The one Rinehart and I and the rest of the public were allowed to attend would be more of a formality, a staged event where already-made decisions would officially be decided.

Rinehart settled into the seat beside me, and I handed her a packet of board items, a thick stack of documents related to the business concerns the elected officials would be discussing. She flipped through the first several pages: all invoices from law firms, six bills in all, totaling a little less than a quarter-million dollars. They were for two months' worth of work, though not *all* the legal work district officials had bought during that time span. For the 2002–2003 school year, the district's legal expenses totaled $3 million, just over $83 per student. By contrast, the St. Louis School District, a similar urban district, with the second-highest legal budget in Missouri, spent $43 per kid. In other districts around Kansas City, the per-pupil expenditure was much lower, from $11 to a mere $2.50. In Kansas City, education leaders spent more on lawyers and legal settlements than they did on curriculum development.

The sight of the bills sickened Rinehart. "My God," she said, adding up the totals in her head. "Meanwhile," she said, closing the packet, "we have to wrap hot dogs to send kids to debate camp."

Gradually the room began to fill. There were a few teens, dressed up in ROTC uniforms, presumably to be officially recognized by the board for some achievement or another. The rest were adults, looking bored and miserable, like us. At about half past six, district administrators began striding down the aisles, some carrying briefcases, others clutching clipboards to their chests. Rinehart spotted Phyllis Budesheim and approached her. A tall woman, Budesheim wore a gray suit and large plastic-rim glasses. They shook hands, and Rinehart gave her a sheet of paper bearing a bulleted list of the Central debate squad's contentions with the state activities association. Budesheim smiled primly as she accepted it. Rinehart thanked her, bowing slightly, and returned to her seat. That was it, the sum total of what she could do for her students.

One by one, the board members filed in, a newspaper reporter following, asking the board's vice president questions and scribbling notes on a legal pad as she walked along. They took their places in the leather chairs on the stage, uncapped the Dasani water bottles that a lesser staffer had set out for them, and promptly started fighting. It was a rehash of the summer's political battle du jour, regarding the district's resource center for parents and the District Advisory Committee, or DAC, Kansas City's version of a PTA. Mundane, but in Kansas City the stuff of venomous dispute. A board member was demanding a public apology from the superintendent and her colleagues on the board, who refused to acquiesce. So they all started yelling at each other. At the peak of the snarl, Rinehart leaned over and whispered to me, "The kids love to come and see this stuff. They talk about it for weeks. They can't believe adults can act like such fools."

As a reporter, I had never encountered such a dysfunctional organization. In my first year covering the district, the board had been found guilty in court of holding an illegal meeting, at which they fired the former superintendent and his top assistant. At the same time, state legislators had introduced a bill in Jefferson City calling for the state to immediately take over the district. A federal judge had ordered an investigation into allegations of patronage and micromanagement by board members. Students had begun the 2001–2002 school year without new textbooks that had already been bought and paid for; when a board member inquired about the missing texts, no one could say for sure where they were. The next year students from all the district's high schools had arrived for the first day of class at a college-prep program for gifted kids without knowing they'd been disenrolled because district officials had balked at the $24,000 price tag for all the program's students for an entire year (which, incidentally, was less than half the price of an average monthly bill from one of the district's many contracted and politically connected law firms). There'd been an ugly fight over the restructuring of school board election districts following the 2000 census; a black political group had muscled in and broken up the district encompassing the predominantly white and wealthy southwest portion of the city, but their actions were reversed by two well-known political operatives—one black, the other white (who happened to have worked on the white board president's election campaign)—who were paid several thousand dollars to redraw the districts themselves, so that the wealthier white district was restored and the district encompassing the poorer white and Hispanic northeast part of the city was broken up. This district was an institution that had, on several occasions, bounced all its employees' paychecks; that had allowed its teacher shortage to increase each year, so students routinely went through entire semesters with substitutes who essentially served as babysitters because they knew little about the subjects they were supposed to be teaching.

The place seethed with incompetence. I had difficulty getting even the most basic documents, such as receipts and contracts; officials would tell me they didn't know where to find them. Once, when I asked for documentation of the district's programs for gifted students, for which it received several million dollars in state grants, I was given three documents showing they'd received the state's money. I asked for a list of gifted and advanced-placement classes at the district's high schools, and I was told they didn't keep such records at the central office. They would have to collect the information from each school's principal (the administrator groaned audibly as she informed me of this, as if my request were superfluous and I was preventing her from doing her work). When I would occasionally stop by the district's offices, I'd find files that were haphazardly arranged, folders buried in dust. And whenever I visited, no matter what time of day, I could hear the sound of televisions tuned to daytime soaps trickling through the halls. As a teacher, Rinehart had the misfortune of having to burrow even deeper into the beast. From her perspective, it was an institution fueled by myriad conflicting self-interests, a collection of bureaucratic lifers whose day-to-day duties, it seemed, were to protect their own turf. These administrators, most of them earning healthy salaries upwards of $50,000, had weathered so many reform initiatives and so-called housecleanings that they were utterly impervious to change. I had talked with many of these would-be reformers who had been chased away, and the stories they told were horrific. A former director of human resources told me she had arrived at an office with "piles of paper on every damn surface." She told me that teachers would sometimes sneak in and purge the files of their own disciplinary records; in some cases, teachers slated for firing were rehired.

To make matters worse, the $2 billion desegregation remedy plan had bloated the institution and split its leadership between the board and the superintendent, who were often at odds, and, perhaps most powerful of all, the legal department, where, naturally, liability concerns tended to trump the needs of students. In this system, even simple decisions, such as allowing a debate team to compete in Omaha, were bogged down for days, weeks, or even months. Sure, the district had some good, competent people working in its central office. I'd personally met one—the guy who ran the dropout-prevention program. Beyond him, I had met no one I would trust with the welfare of the city's children.

AFTER THE BOARD MEMBERS' ARGUMENT finally died out, the meeting dragged on for an hour and a half longer. I felt bad at the end, because there was no discussion of the district's efforts to get the state activities association's rules changed to allow Marcus and Brandon to compete at the Tournament of Champions in Kentucky; Rinehart had only come to the meeting because I'd told her they would be talking about it. That's what the board president, Al Mauro, had told me the day before, when I'd attended a meeting of the board's executive committee, consisting of the chairs of its various subcommittees. They'd discussed the matter that morning, briefly. "I hate to see our students unable to compete on a national level," Mauro had said, sitting at the head of a conference table in a meeting room adjacent to the superintendent's office on the tenth floor of district headquarters. "I think we may need to develop a strategy in case we can't all agree to sing from the same hymnal," meaning if district officials couldn't persuade their counterparts in the activities association to ease up on their rules, the district might have to make rules of its own. "We may have to form our own church to get it done," Mauro said, extending the metaphor.

It was clear from the superintendent's demeanor that this wasn't going to happen. Dr. Bernard Taylor shifted back in his seat and mentioned that this was a matter school districts were struggling with all over the nation, and that they didn't want to risk being suspended from other activities, such as basketball and football. The whole discussion lasted just a minute or so, and soon the board members were fighting over the issue of a tax abatement for Crown Center, an upscale shopping, office, and residential complex just south of downtown, owned by Hallmark, one of a handful of businesses that essentially run Kansas City.

That same evening I happened to take Marcus, Brandon, and Leo to a movie at Crown Center, *8 Mile*, starring Eminem. The guys were huge fans. We got there early enough to grab a bite to eat at the food court. The place was dead, not generating much tax money for itself, much less for the school district. It was an impressive place. Off to the side of the food court, a pair of escalators rose in a broad atrium with high glass walls on one end overlooking a plaza with a fountain and, beyond it, Hallmark's corporate headquarters. The mall's interior was impeccable, though its early-1980s bright color scheme and chrome-and-glass design were beginning to look dated. It was just past seven in the evening, and all the shops were still open, though I wouldn't have run out of fingers if I'd tried counting the number of customers wandering the corridors. The shops offered mostly tourist fare—their racks filled with souvenirs of Kansas City and pricey tchotchkes made of porcelain and brass. There was a large Hallmark store and another full of Crayola crayons (Hallmark owns Crayola). Judging from these offerings, I surmised that most of the mall's shoppers came from the Westin hotel, which is connected to the shopping center by a pedestrian walkway that was paid for with federal transportation funds.

This network of exposed footbridges extended to Union Station, an early-twentieth-century train depot with a vast lobby and spectacularly high ornate ceilings. The landmark had been all but abandoned by the 1990s, until voters on both sides of the state line agreed to a sales tax increase to pay for it to be remodeled. Less than a decade later, the remodel, complete with a science museum, attracted few visitors and was losing public money by the millions. As we strode through this near-vacant palace of shopping and tourism, I felt a momentary surge of taxpayer rage, anger at the city leaders who had privately schemed up this financial flop that drains resources away from kids. They were the same well-connected people who continued to mold the city, mostly white businessmen and attorneys and elected officials who pushed an increasing number of tax-break packages and bond issues to fund big-ticket items that, judging from history—the oft-barren convention center and poorly placed arena and the myriad lured businesses that were earning far below projections—would be failures as well.

Our voices echoed in the cavernous space. In the distance, Brandon spotted a kid he knew making his way out the mall's front doors to a bus stop. He was a former classmate, the previous year's valedictorian as a matter of fact. Brandon shook his head. "Man, he's not even in college," he said.

"He was smart," Marcus said. "He had like a 28 on the ACT."

"So when you gonna take the ACT?" Brandon asked.

"Man, I'll bling-bling that," Marcus bragged to Brandon, making a show of brushing imaginary dust off his shoulders. "I'm good at tests."

"You missed the deadline," Brandon said.

"No, I'm taking it in February," Marcus replied.

"That's supposed to be the last makeup time," Brandon retorted, his voice rising. "You got Rinehart trippin'. Like, you won't get into college."

"I'm in debate," Marcus said, pulling at his collar. "I got scholarships. Besides, all you need is 18. I'll get 18. And even if we don't get 18, we'll get in."

When we got to the theater, only four other people were there, all of them black. The movie is about a poor white kid who lives with his mother in a trailer on the white side of 8 Mile, a road that has historically divided blacks and whites in Detroit. This kid, played by Eminem, is a phenomenal rapper who is trying to make a name for himself at freestyle competitions held in abandoned buildings in Detroit's urban core. The climactic showdown is just like a debate tournament, with Eminem winning his way through elimination rounds. In the final round, he tears apart his nemesis, hurling insults so sharp and funny that Brandon, Marcus, and Leo nearly fell out of their seats, they were laughing so hard. In the end, Eminem's character lands a recording contract and is off to a bigger city where fame and fortune await.

On our way home I told the guys I thought the movie was like them in reverse. Here was a white kid who had learned the lingo of blacks and won at their own game. The Central kids had done the same in an alternate universe, debate, a verbal game long dominated by whites. The main difference was that debate offered greater odds of success; few rappers score lucrative recording contracts, but college scholarships followed by long, successful careers are common among high school debaters. This thought hadn't occurred to the guys, they admitted, but they liked it. I think they were flattered to be compared to Eminem.

It was then that I really understood—naively, I would later realize—how important debate is, that the game is the best education-reform tool I've ever seen, at least for brilliant, slightly rebellious kids like this. It's the greatest trick in public education. It inspires kids who couldn't care less about school to dive into their studies simply to avoid losing an hour-long battle of the minds with someone their own age. Indeed, Marcus and Brandon and, to a lesser extent, Leo had attained celebrity status in a nationwide subculture that roams from tournament to tournament and mingles online at Cross-X.com. And they're still cool, because debate allows them to use their street smarts and pump up their egos. This, it seemed to me, was political power, something I doubt these teens would otherwise have been able to obtain. And like Eminem, they'd earned it in the purest of ways: in face-to-face showdowns, in public, for all the world to see; a way that will gradually disappear as they mature and strive to make their names in so-called real-life venues, be they political or professional.

As we rode east through Kansas City in the dark, past the long-vacant hulls of the sumptuous theaters and upscale hotels and condo towers of yesteryear, Marcus said, "Shit, man, I should start rapping." He pounded a beat on the seat back in front of him. "You best not mess with Marcus Leach," he yelled, "or else you'll be another bum on the beach."

Brandon and Leo doubled over laughing.

"Man, it's hard to come up with the words," Marcus said. "I've got the speed. I just need the words."

THIRTY

MACK DADDY

NOW IT WAS ANTOINE'S TURN TO FRET. Most of the other kids were already on the bus, shimmying down the aisles, holding their day packs head-high to clear the chair backs, staking out the perfect spot for a twelve-hour ride. The bus driver was starting to close the cargo doors, bringing one, then two, down with a jarring slam. Antoine rose up on his toes and craned his neck to peer over the cars in the parking lot. He scanned the traffic moving along Indiana Avenue. None slowed and turned in to Central's parking lot. He looked down and scuffed a heel against the pavement. "Ebony better come," he muttered to himself. "Ebony better come."

It was late November, and Antoine had become a full-on, committed-for-life debate geek. His dad had dropped him off at Central at about 6:30, well before the 7:00 a.m. meeting time Coach Rinehart had set. When his mom knocked on his door at 5:30, he shot right out of bed. Usually he'd pull the pillow over his head to steal a few more minutes of sleep. He'd been looking forward to this day for weeks. He was going to Chicago. The Glenbrooks. One of the biggest tournaments in the country. And his partner was nowhere to be seen.

Antoine gave up searching traffic and muscled his evidence tubs and suitcase into the cargo hold. Ever since that meeting with the woman from the foreign exchange program, where Ebony insisted he'd never go to Azerbaijan, Antoine had worried about his partner. He got more and more worried the closer they got to the trip. Ebony had been freaking out about traveling. He kept asking, "How long the bus ride gonna be? We gonna be on some ratty old school bus? What's the motel like? Like on Independence Avenue? They got TV? A toilet? Towels? Soap? We gonna be the only blacks there?" Ebony's teammates tried to reassure him ("Where you think R. Kelly's from?"). But Ebony seemed genuinely frightened. He didn't hide his emotions well. When he was nervous about something, his eyes widened and his face twitched. "I don't know about this," he kept saying. "I just don't know."

Antoine strode up to Rinehart. She was scowling, deep in thought, eyes narrow as a hunter's. "Man, where is Ebony?" he asked her.

"I'm not worried about Ebony," she said. "I'm worried about Sobek."

She knew Ebony had no life to speak of beyond debate. He'd be there, if a little late. But Sobek was a college kid. God only knew where his priorities were at seven on a cold November morning. He was always late, which she could deal with most days. But not this one. She'd arranged this whole event almost entirely by herself—she booked the charter bus, made motel reservations, coordinated the tournament entry fees. Debaters and coaches from most of the high schools in the city, from both sides of the state line, agreed to chip in on the costs, but it was Rinehart who got it done. Some of the other coaches didn't want to pay their share. Plus, the tournament hadn't even been sanctioned by the state activities association until days before the teams were set to leave for Chicago. Rinehart thought this absurd. Not only was the Glenbrooks one of the nation's biggest high school tournaments (rivaling only Harvard's annual affair in sheer numbers, with more than two hundred schools competing); it was also directed by a man who sat on the board of directors of the National Forensic League. In the eyes of the activities association officials, though, it was a rogue affair so long as the proper paperwork went unsigned. Of course, Rinehart took care of that, too.

EVENTUALLY, EBONY SHOWED UP, then Sobek, all sleepy-eyed with mussed-up hair. Rinehart climbed into the bus and paused to count heads. It was a sumptuous and clean rig, with seats that leaned back and TV monitors mounted every six feet or so on the overhead luggage racks. Antoine and Ebony squeezed past her, Ebony holding his tattered black gym bag and floppy pillow aloft to clear his fellow passengers' heads. He and Antoine sat across the aisle from each other. Ebony rooted through his bag and pulled out a couple of library books, *Constructing a Life Philosophy* and *Ten Philosophical Mistakes*, and propped them up in the window with their covers facing outward for all the world to see, not aware that the windows were tinted.

The bus doors closed and we were on our way, just fifteen minutes behind schedule. We headed north through the forlorn East Side streets, onto the highway, and past downtown and the river and the factories huddled near the rail yards leaking steam into the brisk morning air, and then off across the prairie.

The sun was setting as we passed through the outer spread of Chicagoland, and it was dark by the time we reached the urban core. Rinehart sat in the front row, bolt upright, her hands clasped in her lap. She shook her head. Our destination was the far northern edge of the metro area, and the quickest route was along an outer beltway. But the driver had pushed straight into the city, toward the skyscrapers of the Loop, in the thickest part of rush hour, because, he said, that was the route his supervisors had given him and he couldn't deviate from it. But in the back of the bus it all seemed to be part of the plan. As we cut northward, we got a clear view of the skyline. Antoine and Ebony stared out the window. The night sky glowed red at its lower edges, hugging the broad sweep of towers all glimmering with light. "It's huge," Antoine said. He sized up this downtown against Kansas City's and deemed the latter "itty-bitty" and "gay." He figured you could fit KC in Chicago twenty or thirty times and still have room for an extra skyscraper.

But even the postcard view was no match for the Red Roof Inn. Ebony snatched the room key from Rinehart's hand, and he and Antoine bounded up the stairs. After a couple of awkward attempts with the key card, he popped the door open and peeked tentatively inside. He flipped on the light switch. "A'ight. A'ight," he said. The place was as clean as a photo on a brochure, with a big TV sitting on a dresser. He nodded his head and strode in with a pimp roll, dropping his cargo on a bed, and picked up a video game controller that was sitting on top of the TV, giving it a few practice jabs with his thumb. "This is some fly shit," he said. He strolled into the bathroom, flipped the sink faucet on and off, and gave the toilet a flush. He came out beaming.

"Cro!" he yelled.

"What?!" Antoine replied, a bit startled.

"When the white man offers freedom," Ebony said, "take it."

Then he dropped his pants and flopped on the bed in his underwear.

THE GIRL WORE A SNUG BLACK BLAZER over a low-cut blouse, and her bra pushed her breasts together to form a deep crevasse. Her skin was cocoa brown, like her partner's. Ebony and Antoine stared down her shirt as she leaned over to pull files from her tub. She looked up and caught them gawking, straightened, and extended her hand. Her name was Tiffany. From Chicago. "Where you all from?" she asked.

Ebony and Antoine said Kansas City at the same time and looked away from each other in embarrassment.

"Is that a real jumpin' kinda town?" Tiffany asked, twirling her fists in front of her in a mock little boogie.

"No," Antoine said. "It sucks."

"Are there tumbleweeds rolling down the street?"

"Something like that."

"Hey, you're in Chicago now," she said, smiling and cocking her hip. "So you know we know all about being down and up with it."

She stood with her hip thrust out slightly to the left, her head bent the same way, away from her shoulders, head tilted down. She glanced at Antoine and raised a hand to casually curl a lock of hair around a finger. "I like your hair," she said to him.

Antoine looked down and softly said, "Thanks."

Flirtations aside, the mood darkened once the debate began. After a particularly fierce cross-x period, Antoine leaned over and whispered to Ebony, "That was intense."

"I know," Ebony said. "She was about to kill me."

But when the final buzzer sounded, Tiffany shook her head at Ebony's customary offer of a handshake and spread her arms. "Can I give you a hug?" she asked. "I just sneezed on my hand."

Ebony shyly wrapped his arms around her and quickly released. Tiffany looked over at Antoine and moved toward him, arms open wide. He stepped toward her, angling his head in the same direction as hers. They readjusted at the same time, laughed nervously, and fell into a quick embrace.

Antoine wouldn't realize it for a few months, but he'd just missed a chance to mack a real live lady. In the moment, he was satisfied to have a little touch. The pimping prospects of debate were ostensibly half the motivation for being here. But if this were really the case, he'd be on the speech team; a lot more girls play that game. In fact, policy debate isn't especially popular among females, though reason would suggest it should be. Girls tend to gravitate to academic activities. But debate, with its emphasis on military issues and so many absurd nuclear war scenarios, tends to turn women off. And the uneven representation of genders gives the community a somewhat macho persona that has been known to veer into harassment. With the resurgence of critical arguments, however, the community was beginning to come to terms with these issues, albeit cerebrally. A number of coaches and debaters were crafting cases that challenged sexist notions in common arguments, as well as in the community itself. In the second round of the Glenbrooks, Ebony and Antoine faced one of these cases.

Their opponents were from Vestavia Hills, Alabama, a suburb of Birmingham. They were both girls, one white with Pippi Longstocking braids, the other apparently of Asian descent, and they were both done up in mod suits with tight, short skirts and thin neckties tied loosely around their necks. They were both so skinny their pelvic bones and ribs showed through their clothes. Arguing on the affirmative, they called for Congress to pass a law affording newborn hermaphrodites the right of informed consent before undergoing an operation to become either male or female. This plan was really just an excuse to get to deeper issues of gender, namely to break down the "gender binary" and thus subvert male dominance.

"So you're saying a person can grow a penis and vagina all of their life if they say so?" Antoine asked during cross-x, scratching at his dreads in bewilderment.

"Yes, that's perfectly fine," the first speaker replied. "If they want to remain like that, that's fine."

Feminist arguments have more currency on the debate circuit than ones dealing with race issues. They emerged in the 1980s and '90s as part of the growing popularity of critical arguments, but also because female debaters became more and more vocal about their disenchantment with the male-dominated culture of debate. On eDebate, an e-mail Listserv for college debaters and coaches, there were long, heated discussions about how women are treated in the community. Female debaters complained about being ogled by their male counterparts, enduring sexist comments and overt sexual harassment, being taken advantage of by graduate coaching assistants, and, in some instances, becoming victims of date rape at tournament hotels. A common theme was disrespect. During post-round critiques, judges often addressed only the men in the room. Women held subservient positions in their squads' hierarchies, being made to cut cards for the top, all-male teams, being invited to compete only at second- and third-tier tournaments, and, while there, being made to run errands such as getting food for the rest of the squad.

The game itself, they observed, was skewed toward boys, with its macho emphasis on military issues and the relentless march toward nuclear war. In this culture, women tended to be placed in two categories. If they took to the game with the vigor of their male colleagues, they were seen as bitches. If not, they were seen as weak. In 1989 a pair of graduate students from Wake Forest University, J. Cinder Griffin and Holly Jane Raider (one of whom was told by a debate judge in high school, "I don't usually vote for girl debaters, because debate really is a boy's activity. I am surprised by your ability to handle these issues"), wrote an essay about the problem of low participation by females in the game. They pointed out that men outnumber women four to one in debate. This is particularly noticeable on the national circuit; while there are a number of private all-boys schools competing, most notably Montgomery Bell Academy from Nashville, there's no all-girls school counterpart. Griffin and Raider suggested that in addition to the hostile environment of the community, the subject matter of debates was a turnoff: women, they said, would rather discuss social issues than military ones. "In general, women are not encouraged to discuss military and political issues. Women prefer social and theoretical arguments to military issues, and this is reflected in women's choices of debate arguments," the authors state. "Therefore, even if a female is not discouraged from entering debate itself, she will not remain in the activity for long because the argument discourse either does not interest her or she is actively discouraged from becoming fluent in it."

AS THE ROUND PROGRESSED, Ebony and Antoine grew more and more confused, their speeches mired in long pauses and contradictory arguments. Soon their opponents were covering their faces to hide their laughter. During the cross-x sessions, they were so condescending that I began to take offense.

"Do you know when the Emancipation Proclamation was?" one of the Vestavia Hills debaters asked Antoine at one point, in a patronizing tone.

"Um," he stammered. "I think it was—"

Ebony blurted: "Nineteen sixty-three. Something like that."

"I'm not too sure," Antoine said quietly.

The girl looked at her partner, her face pinched to stifle a giggle.

"Or 1863," Ebony said at last.

"Yeah, that's right," the girl went on in the soft voice of a kindergarten teacher. "And you know when the civil rights movement took place?"

"Nineteen sixties, '50s, '70s," Antoine said.

"That's, like, about a hundred years, right?"

"Something like that."

"So your argument is it was wrong, but it was okay for people to discriminate against African-Americans."

"I never said that," Antoine said sharply. "I didn't say it was okay to lynch people and hang them on a daily basis or things like that."

"But it was wrong, right?" his interrogator asked.

Her partner chimed in: "Isn't it the same with babies getting their genitals cut off?"

Ebony and Antoine stared at her stonily.

EBONY CLAIMED A ROW OF SEATS on the bus and perched himself up high, with arms across two seat backs. "I can't believe it, dude," he shouted to Antoine, above the din of his fellow passengers. "We three and one."

They lost to the girls from Alabama, but they won their next two rounds, as well as the first. Ebony was pumped. "We ain't faced nobody easy yet," he bragged. "I just be telling my boy Antoine, just do what I say, we're all free."

"I know," Antoine agreed. "This shit is real."

"You know what I'm sayin'?" Ebony pounded his fist against a seat back. "You see what good judgin' is? We went oh and five at Turner." A few weeks earlier, while Marcus and Brandon were off winning the Iowa Caucus, the two had competed in a tournament at Turner High School, in the western suburbs of Kansas City. It was just like the Shawnee Mission South tournament Ebony had competed in with Marcus. The judges had voted against him and Antoine in every round, writing on their ballots that they hadn't stood properly, that they were difficult to understand, and, in one instance, that they were "too argumentative." Ebony went on: "Oh and five! Here we in the best competition in the *United States*. And we three and one. What does that tell you?"

"I know." Antoine shook his head. "It's just . . ." He laughed. "Racist."

"*Muthafuckin' Glenbrooks!*" Ebony said. "I waited all year to see this place." He bobbed his head all cool like.

"That's my new thing," Antoine said. "Debate. Eat. Mack down with the ladies."

All afternoon he kept bumping into Tiffany. They ate lunch together. She fondled his dreads a couple of times. She offered her e-mail address, but he didn't have a computer. She asked for his phone number, but he didn't have one. Still, he felt as though he'd scored. *This is tight*, he thought. Here he was in an exotic place, suburban Chicago, with its clean, well-lit streets and stores and restaurants as far as the eye could see. He was surrounded by peers, with no parents around, and had a wad of cash in his pocket.

The bus pulled to a stop at the Red Roof Inn, and he and Ebony bolted up a flight of stairs to their room. Ebony threw the door open and flicked on the light. "It's clean!" he exclaimed. "Oh, my God! It's clean!"

He paced through the room, running his fingers across the clean tops of the tables and the dressers. He tapped the tightly made bed, rubbed the corner of a fresh towel between his thumb and forefinger. "A'ight, a'ight," he said, and he unbuckled his pants, let them fall to the floor, grabbed an ice bucket, and headed out to the balcony hall.

Antoine watched him go and yelled, "You ain't got no pants on! Come on!" He turned on the TV, flipped past a few stations, and stopped on a scene with Chris Tucker and Jackie Chan dealing high kicks and jabs to a dozen bad guys. He shrugged off his blazer, went to the clothes rack, and tugged at a hanger. It wouldn't budge. He peered closer. Instead of a hook, it had a little knob that fit into a notch so motel guests wouldn't steal it. It took him a few seconds to figure it out. "Man," he said, "these Chicago hangers are weird."

The stash of bills was heating up in his pocket. He told Ebony to put his pants back on, and they went out on the town, walking north from the motel across the vast parking lot past Best Buy and the Bally health club to Boston Chicken for a bite to eat. They spotted a yellow Dodge Viper and paused to admire it. "Damn," Ebony said. "You get hella ass in that."

They were dumbstruck in the restaurant. They just stood there frozen, staring at the pictures of roasted chicken and meat loaf. The prices were all in the $6.95 range, almost twice the cost of a McDonald's Value Meal, which they could barely afford on a good day back home. Antoine glanced toward the wall near the door, where a framed photo of Chicago's skyline at night hung. It was the kind of picture he could easily find in his school's library or online. "Man," he said in awe, as if he were really standing amid the buildings.

They decided to go back to the motel and order Domino's. Ebony was eager to shed his pants again. "Freedom, bitches!" he said.

Down the hall the mood was even higher. Marcus and Brandon had gone undefeated. Marcus was jumping up and down on his bed. "We four-oh at the Glenbrooks!" he shouted. "We four-oh!"

No Central team had ever done so well at the tournament. Rinehart had been bringing teams there for five years, and they had yet to claim a trophy. With an undefeated team, and with the decisive victories at the Iowa Caucus and UMKC still fresh in their minds, it was looking as if it might just be their year.

But by the same time the next night, they'd be heading back to the motel with no metal, as down as they'd been all season.

THIRTY-ONE

A FUTURE

EBONY AND ANTOINE'S BUBBLE was the first to pop. For their fifth, and final, round they went up against a couple of Asian kids from a private school in northern California. The opponents were so acerbic and snooty I actually got pissed off watching the round. At one point one of the debaters yelled at Ebony as if he were an idiot. He was questioning their claim that if the plan to help Native Americans didn't pass, all the people in the world would become dehumanized.

"How do you know this?" Ebony asked, innocently enough.

"It's common sense!" She stomped a foot on the ground and slapped her hands against her hips.

"After we kill the Native Americans," Ebony tried to paraphrase, "we'll kill the African-Americans and—"

"We're not saying *kill*! We're saying *dehumanizing*!" She was almost screaming.

And she and her partner kept hoarding Central's evidence. As Ebony prepared for his speech, he searched with increasing panic for a key piece of evidence. He quickly rummaged through the scattered piles of paper lying across the desks he and Antoine had pushed together to make a base camp. He picked up documents that had fallen to the floor but threw them back down again after failing to find the one he needed.

He looked over at the other team. "Hey," he said. "I think you all got some of our cards."

The girl looked up. "Can we just look at it for a little while?"

"Well, like, I need it for my speech."

"Just one second," she said, not even looking up at him.

As soon as the judge cast the ballot for the other team, Ebony spun on his heels and stumbled out the door. "Fuck!" he said under his breath.

He moped the halls until he spotted Rinehart.

"Would you tuck in your shirt and everything?" Rinehart said when Ebony finally arrived at her side. "It looks really bad. And don't give me this senioritis. When you're champion and you've won every round, it's different. So tuck it in and look nice. Please."

He shoved the corners of his tails an inch under his waistband. His shirt ballooned out.

"It's not tucked in."

He sighed, turned around, unbuckled, and stuffed down the excess fabric.

"We lost on theory," Ebony said. "They went to private schools and $2,000 camps and shit. They were whining about how we spread them too much. 'I didn't have enough time to answer y'all's arguments. And it was tough, and me and my partner couldn't—'"

"My partner and I," Rinehart corrected him.

"'*My partner and I* couldn't answer. I'm a little Oriental girl and my mouth doesn't open wide, so I can't answer all the arguments, so I'm just gonna run theory because they don't know what to do and they're, um, and time-suck.'"

"Where did they go to camp?" Rinehart asked, ignoring the racist slight.

"They went to Stanford."

"So you guys weren't debating Harker school. You were debating Stanford University."

"Basically." Ebony shrugged.

"Well, guys, you're running with some really big dogs," she said, her posture softening. "*Really* big dogs. These kids have a lot of advantages. That means that what we have to do is work harder, debate harder, practice our articulation more. We gotta be sharper than they are. We have to be. Because they've got all the advantages."

I CAUGHT A CAB OVER TO GLENBROOK SOUTH, where Brandon and Marcus were debating in the varsity division. When I got there, they were midway through the sixth round against a team from Portage Northern, a school near Kalamazoo, Michigan. They'd already lost one round and were on their way toward losing this one because Brandon had read a card that used the word "man" instead of "human."

They picked up their seventh, and final, round, finishing five-two, in position to advance to out rounds. Now all they could do was wait. Their fate was in the hands of a computer now, as speaker points were being tallied and teams ranked. Brandon put on his headphones and broke off on his own to wander around and look at girls. Marcus spotted Phil Kerpen in the hall.

"Who won?" Kerpen asked.

Marcus gave a thumbs-up. But he didn't look happy. "I wouldn't be surprised if only two five-two teams break," he said. "I've never been to a tournament this big. I don't expect to go at all."

Kerpen felt confident. "I think you got really high points. I think you're gonna be like twelve," meaning twelfth-place speaker overall.

Marcus brightened into a big, silly grin. He stretched out his arms to hug Kerpen and asked, "Can I have your baby? That just means so much to me."

"Hey, congrats on Caucus," Kerpen said. He asked what was being done about the Missouri State High School Activities Association rules forbidding participation in the Tournament of Champions. "You think they're gonna let you go this year?" he asked.

"I don't care," Marcus said. "I'm just goin'."

"Won't they put your whole school on probation, so you can't play football?"

"I don't care. Our football team never wins anyway."

Marcus left Kerpen to find James Holley, his friend from the South Side of Chicago. He spotted him near the cafeteria, with a bag of giant suckers that he was selling for fifty cents or giving to girls in exchange for hugs. They found a wall to lean on and watch the crowd. James kept spotting dark-skinned kids walking by—African-Americans, Latinos, Indians, Asians. "Lot of color here," he said approvingly.

"None of them are going to break," Marcus scoffed.

Despite Central's success in Iowa, Marcus knew that he and Brandon were second-class citizens at a major national tournament such as this. Each season there are just a handful of these big showdowns: the Glenbrooks, Harvard, Berkeley, Emory University's and Montgomery Bell Academy's invitationals, and, of course, the Tournament of Champions. Once debaters attain the highest level of skill in the game, it becomes difficult to differentiate between them. Rounds are excruciatingly close. Judges' reliance on their meticulous notes ostensibly offers a measure of objectivity, but absolute neutrality is nearly impossible. For one, it's a small community. All the coaches and judges pretty much know one another, and they have a shared sense of which programs are the best and which are not quite as good. In this way, some schools on the circuit have become veritable brand names for excellence—Glenbrook North, for example, Greenhill School in Dallas, Pace Academy and Westminster from Atlanta. These schools all have what's known as rep, and in close rounds their clout often tips the scales.

This works in more nefarious ways as well. Since the coaches of these programs have developed friendships over the years, they often help run one another's tournaments. A coach from, say, Colleyville Heritage in suburban Texas might run the tabulation room at Greenhill's tournament, another one of the really big competitions on the circuit. Sometimes, more often than debate folks are willing to admit, these coaches will tweak the pairings and judge assignments to make things more "fair." If the computer spits out a first- or second-round matchup between two teams that everyone expects to advance far in the elimination rounds, the tab room worker might switch them out and match them against lesser teams. They'll also pay more attention to the judge assignments to these powerhouse teams' rounds, making sure that the judges who are most adept at following the high-speed style, and most familiar with the teams' arguments, are sitting in the back of the room when the big dogs compete.

Marcus had no doubt this was what had happened to him and Brandon. He believed they'd gotten a lame judge for round five, when they were sitting on a four-oh record, because the folks in the tab room were looking out for someone else. The big-name private and public schools always dominate these tournaments. It's history, the norm. Any aberration from these norms, such as Kansas City Central going undefeated at the almighty Glenbrooks, would be looked on with shock for sure, and possibly even suspicion. Now, sitting on a respectable five-two record, Marcus seriously doubted they would advance. Their fate rested on the most subjective of all judging standards, speaker points. He suspected that there was no way these judges would rank him and Brandon, two black kids from an inner-city neighborhood in backwater Missouri, among the nation's best.

AFTER THE AWARDS CEREMONY Marcus squeezed into the crowd to look over someone's shoulder at the schedule, to catch a glimpse of the list of teams that cleared. He scanned the page. He looked away and shook his head. "Nope," he said. "Let's pack up."

Near the school's entrance, Rinehart caught up with him. "Did you hear a girl got shot?" she asked.

"From our school?"

"Yeah."

"Killed?"

"Yeah."

"Who?"

"I don't know. Monica knows. Another kid got wounded."

I was struck by how calmly they carried on this conversation. There was concern in their voices, but not much. It was as if the news were not a big deal. I became more aware of our surroundings at that moment, of the sturdiness and cleanliness of the suburban school we were leaving. I wondered what the reaction would have been if a girl from this school had been killed.

I had attended a public school much like Glenbrook South in the suburbs of Denver many years earlier. None of my fellow students was ever murdered. Shortly after I graduated, a teen died of an overdose of Freon in the school's parking lot. The school all but shut down for several days because the students and faculty were so overcome with shock and grief. The incident drew national attention in the late 1980s. In the 2002–2003 season, a far less tragic incident would occur at Glenbrook North, which quickly became the scandal du jour in America. That spring a dozen or so girls were roughed up and doused with buckets of shit, piss, animal guts, and blood at a hazing ritual near the school. It was caught on video and released to a TV station. "The whole world watched in shock," in the words of Oprah Winfrey, who devoted an entire show to the incident. Meantime, the death of one of Central's most promising students would merit a couple of stories in *The Kansas City Star* and be promptly forgotten. Tragedies like this happen all the time in the nation's urban areas.

"Someone dies every year in our school," Marcus said as we boarded the bus. "Always one or two a year." He didn't seem sad. He said this as if it's just the way things are.

A blanket of snow had fallen while we were inside. It clung to the grass and tree limbs and leaves. The change was startling. The air had been merely chilly when I caught the cab between high schools hours earlier.

We settled into our seats on the bus. Leo took a place near Monica, a member of the speech team whose job it was to deliver the news.

"What was the girl's name?" Leo asked her.

"I'm not gonna tell you."

"When it happen?"

"Yesterday."

"Who was the guy? Do I know these people, for real?" Leo asked.

"Yes."

"I don't believe you."

"When I tell you for real, you will know."

Monica waited until the bus pulled to a stop in the motel parking lot. She strode to the front of the bus, and the driver handed her the intercom microphone. "Since we've been here missing and not at home, but—" she started to say.

"Get to the point," someone yelled.

"I think, yesterday, two of our fellow students, something badly happened to them. Kristi Carroll at Troostwood. She was shot in the head and killed. Freddy Ursery was shot in the arm. He's okay."

"Oh, shit!" Leo exclaimed.

"Let's have a word of silence," Monica said.

"Oh, shit!"

We were quiet for a few seconds. Then Rinehart got up and told everyone where they could go for dinner, and when they should go to bed, because the bus would be leaving very early the next morning. She acted as though nothing had happened. She'd trained herself not to dwell on such things; it would only occur to her how callous she'd become when she'd cavalierly tell coaches and teachers from other schools that one or two students get killed every school year at Central and they'd look back at her with shock. Also, Rinehart didn't know Kristi very well; she knew her reaction would be much different if one of her students had been shot, which, thankfully, had never happened.

Leo kept saying "oh, shit." He buried his head in his hands.

"That's Kristi from our first hour, ain't it, Leo?" Marcus asked.

"Yes!" he said. It came out as a wail. "The one that sits right next to me."

"Yeah, the one you really know."

"Oh, shit! This is fucked-up, dude!"

"I know," Marcus said. "She had a future." As if futures were rare at Central High.

THIRTY-TWO

THE GOAL OF LIFE

"**CHECK THIS OUT,**" Ebony said. "There's no God."

We were in my room at the Fairfield Inn & Suites in West Des Moines—Ebony, Antoine, Geoffery Stone, and me. We had a few hours to kill before the first round of the Dowling tournament was set to begin. The guys were dressed up and ready to go, in baggy blazers and crooked ties. Ebony leaned back and laced his fingers behind his head.

"Yeah," Geoffery said.

"Hold up." Ebony suddenly jerked forward. "Check this out. People always have to have somebody that's always higher than them. If there wasn't nobody higher than them, they'd always have these questions like how we got here. We always have to have somebody to pray to for everything because we have to be thankful of something. Like, if we don't have nobody to pray to, like, why are we living for?"

They were quiet for a moment. Ebony scanned his audience. He loved this stuff. When he was a kid, almost all he ever did was read the Bible and books about the Bible. Being in foster homes and homeless shelters, he rarely had anyone to talk with about it. And when he did, he rarely had enough confidence to speak up. Now he was a debater. And not only that, but the *best* debater in the room. It was his *duty* to talk. He waved a hand dismissively in the air. "I'ma stop believin' in the Bible," he said.

"What's you ass mean?!" Antoine wanted to know.

"This is how I figured it out," Geoffery jumped in. "Okay, you got the Bible, right? Certain events that they say in there, they got certain parts of history where it's written down in there."

"It go beyond that," Ebony said, a touch of irritation in his voice. "I'm talkin' about from the beginning." He paused to consider his thoughts and change course. "I got a question. Why y'all believe in heaven and hell for?"

"So when you die you just *stay*?" Geoffery asked, shocked.

"Hold up! Why you all believe in heaven or hell for? And give me three people who been to heaven or hell."

"Okay," Geoffery said. "Jesus. He went to hell *and* heaven."

"Three people you *know*. Your *cousin*, your *past family*, the *slaves*, the *Haitians, anybody*."

"Okay. Jesus," Geoffery said again.

"Don't say 'Jesus.'"

"My uncle Pooky went straight to hell."

"That was for real?! Swear to God?!"

"Did I know of for *sure* sure? My uncle Pooky? He's the baddest man in the world."

Antoine spoke up, his voice low, authoritative: "There are things that go beyond what you see and what you know."

"Yeah," Geoffery said. "Like how do you know the universe exists?"

"How do you know that we are not just—" Antoine tried to say, but Ebony interrupted.

"How do you know we're not living some dream? Some mind?"

"That's what I'm saying!" Geoffery said. "How do you know there's not a universe?"

"There *is* a universe, dude," Ebony said.

"How do you know?!" Antoine demanded.

"We already got proof of it! It's like ten billion stars!"

"They say it's endless, though," Antoine said.

"Yeah." Ebony nodded. "It's endless. It's like taking a piss forever."

"Think about it like this." Antoine raised a finger. He looked like a Rastafarian professor. "You got this earth right now. This itty-bitty speck of nothing in forever. Think if you go that way." He pointed at the ceiling.

"Straight up forever and ever and ever and ever." He sat back and crossed his arms. "Just think for a *long time* about what forever means."

To Antoine this was the essence of everything. That one thought: *infinity*. He'd first thought it when he was a little kid, talking about the world and the universe with his mom, and he hadn't really stopped thinking about it since then.

"Okay," Ebony said, as if he were a teacher who'd been told the right answer. He shifted in his seat and switched the direction of the conversation. "Why do God allow so much stuff to happen on this earth?"

Geoffery didn't hesitate: "Punishment."

"Punish for what? We didn't do nothin'!"

"That's like the top question everybody asks," Antoine said.

"It's guilt," Geoffery explained. "Everybody does something bad. If you never do nothing bad, there would never be—"

"We didn't do nothing bad! We was *born*! Why are we getting punished for something we didn't do?"

Everyone in the room instinctively knew who the "we" was. Ebony was talking about black folks. The "we" was them.

"He gave us the power of *choice*," Geoffery said. "They say God know everything, right? He knew Adam and Eve were gonna do that right before they even did it. Eat of the tree. But he gave them the power of choice because, what would you rather have?"

"Hold on," Ebony said. "I got another question. Adam and Eve had two sons, right?"

"Yeah," Geoffery said.

"Where did the rest of the world come from?"

"He put more people on there."

"No. No. It did not say that in the Bible, a'ight? No. Y'all missed a lot of stuff. Y'all did not read the Bible fully. No. How did they reproduce if he put four people on earth? One woman, and three dudes."

Geoffery looked at Ebony and blinked a couple of times.

"So one dude jacked off and the sperm popped up as a baby?" Ebony asked sarcastically. "What happened?"

"That's a question you have to answer for yourself." Geoffery was on the defensive.

"Y'all didn't read the Bible! I thought you Christians supposed to read the fuckin' Bible!"

"I haven't read the entire Bible," Antoine admitted.

"I did," Geoffery said. "He said, 'Go forth and breed.'"

"It was Adam and Eve, right? Then Cain and Abel. Okay, how did they reproduce? Geoffery? How did we get here? He did his brother in his ass and then he came out the asshole?! Geoffery?!"

Antoine cringed. "I'm not thinkin' about that."

Geoffery was struck dumb.

Ebony leaned back. He'd gotten him. "You say you believe in heaven and hell. And you believe that two dudes done each other in the ass."

"I don't believe two dudes done each other in the ass!" Geoffery was aghast.

"Y'all dumb." Ebony shooed him off with a wave. "Y'all believe in stuff y'all don't know why y'all believe in it. Y'all just talk 'cause someone else told y'all to believe in it."

"No," Geoffery protested. "Someone else did not tell me."

"Y'all followers," Ebony said. "I had to find out for myself."

"Yeah?" Geoffery asked. "What *do* you believe in?"

Ebony raised a hand to his chin. He had to think about that one. "I believe the Bible could be written better," he offered.

"I think that, too," Antoine said.

"I don't know what I believe in, for real," Ebony admitted. "I read so many books that I don't know."

"I wanna hear what *everybody* has to say," Antoine said. "I wanna experience every religion out there. It's more to it than what we are told we can have."

"So shouldn't the goal in life be to seek knowledge?" Ebony asked.

We were all quiet for a moment.

"That should be, like, one of them," Antoine finally said.

"See," Ebony went on, "you can't seek the truth, because the truth has a end. But knowledge has no end. So shouldn't the goal of life be to seek knowledge? You can never stop knowledge."

"If the universe is endless," Antoine said, "there's always somethin' to learn. It ain't no way it ain't."

EBONY WAS NEARING HIS MOMENT OF TRUTH. The city championship, with its promise of a possible trip to Atlanta, was just a week away, and Dowling was the last chance to get ready. We got to the tournament just as the sun was setting; the tall pines surrounding the school swayed in a stiff December wind. Jesus's image was omnipresent at Dowling, a Catholic school—in framed pictures and on posters, his words displayed here and there in giant quotations. Ebony and Antoine's first round was in a room where religious classes were apparently held, because the religious imagery was more prolific there. There was a pencil drawing of Jesus, his head cocked in a look of compassion. We saw the Virgin of Guadalupe, a pop-art poster of a crown of thorns with the caption WON BY ONE, a giant rosary, a wooden sculpture of a man dragging a cross, a picture of Jesus laughing. A sign over the door read, SERVANT ENTRANCE, to remind students that their real work was to be done outside the classroom, beyond school. Near it hung a poster of Mother Teresa that said, "Works of love are works of peace." One of the room's bulletin boards bore the words SOCIAL JUSTICE in bold letters cut from construction paper. Under it, the teacher had tacked up various newspaper articles about people's struggles around the world.

And into this sanctuary walked Ebony Rose, with his file tub bearing a picture of Adolf Hitler. Antoine noticed it and sighed with annoyance. "What are you doing with that?" he asked.

"You don't like my Hitler?" Ebony responded, trying to seem shocked and hurt. "Hitler gonna help us win."

Hitler's image, especially the one he'd taped to his tub, with the murderous dictator looking maniacally toward the sky, his hands outstretched, symbolized Ebony's life ambition. "I'm gonna rule the world," he often said. He knew the picture was shocking, which is why it appealed to him, but he had no idea how truly offensive it would be to many people. Nor had it occurred to him that he got away with displaying the image because he was black in a community of young whites who would be apprehensive about challenging minorities on race issues (at least outside of a debate round). I later pressed Ebony about this choice of iconography, and he said Hitler "was a badass, for real. I mean, he did bad stuff. But he was a genius."

"But, Ebony," I said, "he was responsible for the murder of more than six million people."

"*I know,*" he replied defensively. "I'm not saying I supported him. He was just a genius."

The Hitler image tied together Ebony's earliest impressions of debate and the debate community, the ones he'd gleaned at camp, when he saw it as a training ground for young warriors, conquistadores. The game was so like a war it even had body counts—high death tolls, nuclear war, genocide. And if you're gonna go there, Ebony figured, you might as well go all the way and enlist the baddest of the bad on your side.

But the Führer couldn't quite pull it off for the novice duo. They finished with a winning record, but their low speaker points kept them out of the trophy rounds. Ebony set his sights right away on the next challenge. "If we don't win the city championships," he told me, "I'm gonna be mean." He shook his head sharply.

"It'll be tough," Rinehart told him, then she turned to me. "They'll get spotty judges. Ebony will really have to talk down to the judges."

Rinehart was concerned about Ebony's speaking abilities. They had improved, especially since he'd joined debate. But he was still difficult to understand. He crammed his syllables together in rapid-fire mumbles. He dropped consonants. Rinehart sat in on one of his early rounds at Dowling, and by the end of it she had a long list of words he'd mangled. "Government" he referred to as "gummit." Instead of "I don't know," he said "Iunno"—cramming it all into two syllables. "Saddam Hussein" was "Hoodam Hussein." Rinehart knew she'd have to work with him on that, but she wasn't sure how. She wasn't a speech therapist. The school district had a speech therapist, but Ebony didn't qualify. When Rinehart talked with a school counselor about the problem, he told her it was just a "ghettoized" accent. District rules forbade him from prescribing therapy for it—a mandate from the legal department. She'd gotten the same runaround three years earlier, when she'd sought help for Marcus, who also slurred his words.

It was shaping up to be a painful tournament for Rinehart. None of the novice teams broke. Her second varsity team, Leo and DiAnna, did, but when the pairings came out, Leo snagged a copy, spotted his name, and yelled, "Sucks!" He and DiAnna had been paired up against Marcus and Brandon, meaning one of the teams would have to bow out. Because Marcus and Brandon stood a better chance of winning the whole thing, or at least the TOC bid, which went to the two teams that made it to finals, Leo knew his team would have to step aside.

Rinehart was crushed. Leo had finally made it to out rounds at a national tournament, and he had to bow out. Things didn't turn out any better for Marcus and Brandon. Though they didn't have to debate in the octofinal round, the politics scenario they'd been running all weekend on the negative suddenly became obsolete, when a special election for the U.S. Senate was decided in Louisiana. So they had to unleash the Žižek kritik—fiction. They hadn't lost on it yet, but this was a more conservative judging pool.

By my estimation, they were winning the round. The opponents, two girls from a suburb of Chicago, seemed confused by the argument. But the judges didn't seem to get it, either. It was getting late, and they looked tired. At one point they complained that they hadn't eaten for hours. Someone came to the rescue with bags of food from Burger King. After wolfing his down, one of the judges got up to stretch his legs in the hall. Rinehart was sitting outside, waiting. She was too nervous to watch the round. She overheard someone ask him how the round was going. "Awful," he said. "An hour of bullshit 'speaking for others' arguments."

Rinehart knew then she'd be driving home soon.

OF ALL THE TOURNAMENTS on the season schedule, Dowling, in West Des Moines, was the most meaningful to Rinehart. During her first year at Central, back in the mid-1990s, her teams took beatings from more experienced debaters at schools in suburban Kansas City, such as Blue Springs and Lee's Summit.

After months of frustration, she called a debate director at a high school in Des Moines and asked what tournaments were coming up. He told her about one at Dowling. She signed up her teams and navigated the school district's bureaucracy to score some money for the trip.

Riding into the school's parking lot, her students marveled at the Benzes, Cadillacs, and BMWs. As Rinehart settled into a school desk to judge a round, she began to worry that she'd made a mistake. She hadn't experienced national-circuit debate since her time in Illinois, and these debaters were better than any she'd seen.

After the round she wandered through the halls expecting to find her team dejected. Then one of her younger debaters bounced up to her shouting, "We won and I love Iowa debate!"

By tournament's end, three of her teams had broken into elimination rounds, and three of her kids had nabbed top-ten speaker awards.

But just when things were starting to get good, they also began to sour. Later that school year, with graduation drawing near, Rinehart had received a call from Fred Binggeli, overseer of speech and debate programs for the Missouri State High School Activities Association, who told her she'd broken the state's rules by having her squad compete in too many tournaments. That was 1998, the first year of Kansas City's UDL, when the league offered two-round tournaments almost every Tuesday. Rinehart had known about the tournament limitations going into the season. But she figured it would be okay, because a debate league in suburban St. Louis offered an almost identical schedule. Twenty-five years earlier, the MSHSAA had given those schools written permission to skirt the limits by counting three after-school two-round tournaments as one typical six-round weekend affair.

Binggeli told her he wasn't willing to grant the same exception to her school or any other in DEBATE–Kansas City. (He claimed not to have known about the St. Louis league until I told him.)

"How did you hear about these tournaments?" Rinehart asked Binggeli suspiciously.

"I seen it on the Internet," she remembers his saying.

"What do you mean you saw it on the Internet?"

"I saw it on the Web site," he said. "I saw pictures of your kids."

What Web site? she thought. She hung up and called DEBATE–Kansas City's coordinator, who told her that the University of Vermont had a page dedicated to the UDL on its site. It might have had some pictures.

MSHSAA bureaucrats don't typically conduct that kind of proactive investigation; instead, they respond to formal complaints. Binggeli told me that he contacted Rinehart after receiving a telephone complaint from Sherri Shumaker, a coach at Blue Springs High School who, in turn, was passing along a complaint raised by another coach (whom Shumaker wouldn't name). MSHSAA rules require that charges be filed in writing. But in response to my request under Missouri's Sunshine Law, Binggeli offered no documentation of the complaint.

WHILE THE KIDS SLEPT ON THE RIDE HOME, Rinehart reminisced to me about their first trip to Dowling. They were so charged up by their performance that first year that they schemed all the way home about ways to stick it to the Missouri debate community. They devised a plan to let their Missouri peers know exactly how they felt. They conjured a "Ban Debate" case they would run at the district qualifying tournament for the state championship.

"We started talking about arguing that debate is too stressful, too harmful, destroys too many trees," Rinehart told me as she drove through the Iowa night. "That year the topic was education. We decided to argue that debate was bad for education. And we should eliminate debate. And we should take the money that was used for debate and create a series of festivals, and they would all be held in tropical locations . . . We would just join hands and sing 'Kumbaya.'"

The following spring they showed up at Rockhurst High School eschewing the formalities of dresses and suits and ties in favor of sweatshirts that read, DEBATE IS LIFE, with black tape forming an *X* over LIFE. They hit Raytown South High School, from the southeast suburbs of Kansas City, during the first round. "They were just skunked," Rinehart told me. "They didn't know what to argue. They were furious when they came out of the round. They were purple, they were so angry."

Soon after the first round ended, the tournament's director approached Rinehart and said, "I think you should know that a protest has been filed against your team." He explained that one of her debaters had spoken beyond the time limit, and thus broken the only real rule of debate.

"Why didn't the timer stop her?" Rinehart asked.

"Well, the judge was afraid of being accused of being a racist," he replied.

Rinehart shrugged it off. By the second round, word of their innovative tactic had spread across the tournament. Debaters from other high schools swarmed Rinehart's squad in Rockhurst's lunchroom, telling them, "You guys are so cool!" Their adult coaches, however, were not pleased.

As rambunctious as the tactic seemed, it was in line with current trends in competitive debate. At the college level, teams across the country have recently begun employing "nontraditional" or "performance" strategies. For instance, University of Louisville debaters play rap songs as evidence. And debaters at Kansas's Fort Hays State, which won a national championship in 2002, have been known to jam their rounds with a cacophony of music and recorded speeches or to simulate sex and then pretend to give birth to a book by Nietzsche.

Such creativity doesn't fly in Missouri. A few weeks later Rinehart received a package of letters from the MSHSAA. It included the results of the tournament director's investigation of the formal complaint—which yielded no findings of wrongdoing—and scathing screeds from the Raytown South coach and Shumaker of Blue Springs.

Rinehart was called to the principal's office for a conference call with Becky Oakes, the MSHSAA's executive director. A few days later Oakes shot off a scolding letter to Rinehart's principal. "Adults involved with our young people must be role models," she wrote. "It is our responsibility to encourage our students to have respect for an activity which they have chosen to participate [sic]."

THIRTY-THREE

THE POWERLESS

HE LOOKED LIKE a cross between Rasputin and a homeless man, with his long mane of thinning hair and his bushy white beard. He carried a man purse and wore all-weather jogging pants. He strode through the crowd of kids, who were idling around in their suits, ties, and prim skirts in the commons area of Royall Hall on the UMKC campus, awaiting the start of an early-morning round at DEBATE–Kansas City's championships. He spotted Rinehart and darted over to her, introducing himself as Duane Kelly, school board member. "I know," Rinehart said politely. "Nice to meet you."

In the days leading up to the tournament, I'd called all the board members, urging them to come and take in some of the city championship tournament. I'd been lobbying them, often catching them on their home phones, trying to persuade them to take a more aggressive stance against the state activities association. Kelly was the only one who came.

He asked Rinehart how she was doing, and she didn't pass up the opportunity to gripe. She complained that her kids had been turned away from school that morning because they'd arrived dressed for the tournament. Done up in their Sunday best, they hardly looked like gangstas, but they'd violated the school's dress code nonetheless. Kelly shook his head. "That's one I lost," he said, referring to the uniform policy. "I talked to them about how good Hitler looked in his uniform and how the Nazi youth looked in their uniform. How the Ku Klux Klan has a uniform. And, case denied."

"It doesn't really matter to me one way or another," Rinehart said. "But when a kid's wearing a coat and tie and you're not gonna let them in class because it's not the school uniform . . ."

Kelly said he was concerned about their efforts to get the state's travel rules changed. A few days before the city championship, Phyllis Budesheim gave a presentation to the board about their progress on the matter. Kelly didn't like what he'd heard. It seemed to him that Budesheim was recommending that they fall on their sword. Worse, she had cast Coach Rinehart in a disparaging light, painting a picture of her as a renegade coach whose actions threatened all of Central's extracurricular activities. Budesheim had never sat down with Rinehart to find out her side of the story; instead, she had gone straight to officials at the activities association, who had voiced their misgivings about Rinehart and followed them up with threats. Since then, things had gotten worse for Rinehart. She now had to get every tournament approved through Budesheim herself, which was an onerous task, considering the many layers of bureaucracy she had to navigate to get there.

Kelly didn't like this at all. Rinehart, he reasoned, was exactly the kind of teacher the district ought to support. He was a retired teacher himself, having taught at Northeast.

Standing amid all the pre-round commotion in Royall Hall, he struck a humorous contrast to Rinehart, who was dressed primly in a skirt, blouse, and vest adorned with sequins arranged to form a likeness of Santa Claus. Kelly told her that some members of the board were considering the option of having Central simply go to the TOC, rules be damned, and then see if the state activities association had the guts to punish them. "I'd like to see them try to do that," he said. "The press would tear them apart."

Rinehart smiled politely, knowing she'd never get the go-ahead for such insubordination. "I don't understand," she said. "Why should the football team be penalized because the debate coach makes a bad decision?"

"It could go one of two ways," Kelly continued. "They could all be super-pissed at you. Or they might line up and go with you."

"Not likely," Rinehart answered. "I don't think they're gonna do that. And I don't want to jeopardize anybody else's program. But college recruiters—"

"They're going to this?" Kelly interrupted.

"Well, *sure* they are. And they"—meaning the powers that be at the state activities association—"say you have to prove a hardship."

"Hardship for what?" Kelly asked.

"If we didn't go. They said, well, what's the hardship if you don't go to this tournament?"

"Well, they're kids," Kelly scoffed. "That's why."

"I said, well, there are college recruiters there," Rinehart went on. "There are scholarships that are there. I said, 'I can't tell you that somebody's mom is gonna lose her job if her son doesn't go to a debate tournament. But I can tell you the kid won't get a scholarship to a better school if he's not at this tournament. *That* I can tell you.'"

"That didn't count?"

"Motion denied." Rinehart slashed a hand across her throat. "I mean, it didn't take a heartbeat after I said that."

Kelly turned his head and scanned the crowd, massaging his beard.

"Well, like I keep tellin' people," he said in a thoughtful voice. "We sound pretty good about kids. But we don't give a damn. We don't care."

Kelly returned the subject to the matter of the TOC. "What is it that I could do?" he asked. "How could I help?"

"I guess getting to some people with influence and getting them to pick up the phone and call political people," Rinehart offered.

Kelly was not the most powerful person on the school board. Far from it. To the uninitiated, he came off like a freak. At the first school board meeting I ever attended, he gave a long lecture about a recent eclipse of the sun that was best seen in the Southern Hemisphere. He described how all the animals went silent for a few moments, and he began weeping when he said he wished with all his heart that he could have been there to experience it.

There seemed to be no context for this story in the school board meeting, and it seemed so weird that I found myself wanting to burst out laughing. But no one around me was laughing. All the others in the packed auditorium stared up at the rostrum with serious expressions, listening intently. I wondered for a minute if I had lost my mind, if I were somehow hearing completely different words from what the others were hearing. In time, though, I learned that such digressions by Kelly were commonplace at meetings. He often told stories that only related to the matters at hand in the most oblique terms. He sometimes bought books for his fellow board members, such as *A Sand County Almanac*, in hopes of sparking some intellectual accord among the nine of them. He favored casual clothes—sweatpants and Guatemalan hooded pullovers. A columnist for *The Kansas City Star* once ridiculed the tackiness of his wearing a pair of obscenely tight running shorts to a particularly tense school board meeting. Probably as a result of this iconoclastic nature, Kelly was denied any real position of power on the board. He had fewer subcommittee assignments than most of his colleagues and no officer positions. Despite having been elected to the board twice, he was not given a seat on its executive committee, the group that truly set the district's agenda.

"I'll talk with Al [Mauro, board president] and see what we can scrounge up," he said. He looked back over all the kids bustling around, pushing their carts weighted down with scholarly evidence. "I don't know. Maybe." He ran his fingers through his beard. "Losing scholarships isn't sufficient reason to go?"

"Not a hardship," Rinehart said, shaking her head.

"Well, I don't get it," he said. "I was athletic. I went to college on an athletic scholarship. But I debated. And you know. And all this slobber about the children." His voice was rising with anger; he waved his hands around. "The more emotion they put into 'The Children,' the less I trust them. We got that plastic thing up on the wall. *Is it good for The Children?* Who gives a damn?! *Is it better for the budget?* The budget's what counts! And I don't know about the state. I don't know what you can do. If you can play football in Minneapolis but you can't debate up there, even if scholarships are on the line, I . . . Something's wrong!"

"Uh, I think so," Rinehart agreed.

THIRTY-FOUR

EBONY'S MOMENT

THE KANSAS CITY CHAMPIONSHIP was definitely not the Glenbrooks. Ebony and Antoine were amazed at how lame the competition was. They were clicking like never before. Early in the competition they had a flash of inspiration. They folded up a sheet of paper into a little booklet and wrote on the front, "*The Unofficial Debate Rulebook*, Rose and Lewis 2002." Whenever their opponents made a mistake, like dropping an argument, they pulled it out and read it in a tone of stuffy authority. One judge almost fell out of her chair laughing when she saw this.

As the tournament went on, Ebony kept singing "Dirty south," the chorus of a song by Lil' Flip. He was so close he could almost taste it. "*Hot*lanta," he said. "The Black Mecca." Ebony knew that a win at the city championship would qualify him for the UDL Novice Nationals in Atlanta. He felt more excited than he had all year, perhaps in his whole life. He was confident. Sure of himself. Like he really mattered.

They moved easily through octos and quarterfinals. Then there was a long break before semis for the awards ceremony. Ebony's mind started to work on him. He made his way upstairs, sagging against the rail in the elevator, his brow chiseled sharply in a show of deep thought. He knew his opponents would be a team from Turner High, on the rural edge of Kansas City, Kansas. He paced in the elevator, trying to conjure a game plan. "I don't wanna go negative, and they sweet-talk the judge," he said to me. "'Cause I know that white girl be sweet-talkin' people and shit. Or I go affirmative, I'm probably gonna say we go affirmative because we got answers to everything."

He took a deep breath and exhaled. He squeezed his fists tightly at his sides.

"If we fuckin' break to finals," he said, "I'm gonna piss on myself."

He paced some more as the elevator slowly ascended the building. "Ain't nobody fucked with tax cuts today. I don't know. Bush been winnin' some rounds. I don't know. Bush and spendin' been whuppin' ass today on nega-tive. I shoulda got higher than tenth, but I don't give a fuck. Teams that got speaker awards didn't break, so that's coo. Speakin' ain't shit."

I was feeling it, too. I just knew that they would win. I was beginning to draft a story in my head, one that would make the Missouri State High School Activities Association appear to be the most heartless institution in the Mid-west. My increasingly impassioned phone calls to local elected officials and attorneys weren't having the impact I'd hoped; things were moving too slowly, if at all. But a good story with just a touch of righteous indignation—that could spark action very quickly, I thought. And Ebony's story would be a slam dunk: a kid rises up from foster homes and homeless shelters, over-comes a debilitating speech impediment to win the city championship and a chance at the national championship, only to be denied by some downstate bureaucrats who could care less about the Urban Debate Leagues and the dreams of its kids, like Ebony, for whom a trip to Atlanta would give his life the sense of purpose he craved.

THE OPPONENTS WERE BOTH WHITE. One got up wearing a frilly white blouse. She laid out a case calling for a surtax on condoms, the pro-ceeds of which would be used to pay for sex offender counseling in prison. The Turner girls had written it themselves, and it had stymied opponents throughout the entire tournament. Ebony got up to retrieve one of their cards, and as soon as he started to pick it up, the girl slapped her hand down on it. Ebony recoiled and his eyes widened with shock.

"I'm sorry," the girl said. "Our debate coach strictly forbids me to let you borrow it."

Antoine raised his eyebrows. "Okaaay."

Ebony stood for the first negative speech. He ran a couple of topicality arguments, and then zeroed in on the political disadvantage, claiming that this plan would draw too much political capital from Bush and he wouldn't be able to pass tax cuts, upon which the vitality of the economy depended. He also argued that taxing condoms would cause fewer people to buy them, and that would kill their plan.

The other girl got up to interrogate him. She asked him to explain how the tax would mean fewer people would buy condoms.

"If they don't buy no condoms, your plan won't have no action, right?" Ebony said. She scratched her head. "Am I right? If people stop buying condoms, your plan will have no money, right?"

"What are you saying?"

"Like Bush says, tax cuts are good. They can buy the condoms and your all plan will be enacted. But if the, like you said, you pass your plan, they won't buy them."

She still didn't understand him.

"It's like this," Ebony started to explain again. "If you give tax cuts—"

She cut him off: "People are gonna use condoms whether they want to or not."

"Why would people pay an extra thirty cents for some condoms?"

"It's a sales tax. Thirty cents!"

"What they gonna use?" Ebony insisted. "Aluminum foil?"

She stopped and gave a bewildered look. "*Okay*," she said.

"Well," Ebony pressed on. "You gonna use aluminum? I don't think that's gonna—" His comment broke off as he burst into laughter with everyone else in the room.

The girl was turning red. "Okay," she said, waving a hand in the air to shoo away the intrusion of humor. "Like, on your topicality . . ."

Ebony was looking at her, waiting for her to respond.

"Stop looking at me!" she exclaimed.

Ebony shuddered and stiffened, turning his gaze abruptly to the back wall. "Oh, my bad," he said. "You look good today."

There was an audible groan around the room. Fran buried her face in her hands. The girl looked half-flattered, half-embarrassed. One of the judges, a notoriously conservative coach from Kansas City, Kansas, grabbed her ballot, scribbled a few notes on it, folded it, and placed a pen on it. She sat back with her arms crossed. Her decision had been made.

That left the two college kids.

AS THE ROUND WORE ON, both sets of debaters appeared to be stretched to their mental limits. They clapped their hands together as they spoke, chopped at the air. Ebony was literally drowning in sheets of evidence. They appeared to be flying around him like leaves in autumn. Every move he made would send more documents cascading to the floor. He nervously scratched his head and rubbed his nose every few seconds or so.

During his speech he laid out the case for political capital and tax cuts expertly. In their rebuttal speech the girls barely touched it, focusing instead on the notion that the small tax increase would not deter people from buying condoms.

Antoine, on the other hand, was having a hard time understanding political capital. He kept explaining it like a spending disadvantage, saying that if the government spends money on this program, other important things will be cut. Ebony writhed in his seat, knowing Antoine was blowing it.

During prep, he tried to explain it to Antoine. He handed Antoine a piece of paper on which he'd scribbled, "I am going to kill you after this round!" But during the final negative speech, Antoine once again explained things this way. "If tax cuts are good for the economy, then raising taxes are bad for the economy," he said. "There's no way that you can have both."

The last Turner speaker spent most of her time explaining how their plan would be paid for, and that this extra surtax wouldn't deter people from buying condoms. She barely touched topicality.

The round ended. The Kansas City, Kansas, coach abruptly turned her ballot in. The two college kids studied their notes for quite a while.

Ebony could hardly stand the tension. He paced in and out of the room, his hands balled up into fists. He stopped and stuffed a few cards into a folder, and then he was pacing again. Antoine sat quietly, staring at the judges through the gaps between his dreads.

Eventually, one of the judges folded up his ballot and crossed his arms. The other one did the same a few minutes later. The tournament director collected them, unfolded each one, and rechecked them just to be sure. Then she walked over to the chalkboard and wrote "Turner" on it. Everyone clapped. Ebony slumped down in his seat. One of the Turner girls was startled by the applause. "What?" she said. "Oh, we beat you?" She seemed surprised.

The debaters shook hands. One of the Turner girls said it was the best competition they'd had all tournament. Ebony said nothing in response. It was all over. He'd bet everything on this tournament, and he'd lost.

And little did he know that things were about to get worse. For the previous month and a half, his aunt had been trying to get a loan to buy the house they were living in, the one Ebony thought they already owned. Their landlord was getting ready to put it on the market. Soon after the first of the year, Ebony would learn that he might have to move again, this time possibly outside Central's boundaries, where he'd be unable to stay on the debate squad and continue the one thing he truly loved.

He sat down again and feebly tried to spin a pen between his thumb and his forefinger, the way all the cool debaters do.

Rinehart came over and laid a hand on his shoulder.

"Don't take it so hard," she said. "There's always another debate round."

PART TWO

THE REBUTTALS

ONE

WHOLE NEW GAME

MARCUS COULDN'T WAIT TO GO. He was out the door, lugging his suitcases, before I even parked my car in front of his house. He'd been up since six that morning, already packed. Christmas break was less than a week old and he was bored silly.

He'd spent most of his time hanging out with Richard, who had just gotten a car. They'd driven all over town, but there's not much to do in Kansas City. For a poor kid, though, Marcus hadn't done too bad for Christmas. His mom gave him a cell phone as well as a bunch of new clothes and some spending money. Plus two pairs of new shoes. He had a pair on his feet when he got in my car, white leather with white spiral stripes.

He tossed his luggage on the backseat of my car and plopped down in the passenger seat. He rooted through one of his bags and fished out his portable CD player, which he'd bought at Best Buy when he was in Chicago for the Glenbrooks. He slid the adapter into my car's tape player and cranked the new Dead Prez CD that he'd found at a record store on Troost. That was his main adventure of the break, trying to find a Dead Prez disc. They're a political rap band Sobek had turned him on to. He went to Barnes & Noble at the Country Club Plaza, but they didn't have it. The Plaza is racist, he was convinced. There was no real rap at the music stores. The movie theater never seemed to show black movies, like *Drumline*. At night the powers that be crank country music on the outdoor speaker system, so as to drive urban youth away.

The first song made references to the Black Panther cofounder Huey P. Newton. Marcus clicked forward a few tracks. He was always jumping around, looking for just the right tune. He settled on "They Schools," a screed about how schools perpetuate white supremacy with Eurocentric education. He pressed pause. "Man, I tried to play this for Rinehart and she freaked out," he told me as I drove north through the city. He said she'd turned it off as soon as she heard the chorus: "All my high school teachers can suck my dick." Small wonder. Still, Marcus was incensed by her closed-mindedness. He thought the song had a poignant message, and it was anti-intellectual for her to dismiss it out of hand.

He'd been fighting with Rinehart a lot lately. He was sick of her authoritarian ways, the way she was always on him for the pettiest stuff. The ban on cussing especially bothered him. And she seemed so touchy. She was stressed out with all the MSHSAA and district stuff, and it seemed like she was about to snap. A couple of days before the school break, he asked her what she was going to get him for Christmas and she flipped out. "After all I've done for you!" she shouted, rattling off a list of sacrifices she'd made for him. The plane tickets to Montgomery Bell Academy's tournament in Nashville. The clothes. All the meals. The constant battles with the bureaucratic automatons. They had also gotten into a fight over the spelling of "Žižek," and then another about the pronunciation of "Michel Foucault." She said "Michel" was "Mee-*shale*," with a long *a*. He told her she was stupid. She put her hands on her hips and shouted, "I have a masters in English!" He just laughed at that. "First of all, he's French, so your master's in English is out," he said. "Second, it's 'Mee-*shell*.' I just know."

Things had gotten so tense between them that he skipped her annual Christmas party, which he figured must have pissed her off to no end. At least that's what he said to me, with a touch of macho indignation. The truth is it hurt her feelings, which he knew as well as I did. She never said anything about it. We both just knew.

Clearly, there was deeper stuff at play here. Rinehart was like a mother to him, and he was ready to leave home. It was time for her to treat him like the adult that he was. That's how he saw it anyway. From Rinehart's perspective, he wasn't anywhere near ready. In fact, she worried that he might not even graduate. And she might well be the one who would prevent him from doing so. She'd already dropped him out of college English. He was reassigned to her class for twelfth-grade English, the one for the general student population. He'd only done a couple of assignments, half-assed. He had an excuse, of course. By the time he'd switched to the class, he claimed, all the textbooks had been given out. When he informed Rinehart of this, she said she'd get him one. When she didn't produce the book, though, he'd settled into his school trance, slumping way down in his desk every morning, eyes nearly closed.

As we neared the airport, he recounted the dilemma, and his take on the situation vacillated wildly. "She won't flunk me," he said, leaning back and crossing his arms in a show of confidence and certainty. Then he'd lean over and look at me with pleading eyes. "Man," he said. "She's gonna flunk me out of that class."

After a long pause, looking out the window, he said of Rinehart, "Still, I owe my life to her."

WE WERE ON OUR WAY to Los Angeles, Marcus's trip courtesy of the University of Louisville Debate Society. After the win at the Iowa Caucus, Marcus had become a hot property. Over the previous month or so, he'd fielded numerous notes of inquiry from debate coaches at colleges across the country. The cascade of interest came after Phil Kerpen, the man behind Cross-X.com, had helped him craft an e-mail to send to the eDebate Listserv, the equivalent of Cross-X.com for college debaters and coaches:

> My name is Marcus L. Leach and I'm a senior debater at KC Central—A UDL member school in the Kansas City League. I was talking to a friend and he agreed this would possibly be the best course of action. I guess the next step is to tell a little about myself:

This is my 4th year of debate—both in the UDL and on the national circuit. My partner and I have recently won UDL City Championships and the Iowa Caucus and have competed in elimination rounds of several national tournaments. As juniors my partner and I also did impressive work at tournaments such as Omaha Westside.

Now my non-debate life: I will be concise: I'm poor, son of a single black mother with 9 kids so I can't afford any college expenses and seek scholarship opportunities. I also have poor grades because school has never challenged me and my school lacks qualified teachers outside of debate; now, I'm academically motivated thanks to debate.

I'm interested in any possible scholarship opportunities, and would like to go to the best academic school I can get into. I already have a couple of places that have expressed interest but I'd like to explore as many options as possible before deciding.

Thank you and best regards,
Marcus L. Leach
KC Central '03

He'd gotten bites from coast to coast, the most promising from UMKC, the University of Kentucky, and Louisville. He was most intrigued by the latter. The school's head coach, Dr. Ede Warner, was one of the only black directors of a major debate program in the nation. And his squad was almost entirely black. Warner hadn't responded to Marcus's initial mass e-mail. On Kerpen's advice, though, Marcus e-mailed him to get some ideas about how to beef up his and Brandon's "End Racism" case. Instead of offering advice, to Marcus's surprise, Warner sent back a short note: "How about a trip to LA in December?"

WE CHANGED PLANES IN DALLAS, where we met up with Perry Green, another Louisville recruit from Chicago. He was easy to spot, slender and black in a bright red Louisville T-shirt and ball cap. Marcus and Perry had met years earlier, when they both attended debate camp at Northwestern University. Perry happened to be in Louisville, with Warner, when Marcus's initial e-mail arrived. Warner had asked Perry if he knew Marcus, and Perry had said he was an amazing debater.

We met up with Warner and his squad at the Ontario airport, on the edge of Southern California's Inland Empire. Warner drove us in a rented fifteen-passenger van down the highway into the heart of L.A. A hip-hop beat thumped from the van's stereo. The van's rows of seats were packed with passengers, our legs folded up to make room for suitcases. It was like the Central High debate bus in an alternative universe, its leader a hulking, bald black man rather than a demure redhead with blue eyes and a fetching skirt suit. No censorship, either; unlike prissy Rinehart, Warner was pounding the steering wheel and cussing along with the cranked-up rap. In the backseat beside me, Marcus nodded to the beat and gazed at the fantastic sprawl beyond the whistling windows. The hillsides loomed in the darkness, scattered with lights glimmering like lanterns in a Third World shantytown, making silhouettes of the palm trees. He appeared to feel right at home, as if this were what he'd always been looking for.

Like Rinehart, Warner was a lifelong debate-head. He came to the game in high school, as a young teen growing up in Hammond, Indiana, which lies adjacent to Gary. Together the two cities make up one of the most segregated regions in the nation, Hammond being the white side, Gary the black. Warner's family owned and operated a funeral parlor in Gary, a business that was lucrative enough to finance a home in pricier Hammond. Warner was a gifted student, and in 1977 a counselor at Hammond High recommended he try debate. He joined the squad and has been hooked on the game ever since.

He earned a scholarship to Augustana College in South Dakota, where he competed for the debate squad, on which he was the only black. After his freshman year, when he came home for the summer, he was hanging out one day with a buddy he had known since he was eight or nine. Suddenly his friend stopped and shot Warner a crooked glance. "What happened to you?" his friend asked incredulously. "You *are not* the same cat. You don't *dress* the same. You don't *talk* the same. What happened?!"

After receiving his degree, Warner returned to Indiana with the intention of taking over the family business. But he didn't like the tedium of business ownership, and he found his family's line of work deeply disturbing. At the time, in the mid-1980s, Gary was, in Warner's recollection, "the murder capital of the world." He got so depressed seeing young black men coming in day after day on slabs that for a while he contemplated suicide.

HE'D MAJORED IN POLITICAL SCIENCE IN COLLEGE, but the racial division and oppression of his hometown hadn't factored much into his studies. He'd never given much thought to race issues. Now, amid so many dead bodies in Gary, it was just about all he could think about. So he quit the business and enrolled in graduate school at Wayne State University in Detroit, with the goal of becoming an educator, a debate coach focused on getting black kids involved, to empower them. There he met his wife, Motriyo Isles, whom everyone called Tria. At first, Tria couldn't stand Warner. She thought he was "assimilated. A sellout." Eventually, she became not only his companion in life but his coconspirator in debate.

Before Warner even completed his doctoral program, he was offered a tenure-track position at the University of Louisville, which was desperate to diversify its faculty. Louisville's administrators hired him without even conducting an interview. As the school's head debate coach, he started out by writing cases about race. But he grew more and more frustrated because he'd only managed to recruit a handful of black debaters, and few of them stuck around for long. Eventually, he persuaded the administration to use the debate program as a diversity initiative, and he began handing out debate scholarships to black students. But for the most part, they still didn't like the game. So he decided to shake things up—radically.

LIZ JONES STEPPED UP TO THE PODIUM. "ObservationOne," she began in the queer monotone of a speed-reader. "TheUnitedStatesFederal GovernmentShouldRatifytheOptionalProtocoltotheViennaConventionon

ConsularRelationsoftheUnitedNationsAbolishingtheDeathPenaltyBecause
theDeathPenaltyIsRacist."

She stepped back and cocked her head. "Now that you know we can do
it," she said, "let's debate something real."

Her partner, Tonia Green, clicked a button on her laptop and the room
filled with the sounds of Nas's "Black Zombie." Liz swayed to the beat.

The music stopped, and Liz went off. "Clifford Lewis, Jr.," she shouted.
"Black male. Eighteen years of age. Shot and killed by Louisville police in
January 2001.

"'Obviously we're very pleased.' July 2001 comments of Jefferson County
Attorney Irv Maze after Judge John G. Heyburn II dismissed claims against
the county regarding the death of African-American inmate Adrian Reynolds,
who died of head injuries January 7, 1998, after struggling with corrections
officers outside of his jail cell.

"Rodney Abernathy. Killed by four Louisville police officers in Chicka-
saw Park in June of 2000. Twenty-four total rounds were shot and fifteen
bullets entered his unarmed black body.

"Eighteen-year-old Desmond Rudolph. Another black male. Killed by
Louisville police after they shot twenty-two rounds into his Blazer, stuck
against a pole in a ditch in 1999."

She continued through the long, tragic list, her voice rising in volume as
she chopped at the air with her hands. "And here I sit," she announced,
switching to the meat of her message. "Alive and well. Able to see another
day. A privilege in itself. And in this privileged position on a college campus
debating with tomorrow's leaders, my mission is for you to try and understand at least partially the pain which resides in the streets, and that ivory
towers ignore."

Her speech continued to build in intensity as she shared experiences from
her own life and her observations of the world around her. She paused a
couple of times to play more music, part of a song by Tupac Shakur, another
by Nas. She referred to various scholars, such as Joseph Barndt, Paulo Freire,
and Bernice Johnson Reagon—not long blocks of text read quickly, but para-
phrased ideas and key quotations that cut right to the heart of the matter.

I was absolutely blown away. I glanced at Marcus, and he was staring at her, transfixed. This is why he was so intrigued by Louisville. They were taking this game—upon which his life depended, but with which he was quickly growing bored—to a whole new level.

All along on my journey through debate, I'd viewed the game as a microcosm of the larger power structures in America and the world. And this sudden infusion of emotion and diversity and common sense coming from Liz made me realize in an instant why these power structures are divided and unfair. She was making the case that debate had drifted away from its democratic roots, being a game that anyone ought to be able to play because it's based on arguing and research, which anyone can do. The use of speed-reading, and of evidence culled almost entirely from academic books and journals and news reports, excluded voices and points of view, namely those of oppressed minorities. The music was key to her case. She offered it as evidence from "organic intellectuals," borrowing the phrase from Antonio Gramsci, the early-twentieth-century political theorist and activist. Unlike "traditional intellectuals," who are distanced from the greater population by the ivory towers of academia, organic intellectuals arise out of "aggrieved communities," as Liz put it—in other words, the streets. Gramsci wrote that everyone "carries on some form of intellectual activity . . . participates in a particular conception of the world, has a conscious line of moral conduct, and therefore contributes to sustain a conception of the world or to modify it, that is, to bring into being new modes of thought." The problem, according to Gramsci, and now Liz and the Louisville debate squad, is that these new modes of thought are routinely ignored by higher education and, by extension, policy makers. Just as Gramsci sought in the early twentieth century to build and strengthen a community of organic intellectuals from the lower classes to mobilize the masses and persuade a new generation of traditional intellectuals to join in a revolution (Gramsci was a Marxist), the Louisville debaters were bringing a vital and ever-present component of African-American culture—music—into the policy-making game. They were offering the words of rap artists as evidence to guide policy decisions so that they would respect the concerns and needs of otherwise voiceless minorities. I wrote in my notebook, "This is one of the most incredible things I've ever seen." I looked over at Marcus again. At that moment, I had a vision of him going to Louisville and winning a national championship.

Louisville's approach had fostered quite a few critics on the college debate scene, though, who saw it as grossly inferior to the evidence-heavy style that nearly all other squads in the nation practiced. Some saw it as an overt threat to the game and its importance to the halls of academia. Perry and Marcus both believed, however, that the naysayers were full of crap. At the airport in Dallas, they had talked about their dissatisfaction with debate, and their eagerness to see what Dr. Warner's squad might have to offer. Perry had already made up his mind that he was going to Louisville. He'd even tried some of the squad's techniques at high school tournaments, playing hip-hop and incorporating his personal story into his arguments. He told me it was fun, but far from easy. "It's basically just you for eight minutes," he said of the constructive speeches.

When Perry started complaining about the style of debate on the national circuit, that it's boring and meaningless and it favors kids from schools with copious resources, Marcus nodded and affirmed every word. He told me that in his e-mail to Warner he had said that he'd just won the Iowa Caucus—"like this major national tournament"—and it had meant nothing to him.

Frankly, I was initially taken aback by Marcus's stance. Until then, I'd believed that the win was the crowning achievement of his debate career, and possibly his life. It was certainly one of the greatest thrills of mine. Plus, he'd rearranged his priorities after returning to Kansas City with the trophy in hand.

When I mentioned all this, Marcus shrugged it off as being caught up in the moment. He's just competitive, he explained. Winning is fun. Losing sucks. But in the end, wins don't necessarily mean anything. Perry had agreed. "It's like you get home and you're like, 'What did I just do?'" he said.

Marcus confided that he'd done a lot of thinking over the previous few months. He sensed it was time to move away from debate, beyond it, to find an activity that would prepare him for the real world, preferably as a leader. Debate, with its limited number of shifting positions, had become like a video game for him, one he'd mastered long ago. He was ready to turn it in for a new one.

LIZ CONCLUDED HER SPEECH with an icy observation about diversity in debate. "The truth is you don't want black folks," she scoffed. "You're just looking for yourself with a little bit of color."

Their opponent's first speaker, a white male from Michigan State University, began with a musical selection from the rap artist Deltron 3030, about a scheme to spread a "super-virus" to shut down the system. He offered the song as a metaphor. The virus, he explained, was Louisville's style of debate. He said that debate is no place for advocacy, much less campaigns based on hip-hop, which alienates young black leaders from the generation of the civil rights movement—the very people who made hip-hop possible by creating new opportunities for blacks.

Louisville lost the round, as they had many since trying their new style. Indeed, during the first two rounds of this tournament at the University of Southern California, not a single Louisville team picked up a ballot. Earlier, Marcus, Perry, and I had watched another Louisville team, Corey Knox and R. J. Green, a white kid from rural Kentucky, lose an agonizing debate to a pair from Northwestern University, widely regarded as the most formidable program on the college circuit.

During his first speech Corey had asked his opponents and the judge, "Are you this type of person that fears a group of people of color and group of people standin' on the street in your way in your path when you're walkin' down the street and you walk on the other way? Are you also that person when you walkin' down the hallway and you see someone of color walkin' the same pathway that may dress like I dress, may sag a little bit harder, may have braids or cornrows in they hair, and you look at 'em, you gaze at 'em, but when they look back at you, you kinda straighten up your eyes and you walk and you hopin' and prayin' that they don't say anything to you?

"I've witnessed a lot of that in my life."

Corey looked like the kind of black man whites would cross the street to avoid. His skin was quite dark, his build sturdy, and he wore a ball cap with a flat brim cocked at an angle across his head and baggy jeans with several inches of cuff bunched up around his ankles. His teeth were small, with visible gaps between them. But to anyone who'd spent enough time with blacks to not fall prey to the stereotypes of fashion, it was easy to spot Corey's compassion and integrity. Leaning forward at a school desk, his posture welcoming, he came across as intellectually tough, but peaceful and loving.

He went on to talk about more of his experiences as a black male, sprinkling his speech here and there with references to authors such as Linda Alcoff, Joseph Barndt, and bell hooks. He played a Nas song, "I Want to Talk to You," and then a beautiful chorus of women singing about how they would not bow down to racism, injustice, or exploitation.

The debaters from Northwestern didn't look at Corey as he spoke. They sat staring at the desktops in front of them, their chins resting in the palms of their hands. Marcus watched with widened eyes, glancing back and forth between Corey and his opponents. The disconnect was stunning. From the Louisville side came open-mindedness and willingness, while the Northwestern debaters seemed repressed, as though cowering in frightened resistance.

During their second speech, Northwestern responded by saying that all of Louisville's arguments were irrelevant to Northwestern's case. It was a long monologue about how debate is good. Speaking at an almost unintelligibly rapid clip, and without looking up from his sheets of evidence, Northwestern's first speaker argued that debate builds good communication skills. Corey and R.J. looked directly at him as he spoke. The Northwestern debater never returned their gaze.

As I watched this scene unfold, the whole notion of the way debaters discuss issues seemed utterly absurd to me. I began to question the entire premise I'd been operating under during my travels with the Central debate squad. Until this moment, I had been led to believe that debate offers a race- and class-neutral test of research and thinking skills. Its emphasis on evidence, it had seemed to me, was key to this benefit, because it was the ideas and information that mattered, not how one spoke or looked. It wasn't a perfect system, as I'd discovered at the Glenbrooks, where I learned how the reputation of certain schools sometimes factored into judges' decisions, but debate was as close to ideal as anything I could imagine. But now I was seeing it as white supremacist—not in the white-hood-and-burning-crosses sense, but in the idea that one set of social norms is vastly superior to all others. I recalled my initial reaction to the speedy style of debate and how different it was from my (and, frankly, most folks') understanding of what debate is like, the image of the smooth-talking orator that dates back to Greece in 500 B.C. And I realized, too, that even popular conceptions of debate ignore the fact that academic debate has a history beyond Western civilization; that non-Western cultures have their own debate traditions, and these date back millennia as well. This is especially true for African-Americans. In precolonial Africa, debate was an integral part of the education system, in which adolescents would duel back and forth in front of a crowd with proverbs. In America, this tradition became known as the dozens, where kids would hurl insults back and forth until one, the loser, would betray hurt feelings. Now the game is known as freestyle, where rap artists unleash insulting impromptu rhymes at each other, like in the movie *8 Mile*, which I'd taken Marcus, Brandon, and Leo to see a few weeks earlier.

But until I heard Corey's speech, and observed how the Northwestern debaters responded, it had never occurred to me that debate's focus on evidence—lots and lots of evidence, and the weird speaking style this deluge of info demands—might be exclusionary and elitist. More significant, I'd never thought about how impersonal the discourse of debate had become. True, I'd seen emotion in debate rounds; they can become heated, especially during cross-x. But in the end, debates always boil down to a choice between two detached and disinterested positions. They lack the passion of true advocacy. And this characteristic of the game, it became clear to me as I watched this early-morning round between Louisville and Northwestern, could dissuade a lot of folks from participating, especially blacks.

Louisville's speeches reached such a zenith of emotion and intensity that I found myself profoundly moved. At one point during his second speech, Corey was literally shouting and pounding his knees. "Our whole point is, *Who is the affirmative trying to solve for?* It's only for the best interest of those that sit in the power in the United States federal government! What about the people that's in poverty here in *this* country?! What about the people that's livin' in *these* streets?!"

He concluded by speaking directly to the judge, whose shifting and uncomfortable posture suggested he took this as a threat: "And if you don't believe and buy anything that we saying today, then you vote for them. Go ahead. But I'm gonna let you know now, you continue to support hegemony towards people of color, you continue to support privilege and power, that supports institutional racism for people not only in this country. And if you continue to do that, we, as the Louisville team, will come back not only to this team but to you as a judge and continue to express our feelings and emotions about how we feel about the U.S. leadership, and the way it supports institutional racism."

Afterward, Corey told me he knew they would lose as soon as he walked in and saw who would be signing the ballot. The judge, from Whitman College, had voted against them at an earlier tournament, after which he went off on a bizarre, disconcerting rant, lambasting Louisville for undermining debate's importance as a venue for lofty ideas. The judge even went so far as to say that his mother was dumb, and that if debate were to change so as to allow dumb people like his mother to participate, the entire activity would be ruined.

DURING THE USC TOURNAMENT, I talked at length with debaters and coaches about what Louisville was doing. Most people said that they supported the ideas Louisville was presenting, but they took issue with the way they were doing it. The style is too confrontational, some said. Hip-hop is a bad choice of evidence because it's sexist and violent and controlled by corporate media giants. Others believed, as Michigan State University had argued during the round against Liz and Tonia, that debate is a poor venue for activism because it's a game with winners and losers. Causes such as the one championed by Louisville ought to occur in the so-called real world, such as on political campaigns or through protest. I talked with one assistant coach from Northwestern at length about this. I laid out the oft-argued notion that debate is a training ground for future leaders. I told him of my travels with the Central squad, how I'd come to see debate as a means of empowerment. He agreed to the extent that it provides educational opportunities. But when I tried to suggest that winning is key to that empowerment, that the debate ballot is an instrument of power that can advance individuals as well as ideas, he didn't buy it. He asked, "Are you thinking of power when you play Scrabble?"

Still, I sensed that Louisville's approach was a natural progression of recent trends in the game, most notably the kritik. I floated this theory by one of Louisville's chief allies, Bill Shanahan, who had a hand in first creating these kinds of arguments in the 1980s, when he was a graduate assistant at the University of Texas. And he agreed, to the extent that agreement is possible for a lifelong debater.

He was now head coach at Fort Hays State University, in the tiny prairie town of Hays, Kansas, and he'd led his team to a national championship in 2002 running a very unconventional case that called for the affirmation of the resolution for a U.S. policy for Native Americans, as a "vision." He was a short, skinny man, with big black horn-rimmed glasses, wiry graying hair pulled into a ponytail, and a long scraggly beard. He wore tie-dyed shirts, and shorts, and every time I saw him he had bare feet. A misfit of sorts, Shanahan had been unable to land a job as director of a major college debate program, so he wound up in Hays, a community where he didn't quite fit. The town of thirty thousand, isolated on the windswept plains, is prairie conservative to the core. But it wasn't a bad gig. The university's president respected him and thoroughly supported the program, small though it was, with just four debaters on the squad. And his stock certainly went up when he brought the national championship trophy to western Kansas in 2002.

He got into debate in junior high, when he was diagnosed with asthma and could no longer compete in sports. A highly competitive kid, he immediately took to the game and wound up sticking with it his entire life. As a grad student and assistant coach for Texas, he became disillusioned with debate. He felt as though he were just training lawyers, an uncomfortable and dissatisfying role for him, a born iconoclast. At the time he was reading a lot of political theory and philosophy, such as the work of Michel Foucault and

Paul Feyerabend, whose 1975 book, *Against Method*, outlined an anarchistic theory of knowledge. He was particularly taken with the work of Thomas Kuhn, who wrote voluminously about the notion of paradigm shifts: that science is "a series of peaceful interludes punctuated by intellectually violent revolutions . . . the tradition-shattering complements to the tradition-bound activity of normal science," after which "one conceptual worldview is replaced by another." This was the sort of change Shanahan hoped to bring to the game. He saw in debate "a studied ignorance," he told me. "The style of discourse, it feeds on itself to produce a certain type of thinking. That's power. Debate shapes realities in ways that stay with us for the rest of our lives."

Some of his debaters were turned on by these ideas, too, and they started crafting cases around them. At first, the reaction to these kritiks was hostile, much like what Louisville was facing now. But gradually judges started opening up to them, and the practice spread. Teams won a few big debates, and that was that. Kritiks had become part of the norm.

He told me he felt he was amid a revolution, an intellectual one, of which Louisville was very much a part, though he didn't look on debate in quite as stark terms as Warner and his squad did—as a true institution of power, a sort of farm league for national and world leadership. To him, debate is very much a laboratory for raising and testing new ideas, a free space, detached from the actual policy-making apparatuses that could capriciously wield power against it, or co-opt it for nefarious gain.

AS THE DAY CONTINUED, Louisville picked up a few wins. They'd been trying their approach for a couple of seasons. Though they weren't yet winning enough to be championship caliber, some in the debate community were beginning to cozy up to what they were trying to say. Other squads had even begun experimenting with their own different approaches to the game, and they became allies of sorts with Louisville. One such school was Cal State Fullerton. Indeed, Fullerton's director, John Bruschke, was the one who had encouraged Warner to have his debaters do away with traditional means of reading evidence cards. After judging a round, Bruschke had told Warner to have his debaters put away cards and just speak.

We ended our day watching Louisville compete against Fullerton, and it was like no debate I'd ever seen. Arguing on the negative, Fullerton presented a "fuck the state" counterplan. They played songs by Jurassic 5, Public Enemy, and Rage Against the Machine, which they complemented with personal stories and the theories of Michel Foucault. Music was key to both teams' arguments, and it gave the debate an air of urgency, as though the exchange were taking place in the streets—crowded urban streets, charged with the sort of electricity that precedes an uprising. If I'd begun the first day of the tournament with any doubt that music is legitimate debate evidence, those doubts disappeared during this round. I could see how the music taps into something real, powerful. Music had been omnipresent during my travels with Central—in the van going to tournaments, in the squad room, in the headphones so many of the kids wore. It was a motivator, a pacifier, and, with the right song, at the right moment, a unifier.

Unlike in the earlier rounds Marcus, Perry, and I had watched, there was little discussion of how the teams' plans might spur more diversity in the debate community. The teams checked each other on that front—the two Louisville debaters were black women, and the Fullerton duo was a gay man and a woman, both of Hispanic descent. So the debate came down to two clashing ideas about how to make the world better. Louisville was pushing for the United States to abide by the desires of the San Francisco Bay Area Hip-Hop Coalition to sign an international treaty calling for an end to the death penalty. Fullerton argued that this would just lead to more life prison sentences, which is essentially slavery and is worse than death. The only solution, they said, was a total overthrow of the government: *Fuck the state.*

It reminded me of that early-season round at Valley High in West Des Moines between Brandon and Marcus and Andrew Berg of Fargo North, where the casual atmosphere of dialogue about solutions to racism conjured images of Berkeley in the 1960s. But this, with the music and the personal stories and the urgent language, seemed much more real. I was profoundly moved. The exchange seemed to revive a revolutionary spirit I'd assumed was all but lost on university campuses.

TWO

GEECHY NEGRO

WARNER WANTED TO CHAT with his young recruits, so we skipped the last round of the day and headed to a tiny walk-up taco stand on Figueroa Boulevard, a palm-tree-lined thoroughfare stretching toward the futuristic skyscrapers of downtown, all lit up in neon greens, reds, and blues. Marcus looked wary as we approached. "This is not Taco Bell, hon," Tria said to Marcus with a laugh. "Not at all."

"These are—" Warner started to say.

"This is *real* tacos," Tria finished his sentence. "They're *so* good."

On the way over to the taco stand, Warner had talked some about the debate community's response to Louisville's arguments. "Generally, across the board, the nastiest debates we've had have been against other black debaters," he said. "West Georgia is the other predominantly African-American squad in the country, and our debates with them have just been ugly. Ugly, ugly, ugly."

Marcus knew about West Georgia. One of their top debaters, Rashad Evans, had won a national championship—the first black debater ever to have done so. Marcus had Evans as a lab leader at a camp early in his high school career. He'd found Rashad a bit arrogant, but he respected and looked up to him. When he heard that Rashad had won the big one, he felt proud to have been in his lab. Marcus had also heard about Rashad's run-ins with Louisville; word gets around quickly on the debate scene. In a round earlier that year, Corey had called Rashad an Uncle Tom, and Rashad had started yelling, right in the middle of Corey's speech, "Who you callin' Uncle Tom?!"

"I think it becomes a battle of almost who speaks with the right voice for black America," Warner went on to explain. "And I don't think either one does."

We gathered up our food and headed back to the car. As he drove us to the hotel, Warner said he was excited about the prospect of both Marcus and Perry joining the squad because of their experience debating in the preferred college style of speed and lots of evidence. "I think it takes us to a whole other level," he said.

Marcus thought so, too, not just for the squad, but for himself. He wanted meaning, power—real power, not just bragging rights on Cross-X.com. For that, he knew he had to find his own identity, a voice and purpose. Just seventeen, Marcus wasn't yet sure who he was. He fit in among blacks and whites, but never perfectly in either world. He was half-and-half, in blood and practice, dividing his time between his mom's house and Richard's family, Central High and the debate scene. But in the gut of his soul, he was black. And here was a confident black scholar offering him a chance to embrace his blackness and take it all the way.

Warner looked at Marcus and Perry through the rearview mirror. "Rule number one," he said, "you have to sacrifice personal victory."

He paused to let that thought hang in the air.

"Have you heard about all the debates we forfeited?" he asked.

"No," Marcus replied. *Forfeit?* The word threw him. Until that moment the prospect of voluntary loss hadn't entered his mind. *Isn't winning what it's all about? Not just in the game, but in life?* Winning was Marcus's caffeine, the fire under his ass. His fear of losing was often the only thing capable of slapping him out of silliness, of narrowing his eyes in determination.

Warner said the first time they decided to concede a round for the sake of their cause was two years earlier, when the college topic was Africa. They'd brought with them to a tournament a Pan-African studies professor, whom they placed in the judging pool. After she judged a round, the losing team, from the University of Texas at Dallas, laid into her, calling her incompetent.

"She was in tears after this debate," Warner said. "And that night my debaters were offended."

The next morning one of Louisville's teams was matched up against the same UT-Dallas team, and they decided they would talk about how the professor had been treated. They fully expected to lose. "And the other teams on our squad all wanted to not debate," Warner said. "To show solidarity. Even though most of those teams were either two-two or three-one."

"Whoa," Marcus said, jarred more by the prospect of giving up a ballot than by the comments the UT-Dallas debaters had made.

Warner told us they'd done this once more, at the University of Kentucky's tournament, where Corey and R.J. made it to a do-or-die break round, and the rest of the squad forfeited to watch as a show of support.

Then there was the Pepperdine tournament, a few months before Marcus and Perry's recruitment trip.

"R.J. and Corey debate this team from Texas," Warner told us. "And this guy is pretty much, 'I'm white, but I understand more about black culture than anybody in the room.'"

"Whoa," Marcus said again.

"I mean, he pretty much rolled that way," Warner said. "And I mean, he, he pretty much used 'nigger' repeatedly. Under the argument that 'I'm white, you know. If y'all say it, I can say it.' He talked about 'you people.' Very much in the Ross Perot sense, where he was having a cross-x with Corey, saying, 'Your people spit in their water so they wouldn't have to work in the fields.' Which was an exact quote."

R.J. and Corey won the debate. They cleared to the elimination rounds, and because of an error in the tabulation room they wound up being paired against the same Texas team. Again, all the other debaters wanted to forfeit their rounds to watch in solidarity—including Liz and Tonia, who were the tournament's top seed and were ranked as first- and third-place speakers, respectively. In that instance, Warner didn't let them.

Tria stepped in with the moral of the story: "The broader premise is, it changes the game, where you're not about winning and losing. It is about—"

"Activism," Warner finished for her.

"That's what I wanna use college debate for," Marcus replied. "For me debate . . . Like . . . Like, I feel like it doesn't really . . . Like, it hasn't for me, like, changed, like, the world for me. I think that's, like, a bad thing. I wanna use debate as, like, a transition to, like, serious organizations of change and stuff. Like, get the education on activism and things like that. To actually become someone."

Warner pulled in to the hotel's parking lot and found an empty space. He killed the engine and craned his neck to look right at Marcus and Perry.

"I'm gonna be frank with the two of you," he said. "You're assimilated. You know, you been doin' this four years. And I was assimilated. And if you come to U of L and you debate for U of L, one of the first things you're gonna have to be willing to do is listen to the voices of those that don't have the level of training that we have. And really listen."

Perry nodded.

Marcus stared back at Warner.

Assimilated.

Marcus felt like he'd been punched. He wanted to shout, as Rashad Evans had.

AT THE TOURNAMENT THE NEXT DAY, as I was talking outside with a coach from Northwestern, Perry burst out the front doors of the building and marched up to me. "You just missed the most powerful speech ever," he said.

Liz came out the door right behind him, a cigarette already between her lips. She lit it and puffed away, her body tense.

Perry told me that one of Liz's opponents, from Claremont College, had said that the civil rights movement basically did nothing. Liz went ballistic when she heard this. When it was her turn to speak, she demanded that the judge stop taking notes and look at her. "Their argument is *fucking repugnant!*" she shouted.

I followed Perry into the room to listen to the last two speeches of the round. It was a lecture hall with auditorium seating, and Marcus was sitting near the back, slumped far down in his seat, his legs flopped over the row in front of him. His brow was knit in consternation. I sat down just as the Claremont debater began his speech. Well aware that he'd kicked a hornet's nest, he tried to re-explain his argument as politely as possible. He said he didn't believe blacks shouldn't have been given the rights they'd earned during the civil rights movement, just that, in the final analysis, things haven't really changed so much. He looked over at Liz and Tonia as he spoke, his posture open and submissive, a weary smile on his face, but they were both leering off into the distance.

Honestly, what he was saying made sense to me. In fact, I was carrying a copy of the *Los Angeles Times*, and the lead article that day was a long story about segregated cities. It focused on Milwaukee, beginning with an anecdote about a civil rights march there more than thirty years earlier, in which blacks marched into the white part of the city to demand the right to rent and buy homes there. The march had been a huge success; it battered the legislative vestiges of Jim Crow in that Midwestern town. But now the city had become the most racially divided in the nation. The article asked, *What went wrong?*

Louisville won the round. Afterward, I followed Marcus as he strolled the hallway rather aimlessly. He was quiet and pensive. I asked him what he thought of the round. "It was intense," he said, and then mumbled: "I don't know if I can do this. I mean, I thought that was a valid argument," referring to Claremont's.

He mumbled some more as he turned away from me, so quietly that I didn't understand him. I asked what he said. "I'm going to have to do a lot of thinking," he replied.

THE WARNERS HAD THE TV on when we filed in. It was turned to the modern remake of Jane Austen's *Emma—Clueless*, starring Alicia Silverstone. The young actress stood at a podium, talking about ways to help the Haitians, which she pronounced "Hate-ee-ans."

"They're debating!" Corey exclaimed.

It was New Year's Eve. None of the Louisville teams had made it to the trophy rounds at the USC tournament, so Warner called practice for early in the afternoon, to give everyone a chance to sleep in. Marcus opted not to come. Warner muted the TV set. All the debaters settled in, taking places in every chair, across the bed, and on the floor with their backs propped against the walls and the dresser and the desk. Warner went over the tournament's results. He noted that Liz finished as seventeenth speaker—the highlight for the squad.

"Here's the problem," Warner said all of a sudden. "We're going back to reactive instead of proactive." He leaned forward in his seat and jabbed at the air with his forefinger. "Don't get all into your opponents' arguments," he said, driving a fist against his knee. "Keep pounding your argument home."

I was put off by this; it seemed so unfair and antidemocratic. Louisville was raising valid issues, sure, but it was still just a game. Did Warner expect debaters to argue about nothing but race until the problem of racism is solved? What about the other educational aspects of debate? Learning about the UN or the federal government or mental health policy?

After an hour or so, Marcus and Perry slinked into the room. Perry didn't hesitate to join the conversation. But Marcus seemed distant. Here he was in L.A. on the biggest party night of the year, and he looked like he was ready to go home.

THERE WERE BOTTLES EVERYWHERE. The Louisville squad had settled in, and they were working up a good buzz to ring in the New Year. Marcus walked in all cool like, but Warner made him do an about-face. *No minors allowed.* But an hour or so later, when he found out the seventeen-year-old had been wandering around downtown with a couple of guys from another school as they guzzled beer after beer (chucking their empties into the gutter and shouting, "This is for capitalism!"), Warner did the only sensible thing: he invited Marcus in, with the stipulation that he not drink. But while Warner wasn't looking, Marcus filled a plastic cup with Coke and Malibu Rum.

Marcus had never drunk before, but the sweet cocktails went down smooth and easy. As midnight neared, he found himself in the hallway with

R.J. and two women from Washington State University. They claimed to be cheerleaders, in town for the Rose Bowl.

The women were hammered, slurring their words, and R.J., with the courage of a bottle of Jim Beam, spotted an opportunity to bed a woman who, under normal circumstances, would be way out of his league. But the women seemed more interested in the exotic black man, Marcus. At one point one of them suddenly turned to the seventeen-year-old and said, "I want to suck your cock."

Marcus invited her to Warner's room, into the bathroom, where they could do the deed. But within minutes a man, apparently her boyfriend, burst into Louisville's room with his arms flexed out to the side, carrying a miniature baseball bat. A few steps in, however, his eyes registered the scene—the entire Louisville squad of black debaters surrounded by drained bottles—and his macho posture deflated. He turned tail, grabbed his girl, and fled.

A few minutes before midnight the Louisville debaters began a long series of toasts, with everyone making a drunken proclamation of his or her commitment to the others and expressing hopes for the coming year.

Just then Rashad Evans entered the room. The Louisville crew welcomed him warmly. They poured some liquor into a hotel coffee cup and handed it to him. He came seeking a truce of sorts. He wanted to be friends. He couldn't understand their hostility toward him. He assumed that as blacks on the mostly white debate circuit, they had many things in common. He'd come from the 'hood himself, having grown up in northern New Jersey, near New York City. He wasn't much of a student, but he'd clicked with debate, and it had taken him to college and glory on the circuit. Now a senior, he had his eyes on law school at the University of Pennsylvania.

They continued with their toast, including Rashad in their ceremonial benedictions. "To Rashad," Corey said, raising a glass to the skinny black student. "We've had our little battles. But I just want you to remember one thing. Keep it real. Shit happens to people who don't keep it real."

Sitting in the corner of the room, Marcus was shocked by the remark. He took a sip from his drink, lowered his head, and hunched his shoulders.

Then another debater from Louisville, a white woman named Loran, declared to her teammates, "You all are like a family to me. Sometimes I get sick of you. Sometimes I can't stand to look at you. But that's when you know it's a family. Because when people talk shit about you," she turned and looked right at Rashad, "I want to kick people's asses."

Marcus couldn't take any more. He sneaked out of the room. "Man, Joe," he said to me, his voice quiet and softened by alcohol. "I think they done Rashad wrong. I mean, he won the NDT"—the National Debate Tournament (where Evans had actually finished third, and no black has ever won; West Georgia had won the Cross Examination Debate Association's national championship). "I got mad respect for him."

After the initial potshots, the conversation between Rashad and the Louisville squad went deep and intimate. The Louisville debaters kept filling and refilling Rashad's coffee mug, and together they each tried to understand where the other was coming from.

The Louisville debaters kept working on Rashad, trying to get him to concede that the norms of debate—speed-reading in particular—are racially exclusionary.

"How does speed affect race?" Rashad asked them. "Because everybody can learn how to speed up."

"It's real simple," Tria said. "We choose not to speak fast because we don't want to." Speaking fast, she explained, is an inauthentic form of argumentation developed solely for the sake of competitive advantage.

"But why is speed racist?" Rashad tried again.

"It's beyond that," Tria said. "It's the idea. The essence of strategic advantage is racist"—meaning that strategic advantages based on communication styles in a game tend to favor one set of cultural norms over others. And from the perspective of Tria, a black coach on a black team, this is invariably rooted in race.

During his debate against Corey and R.J., Rashad had argued that racism doesn't exist. This had flabbergasted the Louisville squad. They knew Rashad came from a poor inner-city community. They knew he couldn't possibly believe such a thing. Tria asked him how he could feel justified running such an argument.

"To win the game," he responded.

"At what cost?"

All during the conversation Rashad maintained that policy debate doesn't matter in the big scheme of things. It's just a game. But Tria and the Louisville team kept insisting that it does matter, because it's just like real policy making—especially since many debaters go on to careers where they help shape real policy. "Our mission," Tria told him, "is to force them to listen to different voices."

MARCUS WOKE UP EARLY on New Year's Day and took an extraordinarily long shower. He emerged from the bathroom in his boxers, still high from the proposition he'd received the night before. Eventually the Louisville squad members came out of their rooms, looking beaten down by hangovers and lack of sleep. They'd stayed up until almost four talking with Rashad.

As he drove us to a restaurant for lunch, Warner said of Rashad, "Bottom line is he doesn't want you guys to call him Uncle Tom. He wants you to be nice to him and party with him."

A few of the debaters nodded. It seemed reasonable.

"He was like, 'How can I be a part of this?'" Warner said. "And Tria was like, 'As long as you think it's a game, you can't. It ain't a game now.'"

"I was like, 'You can *nev-ah!*'" Liz said.

They didn't know it then, but they had gotten through to Rashad. He would show up at the next tournament, which would begin the following day at Cal State Fullerton, without evidence, to run a Louisville-style argument. It was an eye-opening experience for him. Not only did he find it more difficult than his usual style of ripping through a huge stack of cards; the emotion of it was tough to contend with. His opponents started crying during his speeches. He thought, *Why are you getting emotional now? When it's me arguing this stuff? When you hit Louisville two rounds ago, you just tried to win. Why's it different now?*

All through the tournament he kept waffling about whether or not he wanted to continue. He drove his coach and his partner crazy. Finally, before the last round, they told him to make up his mind. He decided to go back to debating the way he was used to. They went to the hotel to get their evidence, and when they returned, they learned that Warner would be judging their next round. They were in a position to break to out rounds, and Rashad's coach and his partner urged him to run the Louisville style again. The very idea repulsed Rashad. He told them that his earlier choice had not been strategic; he was doing it so he could understand more about himself and his fellow black debaters. But they kept on him until he finally said, "Bullshit!" and walked away.

"NOW, WHAT DID I SAY that was bashing him?" Liz tried to remember as we headed south on one of L.A.'s highways, toward our New Year's Day meal. "How did I hit him in the nuts?"

Perry chimed in: "You like, 'I can beat you any kind of way. I can beat you our way. And I can beat you fast.'"

"It don't matter," Warner said, waving a hand in the air. "We gon' win this debate. It don't matter."

"Damn," Liz said. "If we debate them, I gotta."

"You talkin' shit," Perry said. "You gotta back it up now."

"You gotta steal somebody's tubs so you can run some politics," Marcus said. He chopped his hands at the air with crooked wrists, gangsta-style.

"Shit," Liz said. "I'll run politics off the top a my head."

"That's true," Marcus said, cocking his head back and nodding.

"He earned enough respect from me to set the stand up," Warner said. "He's not earned enough respect from me to embrace him as down with us."

"Did we call him a geechy to his face?" Liz asked, still foggy about the details.

"You were callin' him *everything* last night," Warner said and laughed.

Marcus stiffened at the "geechy" remark.

I asked what the word meant.

"It's kinda like an Uncle Tom, basically," Liz replied.

"Geechy Negro," Perry said. "Bougie," meaning bourgeois.

"It's not bougie," Liz corrected him. "It's like backward. Tria, break it down. It's a southern term, right?"

"It's a southern term," Tria said, nodding. "'Geechy Negro.' Meaning a shufflin', ass-scratchin', I-will-do-whatever-boss-tell-me-to-do Negro."

"I don't think he even *knows* what a geechy is," Liz said of Rashad.

"A geechy Negro," Tria continued, "is someone who'll say, 'Whatever Boss Man wants me to say I'll say just to make Boss Man happy, 'cause that's gonna make my life easier.' Meaning: 'I'm willing to do and say whatever I have to say to get by. I have no principles.'"

"That's the best I've ever heard it explained," R.J. said, tugging thoughtfully at his red whiskers.

"At first we deployed the term because we liked the sound of it," Liz said. "Then we learned what it meant and we was like, 'Oh.'"

"Well, it applies," Warner said, meaning it applied to Rashad.

"Yeah," Liz said. "Pretty much."

That was the last straw for Marcus. Unless it was the only option remaining, he would not be going to Louisville. As a debater, Marcus was nearly identical to Rashad. He'd excelled at the game the way it's played, and he'd achieved a great deal of notoriety in the community. The game might have left him feeling empty at times, especially now that he was a senior with four years' experience, but he couldn't deny that it had given him a sense of purpose, a feeling of power. He never thought he was sacrificing his blackness to do it. No. He was a black pioneer. Perhaps not the Jackie Robinson of debate. But maybe the Willie Mays.

Fuck Louisville, Marcus thought in the sting of his first hangover. *Fuck Dr. Ede Warner.* From that moment on, he would play the fool.

THREE

CRITIQUE OF IMPERIALISM

MARCUS DIDN'T GET MUCH CALIFORNIA out of his trip to California. It was all debate tournaments and restaurants or driving to debate tournaments and restaurants. On New Year's Day, we spent an hour on Venice Beach. The sun was low on the horizon, the ocean bright with rippling light. People were out enjoying the day, combing the beach, playing basketball, lifting weights in the famous fenced-in gym. Marcus ignored it all and headed straight for the tourist shops, where he scored three T-shirts for ten dollars. After we all climbed into the van, he showed them off. One said, FBI—FEMALE BODY INSPECTOR. Another asked, WHAT'S ON A MAN'S MIND? and offered a picture of Freud with a not-too-subtle image of a naked woman woven into the curls of his head. His would-be teammates, all but three of them female, were not impressed. One of them cringed when he showed them off and looked at him with raised eyebrows as if he were a total creep.

That night, our last in California, we all went out to dinner at a Carrows restaurant, a franchised joint in Fullerton, site of Louisville's next tournament. Having Marcus there was like babysitting a sixth grader. He was hyper and fidgety in his chair, not paying attention to the conversation, blurting out non sequiturs now and then about video games, porn, and strip clubs. He'd blown almost all of his remaining cash on scratch-off lottery tickets, and while everyone else was trying to carry on a conversation, he made a big show of scratching them at the table. When he hit a two-dollar winner, he jumped up and raced off to the convenience store to cash it in for more.

In the morning the squad joined hands in the hotel's parking lot and prayed. Perry had written a letter to the squad that he'd asked Liz to read. It was sweet and naive and full of clichés about family and commitment and the collective struggle for change. He didn't want to leave, so Warner had his ticket changed. Marcus, on the other hand, was off somewhere else doing Lord knows what. It was clear to all on the Louisville crew that he wasn't completely down with the revolution. They wrote it off as immaturity, and they were partly right. But Marcus knew what he was doing. He was making a statement: If they didn't want a "geechy Negro" like him, well, he didn't want them, either.

The morning was getting late. Warner pulled the van around to the front of the hotel, and I loaded in my bags, but Marcus was still nowhere to be found. We made a couple of passes through the hotel lobby, and when we finally spotted him, he had under his arm a fake package he'd stolen from the hotel's Christmas display. I'd never seen that before. In my experience, Marcus was the opposite of a thief. More than once, I'd watched him walk all the way from one end of a sprawling suburban school to the other just to give back a pen he had borrowed from a fellow debater or a judge.

In the van Marcus opened the package to show us more of his pirate's booty, a couple half-pint milk cartons that were getting warm. He closed the package and frowned. "I don't even know why I took this," he said.

"That's all right," Warner said. "You a thief. That's okay. We can deal with this."

He spoke calmly and through a smile, not the least bit pissed. He'd dealt with thugs in his life, and Marcus hardly qualified. He added, "You need someone to put a foot in your ass. And I'm more than willing to be that person."

And he might have been. But after he dropped off Marcus and me at the airport and returned to Fullerton, his squad would decide at a team meeting that they didn't want Marcus to be part of their mission.

I didn't yet know that Marcus had decided against Louisville. I thought he was just riding one of his temporary waves of orneriness. At the airport, as we waited to board our plane, Marcus acted as though he was seriously considering Louisville's offer, but that it wasn't his top choice. UMKC was now in the lead, he told me. He knew Linda Collier was a pro at raising funds, building institutional support for her squad. "They have more money than anyone else," Marcus said. "And they're gonna have the best coaches."

I asked him if winning a national championship was important to him.

He looked at me as if I were nuts. "Joe, think about what you just asked me," he said incredulously. "I wouldn't be in it if I couldn't win it all."

A COUPLE DAYS LATER we were back at Kansas City International Airport, and Rinehart was staring warily at the headphones Marcus was holding out toward her.

"They're organic intellectuals," Marcus said, shaking the headphones at her.

She crumpled her face. "What's an organic intellectual?" she asked testily.

"You have to be a member of the aggrieved community," he told her.

"What *grieve* community?" she asked sharply.

"No," he said. "*Aggrieved* community. It has to offer a different hegemonic discourse. It has to be part of the movement."

She raised a skeptical eyebrow.

"Just listen." He shook the headphones at her again. "There's no cuss words."

She slid the headphones over her ears, and he pressed play. "Nope," she said several seconds into the song, removing the headphones. "They already said MFers."

"That's just at the beginning," Marcus protested. "Besides, you're old enough to listen."

She frowned and put the headphones back on and listened another minute or so. She took them off again. "All I hear them saying is, 'Know your enemy, know yourself. George Bush is worse than bin Laden.'"

"Yeah," Marcus said enthusiastically. "That's right. It's a critique on imperialism. And they quote from *The Art of War*."

She looked away and frowned indignantly. He sneered at her. *Fuck her*, he thought. *If she thinks I'm a fool, I'll give her a fool.*

Once again Marcus was caught between two worlds. He'd been to the front lines of the revolution, only to learn he wasn't black enough. He'd come home to find the white world the same as it ever was, nose turned up to his blackness. *Assimilation.* He hated the word. Acculturation was more his speed. He was good at that: sliding in and out of different social groups, feeling at home in all of them. Except in times like these. Why couldn't the world adapt to him for a change?

We were off to the Southern Bell Forum, the invitation to which he had drooled over months earlier. Now all he wanted to do was sabotage it, at least whenever Rinehart was watching. He was wearing his new FBI—FEMALE BODY INSPECTOR shirt, chosen just to rankle Rinehart. She hadn't said anything about it, but he knew it bugged her, and that was satisfying enough.

IT WAS DARK WHEN WE ARRIVED in Nashville. Rinehart rented a van, and we followed the highway toward downtown's cluster of sparkling towers, not much bigger than Kansas City's. As we exited into the south part of the city, onto West End, past fancy restaurants, boutiques, and stylish shopping centers offering everything from a Borders bookstore and Verizon Wireless to Starbucks and sushi, Rinehart and Marcus got into a fight over the word "fuck." They yelled at each other as we passed the replica of the Parthenon, all lit up in reds and blues, and then Vanderbilt University before arriving at the Holiday Inn. These petty battles were getting tiresome. Brandon and I looked at each other and rolled our eyes.

But again Marcus's temper and behavior were just surface symptoms of deeper unease. He was bored, confused, and pissed off. He didn't know what was coming next. Debate had given him a life, but he was sick of it. He couldn't stand the thought of four more years of it, though he believed it was his only ticket to a college education. Honestly, it wasn't much different from being a slave, he thought. He knew that colleges wouldn't take him simply for who he was. They wanted a competitor who could bring them trophies, prestige for their school, successes to move coaches and professors and graduate students further up the hierarchy of their institutions. Even more, they wanted a black face on their squad, to give them a veneer of diversity and assuage their white guilt. He was just another resource for them to exploit.

He wanted to retreat. Just take the next several months to crawl into a hole, play video games, read whatever he felt like reading, think, and, above all, sleep. But here he was, heading to yet another tournament. *Why? What did it matter?* It was all just the same stuff anyway. Topicality. Genocide. Nuclear war. And more nuclear war. He wasn't learning anything new. And it wasn't fun anymore. Counter-Strike, which he had recently reloaded onto his computer, seemed to offer more twists and turns than debate. None of this stuff—debate, school, cussing—seemed to matter. But then, when you got right down to it, *what did?*

In quieter moments, when he wasn't so tired and cranky, he knew he shouldn't be so hard on Rinehart. She was only trying to make *him* matter. And he knew she was dealing with an incredible amount of stress just for him. "She's about to pop," he'd told me when we were in L.A. It was all because of her battles with the school district and MSHSAA, and he understood that she did this for him. But couldn't she tell that he didn't really care anymore?

At that point I was a lot more sympathetic to Jane's side of the story. I hadn't yet grasped the depths of Marcus's ennui. To me, the equation was simple: Marcus and Brandon and the rest of their teammates were bright kids who, without debate, had nothing educationally. Debate in Missouri, with its more subjective judging standards, seemed to be just more nothing. So Marcus and Brandon *needed* to be able to go to as many national-circuit tournaments as possible. And they needed people like Jane, white adults with white clout, to advocate for them. Indeed, they needed *me*. As a reporter, I had some power. Unlike Rinehart, I could call people in powerful positions—at their homes, even—and they would listen to me. And that's exactly what I did.

A FEW WEEKS BEFORE the Southern Bell Forum, I sat in on Marcus's African-American history class. The teacher passed out a copy of a *USA Today* article he had printed off the Internet, which reported that Senate

Majority Leader Trent Lott of Mississippi had praised Strom Thurmond's stance on segregation at the elder statesman's hundredth birthday party. The students took turns reading paragraphs from the story. They did so haltingly, with no apparent comprehension of the subject matter. Afterward, they looked back at the teacher blankly. He asked them what they thought of it. A few of them shrugged. The rest appeared to be paying little or no attention. The teacher started to explain the article, and gradually the weight of Lott's gaffe began to dawn on them. One of the kids asked, "This is happening *now*?"

"*Yes!*" the teacher said, clearly frustrated. The story had been all over the news. You couldn't pick up a paper or turn on the TV without hearing about it. That the students were unaware only showed how disconnected they were from society and the corridors of power.

Marcus was slumped way back in his desk, bored senseless. He'd heard about the Lott controversy as soon as it broke in the news. He'd already thought about ways he might use it in his debate case.

At the same time, Rinehart was struggling to gain approval to attend the Southern Bell Forum at Montgomery Bell Academy. The irony was incredible. Not only was the tournament's director president of the board of the National Forensic League, but the school was the alma mater of Senator William Frist, who inherited Lott's majority leader position after the Thurmond controversy resulted in Lott's demotion. Of course, the Senate had no black leaders; at that point, there'd been only four in its entire history. But this instance of racially insensitive language had shaken up its leadership, though the change at the top would do nothing to address the larger underlying problem of zero representation in Congress's more powerful chamber. Meantime, in the micro-political world of school district bureaucracy, disinterested adherence to arcane procedures was conspiring to keep two black kids out of Frist's alma mater, even for two measly days of debate.

Throughout December, when Central's trip to Nashville was in doubt, I spent hours talking to school board members, attorneys, and state legislators on the telephone, trying to persuade them to fight the MSHSAA. I had a whole speech worked up that I delivered almost as quickly as national-circuit debaters, but with perhaps a bit more emotion. I'd pace my tiny apartment in midtown Kansas City ranting into the cordless. I got so pissed off about the whole situation that I lost sleep. During the holidays I felt withdrawn from my family because I was so obsessed with the injustice of it all.

But then I went to L.A. with the very person I was ostensibly advocating for, and he told me he didn't care. "The funny thing is, while you guys get all upset," Marcus said, "me and Brandon are calm."

Marcus more so than Brandon. Brandon still desperately wanted to go to the TOC; he just didn't talk about it much. Truth is, they didn't have much hope that MSHSAA would back off from its rules. The previous year, when he and Rinehart had traveled to Columbia to get permission to go to the Tournament of Champions, Marcus had felt a sharp enough sting of disappointment to cover both of them.

In the weeks leading up to the meeting, and on the two-hour drive on I-70 to Columbia, Marcus had really believed that the MSHSAA officials would have pity on him and allow Central to go to the TOC. But the meeting had been short and insulting, lasting just fifteen minutes. The members of the appeals committee weren't even in the room. Rinehart and Marcus had to travel more than two hours to make their case to a speakerphone placed in the center of a conference table. Marcus told them how debate meant everything to him, how he would be nowhere without the game. After less than a minute of thought, the committee members unanimously agreed to deny the request.

Rinehart had known going in that they might be denied. Marcus, however, had held on to hope. He was crushed. After so many debates about the nature of power and the stubbornness of institutions, he should have known better. But now that he was powerless, he finally understood the nature of power. "Everything seemed so corrupt," he told me. "It just fuels one off another. I haven't seen, like, a legitimate political system ever since I started looking into things. I mean, there's nothing that works for everyone. It's always for selfish interests and underlying assumptions. No one does things for others. It's trade-offs for your self-benefit.

"I still believe you can change things politically," he said. "But only social problems. Not, like, education stuff. I learned that day that you can't do anything to change the politics of school."

Marcus would agree that this is a terrible lesson for a sixteen-year-old to learn. But he'd still argue that the underlying premise of the circumstances didn't necessarily matter. The more we talked, the more I sensed that Jane and I might be advocating more for our own good than for Marcus and Brandon's. It was as if we were fighting for them to prove to ourselves that injustice can be overcome, and that we have the power to make that happen. But in the process, we were also providing for these kids a definition of success, molding them into something they might not want to be. Worse, we may well have been contributing to the slow death of a game that's so important to American democracy.

MONTGOMERY BELL ACADEMY'S CAMPUS is spread across a hill just south of Vanderbilt University in Nashville. It's like a small private college, with a half-dozen or so red brick buildings with white trim huddled around a courtyard. Established in 1867, the same year as Central High, it costs $16,000 a year. It's an all-boys school, and its motto is "Gentleman, scholar, athlete." The school's cafeteria has a bank of flat-screen video monitors stacked together to form a single screen. It's called Frist Hall, named after one of MBA's most successful graduates. On the wall opposite the monitors the names of outstanding former students are displayed. William Frist is among those honored, having won "most outstanding boy" in both the elementary and the secondary schools in the late 1960s and early '70s. Frist was a debater for MBA around the same time Karl Rove was debating in high school, and when the national circuit was beginning to form around the faster style of arguing that had already become the norm in college. Occasionally, Frist returns to MBA to deliver a motivational speech to its students, and he describes his debate experience as the best preparation he ever got for his political career.

Like its host school, the Southern Bell Forum is one of the best run, most competitive, and most prestigious in the nation. Invitations are highly coveted, and there is typically a waiting list to get one. The directors, coaches at MBA, pride themselves on offering "southern hospitality." The food is outstanding—barbecue and down-home comfort food such as fried chicken and baked yams. They rent out the bar at the tournament hotel to throw a party for the kids while, down the hall, the coaches partake of an open bar.

The tournament's directors limit the field to seventy-two teams, so each school is allowed to bring just one pair of debaters. It's fun but expensive, once plane tickets and hotel rooms are factored in. Consequently, the field is rather elite; the heaviest hitters on the circuit come out every year. Along with a few of the bigger tournaments, such as the Glenbrooks and the Harvard Invitational, it's a quintessential national-circuit event. In addition to top high school debaters and coaches, national debate bigwigs descend on Nashville every January to check out the action. Coaches from Catholic University and from the universities of Kentucky, Iowa, and Missouri–Kansas City were there to scope out recruits, as well as the entire board and the president of the National Forensic League, who held their quarterly meeting in conjunction with the event.

James Copeland, the NFL's top executive, delivered a short speech to the debaters before the rounds began on the first day. Afterward, I spoke with him, and, like the Louisville debate squad, he made me seriously question everything I had come to know about debate.

I asked him about the tension between national-circuit devotees and debate coaches in places like Missouri and Kansas, where travel is restricted so as to keep the circuit's speedy ways at bay. I didn't mention Central High, only that I was following a team from Kansas City, but he started to answer by saying that his office had received a number of complaints about "that coach," meaning Rinehart, for trying to shirk state rules and take her debaters to national competitions. When I pressed him for details, though, he clammed up. In one of my questions, I suggested that Central was being persecuted by Missouri officials, and he grew testy. "This team isn't being persecuted," he insisted. "My God. It's one of the luckiest teams in the country. Persecution is being a debater in Berger, Texas, where the closest tournament is five hundred miles away."

The six TOC-qualifying tournaments that Central was allowed to attend were "more than 95 percent of the debaters in the country will ever go to," he said. Moreover, the value of a small number of high school kids traveling around the country to compete against the same teams fifteen or twenty times a year was dubious at best. "There's too much whining in this business," he scoffed. "The first thing the urban youth need is a good education," as if he had a clue what kind of education Central had to offer.

No doubt his irritation was due to something deeper than Rinehart's supposed whininess. During Copeland's tenure with the NFL, competitive high school debate had been on a continual decline, the beginning of which coincided directly with the emergence of national-circuit-style debate. Indeed, in Illinois, one of the places where the faster style first became popular, the number of schools offering debate programs in 2003 was less than a quarter of what it had been in the 1960s before the change. Pekin Community High, for instance, where Rinehart had coached early in her career, no longer had a serious program. In fact, the Illinois high school activities association was considering disbanding its state championship tournament because there were so few competitors.

Doug Springer, the man who had coached with Rinehart at Pekin and later accepted a job offer at New Trier, sat on the Illinois association's board of directors. He and I chatted for a while between rounds in MBA's sunny courtyard. Like Rinehart, Springer rejected the dress-down ethic his fellow coaches upheld on the national circuit, opting instead for pinstripes and a silk tie. In the early 1970s, Springer told me, when fast, evidence-heavy debate was gaining favor, a school from a wealthy suburb of Chicago qualified for the Tournament of Champions, which was then just a year or so old. State rules prohibited them from attending. The kids and their parents took matters into their own hands and went to the tournament without their coach. There was backlash from the activities association, which threatened severe sanctions. But the school was located in a stronghold of power. The kids' parents were well connected, and they enlisted attorneys and state legislators to beat back the threat. Soon students from the more privileged communities around Chicago were flying all over the country to compete, taking red-eye flights to make it back from tournaments in time for class on Monday mornings. And these teams began to dominate that state circuit. Downstate teams couldn't keep up. It wasn't fun anymore. One by one, debate programs disappeared.

According to popular wisdom, it's a money thing. Only wealthy public and private schools can afford the debate camps and travel schedules necessary to compete at tournaments like MBA's, so they're the ones that get good. But Springer believed the decline came about because the job had become too difficult for coaches. It takes a lot of time to gather the enormous amount of evidence needed for success. Practices became long and arduous. And the new arguments were weird, counterintuitive, always racing to nuclear war and genocide. It was so much easier before. Just teach the same thing every year: stand up straight, talk pretty, cinch your tie up nicely, and read the same topicality cards everyone has been reading since the 1940s. Now coaches had to learn stuff like Foucault. They had to read dozens of newspapers online just to keep up with all the politics arguments.

To deal with the decline, NFL officials kept trying to adjust. They sought to steer debate back toward its rich tradition—as in the late nineteenth and early twentieth centuries, when academic debates were huge events, drawing standing-room-only crowds and front-page headlines—by establishing Lincoln-Douglas Debate in the 1980s. Named after the debates between Stephen A. Douglas and Abraham Lincoln over the issue of slavery during the 1858 campaign for Illinois's seat in the U.S. Senate, Lincoln-Douglas Debate focuses more on moral and ethical issues than on politics. The topics change several times during the season so as to stifle the amount of evidence production. This change came about after officials from the league's main sponsor at the time, the Ford Motor Company, watched the final rounds of the national championship and were appalled by the speedy speeches and off-the-wall doomsday scenarios.

But Lincoln-Douglas began to speed up as well, so during the 2002–2003 season the NFL offered a third option, tentatively named Ted Turner Debate. When the NFL officials asked if they could use his name for the new division, they promised Turner they'd never ask him for money. They wanted it to appeal to the public, to draw more interest and support for the game, and they believed Turner's name would be instantly recognizable and call to mind the cable pundit shows popularized by Turner's networks. Kids were encouraged to fire opinions back and forth with more emphasis on persuasive rhetoric than on evidence.

FOUR

CO-OPTED

COMPETITION STILL TRUMPED ALL FOR MARCUS. Despite his sour mood, he slipped right into debate mode the second the timer beeped. Their first round at MBA he and Brandon pulled off a huge upset, beating Greenhill, a private school from the predominantly white north side of Dallas that was a consistent power on the national circuit. And though he felt stung by his Louisville experience, throughout the round Marcus kept throwing in little pieces of Louisville's message to the debate community. "You need to recognize your privilege," he argued at one point. "If you do that, the whole system will collapse."

Then he fell apart during the second round, in front of the only black judge he'd face all season on the national circuit: Daryl Burch, the man who'd written his and Brandon's case. Burch had put together the plan to end racism while he was a teacher at the Capital Classic camp Brandon and Marcus had attended in Washington the previous summer. He coached duPont Manual High, a public school for gifted and talented students in Louisville. It was a small program by national-circuit standards—just one team and a tiny travel budget—but Burch had shaped it into one of the best in the nation. His students won some of the biggest tournaments in the country during the 2002–2003 season. They ran a highly evolved version of the case Marcus and Brandon were running.

Burch had a reputation as the best-dressed man on the circuit, a distinction that irked him because people seemed more impressed with his style than with his debate acumen. Still, he looked slick. For the first day of the MBA tournament he wore a crisply pressed olive green shirt with a silk tie of a lighter green. His glasses were narrow and silver-framed, with a light blue tint.

At the Capital Classic camp, the director had pulled Burch aside and said, "I don't want you to feel like I'm asking you because you're the only black coach in camp, but we're having problems with an inner-city kid. He's intimidating kids. Taking lunches. Threatening people."

Then Burch met Marcus, took one look, and thought, *You can't be serious.*

Marcus was wearing a button-down shirt, baggy shorts, and sandals with socks. He had to laugh, it was so absurd. *There was no way this kid was hard.*

Yet the director and a lot of other people at the camp were genuinely scared of Marcus. They couldn't see his behavior for what it was: an act.

Burch took Marcus to a barbershop near the university, in a mostly black part of Washington. "Okay," he said to Marcus. "You got game. Let's see what you got." And he left him there.

He walked up the block for a minute or so, and then came back to peek at Marcus through the window. The wannabe hard-ass looked as if he might piss his pants, all tense and trying to disappear in the corner. Burch went in, laughing.

"Man, you see all those women walk in there," Burch teased as they strolled back to campus. "You didn't run no game on them."

Marcus straightened up after that. Burch had to hand it to him, though. "He convinced people of his identity just through his rhetoric," Daryl told me. "That's powerful."

MARCUS WAS SLOPPY AND IRRITABLE throughout the round Burch judged, and Burch voted Central down. "I probably shouldn't have," he said. "This was just a terrible debate."

He'd later admit to me that he was harder on Marcus and Brandon because it was his case they'd mutilated. Plus, he'd been carrying a bit of a grudge. At camp Marcus kept saying Burch's case was stupid, which offended him not only because it was about race issues, which was rare on the circuit, but because it was the first time he'd been asked to run a case-building lab at a camp. He wasn't furious. He knew Marcus was just trying to show off to his white peers, many of whom were also pooh-poohing the plan. But when Marcus argued the case in front of him, in its original form, with no signs of further development, Burch figured the Central team had pulled it out just to grab an easy win with him in the back of the room, and this offended him more than the earlier criticisms.

"You should go more in-depth on your impacts on racism," he said afterward, during his post-round critique of the debate. "You should make racial politicking offers. Like if you give the GOP and Republicans or just presidents in general the ability to say, 'We don't want to pass minority rights or benefit minorities because it would decrease political capital and not allow us to pass the agenda for things like tax cuts.' Then the president will *always* be able to say, 'I don't want to increase rights for minorities, because it may hurt national security interests.' Like if Bush had a choice of either benefiting minorities and increasing minority rights or increasing tax cuts, he'd always pick tax cuts. Which is actually what the disad is asking to say. That we should reject the plan because we need to save the president's political capital, for tax cuts."

Marcus nodded.

"So in other words," Burch continued, "minorities get sold out for the interest of the GOP." He shifted forward in his seat. "Like when you go over the top on racism, you gotta go over the top. You gotta say we're gonna win racism every single debate. We're gonna stand up, and we're gonna win racism every single debate. So turn everything back with somehow getting back to the impact of racism. Prime example: tax cuts are racist. They say tax cuts are the key to the economy. Yeah, because they put money in the pockets of the most wealthiest people. And they pull money from people with the poor incomes, who are mostly minorities in the inner cities. Tons of liberal Democrats are pushing that all the time. Of why tax cuts push the poor minorities."

Yet Marcus had been making the opposite argument all year. On the negative, he almost invariably argued that Bush's third wave of tax cuts, which the president had been pushing through the whole legislative session, were key to saving the economy and averting nuclear war. When facing these arguments on the affirmative, Marcus and Brandon had always argued around the "tax cuts save the economy" assertions, never addressing them head-on. But in reality, Burch's arguments were truer. The tax cuts Bush was offering that year were, of all his economic packages, the most heavily skewed toward the wealthy, because the most benefits would go to Americans with large investment portfolios. Under Bush's proposal, the mean savings for American taxpayers would be $470 per year. For those earning more than $1 million, however, the savings would be more than $113,000. As such, more than half of the cut would go to less than 1 percent of the population. The plan was so skewed that the billionaire investor Warren Buffett wrote a syndicated column complaining that his $30,000-per-year secretary would wind up paying the same percentage of her income to the government as he would.

Not coincidentally, virtually all of Central's evidence on these political debates came from Phil Kerpen, who, in addition to owning and operating Cross-X.com, worked half-time for the conservative Washington think tank the Club for Growth. I doubt there was an overt conspiracy here; Kerpen seems to be a debater first and a conservative second, and he would never shy away from an argument that contradicted his personal beliefs if he felt it could win. But like any good debate card cutter, he knew how to zero in on the most urgent and persuasive rhetoric. And in the political arena in 2002 and 2003, this tended to come from the right. When I asked him about his methodology for constructing his Thursday Files, which any debater could download the night before a tournament for a few bucks, he said one of his favorite sources was *The Wall Street Journal*'s editorial page, one of the shrillest conservative voices in the country. All season, these scribes had been churning out perfect debate cards, warning of economic doom if the tax cuts faltered and of scores-of-dead-bodies doom if the United States didn't invade Iraq to remove the weapons of mass destruction that, we later learned, were never there.

So if there was a conspiracy, it was much deeper, in the Republican spin machine, whose presumed mastermind was a former high school debater:

Karl Rove. Early in *Bush's Brain: How Karl Rove Made George W. Bush Presidential*, a bestselling exposé of Rove by James Moore and Wayne Slater, the authors go into great detail on Rove's style as a debater. Competing for Olympus High of Salt Lake City, Rove tried above all to intimidate his opponents by coming to rounds with more and more boxes of evidence cards. "Rove figured that if two or three boxes unnerved an opposing team," Moore and Slater write, "why not buy them by the thousands and wheel them in on hand-carts? Why not throw the fear of God into the enemy before the debate even began?" But Rove's secret was that most of the cards were fake, according to his debate partner, Emil Langeland, who is quoted in the book: "We would come in and set up those boxes with file cards in them, color-coded, with tabs sticking up . . . thousands and thousands of them. And you know what? There wasn't a thing on 99 percent of them." The authors conclude that, even back then, Rove's ruthless mindset was fixed: "There was his team and the other team, and he would make the other team pay. He would defeat them, slaughter them, and humiliate them. He would win by any means, but he would win." Appearing early in *Bush's Brain*, this forms a moral base for the book's narrative about Rove's cheating ways as a political strategist.

LATER THAT DAY I watched Burch's top team compete. They were undefeated. Burch watched the round, too, calmly cutting cards at a desk in the back of the room as the kids argued. His students were both white, and they seemed to want to dress as nicely as their coach, with monochrome ties and solid shirts, though they couldn't quite shroud their adolescent awkwardness.

When I came in the room before the round, Burch told his debaters that Central was running the same case. "They run the 1.0 version," he said. "I mean the *one-point-oh* version." DuPont had developed several versions. "One-point-oh, 2.0, 2.5, 4.0, 4.2, and 4.5," he told me. "Three-point-oh is as yet unwritten."

Burch was in his mid-thirties and had been involved with debate since he was fifteen. He grew up in the wealthy community of Radcliff, Kentucky, near Louisville. His father was an Army general, and his mom sold real estate. There were always two Mercedes-Benz cars parked in the garage, he told me. In junior high he got hurt playing football, which pretty much ruined his sports career. He turned to debate, and he loved the game, but he often felt a little uncomfortable as the only black on his high school squad. The same was true when he joined the team at the University of Louisville. Usually, he was the only black at debate tournaments as well. "You're a spot on the team," he told me. "And you're a spot in the larger community."

The school he coached for, duPont Manual, had a lot of black kids, more than the one he'd attended as a teen in Radcliff. But he could never get any of them to join the team, and this frustrated him. To him, debate is an ideal tool for empowerment. He knew it had a lot to do with cliques; blacks were into different things, and, like him, they didn't feel comfortable in a predominantly white activity. But he also knew that the way the game was played was a turnoff.

If he couldn't hook black kids on the game, he figured he could reach white kids. So each season he wrote a case confronting racism. During college he'd made friends with Ede Warner, one of the only other blacks on the scene. Warner was starting to experiment with racism arguments, and Burch picked up a few tricks from him. Warner introduced him to Joseph Barndt's book *Dismantling Racism*, with the "brick by brick, stone by stone" line, as well as Clarence Munford's *Race and Reparations*, which linked racism to an inevitable nuclear war. Burch wasn't afraid to push it. When the topic was education reform, for instance, he had his debaters call for the *Brown v. Board of Education* decision to be overturned. After shocking the other team with this unthinkable proposition, his debaters threw out a bunch of evidence from the Black Power movement, works by the likes of Stokely Carmichael.

The 2002–2003 season was the best of his high school coaching career and, in many ways, the most painful. The experience of writing the "End Racism" case, and running it with two bright, open-minded white kids, had a profound effect on him. They drove to all their tournaments, and he and his debaters would talk about race issues for hours. They even experimented with Louisville's style, sharing their experiences, explaining how hard it was, for instance, to argue that racism is a more important thing to consider than a far-fetched scenario leading to nuclear war. They did this against a team from a private school in Atlanta, one with a formidable reputation on the national circuit. The round got very heated and personal, but duPont Manual had won. Afterward, the other team's coach got upset and started laying into the judge. Later, Burch and his team were in the school's cafeteria when the other coach came in with his team, spotted them sitting there, and said, "We don't eat with *those* people." Then the coach flipped Daryl and his young debaters off. At a different tournament, they had a round against Glenbrook South, from the North Shore suburbs of Chicago. Against duPont Manual's case against racism, these kids had argued that genocide of blacks is a good thing because it curbs overpopulation. Burch was deeply offended. He couldn't understand how a debate coach could teach teenagers that it's okay to argue for the total disregard for human life so long as it wins a round.

All this affected Burch so much that he completely changed his career plans. He was all set to go to law school, but he decided instead to enroll in Louisville's graduate program in pan-African studies and become an assistant coach for Warner's squad. A year later he helped coach Liz and Tonia to the quarterfinals of two separate national championship tournaments. His top debater at Manual, Jeff Miller, was similarly affected. Miller was the top recruit for Northwestern, arguably the best debate program in the nation. But he quit the game right after preseason camp.

FIVE

A LAST ATTEMPT TO SAVE THE SEASON

AFTER BURCH VOTED AGAINST THEM in round two at MBA, Marcus and Brandon lost the very next round on an argument that wasn't even raised by the other team. Marcus got into it with the judge, and afterward he watched her give the other team a high five as they left the room. Central went on to win all their remaining rounds, but, as at the Glenbrooks, the two losses were enough to keep them out of the trophy rounds.

The next two weekends Marcus went along to two tournaments in Nebraska. They were tiny affairs, barely two dozen teams from a half-dozen schools, and he and Brandon didn't drop a single ballot at either. Debate had all but disappeared in Nebraska in the years since its teams started using the national-circuit style. The whole time they were at the tournaments, people kept asking Marcus and Brandon why they even bothered to come and face such easy competition. On the ride home from the second Nebraska event, Marcus told Rinehart he was quitting the team. He announced that he wouldn't be going to their next tournament, in Nebraska again, in two weeks. He wouldn't go to district qualifiers for the National Forensic League's national championship. And he wouldn't go to the TOC, even if the district officials somehow managed to get the rules changed. He was done.

Rinehart was too tired at the time to argue with him; she was looking at a long drive home. The whole way she fretted about it, though. She didn't want the season to end. Marcus and Brandon were the best pair of debaters she'd ever coached. And Marcus was like the son she'd never had. She simply couldn't bear the thought of not taking them to a championship of some sort, be it the TOC or the NFL Nationals. She wasn't naive enough to believe they'd get permission to go to the former, and the latter, she knew, wasn't a given, because they'd have to make it out of their local district qualifying tournament. It wasn't that the other teams might be better than hers; she knew Marcus and Brandon could clean the floor with any debater Missouri had to offer. What she didn't know was if Missouri judges, many of them utterly inexperienced, would see it the same way.

She couldn't blame Marcus for not wanting to go. He'd competed at the tournament twice before, and both times he and his former partner Donnell narrowly missed qualifying because of what they believed were boneheaded decisions by the judges. (They finished fourth their first year; when one of the qualifiers decided not to attend the national tournament, Central was allowed to go instead.) After one of these deciding rounds, one of their opponents actually ran out of the room crying because she knew she'd been beaten decisively. And she was as shocked as Marcus and Donnell to find out she'd won.

But Rinehart had more than just debate on her mind. She still wasn't sure if Marcus would graduate. He needed to pass English, and he was on his way to an F in her class.

Marcus skipped school the Monday after the Nebraska tournament, like usual. When he returned on Tuesday, Rinehart scheduled a private chat with him for that afternoon.

Marcus showed up a few minutes late, and Rinehart was waiting for him, sitting in a student's desk near the middle of the room. He stopped at the door and looked down at the floor. He turned the door's handle a couple of times, making it click noisily. He let go and watched it slowly close, then tentatively sauntered into the room, chose a desk to Rinehart's right, and slumped down in the chair. He stared at a dolly loaded with debate tubs, gave the dolly a push with his foot, and looked back at the floor.

Rinehart turned her desk to face him and crossed her legs. "So, what are we going to do?" she asked.

He shrugged, not looking at her.

"I'm worried that you're not going to graduate," she said.

"What do you mean?" he asked, looking up at her finally and flashing a grin. "Of course I'm going to graduate."

"Not the way you're going now."

"I know, I know." He waved his hand as if to dismiss her. "But that was before I got the books. You're the one who—"

"Don't tell me it's my fault," she interrupted.

"But you—"

"You know you could have gotten those books anytime."

He looked at her for a moment, still smiling, and considered whether or not to push the argument. Rinehart's stare was sharp enough to cut flesh. He allowed a little laugh. "Well, don't worry. I'm on it now. Especially since I'm not debating anymore."

Rinehart's expression softened. She looked away. "That's the other thing I want to talk to you about," she said.

"I already told you," he said. "I'm through."

"I know, I know," she replied, her voice softer now. "And I don't blame you. But I'm not thinking about you right now. I'm thinking about Brandon. He needs this."

She leaned forward and silently met Marcus's gaze with pleading eyes. He locked onto her gaze for several long seconds. He was the first to back down and look away.

"It's just . . ." he said. "It's so boring. I just don't want to have to hear these stupid arguments anymore. You just don't understand how boring it is."

"I do understand," she said. "But think of Brandon."

Marcus curled his lip and gave his head a quick shake. He knew this wasn't about Brandon so much as Rinehart. She was the one who needed it.

"Okay," he said. "So what do you want?"

"I want you to go to NFL districts."

He stiffened. "I can't go through that again," he said.

"I understand," Rinehart said. She was practically whispering. "I know this is beneath you. I know you're better than any of those other kids. And I know I'm not real good at showing my appreciation." She paused for a long moment. Her eyes were red; thick tears formed at the edges of her eyelids.

"But I just want you to know how proud I am of you. It's been an incredible privilege watching you debate. And I understand if you say you're ready to walk away. You've done everything. You've been to nationals. But Brandon hasn't. I'm asking you to do this for him."

"Okay," he said, just like that. "Let's do it."

He stood up and stretched.

"Take me to Church's," he said. "I'm starving."

SIX

HIGH AND LOW IN NEBRASKA

ANTOINE WATCHED THE HILLSIDES glide by in the darkness. A bright moon sharpened the uneven horizon, and he could see dozens of stars. He thought back to the tournament, trying to relive it again in his mind, but it all seemed so unreal he couldn't quite convince himself that it had actually happened.

Just a few hours earlier he had been sitting in the cafeteria of a school in the suburbs of Omaha, listening as the man read through a list of names. Antoine did not expect to hear his. Ebony got seventh place. Geoffery Stone, third. Second place, a kid from Nebraska. Then: "First-place speaker, from Kansas City Central, Antoine Lewis."

Did he say first? Antoine asked himself. He got up and practically floated to the front of the room, the sound of clapping distant and strange, his back numb to all the congratulatory pats. It was surreal—in his words, like "walking through a fluffy cloud of dream."

He and Ebony went undefeated through all five rounds of the Millard North tournament. The other teams were talking about them, and they sounded scared. "Oh, you're going against Central this round?" Antoine heard one say to another when the schedules came out late in the day. "You guys are screwed." It blew his mind to hear kids talking about him like that. *Him.* In this big, beautiful school for white kids.

But then, he had to admit, he *was* on fire. He and Ebony were clicking like never before, beating back all the arguments. *Bap! Bap! Bap!* "I went into Marcus mode," he told me. "I kept thinking, 'Okay, what would Marcus do in a time like this?'"

They cruised easily through the elimination rounds, landing in the final round for a showdown against Omaha Westside, the tournament's second seed. The round started off easily enough, with both sides awkwardly speeding through their piles of case evidence. Then, during their first rebuttal speech, one of the Westside debaters argued, for no apparent reason, that Central's plan would help minorities. "But who cares?" the debater said. "I mean, it really won't matter."

Antoine couldn't believe what he heard. He dropped his pen, stopped taking notes, and leered at the other team. Taking no prep, he got up and devoted most of his rebuttal speech to railing against Omaha Westside. "I take great offense to their argument about how no one cares about the minorities," Antoine said, visibly shaken. "As a minority myself, I feel that we're just as important as anybody, so why shouldn't we? And our plan doesn't specifically do that. We solve for everybody."

He was so pissed off he let his speech wander all over the place, zagging one way to answer one or two of Westside's arguments, then zigging right back to his outrage. When the timer sounded, he realized he'd missed a lot of the other team's arguments. He looked up and met Ebony's cold stare. He felt a pang of guilt. He'd messed up. When he took a seat, Ebony slapped at the back of his head.

For the round's final speech, Ebony nailed everything on the flow. *Bap! Bap! Bap!*

The judges deliberated silently for a long time. Antoine just knew that they'd vote him and Ebony down. He felt bad. Then he felt bad for feeling bad. What kind of game is this where some white punk from Nebraska can say something totally racist and still win just because you did the right thing by getting up there and putting him in his place? Just because you don't argue all the stupid little notes scribbled on a piece of paper? *The line-by-line.* He hated that crap. That was the worst thing about debate. It was like being forced to think like a machine. Take that away and debate would be the greatest game in the world. He was totally down with arguing about big issues. But that's not what the line-by-line was about, he believed. The line-by-line was about arguing the teensy-weensy nonissues. *That's not education*, he thought. *That's* school. *That's mindless obedience.*

Then a judge opened the ballots, read them to himself, and went to the blackboard, where he wrote, "KCC."

Suddenly Antoine loved debate more than anything on earth. His teammates closed in around him to slap his back and take turns holding the first-place trophy. He felt about as high as he'd ever felt as he rode home, gazing at the dark countryside through the windows of the jostling old school bus.

WHEN THEY GOT TO CENTRAL, his dad wasn't there. It was past one in the morning, and it was terribly cold. Antoine watched his teammates climb into waiting cars, their heaters warmed up and running strong, and head off into the night. Then it was just him and his partner and his coach, shuffling their feet back and forth to fight off the chill. He thanked Rinehart over and over again. "A lot of coaches wouldn't have wasted time with us," he said. She laughed, as if any alternative were absurd.

When Jay Lewis finally arrived, Rinehart introduced herself and told him that his son had won the whole tournament and was first-place speaker, and that he should be proud.

"I am proud," Lewis said. "But not surprised."

The hint of a smile crept across his face, and he lowered his head and hunched his shoulders as if to hide it. I'd seen that smile once before, when I met with Lewis at his office in downtown Kansas City. He managed a day-labor shop—a dirty, austere place with no air-conditioning, its lobby jam-packed at all hours with sweaty bodies looking for a day's wages. It wasn't a smiley sort of place; Lewis's clients were often homeless and addicted to drugs. Antoine's mom, Lisa, would sometimes try to get Jay to smile at home, chasing him around the house and showering him with compliments. He'd sometimes flick water in her face to shoo her away.

THEY DROPPED EBONY OFF AT HIS HOUSE. "So, Antoine," Jay asked as they watched Ebony climb the steps to his front door, "is he a good debater? Or is he just there?"

"That's my partner, man," Antoine said. "He's probably better than I am, if not just as good."

There, in a car in the middle of the night, with only his oldest son to see, a broad grin broke out across Jay Lewis's face.

"You know," Lewis said, "Malcolm X debated when he was in prison."

"Yeah?" Antoine replied thoughtfully. He was having a hard time staying awake.

"One of the most powerful things he experienced was imagining yourself as the opposing team," Lewis went on. "And what they gonna say. And you guys do it as a whole, like as a pair. It's better to do it alone. That way you don't have to worry about the other person's plans, their problems. Their ideas, mixed in with yours. You just have yours. You write yours down and think for yourself. And that's like the best you gonna get."

Antoine's dad always sounded so critical. It was like he didn't know how to just give compliments. But Antoine knew that his dad's monologue was an attempt at praise, and he liked it. He knew how much his dad respected Malcolm X and a slew of other black revolutionaries, the names of which Antoine couldn't remember. At their old house in Kansas, his dad had had a whole shelfful of books about Black Power, and he'd read and reread each one. All the Lewises were avid readers. Antoine had his fantasy books, Mom her romance and suspense, politics for Dad. Lewis gave Lisa a hard time for her choices. "That's candy," he'd say, pointing at her latest paperback. He'd wave a copy of some dense book about racism. "This is bread."

AFTER MILLARD NORTH, Ebony and Antoine thought Nebraska was the promised land. They couldn't wait to get back there the following weekend for a tournament in Fremont, a small town northwest of Omaha. But their Nebraskan opponents had spent the week preparing for them, and they lost two rounds early and missed breaking to elimination rounds.

Ebony was depressed when he showed up at the debate squad room the following Monday. He dropped his book bag on the floor with a thud and picked a desk near the far wall where he could sit and sulk and hardly say a word. Later, Rinehart gave him a ride home, and they noticed a FOR SALE sign planted in his front yard.

"Are you moving?" Rinehart asked.

"No," he said. "I don't think."

She looked at him and saw genuine fear in his eyes. She took a deep breath and flashed a soft smile at him. "Don't worry," she said. "Everything's gonna work out."

He stared at the dashboard. "Uh-huh," he said.

"I know you tend to worry about stuff," she said.

"I know."

"But we'll make this work out. I promise."

"I know."

The sign had surprised Shavelle, too, when she got home from work. She knew the landlord was planning to sell. But she hadn't expected him to put a sign up so soon. She immediately went to Ebony's room to finally tell him what was going on. She'd been keeping the situation a secret.

He was on his bed playing video games. She sat down beside him. It wasn't a done deal yet, she assured him. She still had options to get a loan. They were few, but there was still a chance.

"How can you say that?" he asked, looking up momentarily from his video game. "There's a fuckin' sign right outside."

"I know," she replied. "But it isn't sold yet."

He returned his eyes to the TV screen and continued playing his game.

Just as Shavelle had feared, Ebony reverted to some of his old ways. He hardly talked to her or Eddy at all. Each night he'd go straight to his room and shut the door. She didn't hear him laugh as much, that high-pitched, goofy cackle she loved so. Some interested buyers came by one Saturday afternoon when they were all still in the house. She hadn't warned Ebony of the showing. And when he spotted the strangers walking through their house, checking things out, he pulled Shavelle aside and said, "What the fuck?!"

She didn't know how to answer him. The future was a big unknown.

––––––––

EBONY FAITHFULLY CONTINUED going to practice every afternoon, trying to not let on how stressed he was over his tenuous home life. Rinehart noticed he wasn't his old, cheerful self. She tried to get him to talk about it a few times, but he'd just look away from her and say little more than "Everything's coo." She knew it wasn't. But what could she do?

In early February, the squad ventured back to Nebraska for a third, and final, time. Ebony and Antoine worked hard to update their evidence files, to prepare for the new arguments the Nebraska kids had unleashed at the tournament following their triumph at Millard North. They did a little better, going three-two, with high enough speaker points to advance to the trophy rounds. But they immediately bowed out in the quarterfinals. Afterward, Ebony slammed his evidence into his tubs. "Fuck. Fuck. Fuck debate," he said. "I spend all my fucking time on debate." He stared at the floor for a long moment. He shook his head. "Fuck. Fuck. Fuck debate," he said again.

SEVEN

ALL'S RIGHT

MARCUS HAD A KNIFE.

"Hey, Joe," he whispered to me. "Come here."

Marcus and I were becoming friends. We were co-mentors of sorts—he was my guide through the confusing world of debate, and I was an adult who rarely judged, and never disciplined. For a while, he carried around a little notepad, imitating the way I followed the squad, jotting things down. We were co-conspirators, too. Sometimes, near the end of tournament trips, when I was feeling punchy, I'd act a little crazy along with Marcus. So I was often the first audience for his dastardly deeds.

I followed him into a corner, away from the crowd of debaters waiting for the next round's schedule to be released. He reached into the side pocket of his cargo pants and pulled it out. The blade was a good six inches long, with a curved point and a row of disemboweling teeth. I suppose he thought he looked fearsome, but he was dressed up for debate in a green oxford shirt with a black and green tie, and he couldn't hold back his nerdy grin.

"Marcus!" Rinehart yelled from a few paces away. "Put that away! What do you think you're doing?"

She shot him a look to stop time. He laughed, folded it up, and returned it to his pocket. Minutes later he had it out again.

But Marcus's thug games were more than just social commentary. They were a defense mechanism. Even though he, of all the students on the Central squad, seemed the most comfortable among whites, his hoodlum charades betrayed a deep, almost subconscious belief that his success would always be limited because he was black. By acting, however unconvincingly, like an unruly gangsta at the outset, Marcus could dispense with the pain of injustice early. And, in a twisted way, by saying, "The joke is on them," he'd be able to blame the loss on racism. It was a way of controlling something he couldn't control.

It was obvious to me that Marcus was scared, which he confirmed during a talk several months after the NFL district qualifying tournament. In the weeks leading up to this event, he'd made a big show of being put out, that the competition would be beneath him, that he was too big for the local scene. In truth, he wasn't sure if he could pull it off, if he could adapt his game to the preferences of Missouri judges.

Brandon was the only person Marcus had confessed his fears to in the days leading up to the tournament. Brandon was pumped up and ready to take it all. He knew they could adjust and beat all these Missouri suckers at their own game. So they agreed to switch things up. Brandon became the second speaker, or quarterback, when they argued on negative. He felt confident that he could explain the kinds of arguments Missouri judges might find radical, such as counterplans.

Brandon had also been burned at districts, worse than Marcus. The previous year he and his partner were disqualified for reading falsified evidence. They'd gotten the offending evidence from acquaintances on Cross-X.com, a couple of kids from the St. Louis area, who told them that the evidence would beat back a particular argument that had been very popular in Missouri that year. After Brandon read it in the round, their opponents, from Truman High, coached by Chris Adams, director of the tournament, were quick to point out its falseness, suspiciously quick. It seemed like a setup; the debaters were friends with the kid who had given Central the evidence in the first place. When Adams learned of this, she filed an official complaint. Brandon and his partner offered to forfeit the tournament. But Adams pushed for them to be stripped of their NFL memberships and banned from competing for at least a year. The district's steering committee passed on the recommendation for such harsh actions; few of them believed, as Adams seemed to, that the transgression was anything more than a stupid mistake.

It was one of the worst tournament experiences of Rinehart's coaching career. In addition to Brandon's forfeiture, and Marcus and Donnell's painful loss in the final round, her debaters were accused of stealing another team's evidence tubs, which, it was later discovered, had simply been misplaced. There was no proof whatsoever to suggest that the Central kids had done this, other than that they were the only blacks at the tournament.

The early rounds at the 2003 district tournament were worse than Marcus had expected. Their first opponents kept repeating over and over, without warrant, that nurses are poorly trained and underpaid and therefore dangerously incompetent. Another team, one of Adams's, argued that Marcus and Brandon had broken the "rules" because they hadn't read the full citation of their evidence. Debaters almost *never* do this. After the round Adams accosted Rinehart and scolded her for allowing her kids to fudge the rules, while her debaters apologized to Marcus and Brandon for running such a lame argument. Their coach had forced them to do so, they said.

Even I was put off by the whole situation. I wasn't allowed to watch Marcus and Brandon compete at this tournament. This district had a strict rule against observers in the rounds. A few weeks before, I had called Adams to ask permission, and she sternly denied it. When I tried to reason with her, she spoke condescendingly to me, saying, "I'm sure it's disappointing to you." When I pushed a little harder, she immediately grew angry and defensive, saying, "If Kansas City Central is planning on raising a bunch of controversy over this, I can assure you they aren't going to get a lot of support." She was actually yelling at me.

I decided to volunteer as a judge. But they didn't seem to want my services, at least not for policy debate. When I got there, I was made to sit in the judges' lounge, a conference room with rows of straight-back chairs and a couple of tables offering two-liter jugs of pop, chips, and a Crock-Pot full of chili. Adams kept sending other tournament volunteers to ask if I'd judge rounds in the Ted Turner division. I told them I wouldn't feel comfortable doing so because I had no experience with it. They told me they would have a hard time assigning me rounds in policy debate, because I had been struck from so many teams' judge preference lists, which seemed odd because none of these coaches knew anything about me other than my affiliation with Central.

Rinehart had experienced this before. In previous years she'd brought the required number of judges, only to see them not be used for a single round. At another tournament hosted by the same suburban coaches, they had insisted that her husband, Richard, who was there just to supervise the kids, judge. He told them he had zero experience with debate. But they replied that his ignorance was actually a plus. He said that he wouldn't feel comfortable judging, that for all he knew about the game, he'd wind up calling the win with a coin toss. "That's okay," they told him. "We've had judges do that."

I felt insulted by my exclusion, as if these people I didn't know had assumed that I had so little integrity that I would intervene against other teams just to give some sort of advantage to Central. But they eventually acquiesced and gave me some rounds to judge.

I went in expecting complete ineptness, based on Rinehart's and Marcus's continual disparagement of Missouri debaters' skill levels. But I found the opposite to be true. These kids were sharp. They argued a little more slowly, yes, but they did so with a passion that is disturbingly absent from the national circuit. It was as though they actually cared about the positions they were arguing. And their cases were fascinating. I didn't hear any of the generic arguments one finds at national-circuit tournaments. These kids had obviously done their own research and writing, instead of relying on files produced almost entirely at camps or cards they traded with other debaters. I learned more about the topic at this tournament than I had at the previous three national events. One debate in particular interested me, in which the debaters argued that the canonized book of definitions for mental disorders is actually a scam for the health industry, which will tell people that their normal traits are in fact symptoms of psychosis, and that would get them hooked on expensive drugs they don't need. If I'd read it in a newspaper, I would have thought it award-winning investigative work.

And this was a thriving debate scene. Unlike at the Nebraska tournaments we'd attended, there were dozens of schools competing here. And this district covered just half of the Kansas City metro area. Missouri had five such districts, one of the highest numbers for any state. Clearly there was merit to the argument that the old-style kept the game alive.

Indeed, the first day was full of pleasant surprises, the most pleasant being that Marcus and Brandon ended up undefeated. On the way home Brandon hollered, "Four-oh! I've always wanted to go to Atlanta."

THE NEXT DAY Marcus and Brandon won their first round and advanced to face the only other undefeated team. If they won, they'd win it all and be headed for Atlanta.

Rinehart and I couldn't watch, so we bided our time in the cafeteria, nervous. Rinehart was concerned about the judging panel. It had one college kid; she figured they'd win his ballot. The other two were a mom from off the street and an older gentleman who'd been around the Missouri debate scene for years and years. He leaned toward the slower style.

It started to snow outside. Kids were having a snowball fight in the courtyard of the community college where the tournament was being held, still dressed up in their suits and skirts.

Marcus and Brandon came back from the round an hour and a half later, not smiling, but not looking pissed off, either. Marcus said he felt it had gone well, but he wasn't sure which way the two older judges might vote. The man had told them as he left the room that they had adapted well, but he did so in an even tone that didn't betray his secret decision. The mom had quickly filled out her ballot, folded it up, and left the room.

"You better go to the tab room," Brandon told Rinehart. "To make sure there's no funny business."

Rinehart came back a few minutes later, her face twisted into a frown. "Well, same old, same old," she said.

Brandon's eyes widened and he spun on his heels as if he were about to collapse.

She shoved him and smiled. "Wanna go to Atlanta?" she asked.

"Don't mess with me!" he shouted.

She laughed. "You deserve it. Payback is hell!"

"We won?!"

"You won."

"I'm going to Atlanta!"

Yes! We were going to Atlanta! Yet I couldn't quite grasp it. The win was so far beyond my expectations that I felt numb. It was as though I'd just watched a really good debate round, where both sides had me convinced that the right course of action leads in two completely different directions. With Central's victory at districts, every last thing I'd been led to believe about debate at the outset had been turned upside down. In the beginning, I'd seen Missouri debate as backward, an obstacle to progress, only to learn that it was one of the few states in the country where debate continues to thrive—specifically *because* its leaders had resisted progress. At first, I'd thought the national circuit, with its speed and heavy emphasis on evidence, kept racial prejudices at bay, only to hear one of the game's few black coaches, and his mostly black team, blast it as racist. And Rinehart had told me early on, quite matter-of-factly, that her kids would "never" succeed in front of the "soccer mom" judges used at Missouri tournaments. Yet here we were, district champs.

In retrospect, all this contradiction seems obvious—this *is* debate, after all. But at the time all I could do was smile dumbly and try to appear as excited as I should have been. In reality, I wasn't sure what to think anymore.

At the awards ceremony Adams handed Marcus and Brandon their trophy and politely said, "Congratulations. I'm proud of you." She shook hands with Rinehart. Once we got out of Adams's earshot, Rinehart said to me, "It feels so good to stick it to them."

We walked outside to find the ground covered with clean white snow. The sky was breaking to the west, and rays of sunlight poured through the opening, fanning out from the cut of blue sky. The bells in the school's clock tower sounded.

"Look at that," Brandon exclaimed, pointing to the opening in the sky. "It's like a sign from God!"

"God's in His heaven," Rinehart recited from a poem she'd memorized when she was younger. "All's right with the world!"

PART THREE

THE BALLOT

ONE

MEAN GREEN

AS WE PULLED OFF THE HIGHWAY, Brandon noticed the Chicken on the Go restaurant on the corner. "They just have that to keep black people happy," he said.

He was sitting on the edge of the front passenger seat, his face nearly pressed against the window as we rolled onto the campus of the University of North Texas. It was late on a Friday afternoon, and the school was practically deserted, just a few students strolling between the buildings on the balmy spring day. "Damn," he said. "Some hot-looking Asians."

We found UNT's debate coach, Brian Lain, in his office. He'd first started talking to Brandon and Marcus at a college tournament at UMKC in January, right after the two returned to Kansas City from the MBA tournament. They'd skipped school for two days to watch rounds and get a feel for the college scene. The whole time coaches and debaters from Wake Forest and from the universities of Northern Iowa, Kentucky, and Missouri recruited them. Lain seemed the most serious, and Marcus and Brandon were blown away by UNT's top team, Nirav Patel and Johnny Prieur. Patel was by far the fastest and most forceful speaker they'd ever seen, and the duo wound up winning the tournament. Obviously, this was a serious program. When we stepped into Lain's office, Marcus immediately noticed the national championship plaque on the wall, which Lain earned as an assistant coach at

Emory. Lain said he hoped Marcus and Brandon could help him repeat this success at UNT. "I got big plans," he told them. "I have a long-term vision for where we want to go."

Lain gave us a tour of the campus, home to thirty-three thousand students, a third of them in graduate school. It was early spring, and the grass was already turning brown under the relentless Texas sun, though rows of trees thick with pink blossoms tried their best to brighten the place up. A handsome clock tower rose from the center of campus. But overall, it was an austere place, the buildings unadorned, merely functional, not Gothic and inspiring like the settings of college movies. The absence of students made the place feel forlorn, like a nightclub at midday with shades drawn to let the daylight shine in. Marcus asked Lain, "So what does the team do for fun? Besides debate. Like, what are your hobbies?"

"Are you kidding?" Lain joked. "This is the biggest party town in the country." This presented challenges to Lain and his debate program, he later told me; on occasion he had to discipline his debaters for indulging in the local culture too much.

As we strolled across the campus, Marcus asked about the school's areas of specialty, and Lain said that UNT is best known for its music program but is also strong in political science and journalism. Marcus nodded approvingly at the poli-sci distinction; that could fit into his plans.

We passed through a dorm building and looked in on one of the tiny cement-walled rooms, and then the library. "The school can't keep up with bound volumes, so we focus on electronic databases," Lain said. We walked across a shadeless courtyard to a classroom building, entered, and climbed the stairs to the debate squad room. It was a big and tidy space, with rows of tall metal file cabinets along the walls and desks pushed together, each bearing a computer.

Prieur and Patel showed up a few minutes later, followed by John Hines, a graduate student with long hair and a patchy beard who worked as an assistant coach. Patel asked bluntly, "So what's our competition? What other schools are you considering?"

Marcus said that Louisville and Kentucky had made offers, but he had ruled both of them out (this was the first I'd heard about Kentucky; I later learned it was a bluff—there'd been no official offer, just a few e-mails expressing interest). "So it's just UMKC that has a pretty good offer on the table," Marcus said.

Nirav leaned back in his seat. "You've been in Missouri your whole life," he said. "Why not come to Denton?"

Marcus smiled and looked shyly down at his hands. "Yeah," he said quietly.

It felt good to be wanted, especially by a debater of Patel's prowess. This was a program with its eyes on a national championship and a real shot at winning it. Marcus knew these debaters saw in him and Brandon more than a pair of black faces, a chance to assuage white guilt with a bit of diversity.

Lain treated us all to dinner at a steak and seafood restaurant, one of the classier places in Denton, a smallish town on the edge of the Dallas–Fort Worth metroplex. Afterward, we gathered at the house of one of the debaters, a rental in an older neighborhood that he shared with several other students. The living room was immaculate, with a pair of frumpy but clean couches arranged around a large coffee table in the middle of the room. An electronic foosball table stood off to one side, and Brandon went straight to it, quickly losing to one of the UNT guys. Then he sat down on the couch with Lain, who asked him what it would take to convince him to attend UNT.

"I guess if I like the location," Brandon replied tentatively. "But, like, I'm sort of a chronic homebody. But Kansas City is so boring, I guess because I've lived there my whole life."

He added that he'd need a little help with the money.

"My debaters speak very highly of you," Lain said. "I hope you make your decision based on something other than money. But if money is an issue, we can probably tap into our alumni association."

This was all new to Brandon. He'd always fantasized about being sought after, first as a basketball player, then as a debater. But he'd never really believed that it would happen. Now that it was happening, he could barely contain his joy. As he and Lain chatted, he narrowed his eyes and nodded with contrived confidence, but the trace of a grin betrayed his giddiness.

LAIN LEFT US WITH HIS DEBATERS, to show the recruits the best that Denton had to offer. A few more folks showed up, most of them members of the debate squad, as well as a lanky black man with long dreadlocks named Brent. He settled into the couch and pulled out a little box of pot, its buds so dense and sticky he had to cut them with scissors. He rolled a joint as fat as a finger and sealed it with a long, dramatic lick, holding it up for all to see.

The joint circulated the room, passing from hand to hand, blue curls of pungent smoke fogging the air. Marcus stepped out of the circle and crouched in front of the stereo. "What kind of music you got?" he asked.

"Play whatever you want," the host said.

Brandon sat on the end of a couch, slumped way back as if he were stoned, though he politely declined when the blunt came his way. He asked the dude with dreads, Brent, what he was studying. "I don't go to school," Brent replied. "I ain't never went to school here."

He couldn't say enough good things about the town, though. The women, he told Brandon, were easy. Brandon laughed awkwardly. "You don't even have to have no game," Brent said. "Just step up to them, say hi, and you're in."

Brandon later turned to me and said of Brent, "He's like straight off a movie or something." In fact, he was. He played a minor role in Richard Linklater's *Waking Life*, an animated philosophical narrative film in which the characters appear as they might on an acid trip, colors shifting on their skin, eyeballs bulging. In the movie Brent sat in a tree, like the Cheshire cat, and spouted a few lines of far-out wisdom.

Marcus figured out the stereo and put a stop to the throbbing acid jazz the host had chosen, replacing it with the jarring beats of Tech N9ne. *The industry's a bunch of fucking punks!*

He was suddenly hyper. He sat on the couch for a moment, sniffed at the air, and bolted up to change the song midway through. Now Tech N9ne was rapping about Kansas City, "where, nigga, life don't mean shit."

The host, his eyes red from pot, sat edgily on the couch, gritting his teeth and bobbing his head uncomfortably to the abrasive tune. I suggested to Marcus that the others might be in the mood for something a bit more mel-low. He frowned at me and shook his head dismissively. Again he changed the song midway. He got up and paced the room, browsing through the bookshelves, with their selections by Foucault, Aristotle, and an assortment of feminist theorists. The TV was muted, tuned to ESPN's *SportsCenter*. Marcus begged one of the UNT debaters to play him in a game of foosball. Johnny was slumped way back in the couch, and he got up slowly, reluctantly. Marcus won easily and insisted they play another game, but his opponent declined, opting to resume his nearly horizontal pose on the couch.

Marcus paced some more, eventually making his way to the kitchen, where he found a bottle of Malibu rum on the counter. He poured a healthy amount in a red plastic cup with ice and topped it off with some red juice. He took a sip. It didn't taste at all like booze.

The first rush of alcohol calmed him some. He took a spot on the couch. But soon his leg was shaking manically to the beat, and he was perched on the edge of the couch cushion. "Let's go do something," he demanded.

Someone suggested we go to a club where some bands would be playing. "Free music," he said. "How can you go wrong with that?"

"A coffee shop sounds better," Marcus said.

"Coffee shop?!" Brent protested. "You ain't gonna be able to kick it there for long. Hell, you might find Ms. Blue Eyes. She might want to talk to your monkey ass for more than an hour."

The host shot Brent a withering look.

BRANDON AND I RODE WITH ONE of the UNT debaters to the coffee shop, Marcus with another. Brandon studied the sights as we drove through Denton, nodding to the quiet beat coming from the car's stereo. It was your typical college town, small and contained yet cosmopolitan. The lights glowed from the older houses near downtown, making the place feel cozy and warm. "Yeah. I think I could do this," Brandon said to his host. "I like this."

"You like it around here?" his potential future teammate said, pleased.

"I don't know why," Brandon said. "For some reason I don't feel like I'm away from home."

Marcus, on the other hand, wasn't the least bit comfortable. The pot smoking disturbed him. Growing up in Kansas City, he had never allowed himself to be around drugs, not like his brother Jason, who just a few weeks earlier had been arrested a second time, in this instance because he was riding around town with a kid who had vials of crack stashed under his car seat. But what he'd witnessed that night was mild by college standards, and certainly compared with what he'd likely see on the college debate scene.

College debaters are notorious partyers. The culture is perfect for it: a small community of young iconoclastic thinkers from around the country who gather every couple of weeks or so and shack up in the same hotel. Pot and alcohol are the favored intoxicants, but cocaine, nitrous oxide, and various other hallucinogens are also popular. Like Marcus, other black debate veterans have been turned off by this aspect of the culture. Daryl Burch told me he was rattled when he first attended a college tournament as a teen and watched a student snort a line of coke in the bathroom before delivering a speech. It was the first time he'd ever seen someone use the drug. He told me he once went to a post-tournament party where he saw one of the country's top debaters so blitzed on nitrous, booze, and weed that she was slumped on a couch, drooling and babbling incoherently. Rashad Evans, who won a national championship for West Georgia, was taken to a raging party when he visited the school as a high school recruit. His host and elder debater, who was to show him a good time, proceeded to put on a stiff buzz while Evans looked on. Evans grew irritated as he watched her smoke dope all night, wondering if this would be the right choice for him. He told me this was one reason why he tried to strike a peace accord with the Louisville squad, why he believed they might have too much in common to keep on fighting. "Debate is just this community of crazy white people who party too much," he told me.

Sometimes these parties end with more than simple hangovers. The research that goes into debate demands hours and hours of intense interaction among students and coaches. Many of these coaches are young themselves, graduate students with still-fresh bachelor's degrees, the overwhelming majority of whom are male. When travel and drugs are thrown into this mix, lines are crossed, and coaches sometimes hook up with younger debaters, both male and female. Usually, they're consensual affairs, but the power dy-

namics can complicate matters, and the younger of the lovers can wind up
with hurt feelings and a shortened debate career. The issue has surfaced several times on eDebate, the Listserv for the college circuit, where female debaters have complained that they've been taken advantage of—used for sex
and then relegated to the lower rungs of their squad's hierarchy. Some cited
instances of date rape, from which the emotional scars still remained.

These incidents have rarely resulted in disciplinary action, but have become legendary in the community's rumor mill. Throughout my travels in
the debate community, I was privately told that one top-ten program with a
female coach suffered two instances of date rape, and not only was the matter swept under the rug, but one of the offenders was rehired to continue
coaching. I learned that the director of another college program had thrown
a party at his house where an underage male freshman woke up naked in the
coach's bed. The coach left his position, but he continued directing high
school debate institutes and went on to establish a new program at another
university. I was also told that members of a debate squad at a large school
had been implicated in the biggest drug bust in their region. The incident
was the talk of the debate scene for a while, and then the matter simply disappeared when the charges against the debaters were mysteriously dropped.
These situations led to conspiracy theories, in which former debaters in high
positions of power secretly make problems go away so as not to tarnish the
game's good name.

Ironically, debate's darkest moment is forever enshrined in the title of
the game's highest honor. The Rex Copeland Memorial Award goes to the
top team in the nation. Rex Copeland was a talented debater at Samford
University, a Baptist school in Birmingham, Alabama, when he was found
dead in his apartment in 1989. He had been stabbed at least twelve times,
and police who arrived on the scene said his apartment looked as if someone
had gone wild with red paint. Shortly thereafter investigators received a letter
from Copeland's coach, William Slagle, who claimed that he and Copeland
had gotten into an argument about the debater's performance at practice
earlier that day. The coach followed him home, where the dispute escalated
and, in Slagle's words, "just ended up with the murder." Before sending the
letter, Slagle had tried to cover up his crime by calling Copeland's number

and leaving a message on the student's answering machine asking where he was, knowing full well that his bloody corpse was lying a few steps away from the phone. Slagle fled and was found six months later in Nashville when debaters alerted the authorities of his whereabouts. The incident became national news, attracting the tabloid TV shows *Hard Copy* and *America's Most Wanted* as well as the syndicated column "News of the Weird." Slagle was sentenced to life in prison in Alabama in March 1991.

Copeland's parents chose to honor his memory with the award, which carries a $10,000 prize.

MARCUS WOKE UP THE NEXT MORNING full of energy. The UNT folks had arranged for us to stay at the apartment of a debater who was out of town for the weekend. Marcus bragged about his buzz of the night before. "I put like six ounces of rum in my drink," he said. "I put less in Brandon's. And he didn't even finish it."

"Bitch, yes, I did," Brandon said, still in bed and feeling groggy.

"What was that black dude's name?" Marcus said. "Brent? Fucking wigger."

"I liked him," Brandon protested.

"That dude had too much to smoke," Marcus said. "He just kept rolling those blunts."

"That wasn't no blunt, nigga. That was a joint."

"Same difference. You know what else I saw? He wasn't making it right. He didn't even lick it."

"He licked it, nigga."

"Anyway, enough talk about that shit," Marcus said.

"They tried to pass it to me," Brandon said, "and I was like, 'Nah, dog.'"

"Yeah," Marcus agreed. "There's no way I'm gonna smoke pot, especially with a book writer nearby."

At this point, I was straddling the line between detached observer and participant. Though I had been advocating on behalf of Marcus and his fellow debaters through my many calls to elected officials, urging them to challenge the Missouri State High School Activities Association, I was still reluctant to step into the students' lives. Of course, I had already done so when I convinced Marcus to attend the Iowa Caucus, but at the time of our trip to Denton I still viewed this as a journalistic lapse. Looking back, I can see how dangerously naive I was. In practical terms, I was Marcus's and Brandon's guardian on this trip, so it was arguably my responsibility to intervene when the specter of illegal activity arose. But I chose to lay back and let the situation unfold. And the guys chose, thankfully, to sample a little booze and leave it at that.

MARCUS THREW A PILLOW at Brandon. "Get yo ass up."

"Fuck it," Brandon said, slowly lifting himself to the edge of the bed. He sauntered to the bathroom. He emerged a few seconds later. "All right, it's official," he announced. "He's a homo." He displayed a bottle of Mr. Bubble.

Marcus laughed. "Brandon, you didn't have to show me that," he said. "Does he have Herbal Essences, too?"

"No." Brandon laughed. "But this shit is enough."

Marcus took a turn in the bathroom. After a minute or two he poked his head out to share his own discovery. "Dude, this nigga beats off in the shower," he said, probably from experience. "He's got lotion in the shower. Nigga! Why else anybody have lotion in the shower?"

"I'm gonna steal something," Brandon announced. He picked up a dinosaur figurine and knocked over a bunch of pictures in the process. He flinched at the sound of the crash but walked away without bothering to clean up the mess.

We spent most of that Saturday wandering around Denton with Hines, who gave us a tour of the coffee shops and hippie boutiques around UNT's campus. Patel and Prieur met us for lunch, and Patel asked Marcus what he planned to study. Marcus mentioned political science, but said he wasn't sure. Nirav lauded the poli-sci department, where he himself was getting his degree. "We have literally the best environmental ethics professor in the country," he said. "I think it's a really fantastic program."

I asked them if UNT was the sort of place where a kid could skate through doing minimal work. Marcus laughed and asked, "Was that aimed toward me?" The UNT guys shifted in their seats and admitted it isn't the most challenging school in the country, and you probably could get by.

"Is it advisable?" Prieur asked. "You'd be shortchanging yourself. Like, there are certain professors at this university that are just amazing. But then, on the whole, you get very discouraged at not being challenged by the school and by your peers. But really, like really, the trick in undergrad, especially for, like, the first couple years is just: Go to class. You just go to class, you'll get As."

"It's really easy to fall into the trap here that, I don't need to go to class," Hines agreed. "It's not difficult. I've already got it figured out. Because as a debater you're gonna be above all your peers, no matter what school you go to. You'll even get professors where you're like, damn, I know more about this."

After lunch we lolled at Hines's apartment for a while before heading off for a barbecue at an apartment complex on the west side of town. Marcus and Hines talked all afternoon about the current state of debate. John was working on a master's in rhetoric. His apartment was messy and sparsely furnished, with a sagging futon and a low coffee table that served as a desk. On the wall hung a poster of Bob Marley and another of Mumia Abu-Jamal that read: "They kill writers in Bangladesh, Egypt, Iran, Nigeria and USA. SAVE MUMIA." Library books were scattered everywhere. There was one about postcolonial African philosophy, and another by Foucault. Hines said he was working on a paper about the politics of architecture in the post-9/11 era.

They played a game of chess, and Marcus quickly won. "Well, that's enough of that," Hines said, knocking over his king. Hines played some selections by the poet Saul Williams, some of which they planned to pull out against Louisville, should they meet at a tournament. Hines liked what Louisville was doing but sensed it might be incomplete. "I think we're on the cutting edge of debate right now," he said. "It's like two camps—the policy camp and the kritik camp pulling at each other. And here at UNT we're hoping to find the middle ground."

At the barbecue we saw Brent again.

"So do you, like, break-dance?" he asked Brandon, jokingly.

Brandon laughed. "No," he said.

"Do you go out and dance?"

"No. I don't really go out to parties."

"Are you studying all the time?"

"No," Brandon replied. "I just don't go out. Like, this year, one of my best friends from school, a girl, got killed at a party."

Brent was momentarily taken aback. "Wow," he said. "So you deal with some real issues where you're from."

"Yeah," Brandon replied quietly.

"That's cool, though." Brent tried to cheer things up. "Because you're all dope." He smiled. "And when I say 'dope,' I mean with it. On point."

"Yeah." Brandon laughed. "I know what you mean."

"Yeah, because you've been able to live in that place and"—Brent stiffened and raised his chin stoically—"you know, and get something going. Keep your focus. You know what I'm sayin'?"

"Yeah."

"I feel it, too." Brent nodded. "I've lived in lots of places. *Lots* of places, man. And I'm, like, living every ghetto boy's dream."

Marcus sat in the grass a few paces away with Hines. "Debate is all based on liberal democratic theory," Hines said, plucking blades of grass from the ground. "De Tocqueville, and his theories of how American democracy works. But I think that it's wrong, right? To think that the only type of political discourse that happens is what happens in city hall or Congress or in courts. Right? Like, hip-hop is a political discourse. And our architecture is a political discourse. That's the kind of cases I would write if I were debating. That's the shit I would be doing."

"It seems like that would offend the tradition a lot," Marcus said.

"Yeah, people are scared of that," Hines agreed. "Because it forces them to do shit they haven't been trained in."

"And they can't guarantee success," Marcus added.

"But it's also why it's scary to initiate that type of debate in the first place," Hines said. "Because you're not guaranteed success doing that. It's not a formula that's been proven. But I think it has the most potential. For breaking things open. And once you make that move and free debate from those standards, then it makes it a lot harder for the Dartmouths, Northwesterns, and Harvards to continue to dominate the scene. Or the Glenbrooks and Greenhills, you know, those schools that have so much experience in that area and have already set the tone in that area, the ones that are teaching all the doctrine. Like those coaches—Northwestern, Dartmouth, Michigan—those coaches are the ones that are training the next wave of high school debaters to come to college. So their ideology is already imprinted and downloaded, and you already assume that that's the appropriate way to debate."

"Right," Marcus agreed.

"That's why I think hip-hop should happen," Hines said. "It shouldn't be just playing hip-hop but actually doing hip-hop."

"Being an organic intellectual," Marcus suggested.

"Yeah," Hines said. "*Doing* it."

A pause entered the conversation, and they both scoped out the festivities around them. In the distance, a couple of guys tossed a Frisbee. Smoke rose from a Weber grill. The sun shone brightly, and everyone was in short sleeves.

Hines restarted the conversation. "Fort Hays and Louisville say this is what needs to happen in debate," he said. "We're only gonna come in and say we think this is what should happen in debate, but it's up to you to do it. You know, it's about you. So we don't know what our project is yet. We're waiting for someone to tell us."

He looked Marcus in the eyes. "And we think you and Brandon might be the ones to do that," he said.

Marcus smiled and looked away.

WE HEADED BACK TO KANSAS CITY early the next day. Clouds had rolled in, and it felt as though it might rain. As we moved through Denton toward the highway on-ramp, Marcus asked me, his voice deep and serious, what I thought of UNT as an option. I wanted to say that I was worried about all the partying, but I chose to dodge his query. "The more important question," I said, "is, 'What do you think?'"

"If money isn't part of the issue, I'm coming here," he said. "The town is cool. The debate program is a lot better than UMKC's."

"Yeah," Brandon said. "I'm with you. I can do this."

TWO

GROUNDSWELL OF SUPPORT

PHYLLIS BUDESHEIM STRAIGHTENED HER SUIT and entered the large conference room. She had driven for two hours to make it to this mid-morning meeting in Columbia. She felt good about her prospects. For the past several months she had been talking with the nice folks at the Missouri State High School Activities Association. She'd first contacted them during the fall semester to find out how she might go about changing the rules that were preventing Central from competing in the Tournament of Champions. She knew Central had qualified again this year, and that it fell to her to gain the kids permission to go.

She'd been talking mostly with Kent Summers, associate director of the MSHSAA, who was polite and helpful. He suggested she make a case to the MSHSAA's appeals committee. He didn't tell her, however, that Rinehart and a Central administrator had taken the same tack the previous year and been denied.

If Budesheim had asked Rinehart, she might have been spared the long trip to Columbia. But Budesheim hadn't even tried to understand the coach's side of the story until January, when she called a meeting with all the district's debate coaches to find out what changes they wanted from the MSHSAA. The coaches were waved through security, and they made their way up to the conference room on the tenth floor. Budesheim sat at the head of the long conference table. She shot them all a look of cold professionalism and asked them what they wanted. They stared at her blankly.

Rinehart had come in determined not to say the first word, but the silence got to her, so she broke it. "I know this might be a somewhat selfish request," she said meekly, "but I'd like to be able to go to the Tournament of Champions."

Budesheim turned to the other coaches to gauge their reaction, and they nodded in assent. Rinehart threw out a few other possibilities—the National Catholic Forensic League's annual championship, Emory's tournament, Harvard, a couple of tournaments in Dallas.

Budesheim wrote these down, then asked the coaches to prioritize them. To Rinehart's surprise, they put the TOC at the top of the list, though none of the other coaches took their teams out on the national circuit much and were unlikely to ever qualify.

Budesheim kept saying that she wanted to do what was right for the children. Rinehart was leery of this, of course; it's a credo spouted often by top district officials to justify actions that do the exact opposite. But at this meeting Budesheim seemed sincere, once her icy bureaucrat demeanor melted. Budesheim had seemed confident that she would prevail in Columbia. She had assured them that she had a good rapport with Kent Summers. Rinehart still had doubts, but maybe Budesheim, one who spoke their language, could pull it off.

I knew Budesheim didn't have a chance. I'd been talking with Summers, too, and he told me bluntly that there wasn't any interest among the association's members in changing the rules, and that even if there were, the appeals committee wouldn't be the place to get it done. Still, I made the same two-hour trip east on I-70 to Missouri's main college town to witness the proceedings.

THEY CALLED US INTO A CONFERENCE ROOM, and we took our places facing the panel of committee members, myself a ways off to the side. The MSHSAA reps sat in high-backed chairs around a long conference table.

There was just one black person among them—an administrator from a charter school in Kansas City. "We have a long agenda," said John Ihms, the committee chair, "so we ask that you be as brief as possible."

Budesheim took out a written statement and began to read. "Being invited to participate in the Tournament of Champions is rare," she said. "Missouri teams have only been invited two times in the last thirty-two years." (Both teams were from Central.)

She concluded with what she hoped would be a moving appeal. "I've spent thirty-two years in one of the finest school districts in Missouri, North Kansas City," she said. "Yes. Some of those students face challenges. But never have I seen challenges like the ones I've seen in the last eight years," referring to her time with the Kansas City school district.

Emotion began welling in her voice as she said an opportunity to compete at national tournaments would have a huge impact on these kids' lives. "I think we're all familiar with the research on poverty and generational poverty," she said. "For many, college is only a dream. Like many of my colleagues, I consider my work to be a mission field."

"These debates could offer for some of our students scholarship offers," she continued. "This is important. Especially our urban children. It will broaden their horizons. They will offer additional opportunities for research. Also cultural opportunities."

After she'd said her piece, one of the board members said, "We've had this before us three times—1998, 2002, and now again. What have you done to try to get the rules changed?"

Budesheim stammered, "I cannot speak to all that has been done before." She recounted a meeting she'd had with a principal in suburban Kansas City who served on the MSHSAA's board of directors. "That led me to Mr. Summers, and he apparently said this was the best course of action," she said.

"As chairman, maybe I can give you some guidance," Ihms said. "The appeals committee grants exceptions to kids who demonstrate some sort of hardship," he explained. (Generally, school administrators consider a hardship to be, for example, a kid needing to move out of an abusive household. But the MSHSAA has no official definition of hardship, and it grants appeal requests arbitrarily.)

"To say your district has a greater hardship than others in the state," Ihms told Budesheim, "you would have a hard time convincing this group."

He also warned her about the downside of competing in tournaments such as the TOC. "If you talk to schools that do that, they have lots of problems," he said vaguely.

"Do we need to make a motion?" he asked after a long pause.

"I make a motion to deny the hardship appeal," one of the committee members said.

At that, the committee unanimously agreed to deny her request.

I followed Budesheim out of the room. She seemed genuinely shocked. "Why didn't anyone tell me that we'd already been to this committee?" she asked me. I wanted to tell her that it was because she never bothered to ask the person she was supposedly advocating for, but I kept quiet.

It was dawning on her that she'd been played by Summers. As she made her way to her car for the long drive back to Kansas City, she pledged that she would keep up the fight until the rules were changed. I got into my car and drove home knowing that she wouldn't, and that even if she did, she wouldn't have a chance.

A COUPLE OF MONTHS LATER I went to a meeting of the MSHSAA's speech and debate advisory committee. It was an all-day affair, beginning at nine and ending at five, and it was insufferable. I went because I had noticed on the agenda posted ahead of time on the MSHSAA's Web site that they would be discussing Central's debate team. I had asked Rinehart about this, and she said she hadn't requested to be on the agenda. She had no idea what they'd be talking about. She hastily put together a list of concerns she hoped they'd discuss—permission for her team to compete at the TOC, more afternoon tournaments, and so on—and faxed them to the committee member who represented the Kansas City area. The reps didn't get to these issues until late in the afternoon, after nitpicking for hours about the way kids ought to play.

Before the group broke for lunch, Becky Oakes, the MSHSAA's executive director, came in to report on the recently concluded legislative session in Jefferson City. For a while, state representatives considered a bill that would have forced the MSHSAA to back off from some of its rules, including the ones limiting when, where, and how often debate squads can compete.

Jane Cunningham, a representative from the St. Louis area, had introduced the bill. She wrote it because she'd gotten complaints from constituents, which she investigated by attending a meeting of the MSHSAA's appeals committee, where, she later told me, she saw "horrible abuses." At one point, she'd watched the committee grant an appeal to a white male athlete from a small rural school. He told the committee that a school adviser had misinformed him about the number of classes he needed to be enrolled in, and he wound up ineligible to compete. Then, later that day, a black female athlete from Ladue, a school in the St. Louis area, asked for an appeal for the exact same reason, and she was denied.

"I was so astounded I asked if I could advocate for her," Cunningham told me. "They were blown away. I said, 'You just had this white kid this morning with the same circumstance.'"

"But you don't understand," the committee chair told her. "This is Ladue. That kid was from a rural area. They don't understand. Ladue is more sophisticated."

Cunningham knew the real reason was racism. Earlier that day, during a break, she'd chatted with the chairman. After she told him where she was from, he asked, "How can you stand that desegregation plan?" He was referring to the St. Louis desegregation remedy that called for inner-city kids to be bused to suburban schools. "Kids from St. Louis should not be able to play on a county team," he explained. "It's not fair." He told her he would sue if he represented a county school.

Cunningham thought, *Wow. That's extreme.*

Cunningham's bill fell flat, though not for lack of support from the public. During committee discussions, she told me, "person after person came up with horrible stories." She actually sobbed when a track star from Liberty High School, just north of Kansas City, told how he was denied opportunities to compete at Olympic-caliber national meets. "He was a 4.0 student," she told me. "They don't really care about grades. Grade eligibility in Missouri is four Ds. *D* as in dog."

She got emotional during her phone conversation with me as well, her voice a mix of fury and tears. "Kids are being abused," she cried. "Freedoms are being overlooked. And a nonprofit group has taken taxpayer dollars, with no oversight from the state. And they're hurting kids. 'Abuse' is a kind word. It's outlandish."

But officials from many of the association's seven hundred member schools bombarded legislators with e-mails calling for the bill to be killed, at the urging of Oakes and her colleagues. "They were saying the bill is intended to get rid of MSHSAA," Cunningham told me. "That's not true. All we're trying to get them to do is reform."

In the end, the committee chair—a man who had once served on the MSHSAA's board of directors—moved to table the bill so that he could write a letter to Oakes. In it, he meekly suggested that the MSHSAA officials reconsider their travel restrictions. He added, "MSHSAA should seek more diversity in your organization by including minority representation. According to the Department of Elementary and Secondary Education, approximately 17.8 percent of the public school population is comprised of African-American students."

IT WAS LATE AFTERNOON by the time the members of the speech and debate advisory committee got around to the topic I'd come to hear discussed. Fred Binggeli opened the discussion. "This came to us," he said. "We had a request early in the year for travel to five competitions. Basically we wanted to ask you if you're getting these kinds of requests in your areas for exceptions to the 250-mile rule. I haven't received any."

No one responded. The representative from the Kansas City area took off her glasses. "Jane sent this fax," she said. "I really don't as a member feel appropriate speaking about this. It's a disservice to address it with no heads-up at all."

They passed around the letter.

Randy Pierce explained Rinehart's request for more afternoon tournaments. "We got a ruling from MSHSAA over twenty years ago to have a series of Tuesday contests," he said. "Together, three Tuesdays equal six rounds of competition, just like a tournament."

He explained that the contests start at four in the afternoon, so no school time is lost, and he endorsed it as a good program. He looked around the room at his colleagues. "I would respectfully suggest," he said, "you know, I don't know that any action would have to be taken."

Oakes raised an objection. "You can do it in a metro area," she said. "But you probably can't do it out-state at all."

She glanced over at a pair of coaches who represented small-town schools. No response.

She nodded.

"All they have to do is put a schedule together and Fred would work with them," she said.

"This is a healthy alternative," the Kansas City representative said. "And I believe it can be applied to all of us."

"We can just go on the record as being supportive," Pierce said.

As for Rinehart's request to be able to go to the TOC, they were less accommodating.

"What are we deciding here?" one committee member asked.

"It seems to me this is something they ask of MSHSAA, not of us," another said, as if they weren't a committee of the MSHSAA.

Oakes offered the usual caveats: the cost of going to tournaments such as this, loss of class time, loss of teacher time. Far from being subservient, she was running the show.

"If we're looking at charting the direction of Missouri overall," a coach from tiny Neosho in southwest Missouri said, "we don't want to encourage something that would be—"

"Elitist," Pierce finished for him.

They both laughed and nodded their heads.

"I was trying to avoid that word."

"We want to level the playing field," another committee member said.

"I didn't think that was the way we wanted to chart the course of our activity," said another. "Maybe I'm conservative."

Binggeli looked around and said, "I'm not seeing a groundswell of support for this here."

"Even if a hundred schools ask," one committee member said, "it's still a question of what we want this activity to look like in Missouri."

THREE

HOME, BITTER HOME

THE FIGHT STARTED IN A FLASH. Isaiah tagged Ebony with a jab, and a second later Ebony had his brother on the floor. The two writhed about, Ebony smashing Isaiah's face against the carpet. Suddenly they were on their feet again, squared off against each other. Isaiah delivered a hard punch to Ebony's shoulder. Ebony burst into high-pitched laughter. Isaiah struck again. Then again. Ebony laughed harder.

"Pussy!" Ebony said, cackling.

"Bitch!" Isaiah said.

"Fuckin' pussy!!"

Isaiah was home for the weekend, which had become an every-other-week routine. The rest of the time he lived in a boys' home in Independence. In the fall, Isaiah got caught in a stolen car, his aunt Shavelle told me. Ever since moving in with his aunt four years earlier, he had been drifting. He skipped school, stole, and dabbled in drugs, she said. He was becoming the opposite of Ebony.

Comparing the two side by side, one might assume they came from different homes. They were both tall and lanky, and they had similarly puffy cheeks, but other than that they appeared to be polar opposites. Isaiah had darker skin, and he wore his hair longer, his Afro sculpted at an angle, with a pick sticking out the back. In fashion, he preferred extra-extra-large shirts and trousers belted around his thighs to Ebony's loose-fitting but still conventional fare. Isaiah wore an oversize rhinestone stud in one ear, whereas Ebony tended to shun bling. But early on, when they were struggling through the state's social services system, they tried always to act like angels, because they were told they'd be split up if they didn't behave.

After they moved in with Shavelle and her husband, Eddy, however, their resolve unraveled. Ebony hardly spoke at all during that first year, and when he did, it was often in rage. One time, Ebony and Isaiah got into such an intense fight Shavelle feared they might kill each other. Isaiah had found Ebony's journal, and he started reading it over the phone to a girl. When Ebony discovered this, he tore into his brother. When Eddy tried to stop the fight, he broke his hand. Ebony turned around and punched a hole in a wall.

Gradually, Ebony settled in and calmed down. But Isaiah remained restless. The difference boiled down to levels of acceptance. While Ebony accepted that his mother was sick, Isaiah remained hurt at being abandoned and continued to cling to the hope that things would be made right and that the family would reunite. For all the mistakes Tina Marie Harrison made as a parent, she did shower her sons with love during their earliest years. Whether Isaiah could express it or not, this early connection and security were the moral foundation of his life. And when they were taken away from him, he couldn't construct a new one. So he lashed out.

The afternoon fight was over as quickly as it started, with no lingering ill feelings. It was your typical brother brawl, fought to test the pack order and express affection. They still cared deeply for each other, though they never said as much. Indeed, the most prominent image on Ebony's bedroom wall was that of a younger Isaiah, smiling for a grade school picture, dressed in a festive V-neck sweater and turtleneck.

But they couldn't count on each other anymore, not the way they had when they were adrift in the system. They were becoming very different men. Privately, Ebony would admit that he was disappointed and hurt by Isaiah's delinquency. And Isaiah would concede some jealousy of Ebony's success in debate and the likelihood of his moving on to college. They were puzzled and miffed by the disconnection, but they didn't dwell on it. Some things are better expressed with a punch to the arm.

SPRING HAD ARRIVED, and Ebony didn't have much left to look forward to, just one tournament and then the long off-season—a few months
of unchallenging school followed by a few months at a summer job. He still
hung around room 109 after school, though no one was practicing anymore
and Rinehart had stopped offering lessons. He'd chat with Day and Dionne,
play games on the Internet, even stretch out in the corner for a nap. At home
he'd download songs all night, watch cable on the hand-me-down TV in his
room, or read bits and pieces from heady books he'd checked out from the
library.

For the time being, his mom was back in his life. After first reappearing
at the Paseo tournament in October, she had relapsed between Thanksgiving
and Christmas. Shortly after the first of the year, she'd checked into a treatment center, and a few months later she was living in an apartment complex
for recovering addicts just west of Troost Avenue in midtown Kansas City.
She'd befriended a man who had been free from drugs and alcohol for a
number of years. He generously gave her a small restaurant to run on Troost,
a few blocks south of UMKC. It was a tiny place, with just one table, which
Tina stacked with books about recovery and spirituality. The restaurant had
few customers, so Tina spent most of her days sitting at the table, flipping
through books and smoking cigarettes. When she came across a passage that
inspired her, she'd transcribe it neatly onto loose-leaf notebook pages and
hang it on the wall as a sort of reminder to stay steady on the path to recovery. The incantations covered several feet of wall space and were interspersed
with photos of her sons and sisters.

I spent a few afternoons with Tina in this restaurant, sometimes with
Ebony, other times by myself. For all her faults, I found Tina to be a remark-
ably intelligent woman. Her influence on Ebony was plain to see, how her
early nurturing set the stage for his emergence as an intellectual. But, as
Ebony often said, she was "crazy," and she would be the first to admit it.

Without warning, she'd sometimes grow distant during our talks and
start rambling. Her tone would shift quickly from somber and quiet to the
bombast of a preacher. "There is a God," she declared suddenly on one occasion. "Because I should not be here. Just for the guilt alone, I should be ten
feet under. Cuz ain't no pain in the world like losing a child."

She shook her head and stared at the floor.

"Like losing a child," she said again softly. "And I lost them. I let 'em go cuz I had no other choice. I was trapped inside my head, no control. It's so awesome because even though it's such a sad thing, it's a good thing today. Today it's a good thing because when you get off into the Bible and if He opens your mind and your spirit up to revelations and the learned things, He says nothing happens in this world by mistake. And that's some deep shit."

She lit a cigarette and loudly exhaled a cloud of smoke, her shoulders sagging as if collapsing from weight.

"But," she continued, "now that I think about it, Mama used to tell me years ago, early in my addiction, she told me one night in 1994, she said, 'Tina, you're not the only one.' She said, 'There are millions of people out there like you. And if you can one day take all this bad and turn it into good.' And then there's that part in the AA Big Book about the promises or the vision for you. It said there'll come a time in our lives where we won't regret the past and we won't wish to shut the door on it. Because we'll know the reason. And that's some awesome shit. When you sit up by yourself late at night and you come to the conclusion that God predestined you to live the life you lived. For a holy purpose, thirteen years of all I went through. Eight years of abandoning my children, but still he got glory in it. He's gonna take it. And he's got a plan for it all. And I understand that today."

Ebony never said much during our visits with his mother. She'd fix him some breaded chicken strips and French fries, and then sit forward in her seat, forearms square on the tabletop, smiling and watching her son eat, needling him with questions. His answers were little more than grunts and shrugs. It wasn't that he didn't love her; his open body language suggested otherwise. But he wouldn't allow himself to let down his guard. He rarely returned her gaze.

"I miss sleeping together in bed," she told him during one visit. When Ebony and Isaiah were young, they always shared the bed, and she loved waking up in the morning all tangled under the covers. She asked softly, almost pleadingly, "Can we at least one night out the month? Will y'all sleep with me?"

Ebony laughed with embarrassment and looked away. "Mama, we big now," he said, his mouth still full.

"I don't care," she said.

He laughed again, his falsetto cackle.

"Okay," she said, leaning back and waving a hand at the air. "That's all right. Y'all don't remember."

He did, of course. And so did Isaiah. On one of his weekend stays Isaiah opened up to Ebony in a rare moment. He told his brother that he wanted the two of them to live with Tina again. Ebony laughed. "You crazy," he said. "Mama can't even take care of herself. How she gonna take care of us?"

One Saturday that spring Tina invited the whole family over to her apartment for a barbecue. Everyone was getting along nicely when Isaiah suddenly turned on his mother and unleashed an emotional barrage. He blamed her for his turn toward delinquency, saying she'd ruined his life. "You kept telling us you was gonna get better!" he yelled at her. "That we was gonna be together! You lied to us!"

Tina sat there and smiled and took it, forcing herself not to cry, telling Shavelle to "let the boy speak" when her sister tried to intervene.

A few days later Tina disappeared again. I stopped by the restaurant and found the owner there. He said he hadn't heard from her for several days, and he assumed she was back on drugs. When I asked Ebony what happened, he shook his head and said, "I dunno."

MEANTIME, EBONY'S FATHER would have nothing to do with him or his brother. He worked at a RadioShack on the edge of the city, and he never called. Ebony phoned him once during his junior year. It happened to be Ebony's birthday, and when he mentioned this, his father said, "So? What do you want from me?"

"Me, trying to put myself in his shoes," Shavelle told me, "I couldn't imagine how much that would have hurt to have a mother and your father just not be there for you." He was forced to grow up so fast. It worried her that he had to miss out on so many of the carefree joys of childhood. Yet he seemed to be thriving. She was so grateful that he'd found debate. In less than a year the game had helped him emerge as a confident young man—sometimes to an annoying degree. When she'd ask him to help out around the house, for instance, he'd sometimes refer to himself in the third person: "Ebony Rose don't need to mop no floor."

All year Shavelle had wanted to watch him debate, but she could never get away while he was competing in town. During the last tournament of the year, however, she found enough free time to catch what would be his last round as a novice. It was the UDL's Midwest Regionals, held at UMKC, and there were teams there from Chicago and St. Louis. Ebony and Antoine were having a great run. They'd lost just one round in the prelims, and they moved easily into semifinals, where they faced a pair of girls from Paseo Academy. The room was crowded with onlookers when Shavelle came in, mostly kids from Paseo and Central, clustered together on opposite sides of the room. Shavelle took a seat beside me. She was dressed up as if for work, in a fetching black and white silk blouse with sharp black slacks. Barely thirty years old, she still showed a bit of child in her face, with bright eyes and puffy, smooth cheeks. Her hair was permed in attractive ribbons of curls. She sat straight in her chair, arms placed firmly on the desktop in front of her, as if she were at a government meeting that demanded the utmost decorum.

Paseo argued on the affirmative, presenting a scaled-down version of the Portage Northern case Brandon and Marcus had lost to at the Glenbrooks, which called for animals to be given the right of consent before being subjected to experimentation. This torturous captivity, they argued, would ultimately lead to the enslavement of people. Ebony and Antoine were caught completely off guard. The older Central debaters watching the round shuffled in their chairs, feeling nervous for their young teammates. DiAnna leaned over and said to me, "This shit is *crazy*."

During cross-x, Ebony tried to understand what kinds of tests were being conducted on animals. His opponents were vague in answering, though, which suggested that they themselves didn't really know.

"What kind of tests they gonna conduct on these animals?" Ebony asked. "Space test? Drug test?"

"Why would they go to space?" one of the girls answered prissily.

As the round progressed, it became agonizing to watch Ebony and Antoine struggle along. After Antoine's first speech, one of Central's seniors released a loud, exasperated breath and stormed out of the room. Then DiAnna left, saying to me that it was "too messy" for her to sit through. Shavelle politely stayed put, her posture earnestly stiff. She'd never seen a debate before and didn't really know the particulars of the game. But the round was uneven enough for her to tell that her nephew was about to lose, his season about to end. "They're bringing wind to drop the bomb," she said to me about the Paseo girls. "Women like to bring out every point of every argument."

It didn't take long for the judges to decide—three-oh in favor of Paseo. Ebony and Antoine sat still, looking dejected as the judges criticized the round. Afterward, Shavelle cautiously approached Ebony and laid a hand on his shoulder. "I'm proud of you guys," she said.

Ebony said nothing and looked away.

Rinehart was standing nearby. She folded her arms across her chest, her face soft with empathy. "It's been a great season," she said.

Ebony tried to ignore her.

"It's only gonna make you stronger next year," Shavelle agreed, nodding.

Shavelle and I went out in the hall, leaving Ebony to heal his disappointment with the comforting routine of packing his tubs. She was smiling. Things were looking up for her nephew. He had debate, and, more important, she and Eddy had managed to purchase the house they were renting, so now Ebony had the first permanent home of his life. "I'm totally at peace with Ebony," Shavelle told me. "He's one of those success stories that you don't too often hear about in the inner city. He's one of those beautiful success stories."

FOUR

COMMENCEMENTS

MARCUS AND BRANDON'S PLANS were finally becoming reality. All year they'd been arguing for tax cuts. And now they were sitting in the balcony of the Senate's chambers in Washington, D.C., watching the distinguished officials casually cast votes in favor of one of the largest tax cuts in the history of the United States.

We were in the nation's capital for the National Catholic Forensic League's Grand National Tournament, a large competition that, along with the Tournament of Champions and the National Forensic League's championship, is considered part of the triple crown of high school debate.

Actually, the senators were voting to lift restrictions on the nation's deficit to allow for the massive tax break, which, of President Bush's three tax relief bills, was the most skewed in favor of the nation's wealthy. This package eliminated the capital gains tax on investments, so only Americans who could afford a healthy portfolio of stocks would really benefit. Marcus's and Brandon's families would not be among the fortunate. Indeed, the cuts would increase the government's deficit to record levels, threatening the social services that might benefit poorer families. Grover Norquist, one of the chief architects of the president's economic policies, once brazenly said that his goal was to drown government in a bathtub.

Brandon and Marcus were oblivious to this. They sat in their balcony seats, chins resting on open palms, staring disinterestedly at the white readers in suits down below. In the middle of the action stood the former Mont-gomery Bell Academy debater William Frist. He was taller than most of his colleagues. He leaned against a podium, his suit jacket unbuttoned, talking casually with his fellow senators. I kept my eyes trained on him for almost the entire time, which wasn't very long—Marcus and Brandon were bored and eager to leave. I whispered to Marcus that he should watch Frist, and I pointed to the senator, so tall and comfortable in his power.

Marcus scowled and gave his head a quick shake. "Man, this is the most boring thing I've ever seen," he said. "If you say it's not, you're lying."

I couldn't help but feel disappointed by the comment. I was the one who had called Senator Kit Bond's office to reserve tickets for the Senate session. Both Rinehart and I had been looking forward to the Washington visit. We thought the guys would be inspired by it. Especially Marcus. In his more se-rious moments he had spoken of his goal to pursue a career in politics. Rine-hart envisioned him becoming the first black senator from Missouri. In debate Marcus thrived on political arguments. In the heat of rounds he and Brandon would often argue that they were role players in a game of policy making that was less a game, really, than a training ground for future lead-ers. And I'd bought into this argument. I'd imagined Marcus and Brandon as minor-league senators, and I expected them to be electrified by this glimpse of the big leagues.

"This is just another game," I said. "The only reason you think it's bor-ing is because you don't know how to play yet."

Marcus stared back at me for a long moment. He leaned forward, fore-arms flat across his knees, and squinted to sharpen his focus on the scene below.

When I look back on it all, this stands out as one of the most significant moments of the 2002–2003 season, both for Marcus and for myself. In col-lege Marcus would dive headfirst into politics, getting involved with the campus Democrats during the 2004 presidential election and later making a successful bid for student body president. And I would come to seriously question—indeed, nearly reject—the notion that debate is an ideal forum to cultivate new generations of history makers. Of course it is; debaters tend to gravitate toward careers in policy making and law. But Marcus's and Brandon's detachment from these Senate proceedings—especially this particular vote happening before their very eyes, this conclusion of a matter they had discussed all year—convinced me that the game has serious shortcomings. There's a lot of talk in debate about how debaters have agency, especially in the current stage of its history, in which the introduction of critical arguments has shifted some of the focus toward the effects of what is said and learned in rounds. Yet Marcus and Brandon felt utterly disconnected from the real-world game they'd spent the previous four years pretending to play. They didn't know what was happening, and didn't care to know. Worse, they weren't outraged, as I was, by the monumental advance of neoconservative policy borne on this vote, that its passage could further weaken the frail safety net for poor families like theirs. If debate prepares kids to inherit control of the world's most powerful nation, why would two of the nation's top debaters feel so disconnected?

For the rest of the afternoon Marcus and Brandon were insufferable. It was a cold, drizzly day, and they both complained at every step of our tour of the sights around the Mall in D.C. Whenever we passed an entrance to the subway, they both made like they were going to abandon us to return to the hotel, Marcus insisting that his room's bathroom was the only place in the whole city where he'd feel comfortable taking a shit, which his exaggeratedly twisted and squirmy posture seemed to indicate he urgently needed to do. When we finally decided on a restaurant, Brandon took one step inside and announced loudly, "This place fuckin' sucks."

"Mouth!" Rinehart barked.

But this just got them cussing more. Holly Reiss, program coordinator for Kansas City's Urban Debate League, was with us, and the guys managed to darken even her mood, which was typically sunny. "After all you've done for them," she said to Rinehart, "I can't believe they treat you like this. They ought to be smacked."

We walked several miles that afternoon, through the Capitol, past the many buildings of the Smithsonian, the Washington Monument, the Lincoln Memorial, and the not-yet-completed World War II memorial. In their growing tiredness, Marcus and Brandon became more and more irritable and annoying. Only the Vietnam Veterans Memorial quieted them. They silently gazed at the long wall of black marble with the names of 58,196 dead Americans inscribed in it. It was Memorial Day weekend, and the sidewalk beside the monument was packed with somber onlookers. Rinehart walked slowly along, scanning the columns of names. She told us she was looking for the name of one of her high school classmates, a fellow debater. He was just your average kid, not, as the song says, a senator's son. Smart but poor, he couldn't afford college.

"You're never gonna find it," Brandon said softly, sensing Rinehart's tenderness.

But just then, her eyes fixed right on his name. She reached out and ran her fingers across the letters. Brandon sidled up to her and laid his arm across her shoulder. And it occurred to me that this was what was missing from debate: humanness. In a debate round Brandon could coolly evoke the suffering and death of literally millions of human beings without actually feeling the pain of such horror.

In his *Rhetoric*, Aristotle argued that a debater's most persuasive tool is his character, or ethos:

> Persuasion is achieved by the speaker's personal character when the speech is so spoken as to make us think him credible. We believe good men more fully and more readily than others: this is true generally whatever the question is, and absolutely true where exact certainty is impossible and opinions are divided . . . It is not true, as some writers assume in their treatises on rhetoric, that the personal goodness revealed by the speaker contributes nothing to his power of persuasion; on the contrary, his character may almost be called the most effective means of persuasion he possesses.

He proposed that persuasive rhetoric depends on three things: ethos; pathos, or emotion and empathy; and logos, or logic. True, Aristotle's ideals for debate have been the subject of debate for millennia, especially his insistence on debate as a vehicle for defining universal truths, a point he raised in critical response to the Sophists, those professional debaters of antiquity, whom he regarded as rhetorical tricksters. This notion carries potential for demagoguery, which the most celebrated Sophist, Aristotle's nemesis Protagoras, arguably checks with his most famous edict, "There are two sides to every question."

But in America debate has become a churning factory of cold schemes and ideologies, especially on the national circuit. It's Protagorean in the sense that everything—even the idea that racist genocide is best for humanity, as Glenbrook South had argued against Daryl Burch's "End Racism" case—is fair game, so long as it's logically structured and, most important, it wins. And it's Aristotelian in the sense that debate *is itself* the universal truth, because, with its standards of evaluation, it's based on competing evidence that's quantified mechanically with "the flow." It's "objective." It isolates and codifies spoken thought, and rewards the fastest and deepest thinkers.

The problem, however, is that the stuff of debate is real. Genocide actually happens. Bright but poor young men and women actually die in wars. Yet when "future policy makers" consider these phenomena on their supposed "training ground," in their "laboratory for ideas," as I've heard debate described so many times, they're expected not to express—much less feel— the feelings they might experience while standing before a wall of people who died when not much older than they.

No wonder Marcus and Brandon were bored by the Senate vote. It was just another exercise in logic, no more exciting than a debate round between two other teams on the circuit. Neither liked to watch other teams compete. The game was only fun when they were in it. And despite all the talk about agency in debate rounds, somehow Marcus and Brandon had made it through four years of debate believing they weren't players in the American game of democracy.

THE NEXT MORNING we headed off early from the hotel to T. C. Williams High School in Alexandria, Virginia, site of the NCFL's preliminary rounds. The school was the setting for the popular movie *Remember the Titans*, in which Denzel Washington played the part of the school's first black coach, who led the football team to a state championship in the early 1970s, when tensions surrounding desegregation were high. Judging from the photographs of the sports teams displayed in the school's main hallway, this had become a well-integrated school, though the students seemed to segregate themselves by activity, with basketball nearly all black, football more evenly mixed, and soccer almost entirely white.

If the first round was any indication, this would be an easy tournament. Marcus and Brandon had their opponents stammering from the get-go. Afterward, Marcus flexed his face into an angry scowl and complained, "I'm tired of this." His mood didn't change much throughout the day, though he always managed to rouse his competitive instincts just as the rounds began. The tournament's rules prohibited judges from disclosing the winners after the rounds, but Central's opponents seemed to improve as the day went on, indicating that they were moving up in the rankings.

Phil Kerpen, owner and operator of Cross-X.com and a Washington resident, sat in on their final round. Marcus and Brandon argued on the affirmative, advancing their "End Racism" case, and the debate boiled down to a political disadvantage argument based on evidence cards Kerpen himself had produced. During cross-x, Marcus asked one of the kids if he could see his "Phil Kerpen cards," and he grinned at Kerpen, who was sitting beside me in the back of the room. Kerpen chuckled and whispered to me that Central's opponents were mishandling his evidence; he'd cut the cards to answer Daryl Burch's duPont Manual team, who had taken the case far beyond Marcus and Brandon.

During the round's final speech Marcus said, very slowly and clearly, "They argue that civil rights don't work. That is empirically proven false. If it weren't for civil rights legislation, I wouldn't be debating in this room. That's just absurd."

Afterward, Kerpen and I were chatting with Marcus and Brandon as they packed their evidence when one of the round's judges approached. "I don't want to offend you," she said to Marcus, "but I was listening to you and I was thinking about a student of mine who died from a gang shooting. I just wish he would look up to people like you."

Marcus smiled and politely thanked her. As she walked away, he huddled close to Kerpen and said, "I'm not sure if you can deduce anything from that."

I didn't agree. "What if you went up to a white kid and said, 'My cousin is a stoner and I wish he would look up to you'?" I asked.

"Yeah," Kerpen agreed. "It was racist. But she didn't say what I thought she was going to say: 'I wish all black people were like you.' Which is essentially what she said."

THAT NIGHT WE FOUND our way to the Arlington Hyatt, where hundreds of teens bounced up and down and against one another to hip-hop beats. For most of them the tournament was over, and it was time to party before a day of sightseeing in D.C. We weren't much interested in dancing, though. We pushed our way through the crowd to a conference room, where a row of easels displayed the codes of the teams that would advance to elimination rounds in the various speech and debate divisions. The list of policy debate qualifiers was on the display farthest from the door, and the code numbers didn't come into focus until we were standing right in front of it. Central's number was among them, sixth from the top. Rinehart bounced on her feet and clapped her hands.

The next morning Marcus and Brandon squared off against another UDL team from New York City, the Manhattan Center for Science and Mathematics. Marcus was friends with one of the debaters, whose name, coincidentally, was Marquis. Again, Central was on the affirmative. Their opponents ran a feminism kritik, arguing that Central's case perpetuates sexist ideologies, which, as far as I could tell, didn't link in any way to Central's case. Marcus and Brandon bore down on the link and attacked it relentlessly, and by the end their opponents were sputtering almost incoherently. During Marcus's final speech Marquis sat back and smiled and shook his head, as if to say he knew he'd lost.

Afterward, Marquis shook Marcus's hand and asked what his team code was. "I want to watch your next round before we go," he said. While the judges studied their notes, I overheard Marquis's coach say to someone on her cell phone that they would be heading home very soon.

Then Rinehart came in with a grave look on her face. She had just been to the tab room. "You dropped on a two-one," she said. She shook her head, looking for a moment as if she were about to cry. "And you were undefeated. You were the sixth seed. They were the twenty-seventh seed."

Marcus nodded. "I knew it was coming," he said calmly. "I saw them talking after the round. But Marquis is my friend. So that's cool."

Rinehart rushed to her room, called her sister, and sobbed into the phone. Marcus and I caught the subway to the Smithsonian's Air and Space Museum. We challenged each other in games of probability and physics and took a ten-dollar ride on a flight simulator. That night we spotted some teenagers, most of them female, all of them black, lugging their suitcases into the room next to ours. When we opened the door to our suite, the girls caught a glimpse of the sumptuous armchair and love seat. One of them whistled. "You should stop by later," Marcus said coolly.

Marcus quickly spruced up the room. He laid his and Brandon's medals out on the coffee table, and the two of them struck cool, confident poses as they watched TV, waiting for the girls to come by. Before going to bed in the adjoining room, I told Marcus and Brandon how devastated I was that they'd been voted down in a round I thought they'd clearly won.

"We're trying to put that out of our minds," Marcus scolded, his expression hardening for an instant. He fixed his gaze on a spot in the distance. He may have been sick of debate, but his desire for significance remained. He'd always wanted to be "someone important," and debate had taken him part of the way there. The particulars of the game may no longer have mattered to him, if indeed they ever did, but the story of it all did, this chapter in his autobiography. He knew he was in transition, a place of closure and commencement, and its history was his to shape.

His hawk eyes turned back on. "I'm gonna have to win NFL nationals," he said. "I'm just gonna have to use my anger from this to win nationals."

The next morning I found them slouched on the sofa, asleep in their day clothes. The medals were right where they'd left them, perfectly displayed on the table. The girls had never shown up.

———

TWO DAYS LATER Marcus and Brandon were dressed in blue caps and gowns, walking the stage at the Municipal Auditorium in downtown Kansas City. Both had managed to clear the English-credit hurdle, Brandon by knuckling down and submitting to Rinehart's assigned workload, Marcus by transferring to another class taught by a lax teacher.

When the class of 2003 graduates moved single file to their seats on the floor, their family members and friends in the audience screamed crazily. They made the bleachers thunder by pounding their feet against them. On-stage, Principal McClendon took the microphone. "On behalf of the graduates, we would appreciate it if you would hold all applause and shouting until after the program," he said for the first of many futile times throughout the evening. Kansas City graduations are notoriously raucous, so much so that school board members have discussed the "problem" at numerous public meetings with little success at bringing decorum to the ceremonies.

Folks shouted almost nonstop throughout the entire affair—during speeches by the valedictorian and the salutatorian, and songs by the gospel choir, and even the memorial dedication to the slain student Kristi Carroll, whose mother was given an honorary diploma.

Before asking the graduates to cross the stage to receive their diplomas, McClendon declared: "We're going to be the greatest high school in Kansas City, because I'm a graduate of Central High School, and we're going to bring it back to old-school. The way it used to be. At this time, I present the class of Central High School 2003."

Backstage afterward, I spotted Brandon and Leo. They gave each other a brisk man hug. "We're finally grown fuckin' men!" Leo said.

Outside, Marcus posed for pictures with his family. It was a warm late-spring evening, and the receding sun's rays made the skyscrapers around us glow with pink light. Rinehart approached and extended a hand to Evaline Lumpkin, Marcus's mom. She took a picture of mother and son together. "Thank you for giving him to me for four years," she said.

"I wish you could have him another four years," Evaline joked.

Really, she wished Rinehart could have Marcus's younger brother. She worried about Jason every day. It was nearly summer, and crime was rising along with the temperature, as it does every year in Kansas City. Jason was spending more and more time away from home during his hours outside of school. And in her neighborhood this was rarely a good sign. She'd heard through the community gossip wire that the little boy Jason had grown up with, the one everybody called Porky, the one who gave Jason a ride to school every day, had a gun and was going around shooting it. She'd feel so much better if Jason were going to debate camp, the way Marcus did.

Rinehart chuckled at the comment, but she was fighting tears. She hugged Marcus, the best debater she'd ever coached. "I'm going to miss you," she said.

"It's not over yet," he said, smiling. "We got one more tournament."

FIVE

SHOW ME

THE AIRPORT SHUTTLE DROPPED US OFF at a Days Inn on a busy two-lane highway in Peachtree City, Georgia, surrounded by tall pines. "What the fuck is this shit?" Brandon said.

Marcus said nothing as he lugged his bags to their room. The sky was low and a dull gray, the air misty with humidity. The closest sign of civilization was a Wal-Mart across the highway and a good three-quarters of a mile away. The nearest restaurants were a mile and a half down the highway. It was going to be a hassle just to stay fed during the upcoming week.

Marcus knew the setup was lame, but he was trying to make the best of it. It was his idea to sign up for the pretournament camp, so he and Brandon could get into top shape for the NFL national championship. Brandon agreed to go along. But when he saw their digs for the week, he regretted it immediately. "Man," he said, dropping his luggage on the floor and flopping down on his bed. "This shit is jacked up."

The situation worsened the next day, when we were ferried to the pretournament camp at a high school ten miles away in a rented ten-passenger van. There were more campers than seats, so kids had to sit on each other's laps. It was early June and the massive suburban school was eerily empty and even more isolated than the motel. The nearest fast-food joint was a five-minute drive away. Marcus, Brandon, and I found our assigned room, the one set aside for policy debaters, and discovered just two other kids enrolled.

The camp's director was a nationally renowned speech coach from New Mexico, so most of the campers were there to get ready for the forensic events at the national tournament. The debate section seemed to have been added as an afterthought, merely to make more money.

Marcus and Brandon's campmates for the week were two girls from Springfield, Missouri—Danielle, tall and skinny with ponytails and plastic-rimmed glasses, and Veronica, with shoulder-length hair and a delta of bangs fanning down across her forehead. They wore jeans and matching Parkview High School T-shirts. They offered a cheerful hello when Marcus and Brandon entered the classroom. "Sup?" Marcus said as he settled into a desk. Brandon nodded coolly at the girls, sat down, and slid a pair of head-phones over his ears.

Such a contrast. Four Missouri debaters: two schooled in the slow Missouri style; two more familiar with the speedy national circuit. Each pair was looking to move in the other's direction. The NFL national tournament is the melting pot for debate. Two judges decide each round, and the tournament's directors try to pair up speed enthusiasts with traditionalists. To win, teams have to talk the fine line in between.

Their instructor, Ed Williams, a black guy who taught at Woodward Academy in the suburbs of Atlanta, hadn't arrived yet. He would show up a half hour late—his pattern for the rest of the week. When he arrived, he had the debaters jump right into a practice round, telling Brandon and Marcus to argue on the affirmative. "Throw it down just like you would at the Glenbrooks," he said. Both Veronica and Danielle widened their eyes and laughed nervously.

Brandon tore through his case, but disinterestedly, as though greatly inconvenienced just by being there. He mumbled his answers during cross-x, rubbing his eyes, as if he had just been roused from a long nap. While Marcus and the girls delivered their speeches, he laid his head on a desk and fell asleep.

Marcus kept looking over at him, and then at me, shaking his head. He wanted to win the national championship. But he knew that if Brandon got too deep into one of his funks, there'd be nothing he could do.

———

BRANDON GREW MORE AND MORE SULLEN as the week wore on. The next day he slumped at a desk, headphones pulled down over his ears. Williams rapped his knuckles against the desk and waved hello right in front of Brandon's eyes. "Feeling a little tired today?" he asked.

"No." Brandon looked past him.

"You seem a little sluggish."

"I just don't feel like doing this."

Danielle and Veronica walked to his desk and leaned over, their faces nearly touching his, eyes maniacally wide, in hopes of making him laugh. But he looked past them.

"What's wrong with him?" Veronica asked Marcus.

"He's just trying to get attention," Marcus said.

In truth, Brandon was hopelessly homesick. Debate travel was a mixed bag for him. Yes, he'd gotten into debate because he was jealous of his brother's ventures to Iowa, Nebraska, and Chicago. And in the weeks leading up to tournament trips, he was always eager to get on the road. But once he'd reached his destination, he'd immediately pine for home. More than anything he missed his grandpa. Alonzo Dial, though frail with emphysema, was the foundation of Brandon's life. Ever since his parents split up, and his mother died soon after, the old man had been the one constant in his life, the only person he could really count on to be exactly where he was the day before and would be every day after. Bapa rarely left his bed in the living room anymore. An oxygen tank was always at his side, tubes always in his nose. He couldn't even keep up a good argument like he used to. His thoughts would trail off, or he'd be consumed by fits of coughing.

But Brandon found comfort in his granddad's deathly illness. Even more than debate or school, it gave him a sense of purpose. He preferred to stay nearby, whiling away his free hours on the computer that was set up a few steps from his grandpa's sickbed, or sitting on the couch and talking on the phone, occupied but ready to drop everything to wait on his grandpa if there was anything he needed. When Brandon was away from home, he would constantly fret that his grandpa needed his help.

On the second night in the Days Inn, he woke up in the early-morning hours, swearing that he'd heard his grandpa call his name. He skipped camp classes the next day, opting to mope in the motel room with the curtains drawn and the TV on with the volume set low. He spent hours talking on the phone, first with Bapa, then with friends, and then with his granddad again. He caught up on the gossip back home, and the news wasn't too good. The big story was about Porky, a fifteen-year-old Brandon knew mostly as the friend of Marcus's younger brother, Jason. Brandon had never thought much of him. He was just another kid from a broken family, no better or worse than anyone else. But when he got to Central that year as a freshman, he just went crazy, getting involved in some of the school's biggest fights, the ones that had led to the cancellation of the homecoming dance and brought all the cop cars to the school at the end of each day. And now, Brandon learned, word was he'd gotten a gun and was running around town shooting it off. When Marcus returned to the motel from the day at camp, Brandon shared the news from back home. "Damn," Marcus said with the faintest hint of concern. "That boy ain't gonna live long."

Marcus headed off to hang out with Veronica and Danielle. Brandon stayed in the room to brood. He called his grandpa again. The old man wouldn't let on about how he was feeling, he didn't like to get the boy worried, but Brandon could tell he wasn't doing so well because he kept lowering the phone to hack up wads of phlegm. In times like this, Brandon couldn't care less about debate. He just wanted to go home.

THE FOLLOWING WEEKEND we headed into Atlanta, to meet up with Rinehart and check into the tournament hotel. Rinehart had booked rooms at the Marriott Marquis, a sumptuous place with an atrium that soared fifty stories above the lobby. Brandon walked in and craned his neck, squinting at the rows of balconies stretching up toward the glass roof. "Damn," he said. "This is a baller hotel."

The environs instantly shifted his mood. These were the best digs he'd ever had as a debater, and he felt like a political dignitary or a pro athlete who'd just made it to the big time. It was a relief to see Rinehart, who had arrived with his buddy Leo and her nephew Alexander in tow. Brandon sauntered over to the group as soon as they entered the hotel, and he slapped hands with Leo.

"How does it feel to be a graduated man?" he asked.

"Not graduated man," Leo said. "Graduated, *grown-ass* man."

AFTER WE CHECKED INTO OUR ROOMS and dropped off our bags, Rinehart took us to lunch in the hotel's bar and grill. She wanted to go over the tournament's schedule and rules. Instantly, Brandon's mood darkened again. He affected a pissy attitude, pursing his lips and glancing about the restaurant in a show of not paying attention. When Rinehart said that the first speakers on the affirmative would have to pick up the ballots before each round, he blurted, "Fuck that. I'm not picking up nobody's ballot."

Marcus sneered at his partner. "You see what I've been dealing with all year," he said.

Brandon's disengagement at the pretournament camp had really upset Marcus. At times during the week, I could see desperation in Marcus's eyes. This was his last shot, one final chance to really make a name for himself, to prove to everyone who cared to notice that he had mastered this game and was ready to move on to the next playing field. But it was more than that. A month or so before the tournament he had learned that the championship round would be held in the sanctuary of Ebenezer Baptist Church, where Dr. Martin Luther King, Jr., had preached for a while before moving on to Mobile, Alabama, and changing the course of history. How powerful and poetic it would be to read the words of Joseph Barndt in that historic, sacred space: "Brick by brick, stone by stone, the prison of individual, institutional and cultural racism can be destroyed." In the weeks leading up to the tournament, he had visualized just such a moment. He paced his room, practicing delivering his speeches slowly and dramatically, full of emotion and conviction. At times he worked his imagination so hard that he believed it had actually happened, and he felt chills spread across his body as he pictured himself being handed the trophy.

THAT NIGHT WE GATHERED in Rinehart's room, ostensibly to prepare for the first day of competition. But Brandon wasn't there.

Marcus paced the room, frowning. "Can I just say, this is pointless if Brandon isn't coming," he scoffed.

Alexander called Brandon in his room. "You're what?!" he yelled into the phone. "You're pimping?"

Rinehart reached out for the receiver. "Just bring up the case," she said through a forced smile in a sweet, gentle voice. "Then you can go."

She maintained her cheeriness with great effort. Like Marcus, she had set her expectations high. She'd tried to uphold a pragmatic outlook, lest she be utterly disappointed. But she couldn't help picturing her debaters standing at the pulpit of Ebenezer Baptist Church, the very same place where the greatest man of the twentieth century had once stood, arguing for an end to racism. What a perfect ending for her Hollywood story. It was too delicious a vision not to indulge. So if it took sweet-talking Brandon out of one of his bratty moods, by God, she was gonna do it.

Brandon showed up ten minutes later. He stepped into the room with his head cocked back, chest puffed out, eyes narrowed. He let the door loudly slam shut. All he had with him was a half-empty bottle of Coke. No case file.

He silently strolled to the window, tapped a beat against the glass, and gazed out over the Atlanta skyline, the steely buildings glowing orange in the light of the setting sun.

"I wonder if these windows will break," he said. He pounded hard on the glass.

Rinehart stiffened and shifted in her seat on the bed. She stared at Brandon for a full two minutes. Brandon didn't return her gaze. "I'm gonna throw Alexander in these rounds tomorrow as Brandon Dial," she said finally. "*Okay?*"

"He'll be all right," Brandon coolly replied.

"Okay." Rinehart tried to dive into the work at hand. "What is the introduction that you've got right now? We need to tell more of a story in the 1AC."

"Pssh," Brandon said. "What introduction?"

"Joe says you need an introduction. A story."

"What does Joe know?"

"Joe, what was the idea you had?" Rinehart asked me.

While Brandon was skipping class at camp, I had sort of taken his place.

I helped Marcus with some research and partnered with him in a practice round. I was stepping deeper into the story I was covering. I rationalized my involvement as a kind of immersion, a way to experience firsthand the rigors of debate. In truth I was as desperate for a triumphant finale to this season as Marcus was. I wanted these kids to win it all, even if it meant my fudging customary ethical lines.

"I was thinking something like, 'Thirty-five years ago, on these very streets, a mule train carried the body of Martin Luther King to his grave,'" I replied. "'He died trying to achieve a vision of a unified and healthy America where all people would be considered equal regardless of the color of their skin. But today, as we look across Atlanta, we can see . . .'"

I looked over at Brandon. I didn't feel comfortable writing his speech myself.

"Come on," I said. "Brandon, help me out. This is you."

"Striking disparities within mental health care," he answered, not moving his eyes from the city scene.

"Okay," Rinehart said, suddenly encouraged.

"No." Brandon turned abruptly, releasing his attention from the window. "You should do it like, 'While civil rights legislation passed in 1964, it's done nothing to end discrimination in mental health care.'"

"All right," Rinehart said, and she began writing it down. We'd gotten through.

Rinehart finished writing and handed the new speech intro to Brandon. He smiled as he read it. He stuck out his tongue and whooped. "This shit is tight," he said. "You know what would be pimp is if I could remember this."

He read it out loud. "You have to enunciate Barndt," Rinehart said, referring to the speech's moral center: "Brick by brick, stone by stone . . ."

"No problem," Brandon said. "I know Barndt like the back of my dick." Rinehart grimaced.

Brandon looked out the window again. "This style of debate is so gay," he said.

"You can do it," Rinehart said.

"It's harder than you think," he said, his voice pitched with a note of serious desperation.

"What?" Rinehart asked. "To debate stupid?"

"Yeah. I hate debating slow rounds like that."

"Well, we can't help that," Rinehart said. "We've had our fair share of fun, tough rounds this year. We've enjoyed them, and they were fun. But this is a different venue. That's all it is. It's just a different venue. You gotta be smarter than the average guy. That's all you gotta do. And the smarter-than-the-average guy is adapting to the things these people want to hear. They want to vote for you."

Brandon shook his head.

"Yeah, they do," Rinehart insisted.

"Affirmative action," her nephew Alexander said.

FOR THEIR FIRST ROUND the next morning Marcus and Brandon faced a team from New Mexico in front of a pair of older women judges, both of whom took notes on legal pads, a sure sign that they were old-school. Their opponents ran a case calling for the legalization of drugs to allow people with mental illnesses to medicate themselves, arguing that the drug war leads to a loss of biodiversity, which would ultimately lead to the total extinction of life on the planet, because hemp seed is the best source of protein for children.

Both Brandon and Marcus read very slowly, and the other team grew hostile toward them because of it. During cross-x and the rebuttal speeches, the New Mexico kids all but accused Marcus and Brandon of being backwater debate retards.

"That guy was *dissing* us," Marcus said afterward, indignant at the mere suggestion of such a thing.

Brandon laughed. "They sucked dick," he said. "I wanted to stand up and start speeding at the top and talking shit. But I just—"

Marcus interrupted. "If that were a speed round, we would have spanked them."

And so it went for the first couple of days. Marcus and Brandon deftly trod the zone between Missouri and national-circuit-style debate. To make it to elimination rounds, they had to win eight out of twelve ballots. From my perspective, they were trouncing their competition. They both felt fairly confident, too. Their moods were light, they were relaxed. But the judges didn't disclose their decisions, so it was impossible to be sure. Results would be posted during the sixth, and final, round.

On the way to the campus Marcus said, "If I see we only have five ballots and there's no way we're going to break, I'm not going to debate."

Brandon held up his hand for a high five.

The air was as humid as soup, and the evening sky darkened with clouds ready to burst into torrents of rain. Sobek confidently predicted Marcus and Brandon would pick up nine ballots. Marcus seemed doubtful. "Man," he said. "I don't know about these judges."

Midway through the sixth round, Alexander and I stole off to the student union to check the results. We pushed through the crowd that had formed around the posted lists and found that Marcus and Brandon had picked up eight wins. They would break, but if they could pick up one more ballot, they wouldn't have to debate for the first elimination round, and we could all sleep in. Their opponents had six ballots, so it was a do-or-die round for them.

We dashed back to the room where Brandon and Marcus were debating, arriving just before the final rebuttals. Alexander wrote Central's record on a piece of paper and handed it to Marcus. Marcus nodded and softly said, "Cool."

After the final speech the judges took a long time considering their decisions. Finally they signed their ballots and folded them in half. Unlike in the previous rounds, the judges were to disclose their decisions immediately after this one so teams would know if they would be competing the next day. The first judge said he voted negative, against Central. Marcus got into an argument with him over his decision. Rinehart was antsy, irritated that the argument was going on and on. She exhaled loudly, rolled her eyes, looked away. She tapped her fingernails against a legal pad. Marcus's argument with the judge got more and more heated until finally the judge said, "I'm more than willing to answer questions all night." Marcus smiled and said, "Okay."

In an instant, the other judge said, "I went the other way."

Rinehart let out a long sigh of relief. "Too close," she said.

SIX

THE REVEREND JESSE JACKSON
AND THE UNFORTUNATE SURVIVAL
OF HUMANITY

WHATEVER RESOLVE MARCUS had to win the national championship had not awakened with his body on the morning of the first day of out rounds. He'd been up until three in the morning, clowning with the guys in their room.

When I arrived at his room at a little past ten, just before we were to head for the first elimination round, Marcus opened his eyes slightly, and then pulled a pillow over his head. Alexander shook a foot poking out from under the covers. Very slowly, Marcus unearthed himself, moved to a sitting position on the edge of the bed, rubbed his eyes, and locked them on a wad of clothes in the middle of the floor. He remained frozen in that position for several minutes. Gradually he rose to his feet and stumbled to the bathroom, where he took a long, long shower, leaning against the tile wall half-asleep, basking in the rush of hot water. Rinehart called the room twice while he was in there. Both times Alexander answered, and when he knocked on the bathroom door, his voice carried the frantic tone of his aunt.

Marcus emerged in a cloud of steam, a white towel cinched around his bulging waist. His clothes were in a different room, on a separate floor of the hotel, so he threw on some shorts and a T-shirt and wandered casually out into the hall. He spotted Brandon by the elevator.

"You aren't even dressed?!" Brandon said. "Man, Rinehart is going to kill you. She is trippin'."

"Give me the key," Marcus said, holding out his hand palm up.

"I ain't got it."

Marcus let his hand drop to his side. This momentary kink in his plans didn't seem to bother him a bit. He summoned Alexander and had him rush down to the lobby twelve floors below to retrieve a key while he waited in the room watching TV. Alexander returned five minutes later, out of breath from the sprint.

By the time we got down to the lobby, Rinehart had already left.

Now I was starting to panic. I assumed we'd been left behind, that we'd miss the first round and the great Central debate team would go out with a pitiful forfeit. Marcus still seemed unconcerned. His shirttail was sticking out, and his tie draped loosely around his neck. He ducked into the public restroom to straighten up.

A couple seconds later he came running out, energized.

"Joe, come here!" he shouted. "You're not going to believe this! Jesse Jackson is in there!"

We went into the restroom. There were a couple of men in suits lingering outside the stall, where Jackson was relieving himself. The men eyed us warily. Marcus took his time tucking in his shirt, craning his neck to get a peek through the gaps on the stall's door.

"Should I stay in here?" he whispered to me.

I suggested we wait outside.

Jackson emerged a few moments later, talking on a cell phone. His handlers noticed us hovering nearby. "Would you like his autograph?"

"I would love his autograph," Marcus said, smiling.

Jackson ended his conversation and Marcus approached, hand outstretched. "Mr. Jackson, could I . . ."

I tore a sheet out of my notebook.

Jackson seemed put off. "What's your name?" he asked curtly, retrieving a pen from his coat pocket.

I mentioned that Marcus was in town for the national debate championship. Jackson looked Marcus up and down, and his expression softened.

"Keep the faith," he said as he scribbled his name down.

He put his hand on Marcus's shoulder, looked him in the eye, and said, "Keep your head up. Be clear. Be authentic and be precise."

Marcus was at a loss for words. He just stood there, smiling.

As Jackson walked away, he repeated, "Be precise. And keep the faith." He pointed at his eyes. "Eye contact."

We watched them exit the hotel.

"Man," Marcus said to me. "That was a good thing I had to go to the bathroom."

WE STARTED WALKING toward the Georgia State University campus, where rounds were being held. Before we reached the end of the block, Rinehart pulled up beside us in a Buick LeSabre she had rented. "Marcus," she yelled through the open window. "Get in!"

She started laying into him about how late he was, how she had already driven the rest of the guys to the tournament site, how pissed she was to be spending all this money to take him to a national tournament only to have him forfeit out because he couldn't get ready in time.

Marcus paid her no mind. "Guess who we saw in there?"

"Who?"

"Guess."

"Jimmy Carter."

"Jesse Jackson," Marcus said, with a thump of satisfaction.

"Really?" she said detachedly. She was still too pissed to comprehend.

Marcus bounced up and down in his seat. "He gave me a lecture, and his autograph," he said.

"A lecture *and* his autograph," Rinehart said, still unimpressed.

"Yeah," Marcus said. "He was like, 'Keep the faith.' And, 'Be clear, precise.' And some other stuff. And, 'Always keep eye contact.'"

Rinehart looked at Marcus through the rearview mirror. She finally smiled. "Okay, so use that in the negative round," she said. "You know, 'I just met Jesse Jackson. He told me to be clear, precise in the round. And this is why we win.'"

Marcus frowned and looked out the window, peeved that he had to ruin the moment with debate stuff. "I hate going negative," he said.

"Well, I can't help that," Rinehart said.

"So we'll probably drop this round."

Rinehart tapped the brakes and shot Marcus a look through the mirror. "How 'bout we pick up this round? The whole tournament starts at this point. Clean slate."

MARCUS AND BRANDON SAILED EASILY through their first two rounds, picking up three-oh decisions in both. Rinehart pumped her fist after each win. She was starting to believe that her vision of debating in MLK's church would come true.

Throughout the day Marcus kept pulling Jesse Jackson's autograph out of his shirt pocket to look at it. During his speeches he laid it out on the table beside his evidence.

For round three they finally faced a worthy opponent—Iowa City, easily their toughest competition so far. Iowa City was on the affirmative, and their case, which called for the legalization of medical marijuana, had generated a bit of buzz around the tournament because the team ran it so well. Some of Marcus's friends had gone up against them earlier in the day and lost.

Marcus and Brandon huddled with Sobek out in the hall to size up their options. Sobek looked through the list of judges' preference sheets and surmised that they were fairly liberal. The obvious topicality argument might not fly, because Iowa City would be well prepared.

Sobek proposed they try one of the most controversial cases on the circuit: "The Spark." They would seize on the other team's obligatory nuclear war scenario by arguing that allowing a nuclear war is exactly what should happen, because it'll so horrify the world's survivors we'll be forced to rid ourselves of the nuclear menace once and for all. The argument had been around since the mid-1990s, and it had won the Tournament of Champions in 2002 for Pace Academy of Atlanta. A great many coaches believed, with good reason, that this was a horrible argument to teach to kids. They worried that it encouraged a disregard for human life. But kids loved it, especially boys. It appealed to their video game aesthetics.

Brandon nodded approvingly and slapped five with Sobek. Marcus had his hawk eyes on.

Before the round began, Brandon nonchalantly asked the judges how much their personal beliefs factor into their decisions. A tall skinny guy with glasses shook his head. The man beside him held up his hand, pressing forefinger to thumb to form a zero. "If I judged things on my beliefs, none of the teams I judged this year would have won," he said. "I used to work for the nuclear industry."

Brandon and Sobek looked at each other. "Sweet," Sobek said.

The last judge, a woman who had arrived late, said, "Whatever you throw at me, I'll take. If you argue that Martians will eat us on the moon, I'll go for it if the other team doesn't argue it."

The room was packed. "Who are all these people?" one of the Iowa City kids asked. "Are they here to see you?"

Marcus said they were all from Missouri.

"Yeah," the kid said, smiling. "I know they're not here to see me."

The round began. Iowa City argued that when Canada legalized pot for medical use, it caused tension with the United States and jeopardized the most important trade relationship in the world. If that relationship were to sour, the superpowers would clash.

"What happened last time superpowers clashed?" Marcus asked during cross-x. "Hiroshima?"

"Yes," his opponent answered. "Nuclear bomb."

Marcus began to press harder. "So—"

Brandon interrupted. "No. That's enough."

Brandon started off his speech with a few topicality arguments. Then: "Global extinction is inevitable. We must have a nuclear war."

A few of the Missouri kids in the audience flashed thumbs-up, grinning as if they were at a rock concert and their favorite song had begun. Midway through Brandon's speech, one of the Iowa City guys nodded approvingly at Marcus. The game was on.

For the rest of the round they had it out over whether a clash of the superpowers would mean total global annihilation, or more localized death and destruction. It was an incredibly close round. By the end, I had no idea which way it might go.

While the judges pondered their notes, Marcus and Brandon went out into the hall. They bumped into Ed Williams, their teacher from the pre-tournament camp. He shook Brandon's hand. "Nice to see you among the living."

Marcus told them what they had run. Williams chuckled and shook his head. "Why didn't you just go for T?"

Marcus shrugged, looking suddenly doubtful of their choice.

Williams tapped his forehead. "You gotta think," he said. "I told you I know how to play."

"I gotta go in there," Marcus said. "I'm nervous."

All but one of the judges, the bespectacled slender man, had filled out their ballots. The holdout pored over two large computer printout sheets covered with tiny jottings. At last, he sighed deeply and signed his ballot.

More people had come in to see the decision. Kids were lined up against the walls. Rinehart stood in the corner by the door, clutching her purse tightly to her chest.

The woman collected the ballots, then unfolded them one by one.

A two-one decision for the affirmative, Iowa City.

The former nuclear industry worker had voted for Marcus and Brandon. The man with glasses admitted he had let his morals intercede. "Just think for a moment what you're asking me to do," he said. "I had a hard time with that."

Out in the hall Marcus looked tired but not dejected. It was a good round, one of the best they'd had all year.

Alexander slapped five with Marcus. "Good job," he said. "Now you can only lose one more."

"Yeah," Marcus said, his expression serious. "We don't plan to do that."

SEVEN

TOPICALITY

THE SKIES HAD BEEN GRAY and rainy for most of our week in Atlanta, but the next morning they broke open and the sun brightened the trees and flowers on the Georgia State University campus. We were two weeks into June, but it felt like the last day of school, when the promise of months of summer freedom lifts the spirits of students and teachers alike.

When we arrived at the student center, we spotted a large banner made of butcher paper bearing the names of several dozen debaters hanging from the rafters. Marcus's name was among them, listed under a headline that read, "These CX debaters receive an award after finals."

"What does that mean?" Marcus said, staring up at it.

We parted ways with Rinehart. She'd been assigned to the judging pool, so she had to spend the entire day sequestered in a lecture hall, waiting to be sent to a round. Brandon tracked down a copy of the schedule for the morning round. There were thirty-two teams remaining. Five were from Missouri, and five from Kansas. Marcus and Brandon were scheduled to argue on the affirmative against a pair of girls from South Dakota. They'd stayed up late again the night before, and they moved sluggishly through the crowd on the way to their assigned room.

But they both had the look: jaws set at a determined angle, eyes narrowed fiercely. This was the day. The last two teams standing would go head-to-head the following morning at Ebenezer Baptist Church, in front of a packed sanctuary and a panel of a dozen judges from the debate community and the private sector.

Their first opponents threw a tubful of arguments at them. They argued that Central's plan would cause a backlash from the conservatives on Capitol Hill, which would lead us to nuclear war. They said there was no way the case could end racism. And, above all, the case wasn't topical. It was unfair to debate about race issues. The resolution calls for a "public" policy, the girls argued. Central's case is directed toward blacks. Public is *all* people.

Central won easily on a three-oh decision. Now there were twenty teams remaining. All but one other Missouri team, from the small town of Neosho, had been eliminated in the morning round.

In the bustling hallway we ran into Kerpen, who told us that most of the teams that had argued on the negative in the previous round had won, so he predicted that Central would probably get to go affirmative again. Brandon and Marcus smiled and slapped five. They felt like their case was almost unbeatable.

When the pairings for the next round came out, Central got their wish. They were affirmative, against a team from Alabama.

They moved to their assigned room and were surprised to find the place packed with spectators, most of them debaters from the Missouri schools that had been eliminated in the morning round. This run for the national championship was shaping into a touching finale, the stuff of movies. The entirety of Brandon's and Marcus's debate careers at Central had been marred by conflict with the Missouri debate community, based on a fundamental disagreement over how debates should be judged and on when and where high school kids should be allowed to compete. On the online forum of Cross-X.com, Marcus and, to a lesser degree, Brandon had made the debate personal, attacking their Missouri counterparts as inferior and racist. Yet here they were, kids from all corners of the Show Me State, eagerly awaiting a chance to see the team they'd only heard about in the rumor mill. And they weren't hoping to see the Central braggarts be humiliated. They were pulling for a win.

Brandon promptly started things off, belting out the "End Racism" case.

His sleepiness had burned away, and he was in top form, his syllables crisp as they flowed out at high speed. He finished with a good thirty seconds to spare.

The Alabama team's first speaker, dressed in a dashing navy suit with a royal blue shirt and an impeccable silk tie, got up and laid out a political disadvantage with a counterplan and a handful of topicality arguments. Marcus frowned. He was getting sick of topicality. It was like Debate 101, a remedial argument that only green and eager novices like Ebony Rose could get excited about.

I was getting irritated by these arguments as well, especially the one attacking Central for not offering a public policy, because it was based on a disturbing premise of division between whites and blacks. During the pretournament camp in Peachtree City, when I participated in a practice round against Danielle and Veronica, they'd run the same argument, and I'd raised my voice during my rebuttal speech, declaring the argument deeply offensive. Civil rights, I said, are for all people, and when one group of people is treated unequally, it brings all people down. To suggest that Central's plan is not topical is to deny that disparities exist, to avert a conversation that needs to take place at all levels of policy making, be it in Congress or in the national championships for high school debate. Of course debate demands just this sort of intellectual challenge; debaters are supposed to question everything. But having immersed myself in the game and its community for several years, I came to see that it reveals much about American society and the beliefs it upholds. And what I'd come to believe after a year of watching a pair of black debaters argue for African-Americans to have equal access to mental health care is that our nation's youth are either unprepared or unwilling to talk about race.

The guy on the other team was cocky during his speech and both periods of cross-x, but as Marcus kept piling on cards during the second affirmative constructive speech, the kid's eyes widened, betraying his fear. Marcus destroyed their counterplan with the Todd May card: *Don't dictate the revolution!* All his opponents had left to go for was topicality.

Brandon and Marcus responded by arguing, as I had a week earlier in Peachtree City, that "civil rights" are human rights, and that means all people. But they didn't take it all the way. Sitting in the back of the room, I found myself wishing that Brandon and Marcus had delved deeper into Joseph Barndt's book *Dismantling Racism*. Barndt is a white man, and for much of his book he talks about how racial inequality hurts whites as much as, if not more than, blacks, because it fosters an incomplete existence, where whites are imprisoned in veritable gated communities of their own privilege.

When the round concluded with a vintage, blisteringly fast and clear final speech by Marcus, the others in the room applauded.

The judges took longer to decide than I had expected; from my perspective it looked like a crush for Central.

One by one they signed their ballots and handed them over to the judge sitting in the middle.

He slowly unfolded them and read each one.

"We don't have any suspense," he said mischievously. "They do."

Finally he announced the decision.

Three-oh for the affirmative.

Marcus burst into the hall, singing, "Another one bites the dust!"

"Yeah," Brandon said, trotting confidently at Marcus's side. "That girl's in there crying, saying we ended her debate career. I almost feel bad."

"Whatever," Marcus said. "How can you argue about a three-oh?"

WE BUMPED INTO KERPEN AGAIN. He showed us the pairings with the losers crossed off. There were thirteen teams left. Because of the odd number, Kerpen said, one would get a bye.

"Please let it be us," Marcus said. He read over the list. "Neosho's out?" he said. "So we're the last Missouri team. That settles the score once and for all."

"We're the top-thirteen team in the country, dog," Brandon exclaimed.

They slapped hands, and Brandon let out a full-force yelp.

They were starting to generate some buzz. In addition to the Missouri crowd, other friends from the national circuit approached them in the student center to say they were pulling for Central to win it all. Coaches from

Dowling of West Des Moines and Greenhill School of Dallas offered to share evidence and help them strengthen their case for these final rounds on the way to the big showdown at one of America's most historically significant churches.

The pairings were posted in the student center, and we crowded in to get a peek. Central didn't get the bye, but they were assigned the affirmative once again, which, the way things were going, seemed almost as good. Marcus asked Kerpen to decipher their opponents' code. It was Rosemount from Minnesota, the team they had beaten in October at the Iowa Caucus to win their TOC bid. Marcus and Brandon were thrilled.

ON THE WAY TO THE ROOM where the round would be held, Brandon ran into Veronica. "You gonna win this one?" she asked.

"I don't know," he said. "I don't like to predict the future."

She smiled and nodded enthusiastically.

"I pray," he said. Then he closed his eyes right where he was standing and whispered to himself.

When we got to the classroom, we found an even bigger crowd than there'd been for the previous round. The day was moving into the late-afternoon hours, and the sun angled hotly through the west-facing windows. I claimed one of the few remaining desks, and Veronica took a seat next to me.

"You think they're gonna win it?" she asked.

"I don't know," I said. I was as nervous as I had been at the Caucus. My palms were damp.

"I do," Veronica said matter-of-factly. "I think they've got a really good chance."

I feared that she'd jinxed it. Then I tried to force that thought out of my mind, worried that by merely thinking the word "jinx" I had sparked a jinx. I was so anxious for a win that I was becoming irrational.

Brandon got up and laid it out, his voice as smooth as running water. Matt Little, Rosemount's top dog, countered with an attack nearly identical to the one the kids from Alabama had lost on just a few hours earlier—counterplan, a slew of topicality arguments. And the round quickly took a similar shape, with Marcus and Brandon obliterating the political argument, leaving Rosemount with just their beginning-debate T strategy.

This time, however, the topicality complaint didn't center on notions of what's public. Rosemount was arguing that Central's policy didn't increase mental health care. They insisted that all the affirmative plan did was offer access to mental health treatment facilities. Mental health care, they said, is actual mental health care, as in psychological treatment.

Marcus glowered. This may well have been the stupidest topicality argument he'd heard all year. "Access and mental health care are not exclusive," he countered reasonably in his rebuttal speech. "Look, you have to access the hospital to seek the doctor. You have to have the hospital in your neighborhood to go to it to have access to it. We have proved that per capita that doesn't happen in urban areas."

In addition to being intellectually flawed, the argument was even more offensive to Marcus than the "public" arguments he and Brandon had beaten handily earlier in the day. It drove to the heart of his understanding of racism as it has existed in his lifetime. Segregation was no longer upheld by law, but it remained in fact. The history of slavery and Jim Crow had left blacks by and large on the outside, detached from much of what whites take for granted. Quality health care was but one example. So equality had become a matter of access, not in the theoretical sense of legislation and the principles of administrative procedure, but in the unflinching reality depicted in numbers. The facts of Central's case were, in Marcus's mind, irrefutable: blacks simply don't have the access to mental health care that whites do.

But anger showed in his final speech, and I feared it was getting the best of him. Rosemount had hung their inane argument on the fact that Central hadn't offered an exact dollar figure for their plan. This, they reasoned unreasonably, suggested that the access Central's plan would allow wouldn't actually provide an increase in mental health care. It seemed to me an easy argument to beat, and Brandon had effectively covered it in his brutally slick rebuttal speech.

But I kept waiting for Marcus to say one or two sentences extending Brandon's arguments.

He never did.

"I know this is sounding muddled right now," he said as the final seconds were ticking away, "because I have to go over these redundant arguments."

When he finished, Veronica leaned over and quietly asked me what I thought.

I shook my head. I was worried they might lose.

"I don't think so," she said. "I think they're going to win. I think they're going to win it all."

Again the judges took a very long time to decide. The wait was agonizing. Marcus paced nervously. Brandon sat quietly in a chair and stared at the judges.

The judges signed their ballots.

Two-one, for Rosemount.

Brandon looked stunned. "Bogus," he said under his breath.

Marcus leaned against a wall in the corner.

Sobek approached and patted his shoulder.

"It was a good run," he said. "Just clean up and let's head out."

"Why clean up?" Marcus scoffed. "It's over."

MARCUS AND I DRAGGED OUR FEET toward the student union, where Rinehart was holed up in the judging pool.

"Top twelve at nationals is pretty good," Marcus said unconvincingly. "That speaker award better be good."

He stopped and looked me in the eye. His face was twisted, pained.

"How is access not treatment?!" he asked. He began shouting. "How can you get treatment without access first? It makes no sense! That's just the dumbest fucking thing I've ever heard in my life! My final fucking high school round was lost on something that stupid. Makes no sense."

He turned and began walking toward the student center, scuffing each slow step hard against the pavement.

"They would have never made that decision if they thought about what the responsibility of topicality was," he said, his voice now quiet with deep dismay. "About the best way the revolution is to be debated."

MARCUS WAITED IN THE LOBBY while I went into the room where Rinehart was sequestered. She looked up at me expectantly, then deflated when she saw my sullen expression. She lowered her head and came outside, where she stood beside Marcus, saying nothing. The two didn't even glance at each other. Their eyes were turned toward the floor.

"Buy me some pajamas," Marcus said after the long silence, gesturing toward a souvenir stand on the other side of the student union lobby.

"No," she said, her voice soft and gentle, "because they don't have any big enough. Remember, you told me they had already sold out."

"Who said that?!" he barked.

"You did," she replied. There was a dash of pepper in her words.

"I never talked to you about that," he sneered.

She stared him in the eyes and twisted her face into her trademark look of disdain.

"May I *please* have a pair of pajamas?" he whined, dropping his shoulders into a pathetic droop. "*I really want a pair.*"

"I want you to look at them first," she said sternly. "If they don't fit, they don't fit. It'll be a waste of twenty dollars."

"You need to not look at it as a financial issue," he insisted, bristling at the lamebrain financial argument that had ended his high school debate career. "You need to look at it as a moral issue."

And at that she fished through her purse and pulled out a twenty.

Win or lose, Marcus Leach had to have the last word.

PART FOUR

THE POST-ROUND CRITIQUE

ONE

A SHOOTING

MIDMORNING ON THE DAY after their high school debate careers ended, Marcus and Brandon sat in a pew in Ebenezer Baptist Church, watching the final round of the NFL national championship between two all-white, all-male teams from private schools. Brandon whispered in my ear, "I'm in agony sitting here."

Attendance was not optional. Rinehart even made them wear suits and ties. At round's end, they would be called to the front of the sanctuary to claim their trophy. They wound up taking tenth place, and Marcus was named tenth-place speaker as well.

The sight of the tall silvery statuettes lifted everyone's spirits. Rinehart was beaming. The night before she had locked herself in her room at the Marriott, called her sister, and bawled for an hour into the phone.

At several points during the 2002–2003 season, Rinehart predicted she'd never coach a pair of debaters as good as Marcus and Brandon. She'd never have another chance to take a team to the Tournament of Champions. Never again be in a position to win the NFL national championship.

On the other hand, she never imagined she'd have to endure a worse school year. The Missouri State High School Activities Association's second straight denial of Central's request to compete at the TOC, she figured, was about as bad as it could get.

She was wrong on both counts; things were about to get a lot worse.

Likewise, I assumed that the story would end there, with all of us sitting in the church where Martin Luther King, Jr., began preaching. But in the coming year my relationship with the Central debate squad would evolve, and my understanding of this game, which is so intrinsic to a democratic society, would change dramatically. Indeed, my whole life would change.

THE HIGH POINT AND THE LOW POINT of Rinehart's coaching career came within hours of each other on a Saturday night in early November 2004. At a little after seven, Ebony, now the squad's top senior, and his new partner, junior Geoffery Stone, collected medals for winning the Shawnee Mission East Invitational. It was just the second time Central had taken first place at a tournament in suburban Kansas City, a feat she had, just a few years earlier, deemed impossible.

Then, as she slept at her home in north Kansas City later that night, one of her former debaters, Jason Lumpkin, Marcus's younger brother, was shot a few blocks away from his house. He was instantly paralyzed from the chest down.

While the Central debaters were being ferried back from Johnson County, Kansas, all tuckered out from a full day of debate, Jason was getting ready for a night on the town. At about ten o'clock, he'd headed out with his cousin and a couple of other kids from his neighborhood to the Shoppe, a teen nightclub in a warehouse district between Kansas City and Independence. They closed the place down, hanging out and drinking Cokes until a little after one in the morning. Still restless, they decided to cruise the town for a while.

They stopped for a light by the McDonald's at Van Brunt and Linwood. Suddenly a van slammed into their car, forcing it up on the median, blowing out three of its tires. At almost the same instant, shots rang out, and Jason, who was sitting in the backseat, felt his chest jerk forward. He ducked down and kept low as his cousin rode the rims to safety a block and a half away. When they came to a stop, Jason couldn't move himself out of the car, his legs as lifeless as meat.

When Rinehart heard the news the next day, she was devastated. For nearly a decade, she had managed to insulate herself from the tragedies that happened every year among the student body at Central. But this was one of her kids. This was family. She couldn't help but feel to blame, even though it was a random act of violence. When the shooter turned himself in three days later, he admitted that he'd been smoking wet, a psychosis-inducing mix of PCP and formaldehyde. Yet Rinehart knew that if Jason had stuck with debate, he would have been at the Shawnee Mission East tournament. He would have been too tired to carouse the streets in the early-morning hours.

Jason was one who had slipped away. There'd been a lot of those over the past year. Rinehart's conviction that debate is an effective tool for saving bright urban youths from lives of obscurity was being severely challenged. During the 2002–2003 season Ebony had dozens of fellow novice debaters. Two years later Central's varsity squad had dwindled to just three kids. Antoine, one of the brightest students she'd ever taught, became the first Central debater to not graduate on time. He'd gone to summer school to pick up his missing credits, but he wasn't in college—he was just hanging out at home, staying up until three or four every morning, sleeping in until one or two in the afternoon. Brandon and Marcus, who had enrolled at UMKC with the hope of making a serious run for the college national championship, had both quit the squad. Brandon was the first to pack it in. From the start, he felt that he wasn't a valued member of the squad. When research assignments were handed out at the beginning of the season, he was asked to cut just three cards. "That's it," he told me later, clearly insulted. "It's like they thought I was dumb or lazy or something." Worse, he didn't receive any substantive coaching. He traveled to two tournaments, winning one of them, a junior varsity competition in Georgia, and making it to the trophy rounds at his first varsity tournament, a huge accomplishment for a freshman. At both of these tournaments, though, the coaching staff paid hardly any attention to him and his partner; they were spending most of their time preparing the more experienced members of the team. The same thing happened to Marcus, who later told me that he and his partner ended his first season by advancing to the trophy rounds at the Cross Examination Debate Association national championship with almost no attention from the coaches. The squad's director, Linda Collier, openly stated that her priority was helping the female debaters on the squad become the best. After all the praise Collier had showered on them when she was recruiting them during their senior year, Brandon and Marcus both felt as if they'd been snookered. Marcus was doing well. He'd thrown himself into politics and was preparing to run for student body president. But Brandon had dropped out of college entirely. He was working part-time at a movie theater on the Country Club Plaza and was considering enrolling in the police academy as soon as he'd turn twenty and six months.

And, to make matters worse, I had stepped out of my role as an objective observer chronicling the adventures of Rinehart's squad. I'd become an assistant coach, and with a case I built with Ebony and Geoffery, I was forcing Rinehart to question everything she'd devoted her life to for the previous nine years.

TWO

PEDAGOGY OF THE OPPRESSED

COACHING WAS NEVER IN MY PLANS. But after the 2002–2003 season ended, I began spending more time with the debaters to learn more about their lives, and our friendships deepened. I became especially close with Ebony. He lived near my own home, and we hung out together once or twice a week. He'd often come over to my house to watch movies or surf the Web, or we'd go to the library together. Ebony was always trying to get books that the library didn't own, books by Murray Bookchin, bell hooks, and Foucault. He'd call me up and say that his books were in, and I'd give him a ride downtown, where the books were waiting for him, with an interlibrary loan seal wrapped around their covers. We would talk about the stuff he was reading, and politics and race issues. I'd flip through the books, amazed at their denseness. At first, I honestly doubted that Ebony was truly comprehending them; I had to strain to understand them myself.

One day early in the summer before Ebony's senior year, we were at the main downtown branch of the Kansas City Public Library, just killing time, wandering through the stacks, when a book with a red cover caught Ebony's eye. "That's a book Rinehart read," he said, pointing to it. "About teaching or something. I think she said it helped her teach inner-city kids or something. I dunno."

I pulled the book off the shelf and looked at it. The cover was simple—large white words and black words on a red background. *Pedagogy of the Op-*

pressed, by Paulo Freire. I checked it out, took it home, and read it, hoping to learn a little more about Rinehart and her philosophy about teaching inner-city kids. It turns out, I would later learn, that Ebony was mistaken. He'd confused the red cover with that of another book, a more practical manual for educating kids in poverty that Rinehart had been reading.

I devoured the book in a couple of sittings. It put everything I had experienced as a reporter covering race, education, and power into perspective. Every scenario I had witnessed in the previous four years had an explanation in the book, right down to the individual people—the white attorney for the desegregation case, the black city councilman who worked the system for his own benefit, the black children turning against one another, the way the white leaders would beat back black leaders who got too much power. Freire mentioned no specific races or nationalities, no case studies of oppressive regimes. The subjects were simply "the oppressors" and "the oppressed," and the author's aim was to show how these opposing forces interrelate, how systems of dominance are perpetuated, how they morph to accommodate change while still subjugating masses of people to lives of powerlessness and misery. The book would make as much sense to someone in Kansas City, with its Jim Crow past still very apparent in the social and economic landscape, as in Rwanda, where poor blacks butchered poor blacks.

I ordered my own copy from Amazon.com right away and lent it to Ebony. He gave it back to me a week later, its pages covered with highlighter marks and Post-it notes. His take on the book was completely different from mine. Whereas I read it all from the perspective of politics, he zeroed in on Freire's thoughts about education, which, after all, was the book's primary aim. All Ebony wanted to talk about for the next several weeks was Freire's notion of Western education as a "bank deposit system," in which students are passive vessels who receive information from all-knowing, all-powerful teachers. In such a system, what is to be known is decided from on high and handed down, with all the dominance this hierarchy implies. "The banking concept of education regards men as adaptable, manageable beings," Freire wrote. "The more students work at storing the deposits entrusted to them, the less they develop the critical consciousness which would result from their intervention in the world as transformers of the world. The more completely they accept the passive role imposed on them, the more they tend simply to adapt to the world as it is and the fragmented view of reality deposited in them."

So the students aren't really human, Freire concluded, because being human requires "critical consciousness," which, he argues, must be discovered rather than received. What he meant is that in order to truly empower, education must allow students to be agents in the creation of their own worlds through knowledge and understanding. To accomplish this, Freire proposes education based on dialogue, where reality is named and thereby shaped into something the students might actually occupy. It's the idea that knowledge isn't fixed, but rather always changing, forever altered by those it's shared with and shaped by. "In the theory of dialogical action, subjects meet in cooperation in order to transform the world," Freire wrote. "Dialogue does not impose, does not manipulate, does not domesticate, does not sloganize."

In theory, this is a perfect description of debate. In practice, however, debate had become the opposite of what Freire described. That's how Ebony and I saw it anyway. The game had evolved into a banking system, with its perennial cycle of kids jetting off to camp to come home with file tubs full of ready-made evidence, which they'd read like scripts at scorching speeds, as if they were Pentium processors. It was a tradition of obedience to its own tradition, and, it was plain to see, this tradition separated, with few exceptions, the privileged of the oppressing classes from the less privileged of the oppressed.

That summer, before we had discovered Freire's book, I agreed to work with Ebony during his last debate season, not out of a desire to help him and Central achieve the glory I felt they deserved, but as a natural development in my relationship with Ebony as a friend and mentor. As soon as we read *Pedagogy of the Oppressed*, we decided to write our own case, based on Freire's ideas.

Over the next year Ebony and I (and others on the Central squad, including Rinehart) would read nearly all of Freire's books, as well as a few *about* Freire's books, and Ebony would ultimately deem himself a Freirean. Two years earlier Ebony had sat in a hotel room in West Des Moines and declared, "There's no God." He said, "You can't seek the truth, because the truth has a end. But knowledge has no end. So shouldn't the goal of life be to seek knowledge? You can never stop knowledge." In Freire's writing, Ebony found the faith he'd been looking for. He read *Pedagogy of the Oppressed* many times. On the cover of Freire's book *Pedagogy of Hope*, which I'd bought for the squad, Ebony had taped a note that read, "The Holy Bible of Education according to Paulo Freire." Another book he labeled "The Holy Bible of Liberation." He wrote out quotations from Freire's books and taped them on the wall above his bed. And when he was feeling restless at night, he'd read passages to calm himself to sleep.

THREE

ALL THE WORLD IN A GHETTO

EBONY CAME INTO HIS OWN that summer before his senior year. When I first met him, he was a jittery, spastic kid—his mind filled with grand, amorphous ideas, but without enough words to give them shape. He strutted about with presumed self-importance, but this was just a mask barely hiding a desire for something to be cocky about. By the end of the summer before his senior year, he was a seasoned world traveler, having been to Louisville; Washington, D.C.; Baku, Azerbaijan; and all over China on sojourns to learn and share knowledge about debate.

When the prospect of traveling to Azerbaijan first surfaced, Ebony had recoiled. He was nervous about traveling to Chicago, much less an impoverished nation with no cable TV.

By the time May rolled around, and Rinehart was preparing to leave with her students for eastern Europe, Ebony had done a complete 180—he couldn't wait to venture off to a foreign land.

Give credit to a good old-fashioned teenage crush. When the kids from Azerbaijan had arrived in the fall of his junior year, attending Central for three weeks for the first stage of the exchange, Ebony made fast friends with a girl named Narmina. She introduced him to Russian rock, which he played over and over again on his portable CD player. He and Narmina hung out together nearly every afternoon. Their conversations were never very deep—

her English was a bit shaky, and Ebony's fast, choppy diction is hard to follow even for American ears.

Before she left, Narmina left Ebony half of a broken heart pendant, with a note to give it back to her in person, in Azerbaijan. Ebony was touched, but the responsibility seemed enormous. "I always lose stuff," he told me. He went home and immediately taped the pendant on his wall, and next to it a handwritten note that read, in big, crooked letters, "DON'T FORGET! BRING THIS TO NARMINA—AZERBAIJAN!!"

For a while it looked as though Ebony wouldn't be able to make good on his promise, through no fault of his own. District officials were balking, and Rinehart feared she and the students might not get permission to go. Again, Phyllis Budesheim was in Rinehart's way. She hesitated about signing off on the exchange because the country was at war, which was partly true—there'd been a long-running battle in the southwestern part of the nation, though nowhere near Baku, where the students would be traveling, which is safe by any measure. Rinehart, with her zero clout, was powerless to do anything herself. But then a reporter at *The Kansas City Star* caught wind of the matter and started asking questions, insinuating to district officials that they would have two choices: a positive story about the exchange, or yet another bit of bad press about bureaucratic disregard for kids.

The trip to Azerbaijan marked Ebony's emergence as a man. Before he crossed the ocean, he'd known only in the abstract that he was connected to the world. Azerbaijan was as they said it would be: poorer even than the black side of Kansas City. He stayed with Narmina's family, and their apartment wasn't much bigger than his own bedroom. When he went to Narmina's school, he was appalled. The place was as dark and dingy as a cave, the floors warped, the walls cracked, and the bathrooms primitive and foul. The school's library consisted of just a few small bookshelves, and the kids had to share tattered textbooks published in the 1970s. Narmina clued him in to the country's corruption, which she said infested even the school itself. Worst of all was the pollution Ebony saw in the Caspian Sea. The water was so dark and reeking of oil that he imagined it could be set aflame with a single match. Ebony was astounded to learn that Narmina's father earned just less than $100 a week, even though he had a college degree. Meanwhile, he could see that there *was* money in the oil-rich country. On the hillsides surrounding the capital city of Baku stood the ostentatious mansions of the wealthy few.

Yet Ebony found in Baku a richness he hadn't anticipated. Narmina and her classmates and their cash-poor families were not beaten down the way black folks seemed to be in the United States. Despite the poor facilities, the students applied themselves to school with vigor. And they were happy. He'd never been to such a gleeful, friendly place. Wherever he went, strangers would introduce themselves to him, offering friendship and, in some cases, asking for autographs.

His journey continued through the summer. In June he traveled to Springfield, Missouri, for a student leadership camp at Southwest Missouri State, where he read Locke, Hume, and de Tocqueville and became acquainted with the philosophical foundation of American democracy. At the time, his mother, Tina Marie Harrison, was living in Springfield, in a subsidized apartment complex. She'd attended an intensive drug treatment program there, and she decided to stay in the smaller city so as to avoid the temptations of Kansas City's streets. By my estimates, she wasn't doing very well. She'd remained clean and sober, and she drew a modest income from a restaurant job, but she spent most of her time isolated in a small studio apartment, knitting a gigantic afghan out of red, black, and green yarn. As at the restaurant she'd worked at a year before, she'd covered her walls with inspirational quotations culled from the Bible and various books about spirituality and recovery.

Ebony spent just a couple of hours with his mother during the trip, right at the beginning of the camp. He loved her and cared about her, but he had moved on, having accepted that his chance at a normal mother-son relationship was gone. He was grown now, more cautious of emotional attachments. Though Tina was building the longest period of sobriety she'd had since she'd started drugs more than a decade earlier, Ebony had been disappointed too many times to abandon himself to faith in her.

But he thought of her many times during the weeklong camp, not necessarily her, but the oppression her life represented. His mind began to make connections between his experiences as a child of the ghetto, a debater, and a world traveler, on the one hand, and the theories he was learning at the camp, on the other. And these thoughts grew as he moved on to debate camps at Catholic University in Washington, D.C., and the University of Louisville, and, most of all, when he traveled to China at summer's end with Rinehart and his soon-to-be partner, Geoffery Stone.

WHEN RINEHART LEARNED there would be a debate-training institute in China, she decided she simply had to go. Growing up during the Cold War, she'd never dreamed that such a thing would ever happen. The program called on her and her students to serve as ambassadors for the game, to teach Chinese students how to play. They spent ten days there, traveling from Beijing to Xi'an and finally to Shanghai.

The timing couldn't have been better. The high school debate topic for the coming season was U.S. support of UN peacekeeping missions—international relations. All the travel had made the world seem smaller to Ebony, and for the first time in his debate career he was realizing that the subjects he'd be debating weren't distant abstractions, but real human experiences not much different from his own. He was reading Freire religiously during his travels and beginning to develop a worldview.

At the start of his senior season Ebony and I began building his case around Freire's work. One day, while surfing the Web, I discovered that the Democratic Republic of the Congo had banned hip-hop. I suggested we make a case for a peacekeeping mission based on pedagogical dialogue, using rap as a springboard. He cut all the evidence from *Pedagogy of the Oppressed*, and I pulled bits and pieces from news articles and books about American foreign policy and conflict in the Great Lakes region of Africa. Structurally, it was a standard case, meant to be read fast, with links leading to a host of doomsday scenarios: nuclear war, genocide, dehumanization, and, in one card that Ebony was particularly fond of, human roadkill.

FOUR

BREAKDOWN

OUR FIRST TEST was the Mid-America Cup at Valley High School in West Des Moines. A few hours before we headed north, we met with the Louisville debate squad at a public library branch near Central High. Dr. Warner and his debaters were in town for a tournament in Kansas City, Kansas, and they wanted to meet a few local kids to share their radical, hip-hop-based approach to the game, and, in turn, get motivated for the competition. One of the Louisville debaters gave a speech, and then Warner invited us to ask questions. I did most of the asking. At that point I respected and admired what Louisville was doing with debate, but I still had reservations. I couldn't shake the idea that it was unfair, that by pulling all debates, no matter what topic, back to notions of institutional racism within the debate community itself, they were sapping the game of its fun. But the Louisville squad had switched things up a bit since I'd last seen them. They were now addressing the topic resolution as a metaphor, through which they could relate the problems identified in the resolution back to the debate community.

Warner quickly turned all of my questions back on me, challenging their underlying pretenses so effectively that I was struck dumb. It suddenly all made perfect sense to me, especially after having seen Marcus and Brandon abandon their dreams of dominating the college circuit because they couldn't jibe with the culture of their new, all-white squad. Louisville's arguments about the exclusionary norms of the game, it seemed to me at that moment, were simply true.

We left from the library straight for Iowa. Rinehart was sick and couldn't attend, so I took the kids on my own. At that point there were four debaters on the varsity squad: Ebony and Geoffery, as well as Leodis McCray and Shantel Hair, both juniors. The students were all intrigued by the Louisville presentation—especially Ebony, who, having gone to Warner's camp, was 90 percent sure that he'd be competing with Louisville as a college freshman the following year. But we had no intention of embracing Louisville's radical style. The debaters were all eager to bust out their cases and speed-read with the best of them.

During the early rounds Ebony and Geoffery did fairly well, going two-two the first day. Leodis and Shantel, on the other hand, were having a horrible time. Despite the camps Rinehart had sent her to, and all the hours of afternoon practices, Shantel was still just as uneasy with debate as she'd been during her first tournament two years earlier, when I'd watched her timidly take on Ebony and Antoine at DEBATE–Kansas City's Washington High School workshop. At the Valley tournament she kept freezing up during her speeches and under cross-examination. And as the day progressed, she became more and more withdrawn and discouraged. Finally, after the third round, she had a meltdown. She broke away from Leodis and slowly wandered the desolate halls of the massive school alone. I tracked her down. She was near tears. "I suck at debating," she said.

"That's bullshit," I replied, still fired up from our visit with Louisville the day before. "Anyone can debate. It's just arguing. Do you argue with your parents? With your teachers? With your brother and sisters? It's the same thing."

We sat in the hall and talked for a while. I mentioned the Louisville squad's arguments, pointing out how her reaction to the game was just like what Warner had been saying, that the norms of debate exclude diverse voices. I suggested she try doing what they do. Just go into the round and say how she feels.

"What would I say?" she asked me.

"Talk about what you know," I said. "Tell them what Central's like compared to this school. Tell them how you feel when you come to a beautiful school like this and you know it's for white kids. Tell them how you feel coming to a tournament where all the other debaters are white."

Since she and Leodis would be arguing on the negative for the fourth round, I suggested that they approach it like a kritik and argue that their opponents can't advocate changes for the world until they first address the problems right here in their own community.

Shantel thought it over for a minute. Then she nodded her head.

We tracked down Leodis and proposed the idea to him. He shrugged. "Okay," he said. "I ain't got nothing else to lose."

I offered to help them prepare, but they both said they wanted to go in fresh and just let their emotions flow.

The schedules came out. They were paired up against New Trier, the incredibly wealthy public school on Chicago's North Shore where Rinehart had been offered a job many years earlier.

We went to the assigned room together. Shantel asked the New Trier debaters what case they would run, which is the norm at national-circuit tournaments.

They ignored her.

She asked again. Still no answer.

Finally I asked, a little pissed.

"Liberia," one of the debaters, a boy in a sharp shirt and tie, replied without looking up.

I grinned at Shantel, and I called her and Leodis in for a huddle. I told them Liberia was created by American racists for the sole purpose of shipping blacks back to Africa, that its civil war, and need for a peacekeeping mission, stem largely from the turmoil this stirred more than 150 years ago. "Ask them what right they," I pointed at the two unsuspecting kids from New Trier, "from an elite American school, have to advocate for the people of Liberia."

Shantel smiled for the first time all day.

New Trier's first speaker, a girl named Antonia, got up and sped through her stack of cards. Then Shantel took her place beside her for cross-x.

"Have you talked to anyone from Liberia," she asked, "to find out what they want?"

The girl was taken aback. "No," she said.

"Why not?" Shantel demanded.

"Um." Antonia pondered the question, then replied, "Because they're not educated."

"Not educated!" Shantel exploded. "You're just in high school! Are you educated?!"

"I mean," Antonia stammered. "Like, this is just our plan. Um. I'm not saying they're dumb."

Suddenly Shantel asked, "How many black kids go to your school?"

Antonia's partner looked up from his laptop. "Wait a minute!" he yelled. "What does that have to do with our case?"

"It's a *question*," Shantel said. "I'm just *asking*."

The dynamics in the room had shifted. Shantel was standing straight, more confident than I'd ever seen her. Antonia appeared as though she might start crying. Her partner sat in his chair, mouth agape.

"I have no further questions," Shantel said.

Leodis took his place at the front of the room. "I just want to say that I don't mean to hurt anyone with what I'm about to say," he said. "It's nothing personal. I just have to say it."

He cleared his throat.

"Observation one," he began. "I'm half black. When I'm in the white community, I'm not accepted, because I'm feared."

He stopped for a beat.

"Observation two: I'm half white. Black people don't accept me, because I'm not just like them.

"Observation three: I'm young, so I'm feared by the old.

"Observation four: I'm smart, so I'm feared by my peers."

He kept on like this for several minutes, his speech building in intensity as he started talking about the unfairness of the school system, of the debate community, of the crime in his community.

And then he said, "I'm through. I quit."

And he turned around and walked out of the room.

Antonia and her partner were dumbfounded. The judge started to get up. "Wait," she called to Leodis. "Please stay. Let's talk."

He kept going.

Shantel walked to the front of the room. "Hey," Antonia's partner said. "It's not your turn."

"Shut up!" Antonia yelled at him.

"But—"

"Just shut up." She raised a hand at him.

And Shantel went off about Central, about beautiful Valley High, about how dumb she felt at this tournament, how awkward it was to be one of the only black kids there, about how her father had abandoned her, and how her cousin had died playing on a rusty jungle gym. By the end she was screaming and crying, and she, too, turned around and walked out of the room.

We all sat there for a minute—me, the judge, Antonia, her partner—not sure what to do. I got up to follow Shantel and Leodis. As I was leaving, the judge asked me what they should do. "I don't know," I said. "I guess just talk about it."

When I found Shantel in the hall, she was smiling.

In the distance, we saw Antonia flee the room. She was crying loudly. Shantel ran up to her and gave her a hug. She told us that she, too, had grown up poor, as an orphan who had lived most of her life on the predominantly black and poor South Side of Chicago. Now she was living with foster parents in the prestigious New Trier Township school district, one of the most coveted zip codes in the Midwest. It was like hell, she said. Her fellow students—even her teachers—often put her down because she was overweight and couldn't afford the best clothes. Her privileges were a burden, she said. She'd probably feel more at home at Central. And I kicked myself as I listened to her, for presuming that she was a callous rich kid, for subjecting her to our catharsis. But then, Antonia, Shantel, and I would never have learned anything remotely like the truth about one another if that debate had gone as planned.

Throughout the season I'd bump into Antonia at tournaments now and then, and we'd stop for a minute and chat, never about anything serious. She looked happier and more confident each time I saw her. And she seemed happy and pleased that an adult she'd met just once in the debate community remembered her name and cared enough to ask, "How are you?"

After our little exchanges, I'd sometimes wonder if she was aware that she had played a role in an incident that would alter the course of my life. That was the point of no return for me. All remaining pretenses of my being a detached observer of the debate scene were shattered. I was hooked.

MEANTIME, EBONY AND GEOFFERY were having their own epiphany. During their final round of the day, they got into an intense dispute with their opponents after the other team said that racism didn't matter. Geoffery went off. Afterward, during the post-round critique, the judge suggested they go all out on the racism arguments the way Louisville does: put away the cards; don't speed-read; play some hip-hop.

That night we went back to the motel, scrapped everything, and started from scratch. What began as an experiment to salvage the weekend for a de-moralized girl turned into a mini-revolution in the making. We stayed up past midnight, writing speeches and choosing rap songs to play. The next morning the two teams showed up with a couple of CD players, handwritten speeches, and a few books—Freire's *Pedagogy of the Oppressed*, Munford's *Race and Reparations*, and Barndt's *Dismantling Racism*.

The Central teams crushed the competition. Two of Ebony and Geoffery's opponents burst into tears mid-round. Leodis and Shantel's final-round opponents simply quit after the third speech.

Ebony and Geoffery finished four-two, the same record Marcus and Brandon had earned at the tournament two years earlier, but they didn't break, because their speaker points weren't high enough. Still, we drove home pumped up. Ebony was convinced that if they had broken, they would have won the entire tournament. It was hard to disagree. A fire had been sparked in the squad, and we couldn't imagine it extinguishing anytime soon.

AT SCHOOL THE NEXT DAY we filled Rinehart in on the new game plan. She wanted to hear the speeches, so we had a practice round, Ebony and

Geoffery against Rinehart and me. In the heat of competition Rinehart's hostility to the Louisville style surfaced. She took offense at Ebony and Geoffery's claims that debate is exclusionary, its norms rooted in institutional racism. The argument was like a slap in the face. It suggested that the very thing to which she'd devoted her life for most of a decade was wrong. It didn't help that Geoffery and Ebony were intimidated by her heated attack. Their confidence withered, and their arguments came out muddied, contradictory, flawed.

Rinehart protested in her speeches that Ebony and Geoffery were calling for the ballot because they were black and underprivileged, that they were basically asking for a handout they didn't deserve. She argued that this is even more racist than the norms they were indicting because it suggested that blacks can't beat whites at their own game. That got to Geoffery: *Beat them at their own game.*

But the success at Valley was still fresh in their minds, so the squad headed off for their next tournament, at New Trier, with a couple stereos and a boxful of books instead of their usual half-dozen tubs of evidence.

Things didn't go as well at New Trier as at Valley, though. Ebony and Geoffery lost their first round against Westminster, a $26,000-a-year private Christian school in Atlanta with one of the winningest debate programs in the country. The debate was very contentious.

Under the metaphor of Central's case, opponents such as Westminster were compared to wealthy First World nations—in particular, the United States—which, our evidence showed, used twisted norms to dominate dialogue and policy making in the UN (which we offered as a symbol of the debate community). Third World countries were the perennial losers in this skewed game of world peace. And, like countries such as the Democratic Republic of the Congo and Liberia, black inner-city schools were, by and large, perpetual underdogs on the national circuit.

When Ebony and Geoffery framed the debate this way, characterizing Westminster as, in Freire's words, the "dominant elite," the team—and, more significantly, their coach—got upset, despite the win. The scene was just like a page out of *Pedagogy of the Oppressed*, where Freire observed: "For [the dominant elite], *having more* is an inalienable right, a right acquired through their own 'effort.'" Any concession to those who have less, Freire went on to say, is seen as reverse oppression.

Their coach, Jenny Heidt, was a veritable goddess on the national debate circuit. She had led a different Atlanta private school to victory at the Tournament of Champions in 2002, the year Marcus was first denied permission to attend. Now she was co-coaching Westminster with her husband, David, who divided his time between the high school squad and the one at Emory University, easily one of the top five college programs in the country. Their teams enjoyed almost unparalleled success. During Ebony's senior year the squad would claim nine TOC bids and win several of the biggest, most competitive tournaments in the nation: the Glenbrooks, Harvard, the Southern Bell Forum at Montgomery Bell Academy, and ultimately the TOC itself.

When Heidt learned that another one of her teams would be facing Ebony and Geoffery in round two, she called coaches at Emory University to glean strategies for beating a Louisville-style case. Ironically, she had written an article the year before for *Rostrum*, the National Forensic League's magazine, telling coaches how to beat "performance" arguments such as ours, in which she repeatedly referred to the strategies as "unfair." When Rinehart and I read this essay several months later, we found these complaints about fairness, coming from the coach of a private school with more than $250 million in assets, utterly incomprehensible.

By the end of the second round the Westminster team was reduced to whining over and over again, "Why can't you just be complacent?" The judge gave Central the win. I later learned that this particular judge had long been one of the Heidts' favorites, but after his decision in this round they peppered him with e-mails questioning (tacitly challenging) his decision, never once thinking to contact Rinehart to try to understand Central's arguments, smooth over the conflict, and try to find common ground.

FROM THERE EVERYTHING WENT DOWNHILL at New Trier. Ebony and Geoffery went three-three, falling short of the elimination rounds. And Shantel quit before the end of the first day. Leodis tried to brave it on his own, debating as a maverick. But he, too, quit on the second day when one of his opponents accused him of lying in his speech when he said his father had been murdered. He wanted to punch the kid in the mouth. Instead, he just walked away.

That was more than Jane could take. Throughout the tournament she'd felt an air of icy derision from the other coaches she passed in the hall or saw in the judges' lounge. She detected in their glares a mix of pity and contempt. It was hard to deal with, but if the new strategy was important to the kids, she'd support it. She drew a line, though, when it came to her students being hurt. She simply couldn't allow her kids to put their lives out there and risk being dismissed and cut down by suburban kids.

FIVE

PASSIONATE DETERMINATION

AFTER THE NEW TRIER TOURNAMENT the new strategy appeared to be dead. Ebony and I still believed in it, that with a little tweaking it could take the squad further than we could hope to go arguing the conventional national-circuit way. But Shantel was now off the team, having moved down the hall to Mr. Franson's speech team (where, happily, she'd find some of the success she craved). And Rinehart was all but dead set against the new strategy. So, too, were Geoffery and Leodis.

Geoffery was particularly outspoken in his opposition. He felt, as Rinehart had initially expressed, that the new case was a cheap shot, that he and Ebony were calling for a ballot just because they were black and hard off. To him it seemed unfair to the other team and disrespectful to himself, as if to say he and other black kids can't do what white kids do.

So Ebony and I backed off. We agreed to return to the original "Hip-Hop in the Congo" case. And that, it seemed, was that.

Until Jonathan Kozol came to Central High.

KOZOL'S HIGHLY ACCLAIMED BOOK about the injustices of America's education system *Savage Inequalities* came out about the same time Central's $32 million "Taj Mahal" building opened for students, in 1992. He gave a lecture in Kansas City that year in which he lauded the city's costly initiative to integrate its classrooms. But, he warned, "if these terrific inner-city schools in Kansas City don't succeed in attracting whites, we will learn a very sad lesson about America, and it will suggest a kind of message we don't want to hear."

Now he was onstage in the grandest of the most terrific of those terrific schools, and it had failed miserably. He gave a two-hour lecture about the aborted legacy of *Brown v. Board of Education*, culled from research he'd conducted for his forthcoming book, *The Shame of the Nation: The Restoration of Apartheid Schooling in America.* Toward the end of his talk Kozol asked, "Are any of you familiar with the work of Paulo Freire?" Ebony looked at me, eyes widened, and we raised our hands.

Kozol heralded Freire's theory that education is most effective, most liberating, when it's an act of self-discovery, when students are encouraged to come into their own ideas and thus feel empowered to shape the world. He told us how much he loves to sit in on elementary school classes and hear young children ramble about whatever is on their minds, leaping from subject to subject and experience to experience until, in the end, Kozol said, "they wind up somewhere brilliant and wonderful."

The people in the audience, many of them teachers like Rinehart, were nodding along, saying, "Mm hmm." They seemed as caught up as I was in the suspense of the speech, eager for some sort of resolution, a word on which to hang faith. *Kozol must have hope,* I thought, *otherwise how could he stomach decades of a crusade for better, more equal education?* I'd only been immersed in the mire of urban education for less than five years, and I was nearly lost to a sense of despair. Frankly, were it not for debate, I might well assume the battle lost.

At last Kozol spoke of prospects for change. It wouldn't come, he said, from elected officials, from state and district administrators, or from blue-ribbon panels of appointed dignitaries. The change would have to come from the bottom up—from teachers, parents, and above all students. And specifically, better-off white kids. "It's going to take a sweeping upsurge in moral consciousness from young people in this country," he said. "It's going to take passionate determination from the children of the privileged. Theirs is a tarnished victory. They know they couldn't have won if the game was fair."

Ebony walked out of the theater shaking his head, his mind thoroughly blown.

"That was just proof that we gotta keep doin' what we been doin'," he said, referring to the Louisville-style approach to debate. "We just had it confirmed from a disciple of the man himself: Paulo Freire. It's fate."

BUT GEOFFERY WAS HAVING NO PART OF IT. Nor was Rinehart. Leodis didn't have a partner anymore, so it didn't really matter to him. He just wanted to debate. So Ebony and I sucked up our pride and got back to work on the "Hip-Hop in the Congo" case. The day after the Kozol lecture we had a practice round. While Geoffery sped through the first speech, Ebony sat with his head down, looking depressed. When his turn came, he tried to speed-read his cards, but his tongue kept getting tied up. Midway through he just stopped. "Man," he said. "I don't want to be doing this."

I leaned toward Geoffery, folding my hands on a desktop. "Why can't you just give the other way one more chance?" I said. "It's Ebony's senior year. Next year you can do whatever you want."

Geoffery is a natural-born debater, contrarian and stubborn. Once he's dug in on an opinion or point of view, he's almost impossible to persuade because the more arguments you throw at him, the more motivated he is to oppose.

I shifted in my chair and readjusted my attack.

"Geoffery," I said, "remember what Jonathan Kozol said about the children of the privileged? That's me."

I told him that most of the kids he'd be debating at their next tournament, the Iowa Caucus, which Marcus and Brandon had won two years earlier, were just like me: white kids from nice suburban schools who have no idea they're benefiting from a system that's rigged. And we had an opportunity, I told him, to preach to these kids and, hopefully, spark the sort of "sweeping upsurge" Kozol had called for the night before.

Geoffery was quiet for a minute. I could tell I'd gotten through to him. But we argued for a half hour more, until I promised to buy him two two-liter jugs of Coke and a No. 4 Value Meal at McDonald's.

SIX

CONFLICT, AND CONQUEST

EVERYTHING CLICKED AT THE IOWA CAUCUS. In the week leading up to the tournament, Geoffery worked hard on his speech, which he wrote in rhyme and delivered to the beats of Dr. Dre's "Still Dre." It started with a bit about his school:

> *My school is almost 100 percent black.*
> *Just seventeen out of three thousand kids tested proficient in math.*
> *It's the same in English, social studies, and science.*
> *"Academic deficient" is how we're defined.*
> *The only foreign language we get offered is Spanish.*
> *French or Russian? Teacher said I wouldn't understand it.*
> *Walk in my school, it's like goin' to jail.*
> *Metal detectors guard our academic hell.*
> *Early last month there was a fight at my school.*
> *Two girls hitting each other, tryin' to be cool.*
> *Has your school ever had a fight?*
> *Maybe some teachers break it up, right?*
> *Not at my school.*
> *The state believes all blacks are fools.*
> *At Central they treated us like rioters.*
> *They called in twelve cop cars and a helicopter.*

Then he switched to the topic of the resolution, U.S. support for UN peacekeeping missions:

You want war,
Don't go to Liberia or East Timor.
We're the war-torn foreign nation y'all been lookin' for.
Just come over to the East Side of Kansas City,
Where the crime is thick and gritty.

He talked about how stifling Central High is, and how few opportunities kids have besides debate:

I joined debate to give meaning to my life,
To help my mind escape the pain and strife.
But when I come here, what do I see?
Not many people who look like me.
When I joined the team as a freshman, ninth grade,
There were dozens of novices who came out and played.
But now there's just three varsity Central debaters, yo.
I bet you wonder where did they all go?
Don't say they dropped out, 'cause they still in school,
But they're not in debate 'cause it made 'em feel like fools.
Why?
'Cause they can't relate
To the way y'all debate.
And that's a disgrace.

Then he jumped into the heart of Central's case:

The world is like the public school system, divided and unfair.
The UN is like the debate community, where we can gather and share
New ideas, new voices, new points of view.
In debate, judges hold the power to decide what to do,
Same way the U.S. federal government tells the world what to do.

I know you're asking, "What's this jive he's laying down?"
It's a metaphor to bring the resolution to the ground
Where we're all standing.
HERE!
In this debate round,
Where we have the power to change
The same racism that plagues the UN.

The director of the University of Iowa's debate program watched Ebony and Geoffery's first round and afterward offered them both scholarships on the spot. They won three of their first five rounds, and even when they lost, the judges gave them high speaker points. They were especially impressed with Geoffery's speech. One judge told him it was the best deconstruction of debate he had ever seen.

They went into the sixth, and final, preliminary round in a do-or-die situation; they had to win to advance to out rounds. Their opponents were a pair of young debaters from Montgomery Bell Academy of Nashville.

The MBA debaters were immediately offended by Geoffery's speech.

Their first speaker, Charlie Sharbel, began by saying, dismissively, "This is the Montgomery Bell Academy Project." Then he launched into a scorchingly fast-read speech, spewing tons of text at three hundred words per minute. He repeatedly said that Central was "dumbing down" the game. The words were sometimes hard to follow, but the underlying emotion came across loud and clear. He was angry, shouting. The speech felt violent.

The room was full of spectators, Rinehart and all the novices on Central's squad, me, and the head coach from the University of Iowa and his son, who sat on his knee. The man buried his face in his hands during MBA's speech. Rinehart laid her head on a desk and covered it with her arms. She wanted to stand up and say, "Okay, guys, that's it! Pack your stuff. We're leaving."

When MBA's other debater, Jamie Berk, delivered his speech, I stared at him and shook my head. Later, during his final speech, he said I was oppressing him with cruel judgment. "What about *my* voice?!" he demanded, pounding the podium. "What about *my* voice?!"

Ebony took no preparation time before his final speech. In the closing seconds, he paused, looked at his opponents across the room, and said, quietly but firmly, "And how dare you? How dare you call my personal story dumb?"

I was sitting near the judge during the round, and I could see over his shoulder his ballot and notes. He had stopped flowing midway through MBA's first speech. During one of the heated cross-x periods, he jotted on the ballot, "I am about to make the most controversial decision of my life."

Afterward, I went off on Jamie. "What you're arguing for is white supremacy," I said. He gritted his teeth and shook his head.

I pressed on. "You said in your speech that debate trains us to become future policy makers. Well, if that's true, and you become one, someday you'll have to deal with race issues. And if you don't handle it right, you'll have a whole lot of black anger rise up in your face."

WE WON THE ROUND.

We awaited the awards ceremony in the school's auditorium for what seemed like an eternity. Cedar Rapids Washington's brass band played a couple of songs, and Ebony fidgeted in his chair. He'd never won a speaker award at a national-circuit tournament. He felt he had a good shot at this one, but only eight awards would be handed out, out of a field of more than a hundred debaters.

The tournament director took the stage. First he read through the list of top novices. Central had three speakers in the top ten of that division. Finally the host began counting down the top speakers in the varsity division. After reading off the name of the third-place speaker, he said that the second-place speaker had finished far ahead, a full four points (usually the difference is a half point).

"From Kansas City Central," he said. "Ebony Rose!"

Ebony leaped up from his seat, slapped hands with all of us around him, and moved to the front of the auditorium to retrieve his plaque.

Then the director said, "And in first place, just a half point ahead of his partner, from Kansas City Central, Geoffery Stone!"

A HUGE CROWD GATHERED to watch Central's octofinal round, filling all the chairs in the classroom and spilling onto the floor. Far from pissing everyone off, it seemed, Ebony and Geoffery had energized the scene. They were instantly the talk of the circuit.

They won that round, then their next one the following morning, earning their first Tournament of Champions bid. Rinehart was amazed. During all her struggles to persuade the Missouri State High School Activities Association to allow Marcus, Brandon, and Donnell to go to the prestigious tournaments, she had assumed Central would never have another opportunity, believing those were once-in-a-lifetime teams. In her wildest dreams, she'd never imagined that it would happen again so soon, and that the triumphant team would include Ebony, who, despite his brilliance and hard work, seemed hopelessly handicapped by his speech impediment.

Better still, this year Central would actually be able to go.

During the previous summer the MSHSAA members voted to allow speech and debate teams to compete at one tournament each season that falls outside the travel and time restrictions.

We drove home high as could be, Geoffery especially. He kept talking about ways to improve the case, how to run it better at the next tournament.

"Wait a minute," I said. "I thought this was a one-shot deal. Wasn't that the compromise? A couple two-liters for one tournament? We're going back to the old way of doing things for the next tournament."

He looked at me as if I were insane, and Ebony laughed.

Finally, it seemed, Central was truly on the road to the coveted TOC. We felt invincible, certain we would pick up at least one more bid. If someone had told us then that we would eventually decide not to go to that culminating tournament, we wouldn't have believed them.

SEVEN

THE AGONY OF REFORM

RINEHART COULDN'T FULLY ENJOY the Caucus success. She was in pain. Her joints ached intensely, and mysteriously. During the quarterfinal round in Cedar Rapids, she hurt so badly that she wept. No doctor could tell her what was causing the pain. No remedy seemed to work.

In my mind, it was stress. Things had gotten worse for Jane at school. Every day when I arrived at practice, she would corner me and complain at length about the mandates coming down from on high. The staff development meetings she was forced to go to were maddening. Some central office hack would stand before them for two or three solid hours pointing to T charts about *Sesame Street* lessons such as "cooperation" and "respect." Or, more often, they'd talk about more effective ways to discipline the kids. One of her colleagues, who would suddenly quit, just walk out the door with no notice, a week later, complained, "We can't just keep punishing these kids and expect them to work." Rinehart's bosses in the main office were on her about everything, warning her to strictly adhere to every down-to-the-second detail of the mind-numbing curriculum. On several occasions Principal McClendon seriously challenged her worth as a teacher because she never sent her students to in-school suspension. Rather than interpreting this as evidence of her control over her class, he assumed it meant she was hopelessly laissez-faire.

Rinehart's sole joy at Central, the debate squad, was shriveling to nothing. Most years she'd coached dozens of novices and almost as many on varsity. Now there were just a handful on the beginning squad and three on varsity, not even enough to make up two full teams. At the beginning of the fall semester, she had logged on to the school's database and found thirty-two kids who had tested out of the remedial English classes. She offered to take all of them—an uncommonly huge load—into her debate class. Assistant Principal Phillips flatly refused.

Then Marcus's little brother, Jason, got shot, and she had to convince herself that she was not to blame. I'm sure I wasn't helping by coaching Ebony and Geoffery to strengthen a case that was essentially an indictment of the style of debate Rinehart had taught for the last nine years of her career. I kept raising the issue of retention, how at Central, as at virtually all schools in the Kansas City Urban Debate League, there were far more first-year debaters than those with more experience. The fact was kids tended to quit. And the reason seemed to be, as Geoffery said in his speech, that "they can't relate to the way y'all debate."

Rinehart was torn. On the one hand, she knew we were right. High school debate is an activity skewed toward the elite. In order to succeed, kids need thousands of dollars to attend camp. They must learn to argue in a way that's utterly foreign: at breakneck speed, using enough scholarly material to overwhelm a Ph.D. candidate. And even then, she had to admit, there was only so far they could go. The results of any national-circuit tournament show it, with its out-round pairings full of teams from expensive private schools like Greenhill, Westminster, and MBA. These schools have the kind of institutional clout hers would never have. It was like generational wealth.

But then, one of her driving principles was that poor black children can succeed at an intellectual game dominated by the rich, if they work hard enough and have sufficient support. Marcus and Brandon's incredible run seemed to back this up.

What she seemed to have difficulty grasping, though, was that in many cases these kids didn't want to debate this way.

When I first heard about Jason's shooting, my immediate thought was that he would have stayed on the team if Central had been debating the way Ebony and Geoffery now were. I knew that this approach would appeal to a lot more kids, kids like Jason, though I didn't dare tell Jane this, because I knew it would wound her.

But I wanted to know, so I asked Marcus. We were together when we'd first seen what Louisville was doing with debate, slowing the game down, bringing in voices from the street by way of hip-hop. He didn't hesitate to answer.

"Yes," he said. "That's totally Jason's thing."

Later I spoke with Jason himself. He was recuperating in his mother's house, spending his days camped out on the couch in the living room, watching TV, having regained use of his arms but still paralyzed from the waist down. I asked him if he liked debate, and he said he did, especially the cross-x parts, where he could get into real arguments with other kids. When I asked why he quit, he said there was too much reading of evidence that he didn't fully understand or care about. At best it was boring, at worst, humiliating. Jason had always loved school, but by his teens this was more for social reasons. His friends were there. And when the day ended, he wanted to hang with a different crowd from the one that stuck around Rinehart's room until five. And soon he was doing the sorts of things that so many other Central kids do during their free time, mostly a whole lot of nothing spiced up here and there with cheap thrills like smoking weed, shoplifting, and stealing cars. The latter had landed him in jail for a weekend, and out of Central, to an alternative school called DeLaSalle, where his grades improved. But after school, he was still making poor choices, like riding around after midnight, where a bullet stole the movement and feeling from his legs.

When I told him what we were doing on the Central debate squad, attacking racism head-on and using hip-hop along with the usual academic debate stuff, his face lit up.

"Really?" he said, and nodded approvingly. "I definitely would have liked that."

EIGHT

A CHANGE IN CONSCIOUSNESS

TO ME, JASON'S MISFORTUNE was proof of the need for change in debate, and Central's win at Shawnee Mission East hours before the shooting seemed to indicate that the change was imminent. Ebony, Geoffery, and I began to believe that the case was almost unbeatable, that we would go on to win the Tournament of Champions, and history would remember us as mavericks who had forever revolutionized the game.

Then, the following weekend, we traveled to Chicago for the Glenbrooks, the biggest, most competitive tournament we'd attend all season, and we tanked hard.

Ebony and Geoffery lost their first three rounds on what I thought were terrible, reactionary decisions by the judges. Their opponents were indignant about Central's arguments, at the mere suggestion that debate upholds norms that perpetuate social and economic inequality.

There were encouraging moments, though. After the fourth round the judge told us she'd been profoundly moved by the case. Right before it began, she explained, one of her debaters, a black girl, complained, "What do I have to do to have my voice heard here?" After the sixth round the judge stood up and said it was an experience he would always remember. "It probably changed my life," he said. These judges gave Geoffery and Ebony thirty speaker points each, the maximum amount allowed, and we were pleasantly shocked at the awards ceremony when Geoffery was announced as the fifth-place speaker, out of more than four hundred debaters.

But the tides were turning against us. At the very moment we were riding our chartered bus to Chicago for the Glenbrooks, while we were blissfully unaware, an enormous thread in response to Central's case blossomed on Cross-X.com. Within days it contained 108 postings, many from kids who were enraged by Central's case. I spent a couple of days answering their arguments, until it broke down to a tiresome debate between myself and perhaps three kids who just wanted to spout racially offensive views. A month or so later, the issue popped up again on another forum, which mushroomed to more than eight pages with nearly two hundred posts.

I grew angry amid the backlash. At the Glenbrooks, I yelled "Bullshit!" at one of the judges after he gave his decision, and stormed out of the room. I felt as obsessed and outraged as I had two years earlier, when I was pacing my apartment with a cordless phone, urging local leaders to take on the Missouri State High School Activities Association. And at our next tournament, the Ohio Valley Invitational at the University of Kentucky, site of the Tournament of Champions, I went off again, this time in a way that pushed my ethical boundaries as a journalist and fledgling debate coach.

It was the sixth, and final, round. Ebony and Geoffery were sitting on a three-two record; a win would send them into the elimination rounds, a loss meant an early drive home. Arguing on the negative, their opponents, a pair of girls from Celebration, Florida, countered Central's case with a kritik, saying that by mentioning violence in his speech (a fight in his school cafeteria, school buses in Kansas City that had been shot at, war), Geoffery had ruined any chance of creating peace. For the rest of the round, though, the girls sprinkled their speeches with violent images as well. At one point, one of them even went so far as to lightly slap her partner to show what violence looks like. Geoffery and Ebony, on the other hand, refrained from doing so.

Geoffery began his first rebuttal by saying, "Peter Piper picked a peck of pickled peppers, a peck of pickled peppers Peter Piper picked, what's the value of a thirteen-minute speech that didn't say shit?" He went on to explain this admittedly cocky and tough comment by saying that the other team's arguments were irrelevant because they failed to address and provide an alternative solution to the fundamental problems identified in Central's case.

For their final speech the opponents' second speaker said, "And saying 'shit' is violence." That was all she said about the cuss word.

Ebony got up for the last speech of the round and addressed all the other team's arguments, including the one about the "shit" comment, and reiterated, as Geoffery had during his speech, "They've said violent words this whole round. Stabbing. Genocide. They even hit each other."

The round ended, the debaters shook hands, and the judge studied his notes. I was sitting in the back of the room with Daryl Burch. He was now an assistant coach at the University of Louisville, and he'd traveled with us to Lexington to help coach. He had encouraged Geoffery to begin his speech with the "shit" comment, and I agreed it would be a wise strategy because I knew, as Burch did, that this particular judge was a notoriously aggressive debater in college.

He signed the ballot and said the round was very interesting because it made him think of things he does in debate that might keep minorities from participating in the game. Then he voted Central down because, he said, the worst instance of rhetorical violence in the round was when Geoffery said "shit."

Burch moved to the front of the room and started laying into the judge, all in debate jargon. Back and forth they went. I tried to cut in, but they ignored me.

Finally I shouted, "Here's what I saw. All round both teams use violent terms. But then a black man stands up and says 'shit' . . ."

The judge instantly recoiled. And I shot up out of my seat and started pacing the room, just going off about society's image of black men as violent, as mythic rapists of white women. Both Ebony and Geoffery watched me, nodding, as if I said exactly what was on their minds.

I stepped right up to the judge. "I just want to plant a seed in your mind," I said to him, my eyes open wide. I raised my hand toward him, my fingers pinched, as if I actually had a seed to bury in his brain. "I just want to plant a seed, and you can sleep on it, and in a few days you'll understand."

For the "understand" part, I splayed out my hands, making a gesture of a tree of understanding sprouting out of his noggin.

Burch cut back into the dispute, and he and the judge were having it out again, all in debatese, completely ignoring me.

I kicked myself for having come across too strong at the outset. I stepped back into the conversation and tried to recast my comments.

"I know you think I'm saying you're racist," I said.

The judge scoffed and looked away.

"I'm not," I continued. "I just want you to understand the bigger picture that's playing out here."

He shot me a condescending glance and looked away. "I think you're oversimplifying it," he said.

He would listen to nothing more I had to say.

I WAS STILL AWAKE AT 3:00 A.M., lying in bed at the Red Roof Inn just off the highway in north Lexington, furious. I kept thinking, *How dare he suggest that I had oversimplified the decision!* I knew I was right, that the judge had seized on an age-old racist construct, however subconsciously, that black men are a violent threat, especially to white women. I'd seen the world from both sides, as a white who, like the judge, knows few blacks, and then as one who has lived and traveled with African-Americans and now sees the shadows of racism at every turn. I knew that Geoffery, Ebony, and Burch had all seen the judge's decision exactly the same way, and they had confirmed this at the hotel after the round, where we stayed up late eating pizza, joking around, and nursing our wounds.

It hadn't fully dawned on me yet as I was lying there, stewing in resentment, but I had changed immensely over the weekend. My consciousness had shifted. For the first time in my life I was aware of my race with the same intensity that many black people are.

We had spent some time with the Louisville squad on our way to Lexington, during which Burch squared off against Ebony and Geoffery in a practice round while the Louisville debaters observed. Afterward, Dr. Ede Warner had given Geoffery and Ebony a pretournament prep speech. Midway through, he pointed at me and said, "Y'all need to be telling his story! 'Cause I remember when this cat first started coming around, he thought the traditional norms of debate are the best. That they're *not* exclusionary. What made him change? You need to find that out, and say it in the round."

The next day I had awakened at 6:30 with my mind going full sprint. The night before, Burch had told us that Ebony and Geoffery would need to break some of their speeches out into more traditional evidence cards that judges can read after the round. Central would need to ease more gently into what Louisville was doing, he explained, because the high school community probably wasn't quite ready for the change.

I woke up with one thought: *Arbenz*.

Our smoking-gun evidence was a study Casey Arbenz had written for a master's degree at Cal State Fullerton. Arbenz used data from a year's worth of high school debate tournaments in California to show that nonwhite high school debaters, both rich and poor, lose significantly more often and get lower speaker points than rich or poor white high school debaters do. All season long, this evidence had gone unrefuted. Ebony and Geoffery's opponents simply ignored it, and, too often, judges would ignore it as well.

While Burch slept at the Red Roof Inn, Ebony, Geoffery, and I went to a Kinko's downtown to break the Arbenz evidence down to a couple of cards. Looking out the window, Ebony Rose noticed that we were on a street called Rose. We all laughed. Funny coincidence.

As we turned out of the parking lot, we noticed that the next street, one block over from Rose, was called Stone—Geoffery's last name. We began hooting that it was a sign of fate. Tupac's "Changes" was cranked on the stereo. Later we noticed that those two streets intersected—at Kentucky's campus, site of not only our tournament for that weekend but of the ultimate prize, the TOC—a street called Avenue of Champions. Then, in quick succession, we saw a store called Miller's Fine Arts and then a street called Central.

It was just too much all at once to brush off as synchronicity. I felt as though God was telling us that we were going to have a big tournament. I started pounding the steering wheel and shouting like a madman. When Tupac said, "We need to change the way we think," I added, "We need to change the way we debate!"

Then we abruptly got caught in a traffic jam. There was a parade in Lexington that morning.

I found an opening, ducked onto a side street, and got stuck again. Really stuck. Five minutes passed and we hadn't moved at all. Then ten. All of the cars around us were full of white people, and they looked as irritated as I was.

The line moved just enough so I could ease my wheels up onto a sidewalk and squeeze out onto another side street. We zigged and zagged our way past the big, older houses with lush, manicured lawns. Then we crossed a busy street and wound up in a poor neighborhood, near the rail yards, flanked by grimy industry. All the houses were small. Some had peeling paint.

I spotted a kid on a bike, who happened to be black, and pulled up beside him. I leaned out my window and asked, "How the hell do we get out of here?"

He told us he knew how, but he couldn't explain. He knew the names of the first few streets I'd have to turn on, but his memory grew fuzzy the further his imagination took him from his neighborhood.

We ventured off in the direction he suggested, which initially took us farther from our destination, the motel where Burch slept.

I turned to Ebony and said, "God is talking to me."

"Okay, Joe," he said, dubiously.

We drove out of the city and into the suburbs. I ran out of street names the kid had given me. We were on our own. Tupac was now rapping about how there are different hos everywhere he goes. We were passing strip malls with no character. It reminded me of the place where I grew up, a community-less community of convenience stores and cul-de-sacs.

I told Ebony I wanted to hear Dr. Dre. As he pulled out the CD and slid it into the deck, I noticed two black men walking a hundred yards apart along the side of the road. It was a busy four-lane street, not quite a highway, and there was no sidewalk for them to walk on. To their right was a lush country club golf course behind a high fence. The men were bundled up against the cold. They looked vulnerable in this suburban environment so inhospitable to exposed humans.

"Where are we going?" Ebony asked.

"I'm looking for a sign that says Louisville," I replied.

"We're going back to Louisville?!"

"No."

"Oh, okay, I get it," he said. "You still on your God thing."

Just then "Still Dre" came on the stereo, the song Geoffery used as a backbeat for his 1AC. I cranked it so loud that my pant legs vibrated. I loved that song. I used to play it when I was on a hot investigative story at *The Pitch*, when I had the goods on some crony who was playing patronage games, or had just gotten this or that report showing irrefutably that all was not as rosy as the city's leaders claimed, and I knew that soon my name would be on the top of a story thousands of people would read and talk about and even act upon. The song's message is simple: *Fuck you! I'm in charge!*

A few seconds into the song I saw the sign for Louisville. In an instant we were sailing down the highway, minutes away from the motel.

When we returned, I asked Daryl if he believed that God speaks to us through signs. He said he did. I told him the story and my interpretation of it, and he asked me why God would speak to the white man in this instance.

That's when it struck me, as if for the first time in my life: *I'm white.*

Of course I knew I was white, but only superficially. Until this moment I'd seen racism as a force that these kids, the subjects of my journalism project (and later beneficiaries of my activism), suffered through. It was an evil borne, by and large, on an unjust history for which I wasn't responsible, though I felt compelled to confront it. As I got to know these students and their families, I became more and more outraged at the injustices they faced, and I cast myself in the role of savior. But I'd never considered that this is a racist notion in its own right. It assumes a certain superiority, a belief that I, as a middle-class white man, am the standard for liberation.

Daryl had asked, "Why would God speak to the white man?"

The answer was in the details of the message. We'd gotten trapped in a traffic jam full of white people, and later lost in the suburbs. And it was a black kid and a sign for Louisville (with all its black-debate-revolution connotations) that helped us find our way. My message from God, really just a series of mundane events and circumstances adding up in my mind to something meaningful, was a story of liberation. But it was the white guy being led to freedom by blacks, not the other way around.

Here was a lesson I'd heard several times before but that had never sunk in: the victims of racism are diverse. All during the 2002–2003 season Brandon and Marcus had preached the words of Joseph Barndt, a white man, about how the prison of institutional racism can be destroyed. But they'd skipped over the best part of his book *Dismantling Racism*. Barndt's choice of the word "prison" was no mere metaphor. The prison has substance, he insisted; we call it the ghetto. But the ghetto extends beyond the black side of town, Barndt explained, with its cracked sidewalks and high unemployment rates; the apparently pristine suburbs are the ghetto as well, the lives of their inhabitants every bit as deprived.

"To study racism is to study walls," Barndt wrote. "The prison of racism confines us all, people of color and white people alike. It shackles the victimizer as well as the victim."

NINE

DOWN WITH THE REVOLUTION

OHIO VALLEY WAS A THREE-DAY TOURNAMENT, and we were gone for six. As I had done for the Mid-America Cup in Iowa, I'd taken the guys without Rinehart. I'd planned it as a four-day weekend. But I hardly slept the whole time because I was so keyed up, first with ideas about Central's case, then with rage over the sixth round's decision and the judge's disregard of my point of view. On the drive home I got light-headed and dizzy, so I pulled off the highway just east of the Missouri border to check into a motel at three in the afternoon. Tired as I was, my mind was still racing, and I wound up buying over-the-counter sleeping pills to conk myself out. At one point during the weekend I'd overheard another coach in the hall between rounds joking about how addictive debate is. "It's like crack," he said. I'd have found it funny if it weren't so true. I'd been a coach for less than five months, and I was already hopelessly hooked and totally strung out.

I had to ask myself, who was all this for? Was I losing sleep and driving myself crazy for the sake of Ebony, Geoffery, Leodis, and however many more kids might follow? Or was it for my own edification, my own need for power, however tinhorn it may be? Debate is the ultimate role-playing game because it's so real and unreal at the same time. By crafting a debate case, one can recast the world in whatever way one wants. It's seductive, a seemingly perfect forum for ideologues like me. In many ways, the guys on the team were not so much students as agents for my own radical scheme. Never mind that it wasn't even me standing up there speaking to the judge, or that a victory at the end of the round would only resonate in a tiny, tiny subculture of the world's sole remaining superpower, and then only until the next round. This was democracy in its purest form, I had deceived myself into believing. Like crack, indeed.

I suppose I could have taken comfort in knowing I wasn't alone in my insanity. Other grown men and women were similarly addicted, though arguably chasing a different high. As I drove us to Kansas City on that rainy Tuesday morning after the Kentucky tournament, I thought back to the argument after Ebony and Geoffery's final round. While Burch and the judge yelled at each other, and I jumped in here and there to try to plant my "seed" of race consciousness in the judge's mind, the debaters just stood there, not sure what to do. They were aware that these adults were fighting over them—in fact, one of the Celebration girls burst into tears during the most heated moment of the exchange—but they also knew that it wasn't their place to step in and intercede. The kids were like pawns in a peculiar grown-up game, robots we'd tinkered with in our spare time for yet another showdown among obsessed hobbyists. I'd witnessed the same scene many times before during my travels through high school debate, though rarely one quite so intense.

Yet Ebony and Geoffery were very much down with my cause—*our* cause. This case, this new approach to debate, had inspired them like nothing they'd ever experienced, certainly more than school or any sermon they'd heard in church. The change in Geoffery seemed the most pronounced. At the start of the season he was a debater very much in the spirit of Marcus and Brandon: *Just give me the cards and tell me where to read.* The stuff of the arguments didn't necessarily matter. This was a game, and all he wanted was to win. But now the game mattered to him. He wasn't much of a reader when I first started helping coach the squad. Now he was devouring books almost as hungrily as Ebony and I. The words were no longer abstract pieces on a game board; they were true. When he read, for instance, in *Pedagogy of the Oppressed* or in William V. Spanos's *End of Education*, that education is political, he sincerely believed that he was a political agent, that he had the power to create change, no matter how small.

After we were introduced to Spanos's work, in a round we had lost, I sent an e-mail to the SUNY Binghamton professor. We'd heard through the debate grapevine that Spanos was aware that the debate community had appropriated his work, and that he wasn't pleased. He wrote back immediately:

> I am very much aware that the arrogant neocons who now saturate the government of the Bush administration—judges, pentagon planners, state department officials, etc.—learned their "disinterested" argumentative skills in the high school and college debate societies and that, accordingly, they have become masters at disarming the just causes of the oppressed. This kind of leadership will reproduce itself (along with the invisible oppression it perpetrates) as long as the training ground and the debate protocols from which it emerges remains intact. A revolution in the debate world must occur.

And we were going to be the ones to bring it about.

WHILE WE FANCIED OURSELVES REVOLUTIONARIES, though, Rinehart was getting pissed off. She wasn't at all pleased with my keeping Ebony and Geoffery out of school for so many days during our mission run to Kentucky, especially since we came home with not so much as a puny medal to show for it. She'd been uneasy about the change of direction since the beginning.

The following weekend she took the squad to the Dowling tournament in West Des Moines, her sentimental favorite, and, after the first couple of rounds, came close to putting an end to our whole strategy.

In her mind, winning was still what mattered most in debate, no matter how true the arguments seemed to be. And it was agonizing for her to watch her students lose the first couple of rounds to what she believed to be grossly inferior teams. Part of this was her own fault. She'd switched things up for the tournament, to give Leodis a chance to compete, by pairing Leodis with Geoffery, and bringing in a kid named Brandon Davis from her nephew's school, suburban Oak Park, to team up with Ebony. Naturally, the debaters struggled at first to work out their rhythms. But her initial discomfort with the arguments was rising to the surface. It wasn't just the playing of hip-hop that irked her—though she thought playing music was cheap and lazy in a game of persuasive rhetoric and, truth be told, she never much cared for rap to begin with. What bothered her most was the high level of confrontation, all the stark declarations about racist norms. She felt sorry for Central's opponents. These were kids who just wanted to play a game and learn a little bit about logic, civics, and the ramifications of policy decisions. Was it fair to put them on the spot for things they arguably had no control over? Was it their fault they were born white and well-to-do?

The fact that her kids were making these sweeping allegations about debate at Dowling made her all the more uncomfortable. This was, after all, the tournament that had literally saved her program several years earlier. The school's debate director, Tim Sheaff, was one of the friendliest and most accommodating coaches she'd met in the community. And for years she had been operating under the belief that, although not perfect, the style of debate practiced at Dowling and other national tournaments was the most race-neutral in the land. It seemed hypocritical and mean-spirited to be indicting it in the very venue where she and her squad first discovered they could succeed.

She called me at home, returning several messages I'd left on her voice mail earlier that day, flustered and distraught. She wouldn't come out and say it, but I could tell she wanted to scrap the whole game plan and go back to the old way. "Things have gotten out of hand," she told me. "We really need to rein you in."

Yes, this had to do with the case I'd pushed for, but she was more troubled by my self-assigned duties as a preacher. She didn't like my long posts on Cross-X.com. Worse, she was disturbed that I'd sent a terse e-mail to the judge of our sixth round in Kentucky, apologizing insincerely for the way I'd blown up at him and then going off about how I'd felt excluded from the debate community by his dismissal of my comments, arrogantly laying out my credentials as an award-winning journalist who'd been immersed in the debate and black communities for years. In a hardball move, which I now regret deeply, I CC'd my missive to the judge's bosses, the debate directors at a prominent high school and college. The high school coach responded immediately, castigating my aggressive pompousness and threatening to contact her school's lawyers if I dared cast her school in a negative light. On the one hand, Rinehart didn't much care what the coach thought. Aside from offering one friendly comment years earlier after Central had upset a top-ranked team, this coach had never given Rinehart the time of day. But she was a big shot in the debate community, co-director of one of the biggest tournaments in the nation, and she often ran the tab rooms at other big competitions. She was in the in crowd, and no doubt my loose-cannon ways would be circulating in the rumor mill, sullying Central's rep and potentially harming Rinehart's kids.

As for the case, we put off deciding that matter until after the tournament. Rinehart told me she hadn't shared any of her misgivings with the debaters. She said she would suppress her concerns and try her best just to coach.

Then, late the next afternoon, I got another call from her. She was ecstatic. Ebony and Brandon had won four straight and were advancing to the trophy rounds. Throughout the evening I kept getting more updates, each better than the last. They won octos. And then quarters. And with that, another TOC bid.

They lost the next morning in semis. But that was the best any of Rinehart's teams had ever done at Dowling, the most meaningful tournament to her.

She never said another word about scrapping the new approach.

The game was still on.

TEN

REFRAMING THE DEBATE

A COUPLE OF WEEKS LATER I was watching TV at home, flipping through the stations, when I caught a seminar about grassroots political movements on C-SPAN. The speaker was Peter Loge, a director of the Campaign for Criminal Justice Reform, and he was talking about how to frame public debates on controversial issues so as to bring about policy changes that might ordinarily be unpopular. Loge offered the death penalty as an example. He pointed out that public opinion on capital punishment has been historically consistent, with roughly two-thirds of the population in support of it. Yet in recent years, numerous state legislatures have decided to stop executing prisoners. The reason, Loge explained, is that the debate had been reframed to appeal to a deeper sense of justice, that, while most Americans agree that killers deserve to be executed, more believe that everyone deserves a fair shot and innocent people should never be put to death. In Illinois a group of journalism students had discovered that seventeen prisoners on death row were actually innocent, a finding so shocking that the state's Republican governor, George Ryan, who as a legislator had voted to reinstate the death penalty in 1977, pushed for a moratorium on executions.

I immediately called Ebony and Rinehart and told them to turn on their TVs. Afterward, Ebony and I talked about it, and we realized that we could apply Loge's lesson to Central's case, which we had begun to refer to as "our mission." At our next practice we gathered as a squad to figure out what we had in common with the rest of the debate community, which goals in our mission intersected with those of our competitors and, more important, the judges of our rounds. And the answer was simple, obvious: We all loved debate. We wanted the game to grow and to thrive.

We reworked the case, and I sought to transform myself from preacher to diplomat. The results were mixed. We came away from our final national-circuit tournament of the season, in the North Shore suburbs of Chicago, demoralized. Our teams—Ebony and Geoffery, and Leodis and Brandon Davis—went three-three and failed to advance to the trophy rounds. But worse than the losses were the attitudes of our competitors, nearly all of whom seemed indignant about our arguments and stubbornly devoted to the style of debate and the kinds of arguments we were criticizing. All but one of the teams refused to move an inch toward common ground. They all ran the same generic arguments against our case, and we left feeling as though we hadn't learned anything other than that we had no desire to return to Chicago, nor to compete at the Tournament of Champions. We decided instead to reshape our own notions of success. In the future we would compete only at tournaments where our opponents at least respected our arguments, listened to them, and tried to challenge them in creative, thoughtful ways. This had happened at the Iowa tournaments we'd attended, as well as in Kansas and Nebraska.

On the flight back to Kansas City, we schemed ways to break out of the traditional debate box in which winning at tournaments is the ultimate goal. The ideas poured out. The possibilities seemed endless. We could go to the American Bar Association's convention and challenge attorneys to public debates. Or we could do the same thing in Kansas City, inviting local leaders to debate us on policy issues affecting our community. We could get involved in a real policy debate, such as one surrounding a piece of legislation making its way through the statehouse in Jefferson City. We could reach out to debaters at private and suburban public schools to have exchange programs, stage public debates, or work together to build cases that address America's racial inequities, which are mirrored in the school system and the debate community.

This last idea was already becoming reality. In my earliest foray into debate diplomacy, I'd contacted coaches at a couple of the schools Ebony and Geoffery had contentious rounds against, Montgomery Bell Academy and Westminster, to offer an olive branch and to spark a dialogue in hopes of finding common ground. Westminster's coach, Jenny Heidt, politely declined, saying simply that her school's method of debate was "best" and that any suggestion otherwise was an "attack." She said she didn't like what teams like Louisville were doing to the college game and didn't want to see these arguments spread to high schools. The coaches at MBA, on the other hand, Michael Risen and Alan Coverstone, were sincerely interested in understanding where we at Central were coming from, and finding ways for programs like ours and theirs to coexist.

Both Risen and Coverstone were disturbed by the lack of diversity in the debate community, as well as by the overall declining population. As we exchanged e-mails, we discovered that we shared many of the same beliefs about debate and its importance not only as an educational tool but as an essential component of a democratic society. In the late 1980s, Coverstone had written an influential essay about debate's role in developing future leaders, in response to another landmark paper written by Gordon Mitchell, director of debate for the University of Pittsburgh, in which Mitchell had seized on the notion of debaters as agents for political and social change. Mitchell suggested that debaters stretch beyond debate into real-world activism, which we were beginning to do at Central. Coverstone agreed with the idea that high school and college debaters can be agents of change, but he thought it important that debate be detached from actual activism so it may remain a laboratory for ideas. By moving into real policy making, Coverstone warned, the game could be co-opted by overzealous ideologues or it could suffer backlash from people in power. At several points during the season, Central's opponents had used parts of Coverstone's essay to argue against our case, which frustrated Coverstone because his essay really had nothing to do with the arguments Ebony and Geoffery were making.

Initially, my goal was to explain Central's arguments to Coverstone and Risen, but I soon found myself trying to persuade them to use the clout of

MBA's program to advance our cause. I challenged them to join our mission by running a case similar to ours the following season. I suspected the chances of this happening were slim, but I poured it on nonetheless.

In early January 2005 I traveled with the Central squad to MBA's tournament. A few weeks before the trip Jamie, the MBA debater who had been most riled by Ebony and Geoffery's case, had sent Geoffery an e-mail apologizing for how nasty the round at the Iowa Caucus had gotten, and offering to "look out" for us at his school's tournament. Geoffery, Ebony, and Leodis wound up having a good time hanging out with Jamie and other MBA debaters at the tournament, and I had a friendly conversation with Coverstone during a downtime between rounds. Still, I couldn't help feeling a little depressed on MBA's campus. I judged one round, and while the debaters prepared for their final speeches, I glanced through a stack of term papers sitting on the teacher's desk in the room where the round was being held. They were well crafted and full of thoughtful comments scrawled throughout in red ink by the teacher. I recalled a moment earlier in the year when I had worked with Ebony on a paper he was writing for a class. His grammar was atrocious, so I sat beside him and went through with a red pen marking it up as he watched, explaining in detail each of the changes I proposed he make. He quickly caught on, and afterward he told me, "No one has ever done that for me." Now, months later, reading these papers by MBA students, I felt sad and angry. Why does a student need to attend a $16,000-per-year private school, I wondered, in order to learn to write well?

While we were waiting to leave Nashville, I suddenly had the idea that it would be cool to invite Jamie and another MBA debater to visit Central High. They could attend school for a day, to see firsthand the inequality Ebony and Geoffery were addressing with their case, and we could stage a public debate (and, of course, have fun hanging out together). As soon as I got home, I sent Coverstone an e-mail invitation. He immediately accepted, and returned the favor by inviting us to come out to Nashville for a day at MBA.

"Ironically," he replied, "when we worked on our strategy against your affirmative, I suggested a whole host of other things to do (besides voting aff, obviously, :)) that could foster friendship between our students, exchange of ideas and experiences, and promotion of the broader goals we both share. One item on the list of ideas I came up with was to go to KCC for a day of classes and a public or practice debate. While I was serious that we offer this and other ideas, I now feel ashamed that we just held it back for our competitive benefit."

A couple months later Risen arrived with Jamie and his teammate Parkes Brittain. The students attended Central for a day, and Jamie was profoundly moved. He later wrote an essay about the experience, which he posted on Cross-X.com and its college equivalent, eDebate. He was shocked to see that the students in college algebra were working on problems he'd grappled with in seventh grade, and that in English, Geoffery and his classmates were coloring, and that students' grades were determined almost entirely by, as he explained in his essay, "'participation points,' earned not by merit or hard work, but rather by getting up in front of the class and reading the poem that had been assigned the night before. The participation points weren't going to get these kids out of the ghetto, and they knew it. They were a step ahead of their teacher in that regard, but they were resigned to the fact that this was their life and their future.

"I realized that something was drastically wrong here," his essay continued, "and that debate was the only outlet for these guys. For the first time, I saw where Geoffery and Ebony were coming from—they had their backs pressed to the wall, but they weren't going to take it like everyone else. They were going to fight it."

While the kids were at school, I gave Risen a tour of Kansas City, and we talked a lot about debate. To my surprise, he was almost completely on board with my idea of MBA joining Central's mission and running a case like ours. For the public debate round later that afternoon, Risen and his students had written a case based on an analogy, where they offered a plan for the United States to support a cease-fire between Israelis and Palestinians the same way the judges should support a cease-fire between MBA and Central by affirming the very exchange program they were participating in. Incredibly, Risen told me he wanted his squad to run this case at the Tournament of Champions later that spring.

He wanted to do this for two reasons. For one, he thought it would be the best way for MBA to use its clout to support the arguments we were making. Five teams on his squad had qualified for the TOC, and his goal was for all of them to clear to the elimination rounds, at which point they would break out the new case. These rounds have a very high profile, he explained, and the winning arguments typically become the talk of the debate community during the summer, when most kids who compete on the national circuit are at camp. This, he said, is where the norms of debate are created. The other reason was because he wanted to win: he figured that no one would expect MBA to pull out a Central-style case and they'd crush the competition.

He admitted it would be a hard sell for his squad. When he suggested the idea to his students a few days before coming out to Kansas City, some were opposed to the idea—especially Jamie, who had gotten into a heated argument with Risen over it. "It might not happen this year," he said. "But it will. This is where I eventually want to take things."

A few weeks later Jane and I traveled with Ebony, Geoffery, and Leodis to Nashville. Going in, I honestly didn't expect to get anything out of the experience personally. I'd been to MBA's campus several times before, and I assumed I had it all figured out: it's a phenomenal school, where all the students are male and most of them are white. But I felt acute culture shock the instant I arrived. It was a bit like how I'd felt when I first visited Central High several years earlier; at that point I'd never been around so many black people in one place at one time. MBA, of course, was the opposite, and at first it deeply disturbed me. I kept thinking of what Rinehart often says about schools, that their purpose is to mold children into their parents, to inherit their places in society. At Central it had become obvious that the kids were being shaped into servants, soldiers, and prisoners. At MBA I saw the flip side—an all-male, almost all-white crop of future leaders and inheritors of our nation's wealth.

But then something incredible happened. Risen and Coverstone had arranged for Geoffery to deliver his speech to the entire MBA student body. Mid-morning on the day of our visit, seven hundred students filed into the school's auditorium, and Geoffery was handed a microphone. They'd rigged it so Dr. Dre's beat would boom over the PA system, and the MBA kids sat politely in their button-down shirts and ties while Geoffery belted out his message about segregated schools.

I'd heard Geoffery's speech so many times this year that it had become somewhat mundane. But at MBA, with Geoffery facing so many peers raised amid such different circumstances, the speech seemed to regain its power:

> *You know we got the achievement gap*
> *Where blacks score lower on tests, that's a slap.*
> *These kids weren't born dumb, don't you dare say so.*
> *It's 'cause the schools are messed up that their scores are so low.*
> *And there's something else I want you to know:*
> *The longer blacks stay in the system, the further down they go.*

Geoffery ended his speech with a little freestyle flourish, saying what a privilege it was to be at MBA and urging everyone to stick around after school to watch a public debate. And immediately, the entire MBA student body burst into a standing ovation. We were told many times throughout the rest of the day that such a response is very rare at the school.

MBA's headmaster, Bradford Gioia, approached the podium. He appeared to be quite moved. "This reminds us," he said with sincere conviction, "that separatism is wrong."

This is exactly what I had hoped would happen when Ebony and I first started pushing for a radical new strategy, though in my wildest imagination I would never have come up with a scenario such as this.

RISEN STILL WANTED HIS STUDENTS to debate a case like ours at the Tournament of Champions, but they were understandably hesitant. While in Nashville, I tried my best to sell them on it, copying key pieces of evidence and explaining aspects of the case, but I didn't think they'd be persuaded.

MBA's top team wound up going undefeated during the preliminary rounds at the TOC, and Risen sent me an e-mail during out rounds saying that if they won quarterfinals, they would likely face Westminster's top team in semis, and that this would be the perfect moment to run a nontraditional case like ours.

But they lost quarterfinals, and Westminster went on to win the whole thing.

That was that, I figured, until I got a call out of the blue a month later from Risen. He told me two of his teams had won both semifinal rounds at the National Forensic League's national tournament—they'd closed it out. At a typical tournament this would mean the end of the festivities. But at NFL nationals the final round is a big deal, one of the only debate events in the country that draws a large crowd. And it's taped every year, and those tapes are sold to debate coaches across the country.

Risen told me he and his debaters were going to use the opportunity to talk about the issues we at Central were addressing with our case—how the institutional structures that keep races separate and unequal are mirrored in the debate community itself.

I hung up the phone and called Ebony and Geoffery and Jane, breathless with excitement. We'd made quite an impact on MBA, a veritable Goliath of high school debate, and, by extension, the debate community as a whole. Things were happening because of us. I was receiving e-mails from coaches and students who shared with me how our case affected them, sometimes even spurred them into action. One coach, a stranger before we began e-mailing each other, told me one of his students was so moved by Geoffery's speech that he was now working to establish an Urban Debate League chapter in his home city.

And things were happening at home in Kansas City. Several coaches in the Urban Debate League formed a collective, pooling their resources to help one another's students prepare for national-circuit tournaments. We began reaching out to the larger community to get more support, both financial and political, for high school debate. I say "we" because I was now among them, a bona fide coach, soon to have a program of my own. Later that summer I would persuade administrators at DeLaSalle Education Center, an alternative school attended by many of the students who have been kicked out of the Kansas City school district, to allow me to start a debate program there.

I was following through on a promise I'd made.

While Risen was in Kansas City months earlier, he asked me about my future plans. I tossed out a couple of book ideas I was pondering, then he cut to the chase: "You're still going to be in debate, aren't you?"

"Yeah," I said. "I'm gonna stick around."

ACKNOWLEDGMENTS

I have enormous gratitude for the people who made this book possible by opening their lives to me: Jane Rinehart and Richard Bulman; Marcus Leach and Evaline Lumpkin; Brandon and Bryan Dial; Ebony Rose, Shavelle Christian, and Tina Marie Rose; Antoine, Lisa, and Jay Lewis; Geoffery Stone and Leodis McCray. Many thanks also to William McClendon and Edwin Birch for granting institutional access.

I'm grateful to those who brought the story into print. I thank God above for my agent Lydia Wills, who totally kicks ass, and her assistant, Jason Yarn, and Justin Duda, who put me in touch with her. I have the deepest gratitude for the brilliant folks at FSG: Ayesha Pande, who bought the idea and helped me through those shaky first steps; Eric Chinski, who deftly brought the story into focus; Gena Hamshaw, Jeff Seroy, Joshua Rubins, Sarah Russo, Kimberly Criner; and Mickey Duzyj for his fabulous artwork. And thank you, CJ Janovy and Andy Van De Voorde, at *New Times*, for giving me the space to pursue this story.

Several veteran journalists and writers graciously shared their wisdom with me. Thank you to Leon Dash, David Margolick, Whitney Terrell, Adrian Nicole LeBlanc, and Susan E. Eaton. Likewise, I had many mentors in the strange and wonderful world of debate. I am especially thankful to: Dr. Ede Warner, Tria Warner, Daryl Birch, and the whole Louisville crew; Linda Collier, Holly Reiss, and Gabe Cook at DEBATE–Kansas City; Michael

480   ACKNOWLEDGMENTS

Risen and Alan Coverstone at MBA; and Bill Shanahan, Scott Deatherage, Doug Springer, Melissa Maxcy Wade, J. Scott Wunn, Don Crabtree, Randy Pierce, and David Song.

A project such as this is impossible without the support of family and friends, and I thank everyone who encouraged me along the way—in particular my late grandfather Carl S. Miller, a deft editor who put the ink in my veins, my aunt Lora Minichillo, who helped me out in a tight spot, and the love of my life, Allie Johnson, whose firm hand carried me when I thought I couldn't go on.

Lastly, in the spirit of this book, I honor a high school teacher. I never even had a class with Paul Epstein, but he still took the time to meet with me after school and during lunch period to teach me what it takes to be a writer.